© James Estrin

WILLIAM GRIMES
APPETITE CITY

William Grimes was the restaurant critic for *The New York Times* from 1999 to 2003. He is the author of *Straight Up or On the Rocks* (NPP, 2001) and *My Fine Feathered Friend* (NPP, 2002), and the coauthor of *The New York Times Guide to New York City Restaurants 2004*.

Also by William Grimes

Straight Up or On the Rocks: The Story of the American Cocktail

My Fine Feathered Friend

The New York Times *Guide to New York City Restaurants 2004* (coauthor)

Eating Your Words: 2000 Words to Tease Your Taste Buds (editor)

Appetite City

Appetite

North Point Press • A division of Farrar, Straus and Giroux • New York

City

A Culinary History of New York

WILLIAM GRIMES

North Point Press
A division of Farrar, Straus and Giroux
18 West 18th Street, New York 10011

Printed in the United States of America
Published in 2009 by North Point Press
First paperback edition, 2010

The Library of Congress has cataloged the hardcover edition as follows:
Grimes, William.
    Appetite city : a culinary history of New York / William Grimes.
        p.   cm.
    Includes bibliographical references and index.
    ISBN: 978-0-86547-692-9 (hardcover : alk. paper)
    1. Food habits—New York (State)—New York—History.   2. Food—
Social aspects—New York (State)—New York.   3. Cookery—New York
(State)—New York.   I. Title.

GT2853.U5G75 2009
394.1'209747—dc22

                                                          2008054288

Paperback ISBN: 978-0-374-53249-9

Photo research by Laura Wyss

Designed by Jonathan D. Lippincott

www.fsgbooks.com

P1

To Nancy

Contents

Illustrations

Appetite City

Before there were restaurants, coffeehouses like the Gentlemen's and Exchange at the foot of Broad Street offered rudimentary meals.

1

The City Without a Restaurant

In the late 1820s, a Columbia College student by the name of Sam Ward often stepped into a small café in lower Manhattan for a bite to eat. Ward, the son of a prominent banker, would later achieve fame as a big political fixer in Washington and eventually go out in a blaze of scandal. This was no mean feat in the lax moral atmosphere of the Gilded Age, but Ward had great flair.

He also had, even as a young man, a highly developed taste for the finer things in life. Unfortunately, the finer things were in short supply in the New York of his youth, especially when it came to the pleasures of the table. The city, awkwardly poised between the Dutch village it had so recently been and the teeming commercial city it was soon to become, offered little more than the basics to the New Yorker in search of a meal, or the traveler in need of a place to stay and a decent dinner. Visitors and residents alike, their numbers increasing daily, made do with the grim fare served at the city's boardinghouses, or dined on plain English-style meals at the handful of taverns and chophouses scattered around town. The city that would one day boast many of the finest restaurants in the world was, in the early nineteenth century, a culinary desert.

The old Knickerbocker families, solidly conservative in their manners and their tastes, did just fine. They ate at home. Meals usually were made in the kitchen, but coffeehouses and taverns also functioned as catering shops. When John Battin opened the Eastern Coffee House at Burling

Slip and Water Street in 1813, he took out an advertisement in the *New York Post* that itemized the fare—beefsteaks, mutton chops, broiled chicken, and oysters—and noted pointedly that "families can send servants with dishes to pick up cooked items." This was, in effect, take-out food, a category that would eventually become one of the city's hallmarks.

The commercial travelers, foreign merchants, and ambitious young men pouring into New York from the hinterlands found the culinary landscape forbidding. The handbooks for visitors that first appeared in print around this time offered scant hope for the hungry. The purportedly comprehensive *Blunt's Stranger's Guide to the City of New York*, published in 1817, listed no restaurants at all, just boardinghouses and hotels: the City Hotel, the Merchants Hotel, and Merchants Hall.

All the more thrilling, then, for a young dog like Sam Ward to discover a little French confectionery and café on William Street, in the heart of the commercial district. It was called Delmonico's, and it was run by two French-speaking Swiss brothers of that name, John and Peter. "I remember entering the café with something of awe, accompanied by a fellow student from Columbia," Ward recalled in the 1870s. By then he was a legendary bon vivant, and an inspiration for a generation of younger men keen to receive instruction in the arts of fine dining and sophisticated conversation. Delmonico's, now in its prime, was universally regarded as the finest restaurant in New York, which had also undergone a remarkable transformation, evolving into a restaurant city to rival Paris. But even from this distant vantage, Ward remained enthralled by the humble café that set him on the path of pleasure, a little temple where, he wrote, "the dim religious light soothed the eye, its tranquil atmosphere the ear."

Innocent impressions, recollected in sentimental old age, might have influenced Ward's description. In his private papers, which include an attempted history of Delmonico's, he characterized it as "a very primitive little café," an opinion seconded by the New York brahmin Abram C. Dayton. "The little place contained some half dozen pine tables with requisite wooden chairs, to match, and on a board counter covered with white napkins was ranged the limited assortment of pastry," wrote Dayton, the son of a prosperous merchant. "The silverware was old-fashioned two-tine forks and buck-handled knives, the cups and plates solid earthenware." In Delmonico's early days, the chef himself brought the food to the table.

Primitive it may have been, but from the outset, Delmonico's struck a distinctive note. Like the spire of Trinity Church, it towered over its surroundings. Service was prompt and deferential, for one thing, a marked departure from the "democratic nonchalance" of chophouses and lunchrooms like Clark and Brown's on Maiden Lane, George W. Brown's Auction Hotel on Water Street, or Holt's Ordinary on Fulton Street, where diners had two choices: a shilling plate (a shilling was worth twelve and a half cents) or a two-shilling set menu known as an ordinary. This was the "meat and two veg" special of its day, a slab of beef or mutton with potatoes and gravy, served up fast with no frills. At its best, the chophouse could be excellent, in the British way, but a steady diet of meat and potatoes, day after day, did have its limitations.

Delmonico's brought a whiff of Paris into the crude, bustling streets of a city long on ambition but short on amenities. Ward was smitten. "I reveled in the coffee, the chocolate, the bavaroises, the orgeats, and petits gateaux and bon-bons," he wrote. The "foreign element," as Dayton described the patrons, only added to the attraction for young New Yorkers in search of atmosphere and romance. The youngbloods made their way to Delmonico's on Saturday after-noons to indulge in a cuisine that their parents regarded as pretentious and possi-bly health-damaging. There they mingled with European traders and merchants keen to make a killing in the promising New York market, attracted by "the *filets*, *macaroni*, *café*, *chocolate*, and *petit verre*"—the last an aperitif.

Dishes like these came as a revelation. The Bank Coffee House, run by the Irishman William Niblo, ranked at or near the top of the city's eating houses, also known as refectories, but that was not saying much. Thomas Hamilton, a Scottish visitor, remarked that the fare was "more excellent in point of material, than of cookery or arrangement." The Bank menu sounds enticing enough, though plain, with the inevitable starter of oyster soup followed by a choice of meat or fish: shad, venison, partridge, grouse, "wild-ducks of different varieties, and several other dishes less notable." Unfortunately, Hamilton wrote, "there was no attempt to serve this chaotic entertainment in courses, a fashion, indeed, but little prevalent in the United States. Soup, fish, flesh, and fowl simultane-ously garnished the table; and the consequence was, that the greater part of the dishes were cold, before the guests were prepared to attack them." The Del-monico brothers sensed a need, and they addressed it with distinction.

Ward remained a regular at Delmonico's for the rest of his life, watching with approval as the café prospered, grew into a full-fledged restaurant, and fol-lowed the movement of wealth and power farther and farther uptown. By catering to the tastes of Manhattan's leading businessmen and the social elite, the restaurant quickly became an emblem of New York sophistication and cosmopolitanism. Not just a gastronomic shrine, it functioned as a clearinghouse for anyone aspiring to the upper reaches of society. To have an account at Delmonico's meant that you had arrived. For nearly a century, it reigned supreme among New York's restaurants. This meant little in the 1820s but quite a lot as the century wore on and New York evolved into the undisputed dining capital of the United States.

In 1827, when John and Peter Delmonico opened for business, the glory years lay far in the future. Their fledgling venture, originally a wine shop serving foreign traders and merchants, was a risky proposition. It assumed that New York could support a real restaurant run along French lines, with a serious kitchen, a printed menu (in French), and an atmosphere of refinement and leisure. In other words, a restaurant such as might be found in Paris, where diners entered expecting to spend two hours or more savoring fine food served by attentive and knowledgeable waiters.

This was a big assumption. Local tastes ran to beef, beer, oysters, and bread. Moreover, dining was not thought of as a leisurely activity. Americans ate fast—they still do—and New Yorkers ate even faster. Time spent eating was time wasted, distraction from the serious business of making money. It was not at all uncommon for a broker or clerk to wolf down lunch in less than twenty minutes at a downtown eating house, standing up if there were no seats to be had, which was often the case. The dominant dining philosophy was simple: feed as many people as possible, as quickly as possible. At the Auction Hotel, pies were spread out on a counter, already cut into slices, so that customers could grab lunch on the run. Table manners remained a work in progress. A fastidious New Yorker, reminiscing about the city of his youth, recalled with amusement diners who liked to crumble up their apple pie and drop it in a glass of milk.

If dining in New York was a commercial rather than a leisure proposition, it was also, more than in any other city, public rather than private. Early on, as businesses proliferated at the tip of Manhattan Island, residents began moving uptown. Elsewhere, Americans walked home for lunch, but in New York, most laborers lived too far away from their jobs for a home-cooked meal. This created a booming lunch trade for the handful of plain-fare establishments serving crowds of customers at lightning speed and rock-bottom prices. Most closed in the afternoon, their work done for the day.

Old Tom's, on Thames Street, was one of the first English-style chophouses.

Clark and Brown's, at the Franklin Coffee House on Maiden Lane near Liberty Street, was typical of the breed. The proprietors, both English, had made their mark at the Auction Hotel, which pioneered the shilling plate and sold pies and pudding at sixpence, drinks the same. At their chophouse, the men presided over a no-frills dining room with a dingy bar up front and mahogany booths in the rear. John Brown, "a stout, burly, red-faced Englishman," stood at the head of a stairway in the middle of the dining room and carved the meat. One shilling bought a substantial meal of sliced roast beef or beefsteak with plum pudding and a tankard of half-and-half (brewed in New York or Pennsylvania but labeled Burton Stock Ale) or London Dock brandy. With each order came a hefty slice of bread speared on a two-tined fork and a pickled walnut or mushroom catsup for zest.

There was nothing fancy about the food or the service at Clark and Brown's. Picky diners learned to keep their opinions to themselves. One customer, upset at being served his bread on an archaic horn-handled fork, complained to Clark. The owner, after putting on a show of concern, told him, "Well, Sir, it's a rule of our place to serve bread on a fork, and them as don't like our ways of course has the privilege of going elsewhere." A young diner, requesting a silver fork, drew a withering stare from Clark. "Steel forks was good enough for your father, Sir—your father as made the money you are now a-spending," he said. "If you wants silverware you must go somewhere else, for as long as I keeps this place I'll keep steel forks." And that was that.

Basil Hall, a British naval officer and traveler, took lunch at Clark and Brown's in the late 1820s and reported to English readers on the joys of dining out, New York style. The dining room was long, narrow, and dark, with wooden booths arranged along a center aisle. As diners took their seats on the pewlike benches, a small boy would poke his head into the booth, taking orders and shouting them over to attendants near the kitchen. Hall, advised that the corned beef was good, ordered accordingly, as did his two companions. "Three beef, eight" rang out—three corned-beef lunches for booth eight. In an instant, a tray supporting three sets of covered dishes made its way down the aisle, held aloft by a jacketless waiter. Each diner was handed a plate with a slab of beef and a second plate heaped with mashed potatoes, along with a knife and, of course, bread on a fork.

"The multiplicity and rapidity of these orders and movements made me giddy," Hall wrote. "Had there been one set to receive and forward the orders, and another to put them into execution, we might have seen better through the confusion; but all hands, little and big together, were screaming out with equal loudness and quickness—'Half plate beef, 4'—'One potato, 5'—'Two apple pie, one plum pudding, 8' and so on."

New Yorkers loved places like Clark and Brown's, which endured for decades serving the kind of simple fare—what would now be called comfort food—that lingered forever in the imagination. The playwright Charles Gayler fondly recalled the chicken potpie and rice pudding "with lots of raisins in it" at Holt's Ordinary in the 1830s. But the old chophouses and ordinaries, self-consciously anachronistic, outlived their time to become relics and curiosities.

Abram C. Dayton, the merchant's son, observed the proliferation of the city's eating houses with an amazed eye. Born in 1818, he attended schools in Germany and Holland and returned to a place he barely recognized. The over-grown village of his youth was now a tumultuous commercial city. Shortly before his death in 1877, he took a fond look back at the city's Dutch-inflected manners and customs in *Last Days of Knickerbocker Life in New York*. Since the publication of Washington Irving's *History of New York*, ostensibly written by one Diedrich Knickerbocker, "Knickerbocker" had gained currency as a synonym for stolid, determinedly insular, frugal Dutch ways. Dayton, a product of this vanishing culture, wanted to memorialize it before it disappeared entirely.

For Dayton, eating houses were evidence of the foreign presence in the city, and a measure of its transformation from "primitive Gotham" to "metropolitan New York." Knickerbocker taste did not run to public dining, and the cuisine on offer, whether chophouse English or Delmonico's French, did not entice. English-style rare roast beef, for example, encountered resistance—the Dutch liked their meat well cooked. Clark and Brown's, Dayton pointed out, was patronized mostly by Yorkshiremen in town to sell manufactured goods. In 1835, when James Thompson moved his confectionery shop to 171 Broadway, a prime location near the main shopping district, he hoped to lure female customers with fetchingly displayed cakes and pastries. To create a welcoming atmosphere, he installed his middle-aged sisters behind the counter. For years the shop struggled. Women would peer in the window, curious, but they stopped short of entering and eating a piece of cake. It simply was not done. Thompson persevered, and eventually prospered, but no thanks to Knickerbocker patronage.

Knickerbocker society was already becoming quaint by the time Dayton returned from Europe. Public business and public appetites defined the new New York, and it is hardly surprising that momentous changes were afoot. The real wonder is why a restaurant like Delmonico's had taken so long to arrive, especially in a city with no shortage of French émigrés, or foreign businessmen desperate for a good meal.

In fact, Delmonico's did not arise in a vacuum. It was not the only pastry shop in town, for one thing. François Guerin, just around the corner on Broadway between Pine and Cedar streets, strategically facing the City Hotel, had opened in 1815 and carried on for decades. Like Delmonico's, Guerin's served pastries, confectionery, chocolate, and liqueurs. In a bid to capture the female lunch trade, Guerin added a small ladies' dining room. He was premature. The ladies shopped, or took the air, and then walked to their homes for lunch. But as the residential district moved northward, and the dinner hour grew later, Guerin reaped the rewards, although, unlike the Delmonicos, he had no ambitions beyond quietly amassing a fortune.

The dashing Auguste Louis de Singeron, a French nobleman who fled revolutionary France, chanced into a career as a confectioner when he made some molasses candy for a pupil he was tutoring. The boy's family was delighted. Singeron, a brisk, energetic man ("his walk," one contemporary wrote, "was that of a man who walks for a wager"), spied an opportunity. He opened a French-style confiserie and pâtisserie on Pine Street and gave New York an eye-popping demonstration of French inventiveness in the culinary arts. It was Singeron who introduced the practice of stamping New Year's cakes with hearts pierced by arrows, and cupids cavorting among roses. In his shop windows, passersby marveled at gilded gingerbread figures of Louis XVI and Marie Antoinette, or blancmange in the form of bewigged gentlemen and ladies in court costume. Singeron's pièce de résistance was a marzipan version of the façade of the Tuileries, which he had helped defend against attack by a revolutionary mob in 1792.

New York's torrid summers made ice cream a precious commodity. They also created a windfall for European entrepreneurs reared on the pleasures of the outdoor café. John H. Contoit, a Frenchman with an English wife, came to New York in the 1790s and originally set up as a confectioner. In 1799, he opened an "ice house" on Greenwich Street, where he sold ice cream, syrups, punches, and coffee. This proved to be just the thing. A decade later, Contoit opened the New York Garden, a pleasure spot on Broadway between Leonard and Franklin streets in present-day Tribeca, where New Yorkers could take a stroll and then sit down for refreshments. The "garden" was little more than a few trees in a long, narrow plot squeezed between two buildings, but it offered relief from the summer heat. A walkway led between two rows of green-and-white wooden booths attended by black waiters, who raced back and forth, carrying lemonade, pound cake, and ice cream in three flavors: vanilla, strawberry, and lemon. Officially no liquor was served, but a discreet quarter slipped to the waiter would produce a lemon ice spiked with cognac.

Ferdinand Palmo, an Italian, came to New York in 1808, when he was in his early twenties, and, after scrimping and saving, opened Palmo's Garden, known for its gilded columns multiplied ad infinitum by mirrors lining the walls. (A subsequent owner, a Frenchman by the name of Pinteux, rechristened it the Café des Mille Colonnes.) The café, at Reade Street and Broadway, attracted French and Italian expatriates who gathered to play dominoes, drink chocolate, and nibble at ices, as well as the gay blades of the town, who took in Broadway's gaudy spectacle just outside the door. As an Italian band played, patrons enjoyed

Palmo's authentic Italian frozen treats, unrivaled, a visitor exclaimed, for "variety, quantity and quality," and "not inferior to those of Tortoni in Paris." Another ice cream parlor, the Café Français, just a few doors down, on Warren Street, served as an unofficial headquarters for the city's wits—men like the poet Fitz-Greene Halleck and the writer Charles Fenno Hoffman, editor of the *Knickerbocker Magazine*.

Ice cream—vanilla, strawberry, and lemon—was the draw at the New York Garden, which opened in 1810 in what is now Tribeca.

Palmo prospered. He became one of the city's notable figures, but he nourished a larger dream: to establish Italian opera in New York permanently. Accordingly, he sold his restaurant and in 1844 opened Palmo's New York Opera House in the renovated Arcade Baths, on Chambers Street, just north of City Hall Park. New York, alas, was not ready. Palmo, financially ruined, returned to the stove. It was a long, hard fall. He wound up working, it was said, at Charley Abel's, a Broadway restaurant whose character may be deduced from one of its advertisements: "Here meet daily the wits, fast men and bloods of the town. It offers all the attractions of 'the Old House at Home,' to strangers, while to 'men about town,' who are 'up to a thing or two'—who know the difference between Heidsieck and Newark Cider—Havana Cigars from Down East 'long nines,' at a penny a grab—it is *the* place of any other in the city, for an occasional 'drop in.'" Fate was unkind.

Ices were not the only way to cool off in the hot New York summers. In 1808, the Lynch and Clark company, which owned the Congress Water Springs at Saratoga Springs, opened a soda-water shop on Wall Street that catered to thirsty brokers. After being taken over by Albert J. Delatour, the little soda-water business became a huge draw, with brokers and bankers forming a line outside that snaked all the way down Wall Street. "It were curious to know how many sixpences and shillings have gone into the exchequer of the landlord [i.e.,

Delatour] the two days past," the *Times* wrote during a heat wave in the summer of 1852, "but we have referred the point to our money reporter, and he won't tell—simply because he is not disposed to have his veracity questioned by stating the enormous number." Glasses were chilled in tubs of ice, then filled with soda by one attendant as another added flavoring from bottled syrups. One by one, customers would enter through a narrow alley from Wall Street and exit on Broad Street, inspired, on hot days, by the hourly temperature readings that Delatour, a scrupulous weather watcher, posted in the window.

A powerful symbiotic relationship developed between theaters and eating houses (the term "restaurant" did not enter into common usage until the middle of the nineteenth century), one that continued throughout the century and persists to this day in the streets around Times Square. The earliest and long the most famous was Edward ("Ned") Windust's basement restaurant at 11 Park Row, which opened just a few steps from the Park Theater in 1824 or 1825. The theater, built in 1798 by a consortium of wealthy citizens, presented performances by English stock companies and, beginning in the 1820s, classical music. (In its 1825 season it introduced Italian opera, no doubt inspiring Palmo.) Before long, it became the nucleus of a thriving commercial strip, with hotels, coffeehouses, and Windust's among the attractions.

Windust's quickly became a rendezvous for actors, writers, and lawyers (and a refuge for Horace Greeley, editor of the *Tribune*, fleeing from a howling mob during the draft riots of 1863). Theatergoers crowded in, hoping to catch a glimpse of the stars dining on the restaurant's English menu of beefsteaks and chops. In the ensuing decades, theaters all over New York would inevitably acquire satellite restaurants, some of them owned and operated by actors. The audience for theater was enormous. Gathering before performances and spilling onto the streets afterward, playgoers provided the critical mass that allowed hundreds of saloons and restaurants to prosper. Just as important, the presence of actors and other theater folk brought color and excitement to the city's emerging dining culture. Appetite and celebrity turned out to be a powerful combination.

As one eating house after another opened its doors, New York gained confidence. Restaurants reflected the surging prosperity of a port city open to new markets with the inauguration of the Erie Canal in 1825, and their increase changed the city's image of itself. "New York abounds beyond all other places in the universe, not excepting Paris, in consummate institutions for cultivating the noble science of gastronomy," James Kirke Paulding boasted in *The New Mirror for Travellers*, an 1828 guide to the city. "The soul of Heliogabalus presides in the kitchens of our hotels and boardinghouses, and inspires the genius of a thousand cooks."

The claim was preposterous on its face. Even before the revolution of 1789, Paris was well on its way to creating a highly sophisticated restaurant culture. Its growing population had put stress on the old guild system, under which caterers, poulterers, pastry makers, roasters, and the like jealously guarded their exclusive rights to perform specific functions. Gradually, they began poaching on one another's territory. At the same time, the idea took hold of preparing food intended to be eaten at table, rather than taken away. For decades, certain specialty purveyors had operated rooms serving a concentrated beef broth known as a *bouillon restaurant*, or restorative, intended for Parisians with delicate stomachs and weak nerves. The name attached itself to a new kind of establishment, appearing with increasing frequency, that offered meals more varied than the set-menu table d'hôte found at inns—not to mention the pleasure of dining at a small table, rather than rubbing shoulders with complete strangers. The newfangled restaurants also featured flexible hours and publicly displayed prices, thereby eliminating the unwelcome element of surprise.

Contrary to myth, the French Revolution did not create the restaurant by driving chefs from their positions in aristocratic kitchens. Rather, it accelerated a process well under way. Antoine Beauvilliers, a chef to the Count of Provence who would go on to write the seminal *L'Art du cuisinier*, had opened the city's first luxury restaurant, the Grande Taverne de Londres, on the rue de Richelieu near the Palais Royal, as early as 1782. In short order, a cluster of culinary jewels found their setting nearby: Les Trois Frères Provençaux, Méot, the Boeuf à la Mode, Véry. By 1805, there were fifteen restaurants and twenty cafés in the Palais Royal, one of which, Véfour, is still in business today. At the time of the Revolution, Paris boasted a hundred restaurants, a number that would increase fivefold by the turn of the century. Paris even had a great restaurant critic, Grimod de la Reynière, whose coterie of fellow gourmets pronounced judgment on the city's restaurants—three thousand of them in 1815—in a more or less annual guide, the *Almanach des gourmands*.

New York a rival of Paris? Hardly. In the heady years after the opening of the Erie Canal, New York held some strong cards, but Paulding was a little ahead of himself. The truth was quite different, as anyone in search of a respectable meal knew all too well. And with each passing month, the lack of dining amenities assumed the proportions of a scandal.

New York, in the 1820s, was quickly outgrowing its bounds. As a burgeoning commercial center, it attracted a large transient population desperate for hotels and restaurants. Young men in search of work were streaming in from the countryside. Increasing numbers of foreign businessmen were making their way to New York, along with travelers keen to see for themselves the largest, most go-ahead city in the United States. In 1835 alone, with a population of 270,000, the city played host to about 60,000 visitors, each of whom stayed for an average of three days.

What did they find? A handful of hotels, a motley assortment of boarding-houses, and a scattering of restaurants that catered mostly to the lunch trade. The ices at Palmo's café and the exquisite bonbons at Delmonico's attracted attention precisely because they were rare exceptions.

The city's hotels, run on the so-called American plan until after the Civil War, confounded foreign visitors, who were used to dining when and where they pleased. The price of a room included all meals, so a guest who chose to eat outside the hotel was in effect paying twice over for his food. Mealtimes, announced by the ringing of a gong, were strictly regimented. Typically, breakfast was served at eight, dinner at three, tea at seven, and supper at nine, which sounds like a lot of eating, but in practice, as one English traveler wrote in 1833, the last was "frequently dispensed with."

European guests were startled at the American habit of rushing the dining room and gobbling down meals in silence. "On the first occasion of my dining at the public table," Henry Tudor, an English barrister, wrote in 1834, "I had but just received a plate of fish, after partaking of soup, and was leisurely commencing to dispatch it, and was comfortably settling myself in my chair for a couple of hours to come, when, casting my eye along the line of the table, I was immediately startled to find that half the chairs in various portions of its length, and which but a few moments before were fully occupied, had been deserted; and in five minutes afterwards, I was left in a state of solitary abandonment, with the exception of three others, out of a large company of perhaps 150 persons." Determined to be charitable, he interpreted the stampede as evidence of "the striking activity and economizing diligence of the people."

In that same year, Thomas Hamilton, a Scottish officer turned novelist, provided an even more detailed picture of dining on the American plan. The day began with breakfast, an abundant repast, replete with weighty dishes supplemented by "rolls, toast, and cakes of buckwheat and Indian corn" continually delivered to the table. One custom caught him unawares: "Eggs, instead of being eat from the shell, are poured into a wine-glass, and after being duly and disgustingly churned up with butter and condiment, the mixture, according to its degree of fluidity, is forthwith either spooned into the mouth, or drunk off like a liquid."

After attending to business about town, Hamilton returned to his hotel for dinner at 3:00 p.m. and sensed a general drift toward the hotel's bar, packed with guests itching to get at the dining table. The dinner bell rang, and he was swept by the human tide to the dining room, where, once again, he marveled, then complained. "The number of dishes was very great," he wrote. "The style of cookery neither French nor English, though certainly approaching nearer to the latter, than to the former. The dressed dishes were decidedly bad, the sauces being composed of little else than liquid grease, which to a person like myself, who have an inherent detestation of every modification of oleaginous matter, was an objection altogether insuperable."

In time, Hamilton learned to pick and choose, thereby constructing a palatable meal. But he never managed to keep pace with the "gulping and swallowing" American diners around him, attacking their food in silence. "If you asked a gentleman to help you from any dish before him, he certainly complied, but in a manner that showed you had imposed on him a disagreeable task," he wrote, "and instead of a *slice*, your plate generally returned loaded with a solid massive wedge of animal matter."

As Hamilton's account suggests, the hotels did not stint. The typical spread was lavish, and at top establishments, like the Astor House, the city's first luxury hotel, it could reach Roman heights of indulgence. The table d'hôte menu on March 21, 1838, ran to thirty-seven items, most listed in French, with no divisions into appetizer, main course, or dessert. Vermicelli soup was followed by oyster pie, veal breast in white sauce, an assortment of roast meats (including wild duck, goose, and guinea fowl), squab compote, lamb steak with onions, and three desserts (queen of puddings, mince pie, and cream puffs). Of course, a room at the Astor cost an astronomical two dollars a day, which guaranteed comforts like running water even on the upper floors.

The American plan remained the norm until after the Civil War. By that time, the slapdash style remarked upon by so many British visitors in the 1830s and 1840s had evolved into a carefully choreographed ceremony. Carl Schurz, the great social reformer, dined at the Union Square Hotel soon after arriving in the United States from Germany in 1852, and the experience made a deep impression. "It was a table d'hôte, if I remember rightly, at five o'clock in the afternoon," he wrote in his memoirs.

> Dinner-time was announced by the fierce beating of a gong, an instrument which I heard for the first time on that occasion. The guests then filed into a large, bare dining-room with one long row of tables. Some 15 or 20 negroes, clad in white jackets, white aprons, and white cotton gloves, stood ready to conduct the guests to their seats, which they did with broad smiles and curiously elaborate bows and foot scrapings. A portly colored head-waiter in a dress coat and white necktie, whose manners were strikingly grand and patronizing, directed their movements. When the guests were seated, the head-waiter struck a loud bell; then the negroes rapidly filed out and soon reappeared carrying large soup tureens covered with bright silver covers. They planted themselves along the table at certain intervals, standing for a second motionless. At another clang of their commander's bell they lifted their tureens high up and then deposited them upon the table with a bump that made the chandeliers tremble and came near terrifying the ladies.

Most visitors to the city did not stay at the Astor or the Union Square, needless to say. In the early years of the century, and in the decades immediately after the opening of the Erie Canal, newcomers seeking work found accommodations, and meals, at boardinghouses. Some were high-class, offering all the creature comforts later associated with first-rate hotels, including generous, well-prepared meals. John Bernard, an English actor and stage manager visiting New York in the early nineteenth century, was delighted at the quantity and variety of dishes at his boardinghouse, especially the breakfast. Arrayed on the table were fish, ham, beef, boiled fowls, eggs, pigeons, lobsters, and assorted vegetables. There was pumpkin pie for the sweet tooth, and coffee, tea, and cider to drink, along with alcoholic beverages like cherry brandy and sangaree (a wine punch similar to sangria).

Edgar Allan Poe, arriving in New York in 1844 with his bride, Virginia, had the good fortune to find a boardinghouse on Greenwich Street near Cedar Street where, he exulted in a letter, "we had the nicest tea you ever drank, strong &

hot—wheat bread & rye bread—cheese—tea-cakes (elegant), a great dish (two dishes) of elegant ham, and 2 of cold veal, piled up like a mountain and large slices—3 dishes of the cakes, and everything in the greatest profusion. No fear of starving here."

But these were not the boardinghouses typically described in travelers' diaries and snide newspaper articles, or that haunted the memories of former clerks and scriveners toiling in brokerage houses, shipping offices, or dry-goods firms on Pearl Street, a bustling commercial thoroughfare running through lower Manhattan. This army of underpaid young men roosted in private homes that once housed the city's lesser gentry and mercantile elite, and now, crumbling at the edges, provided room and board at rock-bottom rates. In 1817, a top-class boardinghouse charged two dollars or more a day, but at the bottom of the scale, room and board could be had for two dollars a week.

Asa Greene's novel *The Perils of Pearl Street* presents a somber picture of boardinghouse fare in the early 1830s, seen through the eyes of Billy Hazard, a raw recruit from the provinces. With his clerk's salary, Billy finds a boardinghouse for four dollars a week. He quickly notices that his landlady economizes by buying half-price provisions. The meat is suspect, the fruit damaged. Breakfast leans heavily on salt shad or mackerel and a piece of beef that the coal fire seems to have dried rather than roasted. "No fowls, no eggs, no oysters, ever made their way to the breakfast table," Greene wrote. There are no rolls, buckwheat cakes, or toast. The bread, baked on the premises, is "thoroughly soured, and heavy as a grindstone." The butter, salted heavily by the dealer to add weight, is salted again by the landlady to discourage overconsumption. The coffee grounds are stretched with burnt bread crust or roasted rye.

Dinner is a slight improvement. The cheaper cuts of meat prevail, "dry as a chip" and served without gravy. Roasted mutton, "smelling strongly of its sheepish qualities and reeking in its own grease," takes pride of place, accompanied by watery potatoes, sliced beets, or boiled cabbage. Last, and surely least, is the dessert feared by every boardinghouse resident, a sour baked apple surrounded by a casing of tough dough.

The notorious baked apple loomed large in the bitter recollections of many a New Yorker of the time. At Billy's boardinghouse, this dread invader takes its place on the table alongside crunchy rice pudding served with molasses, and a leather-crusted apple pie. Loose tea is measured out in the pot by the thimbleful and rinsed by repeated additions of boiling water as the dinner progresses. The milk (well watered) and the sugar are held firmly in the grip of the landlady.

By midcentury, the culture of boardinghouses had become a rich source of comic material. Nearly every newcomer to the city, whether down-at-heels or well-to-do, native-born or foreign, had spent time in them and suffered at their tables. "Like death, no class is exempt from it," Thomas Butler Gunn wrote in his *Physiology of New York Boarding-Houses*. Gunn, a British journalist who came to New York in 1849 and later covered the Civil War for the *New York Tribune*, lived in boardinghouses of every description, taking careful notes along the way. At the lower end of the scale, he described boardinghouses in which hard-pressed families took in a solitary guest. At the upper end were large-scale operations with eighty or more residents. In between, every variation could be found, each with its own tone. There were moral boardinghouses run by stern evangelical Christians, and boardinghouses with marriageable daughters whom the guests were expected to court. There were French *pensions* and German *Gasthausen*. For a time, fastidious diners could patronize vegetarian boardinghouses, although, Gunn noted, these had mysteriously disappeared by the early 1850s.

All had one thing in common: unsatisfactory food. At the high end, where the landlady was always referred to as Madame and guests were awakened by a soft knock at the door at 9:00 a.m., in sharp contrast to the peremptory 7:00 a.m. gong at cheaper establishments, the quality was higher but the portions much smaller. Gunn dealt with these establishments in a chapter titled "Fashionable Boarding Houses Where You Don't Get Enough to Eat." The day started with tiny mutton chops, slices of pâté, French bread, and French-style coffee. Lunch consisted of "delicate shavings of cold meat" and coffee. The fare, overall, was "light, tasty, and insubstantial."

At the "mean boardinghouse," liver and salt fish dominated, with the occasional ox heart on Sunday, surrounded by overboiled carrots, greasy cabbage, and potatoes that tasted "like something between yellow soap and bad artichokes." The landlady at this particular house took special pride in her pastries, which were "of solid construction, and damp, putty-like material." Guests who passed their plates to the head of the table for second helpings would receive a portion even smaller than the first. Only by repeating this humiliating ritual four or five times could they hope to fill their stomachs.

Showing great ingenuity, boarders at an especially stingy house sent their smallest member down into the locked subterranean kitchen via dumbwaiter, where he discovered what many had long suspected. The family, while their guests made do with tough meat and thin soup, feasted like lords below. A juicy turkey sat invitingly on a table, and the guests, let in by their advance man, set about stripping the carcass until the bones shined.

Gunn, after surveying the terrain, judged boardinghouse cuisine rather tolerantly. True, he wrote, "we have known the beef of tougher consistency and more *veiny* construction than was desirable, and the potatoes had more eyes than Argus; but on the whole, the diet was endurable."

Further down the economic ladder, street vendors catered to New Yorkers short on cash or time. For generations, their cries formed part of the aural backdrop of the city, along with the clip-clop of horses' hooves and the shouts of drivers trying to squeeze their carts and wagons through narrow, crowded lanes. In the early years of the century, clams, oysters, hot gingerbread, and tea rusks were sold on the street, with each vendor crying his wares. Oyster peddlers shouted, "Oysters, here's your brave, good oysters!" Clam vendors sang out: "Here's clams, here's clams, here's clams today / They late came from Rockaway; / They're good to roast, they're good to fry, / They're good to make a clam pot pie. Here they go!"

On the Bowery, vendors did a brisk business selling ice cream, apple pie, and baked beans in syrup. Hot yams were a favorite food, and continued to be sold on the streets of New York well into the twentieth century (the narrator of Ralph Ellison's *Invisible Man* recovers a powerful taste memory of the South courtesy of a hot-yam vendor in Harlem). Baked pears were sold from an earthenware dish filled with homemade syrup. Most famous of all were the hot-corn girls, New York's version of the pitiful match girls of Europe, selling corn on the cob from cedar pails filled with hot water. "Here's your lily-white corn; / All you that's got money / (Poor me that's got none) / Come buy my lily-white corn / And let me go home." Sam Ward, the epicurean, left no record of the pleasures of hot corn. That New York was a world away from the tables at Delmonico's. But it, too, was no less a part of the city's great feast.

2

From Field to Market: The New York Feast

When James Kirke Paulding proclaimed New York a second Paris, he indulged in a form of speech recognized around the world as peculiarly American. He was bragging. The New York of top-quality restaurants, luxurious cafés, and renowned chefs would eventually come to be, but not yet. Paulding was building castles in the air. But when he praised the bounty of New York's rivers and fields, and the splendors of its food markets, he stood on firm ground.

The cooks of New York had at their disposal a wealth of local and imported ingredients, a culinary palette that present-day chefs can barely begin to imagine. There was game galore: canvasback ducks from the Susquehanna; venison from the plains around Hempstead, Long Island; snipe, plover, and woodcock from the meadows near Newark. The bays and inlets of New Jersey, Staten Island, and Long Island nourished oyster beds of surpassing richness, while the market gardens of New Jersey, Long Island, and southern New York produced bumper crops of fruits and vegetables. And the fish! "O for a mouth to eat, or to utter the names of fish that flutter in the markets of New York, silently awaiting their customers like so many pupils of Pythagoras," wrote Paulding, who singled out "the delicious bass," "the toothsome black fish," "the sea-green lobster of the Sound," and "the amiable sheep's-head"—a striped fish, *Sargus ovis*, not to be confused, he hastened to explain, with the head of a sheep. All these and more "may be seen of a morning at Fulton and Washington Markets."

All cooking begins with raw materials, and in this respect, New York was blessed. Field and forest, wetlands and farmland, bay and ocean and river all yielded a surfeit of ingredients to overwhelm even the most demanding appetite. What could not be procured locally arrived by ship or rail from New England, the Chesapeake Bay, the southern states, and the Caribbean, source of the sea turtles that nineteenth-century New Yorkers demanded for soup.

As the city grew, the supply system expanded. Early on, food came to New York by farm wagon, canal barge, oyster boat, and a motley assortment of fishing vessels. Beef arrived on the hoof, pushed along in great cattle drives from as far away as Ohio. With the advent of the railroad and faster oceangoing ships, the world shrank, and New York fattened on meat and produce from the four corners of the earth. Between 1840 and 1860, the value of produce grown in the market gardens around New York increased eightfold. Transatlantic ships sold their surplus food to restaurateurs, who could then offer their customers such delights as real English mutton. In 1850, a journalist touring Fulton Market saw Sicilian oranges, Bahamian pineapples, Cuban bananas, Virginia watermelons, Chilean pumpkins, and Vietnamese hens.

The inventory of ingredients seems fabulous. It was a time when whales swam in New York Bay, oysters grew as large as dinner plates, and bear meat appeared regularly at the city markets. Before industrial pollutants and overfishing depleted local waters, fish and crustaceans reached stupendous sizes. An early Dutch settler, marveling at the shellfish in New York Bay, was moved to poetry: "Crabs, lobsters, mussels; oysters, too, there be / So large, that one does overbalance three / Of those in Europe; and in quantity, / No one can reckon." Hudson River sturgeon achieved remarkable proportions—one specimen, caught near Saugerties in 1836, measured eight and a half feet and weighed 150 pounds. Even its lesser brethren, leaping from the water, could knock a fisherman overboard with a thrash of the tail.

In the 1890s, the historian James Grant Wilson described the great days of abundance with a nostalgic pen. "The elders of the passing generation have seen armies of geese on their southern migration, and flocks of ducks hanging over the Harlem flats, so thick as to cast their shadows on the plain like obscuring clouds," he wrote. Wilson recalled the herds of deer roaming Long Island, and woodcock in Jones Wood, near present-day Eighty-sixth Street. Hunters heading out to Moriches, in central Long Island, would return with bags full of partridge, quail, plover, snipe, wild geese, and ducks. This New World bestiary confounded foreign visitors. Peter Neilson, a Glaswegian merchant reporting on his stay in New York in the 1820s, claimed to have seen bear, wildcat, raccoon, possum, squirrel, heron, bald eagle, vulture, and owl on one hotel's menu.

New York's bounty was on full display in the markets that were the city's pride and shame. It was there, in squalid surroundings, that housewives, boardinghouse operators, and restaurateurs jostled and competed for the day's provender. Without exception, the markets were noisy, dirty, and overcrowded. Small fishing boats converging on the markets created maritime gridlock as they battled with larger vessels whose churning side wheels threatened to swamp them. Cattle and oxen, floated across the East River or the Hudson on flat scows in the early days, often fell overboard and drowned. Hundreds of carts and wagons, bearing fruits and vegetables from the hinterlands, clogged the streets and jammed the entrances to the ferries. One of the more picturesque sights of old New York was the nightly gathering of wagons near the ferry slips as farmers set up for the next day's market. While snoozing on a tarpaulin thrown over turnips and potatoes, they made inviting targets for the thieves who roamed the waterfront and haunted the all-night saloons nearby.

During the Christmas rush, the game stalls at Fulton Market, on the east side of Manhattan, did a booming business. The engraving is from the 1870s.

Graft at the markets was widespread. As Tammany Hall and its me-first ethos began to define New York's political culture, the rents and fees generated by the city markets found their way into the pockets of market clerks and their overlords. For decades, the dire state of the markets would be a constant theme in the newspapers. Readers fired off outraged letters to the editor. Publishers responded with thundering editorials. The market buildings, the *Times* complained in 1858, "are ricketty, rotten, tumble-down rat-holes, which Providence, in its chastening trials, never permits lightning to strike, and which, as if in mockery of men's hopes, fires never will consume." Exposés appeared regularly. Nothing changed.

Almost from the time they were built, the markets were an eyesore and a disgrace. Before refrigeration arrived in 1835, the aromas on a hot summer day could be pungent. Flimsily constructed, the markets offered no protection from the weather, or from human predators, either, as speculators, agents, and middlemen connived to gain control of stalls and manipulate prices by strategic large-scale purchases.

Tension among vendors was rife. Local tradesmen paid rent on their stalls, while out-of-town farmers and fishmongers, allotted their own section of the market, did not. This inducement was designed to draw "countrymen" to the market and make their produce available to city dwellers. Out-of-town butchers were also allowed to sell "small meats": sheep, lamb, and calves sold by the quarter.

This system of incentives encouraged schemers. The shirk (or shark) butchers, posing as farmers, infiltrated the country stalls. So too did the middlemen, known as hucksters or forestallers, who met farmers driving their cattle from Long Island or the lower New York counties and used every possible ruse to buy cheap. Then, posing as agents for the farmers, they set up at farmers' stalls in the market and sold the meat at marked-up prices. The countrymen who did make it to market often found no stalls and were forced onto the sidewalk. In 1818, the Market Committee, a standing committee of the Common Council, reported: "It is a rare thing to see a farmer in the market with meats etc., of his own raising; the truth is, that nearly, if not all, these agents are butchers or hucksters in disguise." Enforcement of the rules was up to the market clerks, who as often as not were colluding with the rule-breakers.

Only the strong survived, whether vendors or customers. It had always been thus. "I have frequently observed, and sometimes felt, great rudeness in our public markets, especially when any kind of provision appeared of which there was a scarcity," an offended female marketgoer wrote to the *New York Gazette* in 1763.

I have seen people press and shove with such rudeness and violence, as sufficiently shew'd an intention truly hostile, and that force alone could determine the purchasers; and sometimes the prey has been seized, and in danger of being torn to pieces, by two furious combatants, equally voracious, who seemed, by their actions, to be upon the point of starving, and to contend for their lives. I, who am a woman, unused to war, and of a peaceable disposition, have been obliged to give up my pretensions to the goods, half purchased, and give place to one of more strength and resolution, being not quite reduced to the necessity of fighting or starving.

New York's first great food market was the Fly Market on Maiden Lane, which operated, in one form or another, from the beginning of the eighteenth century until 1822. Its peculiar name derived from the Dutch word *vlie* (meadow), a reference to the saltwater marsh that once ran along the shore of the East River from Wall Street to Beekman Street.

The Fly had its shortcomings, not least of which was its location over a common sewer that carried water from Maiden Lane and surrounding streets to the East River. Along the way it picked up the refuse from nearby taverns, fruit stands, and cookshops. Nevertheless, the butcher Thomas De Voe wrote in his 1862 history of the city's markets, "it could claim the merit of being the best, and the most liberally supplied with all the various articles used for human food, in the United States."

The Fly's vendors loved it against all reason, and when the end came, some clung desperately to the old place. Several butchers continued to sell their meat even as the market was being dismantled around them. John Seaman, at stall 71, became the last to vacate when a piece of the roof fell down between him and his father as they were completing a sale.

In 1821, Fulton Market opened. Its strategic location, near the Fulton Ferry, made it much more convenient than the Fly Market, three blocks to the south, whose business it completely absorbed. The Fly Market had already lost business to the Washington Market across town, which opened in 1813. Fulton Market killed it off for good in little more than a year.

When it opened, Fulton Market presented a handsome appearance. Stalls were arranged in three two-story brick buildings. The main building was topped with a wooden tower whose bell tolled at 2:00 p.m. every day, the signal for the meat stalls to close down. Over the years, wooden sheds filled in the open spaces between the buildings, and makeshift stalls crowded the sidewalks outside. It became an ordeal for pedestrians to pass by, and the market took on a ramshackle aspect of "an aggravated shanty," the *Times* complained. Maybe, but it was a shopper's paradise. Fulton Market offered every food imaginable, and more besides: shoes, stockings, used hats, cheap jewelry, racy novels. Its stalls and restaurants sold everything from fried doughnuts to oyster stews. (The famous fish market was a much later addition; it did not come along until 1869.)

Across town, Washington Market received the heavy traffic coming from New Jersey and the lower New York counties. New Jersey farmers had chosen the site as a convenient spot to sell their butter and eggs, and "Grand Country Market," emblazoned over the doorway to the original structure—a brick building with rough timbered floors—reflected the market's rural roots. By 1858, Washington Market had nearly a thousand stands. In peak season, farm produce was also sold from as many as two thousand wagons crowded outside the market. By the late 1870s, it was the largest of the city's ten food markets, doing $100 million in business annually. And, like Fulton Market, it soon gained a reputation as an unsightly, chaotic mess. Nevertheless, it continued to do business until the 1960s.

Scribner's Monthly captured the flavor in 1877:

LEFT: Opened in 1821, Fulton Market evolved into a ramshackle labyrinth of food stalls and oyster stands. RIGHT: Wagons from the market gardens of New Jersey and New York rolled into Washington Market, on the west side of town, laden with produce for the city's restaurants, hotels, and boardinghouses.

Choose a Saturday morning for a promenade in Washington Market, and you shall see a sight that will speed the blood in your veins—matchless enterprise, inexhaustible spirit, and multitudinous varieties of character. The best of stock is on sale—prime beef, the fattest poultry, the freshest vegetables—and the prices are the lowest. New Yorkers endure all the inconveniences of a street-car ride from Manhattanville or Harlem that they may have the traditional benefits of Washington Market in replenishing their larders. As you drift through the aisles—gangways, the market-men call them—the traders, who appear to have already more business than they can attend to, cheerily call your attention to their stock. "Nice quarter of mutton, sir?" "Prime sirloin of beef, twenty cents a pound?" "Here you are, sir! Haunch of venison, or a brace of ducks?" And so on through a long catalogue. There are avenues with crimson drapery—the best of beef in prodigious quarters; and avenues with soft velvet plumage of prairie-game from floor to ceiling; farther on a vegetable bower, and next to that a yellow barricade of country butter and cheese. You cannot see an idle trader. The poulterer fills in his spare moments in plucking his birds, and saluting the buyers; and while the butcher is cracking a joint for one purchaser he is loudly canvassing another from his small stand, which is completely walled in with meats. All the while there arises a din of clashing sounds which never loses pitch. Yonder there is a long counter, and standing behind it in a row are about twenty men in blue blouses, opening oysters. Their movements are like clock-work. Before each is a basket of oysters; one is picked out, a knife flashes, the shell yawns, and the delicate morsel is committed to a tin pail in two or three seconds.

The market system was no system at all, but a makeshift response to overwhelming demand, which, against all odds, it met. New Yorkers willing to navigate the crush and endure the insolence of the vendors could get their hands on the best and the most varied meats, fruits, and vegetables available in the United States. Thomas De Voe was a harsh critic of corruption, but even he admitted that slovenly, overcrowded, ramshackle Washington Market "is without a doubt the greatest depot for the sale of all manner of edibles in the United States."

The bounty is reflected in the earliest surviving menu from Delmonico's, a bilingual French and English bill of fare, printed in 1838, that indicates just how far the restaurant had advanced in the decade since it had started out selling coffee and pastries. Diners could feast on squab, hare, quail, pheasant, woodcock, grouse, venison, and wild duck. The fish included sheepshead, blackfish, striped bass, sole, trout, salmon, ray, shad, mackerel, and whiting. The vegetable dishes included salsify au jus, asparagus, eggplant, spinach or chicory in cream sauce, artichokes à la Barigoule, and cauliflower.

Besides selling raw ingredients, the markets attracted small food stands and low-cost restaurants that profited from the foot traffic. Some operated within the markets, others on the sidewalks and streets nearby. A few of the temporary food stands evolved into celebrated restaurants, especially at Fulton Market.

Most food vendors operated nothing more complicated than a little stand selling hot coffee and cakes, or soup and pig's feet. In 1801, Elizabeth Kline petitioned the governing board of the Catherine Market for the privilege of selling coffee and chocolate, "where nothing of this kind is at present sold by any person." Fish was the main commodity at Catherine Market, especially the eels brought in by fishermen from Canarsie, which the city's handful of Chinese residents bought fried or smoked.

Elizabeth Kline's counterpart at the Oswego Market on Broadway and Maiden Lane, which flourished at the end of the eighteenth century, was a certain Mrs. Jeroleman, who set up a table to sell hot coffee at threepence and doughnuts for a penny each. With a reported weight of 225 pounds, she was apparently an enthusiastic sampler of her own cooking. "As she moved about the market with her broad Dutch face," Thomas De Voe wrote, "the butcher-boys sung out, 'There goes the large dough-nut.'"

Kline and Jeroleman were pioneers. Before long, the city markets would swarm with coffee vendors, a familiar sight to shoppers like the two main characters in Cornelius Mathews's *Big Abel and the Little Manhattan*. Off to take in the sights, they pay a visit to Fulton Market and see a man with a tin box balanced atop "four thin legs." On top of the box is an assortment of cakes. A bed of coals inside the box heats the coffee, which is served in white cups. Writing for the New York *Aurora* in the early 1840s, Walt Whitman ventured into the Grand Street Market and noted "the savory fumes of the coffee and the rich 'kraulers'" that tempted street urchins and businessmen alike.

Washington Market, for the hungry visitor, was a city within the city, its winding gangways an invitation to penetrate deeper in search of delicious foods at its stalls. Outside the market, Smith & McNell's, one of the city's most famous restaurants, fed thousands of marketgoers and vendors in its cavernous dining room. Fulton Market, too, grew both by accretion and subdivision, with small snack shops carving out a tiny niche in the cellar. Some started out on the sidewalk and then, when the city tried to chase them away, burrowed inside the market.

For the shopper in a hurry, or the New Yorker with only a few pennies in his pocket, the market stalls offered a quick meal for next to nothing. "There is no privacy in those humble refectories (privacy must be paid for), and the passer-by may see street vagabonds and many a poor devil enjoying, for a pittance, the ordinary fare for which appetite is the best sauce," wrote a nostalgic journalist in 1879, when Fulton Market was about to be torn down to make way for a new one. "Men who are now prosperous, men who have acquired position and reputation, have, in their early days of struggle, satisfied their stomachic cravings at those lowly trenchers." He named them: James Gordon Bennett, editor of the *Herald*; Horace Greeley, editor of the *Tribune*; Henry Raymond, editor of the *Times*.

Smith & McNell's had begun life in 1853 as a coffee-and-cake restaurant on Washington Street, opposite the market. It was a modest establishment, capable of seating about fifty diners, but at the time there were few restaurants in the neighborhood, and its low prices attracted customers. By 1880, the original restaurant, heavily patronized by market men and produce dealers, had become an enormous hotel whose restaurant, open round the clock, could feed eight thousand diners a day. The loyalty of the market men ensured a steady supply of top-quality ingredients. Plain fare was served in the downstairs dining room, where market men and farmers ordered steak, chops, or ham and eggs for a nickel or a dime. Amazingly, these prices held until 1907. Upstairs, more elaborate meals were served to businessmen, but even there, the food was a bargain. Smith & McNell's did a roaring trade for more than half a century, right up until the First World War. By then the price of an entrée had risen to fifteen cents, but the general tone of the place remained remarkably constant.

The markets fed rich and poor alike. Roasted and bathed in fancy French sauces, their game seduced the palates of the city's gourmets; day-old vegetables found their way to the boardinghouse table. But in time, progress swept them all aside as civic improvers, hygiene fanatics, and supermarkets gained the upper hand. Only recently have New Yorkers become aware of what has been lost—a

The teeming waters of the Atlantic and Long Island Sound provided an abundant daily catch for the fish dealers at Fulton Market.

Fresh watermelons draw a crowd at Fulton Market. Note the oyster saloon across the aisle.

time-honored system for delivering flavor from the country to the city. In a frantic scramble, chefs and shoppers have tried to recapture the past. Through the city's greenmarkets, the link between farmers, consumers, and chefs has been forged anew. Some restaurants, on their own, have struck deals with local farmers to supply the fruits and vegetables that once came into the city by the wagonload each morning. In neighborhoods all over New York, hungry citizens have banded together to buy directly from farmers in share-purchase arrangements. Fine dining depends, ultimately, on the small-producer system. For generations, New York had the best one in the United States. Not coincidentally, it had the best restaurants, too.

Wholesale oyster dealers at Fulton Market quickly realized they could make money selling oysters on the half shell and oyster stews.

3

New York on the Half Shell

When the novelist William Makepeace Thackeray traveled to New York in 1852, he was given the star treatment owed to the author of *Vanity Fair*. He was feted publicly and privately, introduced to the cream of literary society—such as it was—and exposed to the great sights of America's most dynamic city. He sampled the fast-paced delights of Broadway and, at his own insistence, approached a genuine Bowery boy to enjoy some of the salty vernacular he had heard so much about. "I want to go to Brooklyn," he said, approaching a likely-looking loafer in the street, who, appraising the great writer coolly, said, "Well, why the hell don't you, then?"

One bit of the city's culture could not be ignored: the oyster. Oysters, as everyone knew, were to New York what the lobster was to Boston and the crab to Baltimore—the local food par excellence—and nowhere were they served in a fresher, more succulent state than at Fulton Market. For Englishmen used to the small, coppery-tasting oysters of the North Sea, the New World bivalves were a marvel, and Thackeray was fascinated by tales of their astounding dimensions. Already, at Boston's Tremont House, he had partaken, and the experience was unforgettable. Asked how he felt, Thackeray replied, "Profoundly grateful, and as if I had swallowed a large baby." In New York, the renowned oysters of A. P. Dorlon in Fulton Market produced a similar reaction. "Why, they are perfect beasts of oysters," Thackeray said.

Indeed: the bays and inlets of New York Harbor, the Raritan River in

New Jersey, and the entire length of Long Island Sound provided some of the most encouraging habitats an oyster could hope to find, and the species prospered accordingly. Up and down the shoreline, New York oysters grew fat and sweet. They were perfect beasts.

"There are a few places which have oysters of such an exquisite taste, and of so great a size, that they are pickled and sent to the West Indies and other places," wrote Peter Kalm, a Swedish naturalist who visited the Middle Atlantic states from 1748 to 1751. New Yorkers ate plenty of pickled oysters, too, although the appetite for them seems to have waned after the mid-nineteenth century (for mysterious reasons, since they sound delicious). The oysters were boiled, then steeped in a fragrant bouillon of their own juices seasoned with allspice, mace, pepper, and vinegar. Sometimes, oysters were fried in butter and then packed in a butter-filled jar.

Foreign travelers never failed to exclaim over the ingenuity that Americans applied to their oysters. "The New Yorkers alone have, I believe, twenty different ways of cooking oysters," wrote Francis Grund, a German visiting the city in the 1830s. "This in a country in which there is but one way of dressing meat." In his rambling tour of the city's oyster cellars in the 1850s, Charles Mackay, a Scottish journalist and songwriter, sampled "oysters pickled, stewed, baked, roasted, fried and scolloped [*sic*]; oysters made into soups, patties, and puddings; oysters with condiments and without condiments; oysters for breakfast, dinner, and supper; oysters without stint or limit—fresh as the fresh air, and almost as abundant— are daily offered to the palates of the Manhattanese, and appreciated with all the gratitude of which such a bounty of nature ought to inspire."

Before the era of restaurants and oyster saloons, oysters were sold any which way. On the streets, free blacks sold oysters from small cellars under the sidewalk, from market stalls (especially at Catherine Market), and from moveable stalls at the wharves. Most New Yorkers bought their oysters straight off the boat or in the markets. As late as 1830, a single wholesale business was enough to supply all the city's eating houses. Benjamin Story's provision shop at 64 Barclay Street put away 200 to 500 bushels in the fall and sold them off during the winter to eating stands in Washington Market or to grocers' shops.

By the middle of the nineteenth century, however, New York was consuming huge quantities of oysters, both local varieties and imports from Virginia. It was also supporting a major industry whose dimensions were impossible to measure. The *Herald*, in a series of articles on the oyster industry that ran in 1853, counted

1,500 boats of between 45 and 200 tons supplying dealers with oysters from Virginia and from local waters. Untold quantities of oysters were sold directly from boats and never passed through a dealer.

This thriving trade provided a ladder to success for black entrepreneurs like Thomas Downing, a free black from Virginia who ran a celebrated oyster saloon at 5 Broad Street that catered to politicians and clerks at the nearby Custom House. Downing counts as one of the more remarkable success stories in early New York. Black tavern owners were hardly unknown. Cato's Tavern, a roadhouse at what is now Fifty-ninth Street and Second Avenue, was owned by a black bartender. Nor were black oystermen a rarity—quite the contrary. Of the twenty-seven names listed in the 1810 city directory as oystermen, at least sixteen were black, and several, like Downing, opened their own oyster saloons. In 1830, Thomas M. Jackson opened an oyster cellar on Howard Street, west of Broadway. It was, the civil engineer Charles H. Haswell recalled, "a favorite and very popular resort, and deservedly so, as he kept good articles and was very civil and attentive to his customers. He also was popular as a caterer for public and private festivities."

At street stands like this one in an 1840s watercolor, rich and poor alike could enjoy oysters with a sprinkling of salt or a dash of vinegar or lemon juice.

But Downing achieved a rare level of wealth and prominence thanks to the oyster, which he had come to know and love growing up on Chincoteague, in the heart of Chesapeake oyster territory. After heading north to join the army in 1812, and working as a domestic servant in Philadelphia, he made his way to New York in 1819, where he set up as an oyster dealer in a small way, rowing a skiff across the Hudson to the New Jersey Flats. "There he would tong as many as time admitted," his son wrote in a brief biographical sketch, "and row himself back across the river and offer his delicious bivalves to a continually increasing number of customers" from his home on Pell Street. He prospered, and in 1825 he opened an oyster "refectory" at 5 Broad Street, where he roasted his oysters on a large gridiron over a fire of oak shavings. "Ladies and gentlemen with towel in hand, and an English oyster knife made for the purpose, would open their own oysters, drop into the burning hot concaved shell a lump of sweet butter and other seasonings, and partake of a treat," his son recalled. "Yes, there was a taste imparted by the saline and lime substances in which the juice of the oyster reached boiling heat that made it a delicate morsel. Truly, one worthy to be borne to the lips that sipped from the shell the nectareous mite."

The humble refectory became a favorite haunt of local merchants, stockbrokers, and politicians, for whom it functioned as an informal club and message center. A good listener, with a courtly manner, Downing acquired an almost mythic reputation as the man who knew all the secrets of Wall Street and City Hall. In 1835, Downing expanded his enterprise, absorbing the buildings on either side and remodeling lavishly with chandeliers and carpets.

By the 1840s, Downing's reputation was secure, his elaborate menu an irresistible draw for the discriminating diner. Along with the usual offerings of oysters on the half shell, and oysters stewed and roasted, he served scalloped oysters, fish with oyster sauce, and poached turkey stuffed with oysters. Philip Hone, the diarist and mayor, called him, simply, "the great man of oysters." Others called him the Prince of Saddle Rock—a reference to the largest, most sought-after oyster of the day. In 1842, it was Downing who was selected to cater the Boz Ball at the Park Theater. Given in honor of Charles Dickens, then on his first American tour, it was one of the most lavish affairs the city had ever seen. Downing's once-humble cellar became one of the city's preeminent "power restaurants," a position it held until 1857, when its owner retired with the sizable fortune of $100,000.

Brooklyn had its own Downing, the famous John Josephs, better known as Johnny Joe. Born a slave in Martinique, he was brought to New York as a boy and then freed by his master. For several years he served as a waiter in private homes, and later as an army servant, serving under General Winfield Scott during the War of 1812. In 1825, he married Louisa Britton, a former slave from Martinique, who did the cooking when he opened a small oyster saloon on Prospect Street. When the Hamilton Literary Association was founded in 1830, its members made Josephs's saloon their headquarters for meals and reunions.

The relationship turned Josephs from a mere purveyor of oyster stews into a local legend, as judges, lawyers, and newspaper editors followed, attracted, according to the *Brooklyn Eagle*, "by the best company, the best wine, the best oysters and the best cookery." At gatherings of the club, members would sing an official song of praise: "Our trysting place in Prospect Street. / Our glorious John

Joe's, / Where we all ate the oyster fries, / Down there at Johnny Joe's." The glory years lasted until Prospect Street was buried under the main entrance to the Brooklyn Bridge. "This vestibule of the great structure should properly be christened as Johnny Joe's monument," the *Eagle* proposed in its 1880 obituary of Josephs, "for who of all mortals more enjoyed his wine and oysters (and was more royally treated by him) than the immediate President of the Bridge Company, who is a distinguished Hamiltonian and whose portrait hangs in its ancient hall?"

The first oyster saloons were makeshift stands set up by bargemen, who converted their ship's hatches into trestle tables from which they sold oysters and clams on the half shell. In Fulton Market, wholesalers gradually realized that by setting up a few tables and chairs, and firing up a charcoal stove, they could do a brisk business in oyster stews in addition to raw shellfish. In the months when oysters were not eaten, steaks and chops were added to the menu. Eventually, full-blown restaurants evolved.

"All a man wanted for a start in the business was pepper, salt, vinegar, and a board on which to set out the dishes," the *Tribune* wrote in a history of the market. The great Alfred P. Dorlon, another whose name became synonymous with oysters, got his start in precisely this way. Described by a contemporary as "a tall, compact, well-made man, with sandy hair and complexion, and the look of a pilot, or one accustomed to the sea," he worked at his father's stall in Fulton Market and in 1844 set up on his own as a wholesaler, selling a few bushels of oysters a day. Soon he opened a stall with a few tables, where he sold oysters stewed, fried, and broiled. With his brother Philetus, he founded A. & P. Dorlon, whose stall—number 96—flourished until the 1880s.

It was at Dorlon's that distinguished European visitors, including the Prince of Wales, ate their first Manhattan oysters. Thousands of New Yorkers picked their way through the market's maze in search of the renowned Dorlon stews. For the newcomer, it was a challenge. "Dorlon's oyster stand is inside of the market, not far from Beekman Street and close by the stand of the millionaire chicken man, if you know where that is," a reporter wrote for the *New York Evening Gazette* in 1867. Those who did not were advised to join the crowd heading toward the ferry to Brooklyn,

> pass a dozen soup stands, pie counters, cake tables, and lunch rooms (remember you are inside that village of shanties known as the market), wind your way through several Yankee notion

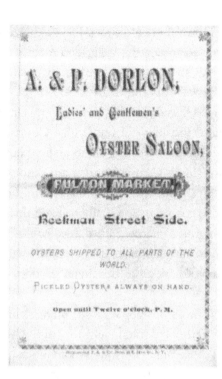

A menu from Dorlon's at Fulton Market, one of the city's most renowned oyster saloons

shops, and book stores . . . behold all the wonders of the tropical fruit department, with its heaps of flaming bananas, yellow lemons and golden oranges; pass the watermelon tables surrounded by a crowd of hungry New York merchants, each with a knife in one hand, and a bloody slice of the fruit in the form of an alligator's jaw, in the other, wander through the never-ending peach department, with the peaches piled up like cannon balls in the Brooklyn Navy Yard, while baskets of them stand on the floor wreathed in the living green of the peach tree, and innumerable small baskets hang over head, the blushing New Jersey maidens meanwhile standing behind the benches, as fair and sweet as the peaches they sell—pass by all this, if you can, . . . turn to your left, glance at the fishes of a thousand species, and the crabs and lobsters that will thrust out their antennae as you pass by; shudder slightly; ascend a second flight of stairs, wander through a maze of meat stalls, fish benches, clam stands, etc., and finally turn to the right and find yourself in the cozy oyster saloon of Dorlon.

Never had so many traveled so far for the humble oyster.

Dorlon's success begat Dorlon and Shaffer, a partnership between the third Dorlon brother, Sydney, and George H. Shaffer, an employee of A. & P. Dorlon. Sydney, who had been working for his brothers during the winters, opened a small saloon when a stand at the market became vacant in 1858. Soon he emerged as a rival. By serving no alcohol other than ale, he attracted a more mixed clientele. Couples and even unescorted women would travel all the way from uptown Manhattan to eat an oyster stew and, perhaps, to get a glimpse of Sydney, a character much remarked upon for his "large and unfashionable" clothes and his odd manners, described as "eccentric but pleasant." He was easy to spot. A lover of beautiful flowers, he usually had a small bouquet affixed to his lapel.

Guidebooks often confused the two Dorlon stands. Their task became even more difficult when a third Dorlon's, unrelated to the two Fulton Market restaurants, opened across from the south side of Madison Square in 1875. Its large clock on the sidewalk soon became a city landmark, with letters instead of numerals on the face spelling out DORLON OYSTER. The house specialty was its Gunther's Cove oysters—mysterious because no Gunther's Cove appeared on any map. The infuriated Dorlons of Fulton Market carried on a press campaign disavowing any connection with the upstart. In their contempt, they declined even to identify its location, other than "somewhere uptown." They failed. The new Dorlon's became a beloved New York institution, in large part because of the excellence of its grill.

No uptown rival, though, could cut into the business of the downtown restaurants, whose mystique grew with the years. Ambience could not explain the attraction: both establishments were spartan, dispensing with such niceties as napkins, tablecloths, and butter knives. This did not deter fashionable New Yorkers. "Fastidious ladies, who at home dwell in splendid boudoirs and sit in perfumed chambers, take Dorlan's [sic] on their way from the opera, for a stew or a saddle-rock roast," wrote one observer in 1868. "Gentlemen who have rosewood tables on Turkey carpets, eat off of porcelain and silver ware, whose dining-rooms are perfumed with the choicest flowers, thankfully accept a stool without a back to it at Dorlan's, and are jostled by the crowd. The belles and madames of the upper ten often stand in a row awaiting their turn."

When A. & P. Dorlon's remodeled in the late 1870s, as the original Fulton Market was being readied for the new, it lost some of the old atmosphere. When it was little more than a shack, Dorlon's exuded a raffish charm. Patrons accepted the brusque service as part of the experience. At the new Dorlon's the menu still ran heavily to oysters, served raw or in stews and fritters, but patrons could now also order a porterhouse steak, fried tripe, or game in season, including canvasback duck, partridge, woodcock, or venison, with pie or strawberry shortcake for dessert. Besides shellfish, the restaurant offered eels, bass, smelts, and shad, with Bass ale on tap and five brands of champagne. With the introduction of silverware and napkins, Dorlon's entered into competition with the fancier oyster restaurants uptown, and became just one of many.

Another leading oysterman was Captain Demorin Libby, of Libby's Oyster House. In 1839, Libby, after heading out to sea from his childhood home in Wellfleet, Massachusetts, opened an oyster saloon in New York at 6 Broad Street, later moving it to 19 Wall Street and, finally, 59 Murray Street, where he stayed in business for thirty-eight years, building a faithful clientele—Cornelius Vanderbilt, Horace Greeley, and the soprano Jenny Lind among them—with his pickled oysters and lobsters boiled in seawater. Libby, who neither smoked nor drank, was a hardy old coot. At ninety he was spotted ice skating on the Orange Oval near his home in East Orange, and he lived for another five years after that. Along the way, he managed to survive a bizarre incident at his Wall Street saloon in 1852. While cooking at the stove, the *Times* reported, "his attention was attracted to a heavy mass rolling in the air." The mass was a nearby lodger who slipped while covering a hole in his roof and fell straight to his death through Libby's skylight.

The oyster stands at Fulton Market, open late, did a roaring business catering to parties heading back to Brooklyn on the ferry after a night at the theater. At a proper stand, patrons ordering a half dozen oysters paid fifteen cents if they ate standing up, twenty cents sitting down. A "half dozen" meant seven oysters, and a dozen meant thirteen. At the cheaper stands, a half dozen cost a dime. To signal the attendant, patrons would take a two-pronged fork out of a glass of water and wave it.

Elsewhere in the market, hungry patrons sought out oyster pies, a popular food but not one for the weak of stomach, evidently. "It is like a small cart-wheel, of pale complexion, and most uncertain age," wrote a roving reporter for the *National Police Gazette*. "When one is called for, it is steamed a little to take the rheumatism out of the oysters, and then, after being drowned in a milky compound, is placed in a condition of fragrant hotness and pliability before the devourer."

Oysters were the great leveler. At market stands, the New Yorker with a couple of nickels rubbed shoulders with the gay blades known as "howling swells." In humble cellars and lavish oyster palaces all over the city, oysters were consumed voraciously for as long as the oyster beds held out. Theaters nearly always had an oyster saloon nearby, precursors of the boisterous Times Square restaurants known as lobster palaces that would appear around the turn of the century. One veteran restaurateur recalled selling five hundred "shilling stews" every night near the Park Theater in the 1830s.

Along Canal Street, cheap oyster saloons hung out a muslin balloon stretched over a wicker or rattan frame and illuminated by a candle within— "the red-white oyster moons, to light the seeker down," as one novelist had it. Inside, as at the beef saloons, diners sat in a wooden booth where, for privacy, they could draw a thin curtain hung on a rod. Prices were scaled to the common man. The "Canal Street plan" was a catchphrase for one of the best deals in town: all the oysters you could eat for six cents, usually sprinkled with vinegar or lemon juice, or perhaps just a little salt. By the 1880s, ketchup and horseradish were standard as well. Along the East River, longshoremen, sailors, and stevedores patronized rickety shacks selling raw oysters at a penny apiece. Inside, they could order oyster soup for a nickel and oyster stew for a dime.

George G. Foster, a writer for Horace Greeley's *Tribune*, sauntered into one of the deluxe oyster saloons in the late 1840s, an "Aladdin's cave" of sensory delights that inspired an almost delirious account of its splendors, from the "gorgeous labyrinth of many-colored glass" that pleasantly disoriented first-time customers, to the damask curtains, plush carpeting, shaded lights, and "long row of mirrored arcades, festooned with costly blue and crimson silk, wreathed with golden carved work." Foster also noted the "exquisite and voluptuous" drawings on the wall—a woodcock here, a half-nude woman there. Perhaps a half dozen oyster saloons in the city measured up to the standards of this one, which Foster regrettably failed to identify. In 1872, the *Brooklyn Eagle* reckoned that there were 750 oyster saloons in New York and 100 in Brooklyn, while a veteran oyster dealer talking to the *Times* in 1883 put the number at a scarcely credible 4,000. Whatever the precise figure, New York had a lot of oyster saloons. As an 1853 guidebook put it, "One might think that the people of New York should essentially be classed as an oyster-eating community."

At the lower end of the scale, the oyster saloon carried connotations of vice and prostitution. Florence's, on the southwest corner of Broadway and Houston Street, gained a citywide reputation not only for its oysters but also for the louche atmosphere it absorbed from its surroundings. "A sort of half-light of criminality has seemed to hang over [Houston] street for all its history," one reporter noted in 1875. Readers no doubt nodded in silent agreement, thinking immediately of Harry Hill's concert saloon a few doors away. Hill put on popular acts, most of them risqué or vulgar, that would later be cleaned up and sold as family entertainment under the name of vaudeville. The occasional boxing match was staged as well. Fights were common and prostitution rife, helping set the tone for a district that soon specialized in tough bars, late-night restaurants, and dubious entertainments.

When John Florence, an Irishman, set up shop in a cellar in the 1830s, he intended his restaurant to be a top-drawer oyster saloon for the higher class of sporting gentleman. And so it was, its rich appointments "worthy of the approving nod of Sardanapalus," as the journalist and man-about-town Nathaniel P. Willis put it in 1843. Florence's private supper rooms were, the *Times* reported, "the resort of fashionable and fastidious parties." As Houston Street declined, Florence's began attracting the lower class of sporting gentleman, lured by the keno, faro, and roulette action. A favored haunt of gamblers and thieves, it was the first establishment pounced upon by the police in the Great Keno Raid of 1871.

Florence's was also the scene of some of New York's more famous fistic altercations—not organized bouts but out-and-out brawls. "It was here," according to the *Times*, "that the celebrated fight between Andy Sheehan and John Morrissey occurred, in which the latter well-nigh killed his assailant with his fists, and established for himself such a reputation that never afterward was he attacked physically, except in the ring." Morrissey went on to work as an enforcer and street-level political fixer for Boss Tweed and develop a close (and lucrative) friendship with Cornelius Vanderbilt. Eventually, he opened a swell gambling house across from the Fifth Avenue Hotel on Madison Square before serving two terms in Congress.

Less celebrated, but just as stirring, was the face-off between James Haggerty and the notorious William Varley, better known as Reddy the Blacksmith, who "indulged in an interchange of courtesies which terminated for the time by the breaking of a heavy cut-glass decanter over Reddy's head, and his complete and instantaneous insensibility." The fight later resumed across the corner at Patsy Eagan's saloon, where Reddy, armed with a pistol, shot Haggerty dead. Such were the pleasures of Houston Street.

The oysters sold in New York went by many names but all belonged to the same species, *Crassostrea virginica*, which developed different taste characteristics depending on where they fed. Some of them were whoppers, like the one that turned up in 1869 at Crook and Nash's, a chophouse in the New York Times Building on Park Row. Upon being opened it revealed a five-inch smelt "curled completely round the edge of the molusc [*sic*]." The "enterprising oyster" had gone for big game, and at the time it was shucked was in the process of consuming its oversize prey.

A few of the local oyster names, like Blue Points, from the Great South Bay of Long Island, can still be found today. Others no longer stir even the faintest of memories: the once-prized Shrewsburies (from the Shrewsbury River in New Jersey), with their distinctive yellowish color and sweet flavor; Rockaways (from the south shore of Long Island); Prince's Bay (off Staten Island); and the fabled Saddle Rocks. The annual August reports on the impending oyster season, a standard newspaper feature, listed names that have vanished forever: Amboys and Keyports from Raritan Bay (called Sounds by Staten Islanders); Bayvilles; East River Hills; City Islanders; Oak Islands; and the many subvarieties of the Rockaway: Millcreeks, Cinderbeds, Brokerboilers, Flatlands, and

Eastern Shoos. (The Rockaways were famous for more than oysters. The fine sand from their beaches was sold to saloons and eating houses, where it was scattered on the floor.) "The Rockaways and Blue Points have spawned and are rapidly fattening," ran a report on the 1889 season. "The Bayvilles and East River Hills are in good enough condition to rejoice the heart of the oyster farmer intent upon the financial probabilities of the year." Better yet, "there will be little trouble this year from starfish, mussels, drumfish, borers, and other foes of the oyster's happiness."

Most famous of all were the Saddle Rocks, named for a natural outcropping about twenty feet high, with a saddle-shaped crown, near the head of Great Neck, on Long Island. In the autumn of 1827, one story had it, a strong northwest wind blew for three days, resulting in an exceptionally low tide that exposed a bed of oysters just below the rock. Unusually large (three to four inches on av-

Oyster barges with storefronts once lined the waterfront. There were only a few left by the 1930s, when Berenice Abbott took this photograph on South Street near Pike Slip, under the Manhattan Bridge.

erage), with a thin shell and flavor described as "delicate" and "luscious," they attracted hordes of oystermen, who quickly stripped the bed bare. By the 1840s, nary a Saddle Rock was left, but the name lived on, since dealers and restaurants could use it profitably. "Nowadays any big fat oyster answers to the name of Saddle Rock, whether he comes from Blue Point, the Shrewsbury or the Sound," the oysterman J. W. Boyle told a reporter in 1883. "You and hundreds of other New Yorkers never know the difference."

Local oysters were prized above the blander Virginians, which went into stews rather than being served on the half shell. A "northern stew" commanded a premium price. Fried oysters required the large "box" size, so called because they were shipped in boxes rather than barrels. As the decades wore on, though, large oysters on the half shell fell out of fashion. "They belong in fries and broils and nowhere else," one dealer argued in 1882.

> They have no more business to be eaten raw than big pumpkins have. Nobody thinks of eating them on the half-shell nowadays but countrymen. When a real hay-maker comes to town he goes for his oysters before he strikes even a cheap theater. And he wants them just as big as he can get them. So we always keep some large ones on hand, though there is not much demand for them. Sweet? It's just like eating a piece of alligator to chew one of the biggest oysters. There's just the difference, Sir, between a large and small oyster that there is between a codfish and a trout. The only merit of the one is that he weighs 20 pounds; the other, though small, is sweet, tender, delicious.

Like the game birds of the New Jersey Meadowlands, the oyster retreated before the encroaching human tide. Avid consumption and pollution depleted the great natural beds around New York early on. From time to time, new ones were discovered, but after 1850 most New York oysters were farmed, often using Virginia seed oysters from the Chesapeake Bay. Once king, the oyster became simply another kind of seafood. The oyster carts and the oyster cellars disappeared, as the Libbys and the Dorlons died off.

Today, only one restaurant in New York offers an approximation of the old oyster cellars: the Oyster Bar at Grand Central Terminal. Its oyster pan roasts, oyster stews, and oysters on the half shell in dozens of varieties recall a New

York that vanished more than a century ago. At a window facing one of the station's teeming passageways, stand-up diners slurp a quick stew before rushing back to work or racing for a train. At low-slung counters, hordes of lunchtime diners wave for stews and iced oysters the way their forebears must have done at Fulton Market in the middle of the nineteenth century, but now the oysters come not only from Long Island but from Newfoundland and Washington State. Bustling and vibrant, the Oyster Bar is sacred ground, a last link to the bivalve that defined New York dining for generations.

4
A Little Restaurant and How It Grew: The Delmonico's Story

The Delmonico's story begins, like a fairy tale, in the mountains of Switzerland, where three brothers lived on a small farm in the canton of Ticino. Francesco, the eldest, tilled the soil. Pietro, his younger brother, apprenticed himself to a pastry chef in Berne. Giovanni, the youngest, left landlocked Switzerland in search of adventure on the high seas.

Giovanni prospered. As captain of the three-masted schooner *Fidelity*, he made commercial runs between Cuba, Spain, and the United States. At thirty-eight, however, he began thinking of how to make his living on land. Around 1824, he Anglicized his first name as John and set up in New York as an importer of French and Spanish wines. Almost immediately he sensed that the city around him throbbed with potential. On a visit home, he convinced Pietro, now firmly established as a confectioner in Berne, to uproot his family and bring his pastry business to the New World.

In 1827, the two brothers opened a café and pastry shop at 23 William Street. As we have seen, the place was not much to look at. A simple pastry counter ran along one side of the room, presided over by John. Customers took a seat at one of a half dozen pine tables and ordered a cup of chocolate or coffee with a small cake or a bonbon, followed, perhaps, by a glass of brandy and a cigar. As Abram Dayton pointed out, the dishes were earthenware and the forks two-tined.

Ticino is an Italian-speaking canton, and the Delmonicos bore an Italian name, but the family, for whatever reason, spoke French, and the

Delmonico brothers ran their business along strictly French lines. Foreign businessmen soon took note of the little café with the distinctive French accent. Would-be sophisticates like Sam Ward also found their way there, usually on the sly. "On these occasions unusual secrecy was indispensable," Dayton recalled, "for if detected we were certain to incur the marked displeasure of our grandmothers, and to be soundly berated in the first place for our foolish extravagance, and secondly, pitied for our lack of taste by giving preference to 'such vile greasy compounds,' which we were assured would destroy our stomachs; while if we dared to mention the cool, refreshing *vin ordinaire*, that delightful beverage was denounced as a miserable substitute for vinegar."

Delmonico's thrived. Within four years, the two brothers took over the building next door and opened a full-fledged restaurant to complement the café. Here was something new: fine French food, courteous service, and the opportunity to eat at an hour of one's own choosing. Instead of a set meal at a set time, as was offered at the city's hotels and ordinaries, Delmonico's gave its customers an à la carte menu (alas, none survive from the period before 1838) and, just as important, the freedom to dine when they felt like it. For households putting on a fancy dinner, they provided catering services. At Christmas, Delmonico's sold imported French toys. Business took off immediately. In need of reinforcements, the brothers sent to Switzerland for yet another member of the family: Lorenzo, one of Francesco's sons.

Lorenzo, only nineteen years old, would soon become the face and future of the Delmonico empire, which now included a 220-acre farm in Williamsburg, Brooklyn. In the coming years, with uncanny prescience, Lorenzo would anticipate, and capitalize on, New York's growth, hopscotching uptown as the city expanded. A stickler for detail, and a keen student of the tastes he catered to, he earned the undying loyalty of the city's ruling class. He was, as one obituary writer would note, "more of a Yankee than either of his relatives; he was enterprising, he was sharp-witted, quick to discover an advantage and earnest in its pursuit."

Just where the Delmonicos learned the French style of cooking and service remains somewhat mysterious. John, sailing between Spain, Cuba, and the United States, spent no time in France, and Peter never left Berne. Nevertheless, their approach was uncompromisingly French, at least at the outset. They spared no effort to acquire the best French wines, and they kept abreast of the latest fashions in Parisian cookery. As their business grew, they became a constant source of employment for French chefs, who brought with them the latest innovations from the top Parisian restaurants. New Yorkers ranked Delmonico's with the best in Paris, and foreign visitors were not inclined to dispute the claim. With time, Delmonican tastes became more cosmopolitan, embracing dishes and ingredients from around the world, and from distant points within the United States. "The metropolitan education of an intelligent visitor, foreign or American, was incomplete," Sam Ward wrote, "until he had partaken, on a major or minor scale, of the creation of this culinary world, fare in which the delicacies of every zone, from the caviare of Archangel to the 'polenta' of Naples, the 'allia podrida' [sic] of Madrid, the Bouillabaisse of Marseilles, the 'Casuela' [sic] of Santiago Chili, and the Buffalo hump of Fort Laramie were at command."

But it was with French cuisine that Delmonico's first made its impact, inspiring some dissenting rumbles. At the time, French food did not inspire universal admiration. Philip Hone, merchant and (very briefly) mayor, whose diary provides a detailed picture of social life in New York from 1826 to 1851, pronounced the city's latest dining sensation an overrated dud after a visit in 1830. "We satisfied our curiosity but not our appetites," he wrote, "and I think are prepared, when our opinions are asked, to say with the Irishman who used lamp-oil with his salad instead of olive-oil, that if it were not for the name of the thing he would as lief eat butter."

On December 16, 1835, disaster struck. Fire swept through lower Manhattan, destroying nearly seven hundred buildings in a matter of hours. Most merchants could only watch as their businesses burnt to the ground. The fire spread erratically. Buildings that seemed safe would suddenly become engulfed in flames. Delmonico's was one of these. A group of men who had ducked into the café for a cup of chocolate had to leave immediately when someone noticed flames licking the corner of the room. Within hours, the city's first and finest French restaurant was a heap of cinders.

The canny Delmonicos, expansion-minded from the start, had opened a hotel at 76 Broad Street the previous year. They now shifted their restaurant operations to this location. At the same time, at the corner of Beaver and William streets, they began constructing a new restaurant, which opened to great fanfare in 1837. The Beaver Street Delmonico's, a brick-and-marble building popularly known as the Citadel, reflected the prestige and the ambitions of the family enterprise, with marble floors in the first-floor dining room and expensive parquet upstairs. On the third floor, patrons beheld a marvelous French innovation: private dining rooms.

The Delmonicos had invested heavily in this new venture, which, Ward recalled, soon became "the resort of the businessman, the 'bon-vivant' and at times of the reveller." Their timing was impeccable. Even in the financial panic year of 1837, New York was a go-ahead city, swelled by an influx of Americans on the make and immigrants eager to start a new life. When the restaurant opened, the city had a population of about 160,000. By 1830 that number had risen to just over 200,000, and it would reach 300,000 by 1840. Foreign traders and a rising native merchant class made a natural constituency for a restaurant that, almost from the outset, courted elite customers and spared no effort or expense to please them. Generations of well-to-do New Yorkers took family meals at Delmonico's; they danced at its balls and cotillions. The high and the mighty were feted at its ceremonial dinners, and the daughters of the prominent were presented to society at its balls.

The contrast with François Guerin's pastry shop is instructive. The rival confectioner carried on at his original location, refusing to budge. The shop was dingy, the presentation crude, and the hygiene suspect. "In the window he displayed confectionery (imported and domestic), pastry, cakes, bottles of cordials, Parisian bonbon boxes, fruit," Abram Dayton recalled. Inside, Guerin sold fruits preserved in sugar and brandy and, from a long counter, tarts and confections. The bill of fare was limited to sardines, sandwiches, and sweets. At the rear of the store was a small room where diners could enjoy coffee, chocolate, and ice cream, "but it was at best a dingy place," Dayton wrote, "and as it had no entrance except through the store, it was but little frequented, and never by ladies." Business was good, nevertheless, and Guerin grew rich.

Of course, Guerin must have found it hard to keep his mind on pastry display. In 1833, in one of the more sensational court cases of the day, he sued a certain William A. Strozzi, seeking large damages for offenses that were more than any Frenchman could bear. It seems that Strozzi, a "linguist" who had taught at the Washington Institute, developed a taste not only for Guerin's mille-feuilles but for Madame Guerin as well. Stationed behind the counter, she initially repulsed his advances, but he persisted and in the end won her heart. According to court testimony, Strozzi then began pestering his beloved to supply "money, segars and other articles from the store." He also coerced Madame Guerin into signing an agreement to marry him within a year of her husband's death. Impudently, he began referring to her as his wife.

When the affair came to light, Madame Guerin tried to take her own life with a dose of laudanum. Her aggrieved husband went to court, a course he was soon to regret. Lawyers introduced correspondence between Strozzi and Madame Guerin—"probably the most curious specimen of love letters ever produced in a court of law," according to the *New York Courier and Enquirer*. Alas, the contents were either too steamy or too bizarre to be reprinted or even paraphrased. Still, the house of Guerin carried on, shaken but resolute. As late as 1851, the city directory listed an Edward Guerin, confectioner, at the pastry shop's address, 120 Broadway.

Free from such distractions, Delmonico's established the tone for fine dining in New York almost overnight, and it would remain preeminent until the 1890s. This was no small feat. As the city grew, it added hotels, and those hotels, vying to outdo one another in the luxury of their accommodations, opened dining rooms intended to compete with Delmonico's. Leading the list was the Astor

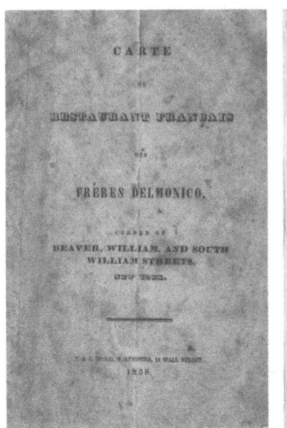 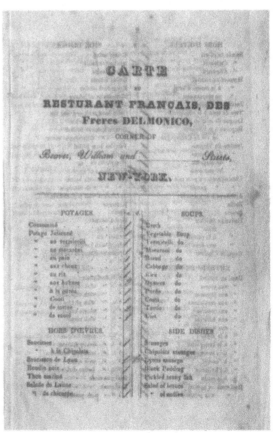

ABOVE AND FOLLOWING PAGES: The earliest known Delmonico's menu, from 1838, shows the ambitions of its kitchen and the profusion of ingredients available. Prices are given in shillings and pence.

ENTREMETS SUCRÉS. | s. | d. | PASTRY, CAKES.

French	s.	d.	English
Crème au bain marie			Fried cream
" frite			Currant jelly
Gelée de groseilles			Rum do
" au rhum			Rice soufflay
Soufflé au riz			Omelet do
Omelette soufflée			" with preserves
" aux confitures			" with sugar
" au sucre			Rice pudding
Puddin au riz			Rice Balls
Croquette de riz			Potato do
" de pommes			Rice Cake
Gateau au riz			

DESSERT. | | | DESSERT.

French	s.	d.	English
Orange et sucre			Orange and sugar
Salade d'oranges			" salad
Fraises et sucre			Strawberries and sugar
Framboises et sucre			Raspberries and sugar
Gâteau de pommes			Apple cake
" à la crème			Cream cake
Compote de pommes			Stewed apples
" à la Polonaise			" " Polish fashion
" de poires			" pears
" de pruneaux			" prunes
" de pêches			" peaches
Pêche			Peach
" à l'eau de vie			Brandy peach
Meringues à la crème			French kisses
" aux confitures			" with preserves
Macarons			Macaroons
Biscuits au moule			Sponge Cakes
Fromage de Chester			Chester cheese
" Parmésan			Parmesan do
" de Gruyère			Gruyere do
" tête de mort			Dutch do
La demi-tasse de café			Cup of coffee
Punch au rhum			Rum punch
" à l'eau de vie			Brandy do
" au whiskey			Whiskey do
" à la Romaine			Roman do

LIQUEURS.

Extrait d'absinthe	0 6		Crème de chocolat	0 6
Eau de vie de Cognac	0 6		Vanille	0 6
" " d'Andaye	1 0		Huile de rose	0 6
" " de Dantzig	1 0		" de Vénus	0 6
Kirschenwasser	0 6		Crème de Moka	0 6
			Parfait amour	0 6
Rhum vieux	0 6			
Anisette de Bordeaux	0 6		Anisao de Majorca	0 6
Noyesu	0 6		Angelique	
Canelle	0 6		Al kermes	1 0
Crème de menthe	0 6		Elixir	1 0
" d'absinthe	0 6		Ratafia de Grenoble	0 6
Curaçao de Hollande	0 6		Scubac	1 0

VINS—WINES.

Red Bordeaux—Bordeaux Rouge.				*Rhône Blanc—White Rhône.*	
Lafitte,	1825	20		Hermitage	12
Chateau Margaux,	1825	20		Cotillon	8
Latour,	1825	20		Condrieux	8
Haut Brion,	1825	16		St. Peray	8
Léoville,	1825	12 & 16		*Bourgogne—Burgundy.*	
Larose,	1825	16		Clos Vougeot	20 & 24
Mouton,	1825	16		Chambertin	16
Rawzan,	1825	16		Nuit-Richebourg	16
Chateau Langoa,	1825	12		Beaune 1ᵉʳ	16
Pichon,	1825	12		Volney	16
Duern, 1825		12		Chablis	8
Callon, 1825		12		*Blanc du Rhin—White Rhine.*	
Chateau Beycheville		12		Laubensheimer	12
Batailley		12		Rudesheimer	12
St. Pierre		12		Hochheimer	12
L'Aux		12		Stein-wein	12
St. Julien		4 & 8		Johannisberger, 1822	16
St. Estephe		8		*Champagne.*	
Vieu Claret		8		Delmonico Brand	12
Ordinair				Sillery	12
Bordeaux Blanc—White Bordeaux.				Anchor	12
				Montebello	12
Barsac		16		Key brand	12
Sauterne		4 12 & 16		Oeil de perdrix	16
Grave		8		*Madère.*	
Blanc ordinair		3		Faquart	48
Rhône Rouge—Red Rhône.				Old Reserve, 1822	40
				Old Madeira	12 & 16
Hermitage		12		Romanée—Sherry	32
Côtes rôties		12		Sherry	12 & 16
St. Joseph		8		Porto	12 & 16
Roussillon		8			
La Nerthe		4			
St. George		8		Brown Stout	4

House, New York's answer to Boston's Tremont House. In addition to hot and cold running water in every room, the Astor boasted water closets on every floor and gas lighting throughout the building (not just in the public rooms). A printing press turned out fresh menus daily for the hotel's dining rooms, which served American cuisine at a level appropriate to its select clientele. Sarah Mytton Maury, an Englishwoman staying at the hotel in the 1840s, encountered a dinnertime feast of turtle soup, oyster pie, sliced ham, poultry, and game, followed by a variety of sweets, jellies, and blancmange. If inclined, she might have extended the meal with shad or sheepshead, partridge, canvasbacks, and venison "cooked on the table before you."

In the Broad Street rooming house that the Delmonicos converted into their hotel, Joseph Collet, a Frenchman, had made a stab at running a French restaurant. He failed, but the Globe Hotel, on Broadway just below Wall Street, mounted a serious bid when François (Francis) Blancard took it over in 1836, breaking with American practice and operating under the European plan, meaning that guests paid for room and board separately. If and when it pleased them, they could take their meals in the dining rooms, which were also open to the public. Judging by the fare on offer, it seems highly likely that they chose to eat at the hotel. At Blancard's, the discriminating diner could feast on suprême de volaille aux truffes (chicken breast larded with thin slices of truffle), pâté de foie gras, and woodcock salmis, or stew.

The Globe filled a desperate need. Delmonico's was already "crowded to excess," despite a clutch of competing restaurants. A continuing influx of foreigners, and the new efficiencies of steamboat navigation, would require more such restaurants, the *Spirit of the Times* predicted, pointing out reasonably that "Delmonico's cannot dine all the town."

Up and down Broadway, the French tone was unmistakable. New York's increasing wealth made it a natural market for luxury goods, France's stock-in-trade for centuries, and it quickly succumbed to an infatuation that continues to the present day. The journalist Charles Briggs, in a fit of comic pique, surveyed Broadway's signs and storefronts and complained of "Madame Grand-this and Mons. Grand-that" over every shop door, along with "the French shoes, the French gloves, the French clocks, the *liqueurs*, the *bon-bons*, the *bijouterie*, the *meringues*, the *pates-de-foie-gras*." French audacity knew no bounds. "Not long since," Briggs wrote, "we saw on a sign-board, stuck up at the entrance of a cellar on the corner of Reade-street and Broadway, '*Au Rocher de Cancale*,' painted in very soup-maigreish looking letters, with an attempt at the representation of an oyster." New York, the world capital of oyster consumption, renowned for its Shrewsburies and Blue Points, encroached upon by a Parisian! Imagine the tables turned, he suggested—an American setting up a "house of refreshment" in Paris with a menu featuring clam soup, pumpkin pie, waffles, hoe cakes, and mush and milk.

Briggs found the French irritating but American Francophilia even worse. In his satirical novel *The Adventures of Harry Franco*, he sends his hero, a luckless broker in the panic year of 1837, into a pretentious restaurant serving "potage au lay de mush" and, for dessert, "pattey de pumpkin." Franco cannot help noticing that his "bif au naturel" and "pomme de terre a la maitre d'hotel" bear a striking resemblance to beef and potatoes.

In 1839, flush with success, Blancard opened a newer, grander Globe on Broadway just a few steps north of the old hotel. Designed to impress, it was an imposing five stories tall and clad in Quincy granite, just like the Astor House. The new Globe offered a five o'clock table d'hôte for diners who liked the idea of a fixed dinner hour, as well as more flexible French hours for European guests. Already, however, the ground was shifting. An explosion of new hotel construction was adding hundreds of restaurant tables every year. New York, which had 8 hotels in 1818, had 28 in 1836, and 108 in 1846. That year, Blancard and his beloved Globe went under as the city's bon ton migrated northward. Lower Manhattan, once a tightly integrated business and residential neighborhood, was rapidly becoming a purely commercial district.

By the 1850s, certain downtown streets were already deserted after business hours. By the 1860s, the neighborhood had been transformed beyond recognition. "If a New Yorker who had been absent from the city fifteen years were to be set down at Bowling-green for a walk up Broadway," the *Times* wrote in 1860, "he would hardly find, in the whole distance thence to Grace Church"—that is, to Eleventh Street—"half-a-dozen objects with which he is familiar. St. Paul's Church, the Astor House, Barnum's Museum, St. Thomas's Church, the New-York Hotel and the Church of the Messiah would comprise about the whole list." New York was a different city, but one thing remained unchanged. Delmonico's was still its leading restaurant.

In 1842, John Delmonico died. Lorenzo, now twenty-nine, took over as manager of the family empire, which would expand and flourish under his watchful eye. For the next forty years his routine never varied. At 4:00 a.m. he shopped the

Washington and Fulton markets. Four hours later he returned to the Citadel, his purchases trailing behind him in rolling carts. After drinking a cup of coffee and smoking a cigar, he would go home to nap, returning in the evening to the restaurant, where he sat with friends until midnight. In 1848, Peter sold his interest in the restaurant, and Lorenzo became sole owner of Delmonico's and curator of its mystique.

In 1856, Lorenzo made a typically bold move. He decided to move uptown yet again. The Citadel remained in place, serving lunch to the financial district, but henceforth the flagship restaurant would be located at the corner of Chambers Street and Broadway. The location was artfully chosen—just north of City Hall, across the street from the splendid A. T. Stewart department store, and within arm's reach of the newspapers on Park Row. In the grand second-floor dining room, leading merchants, editors, politicians, and lawyers ate at their leisure, while downstairs an anonymous army of dry-goods clerks, lawyers' assistants, and journalists hurried through lunch or ordered cocktails.

No sooner had New York grown used to thinking of the "uptown" Delmonico's as the last word in culinary fashion than Lorenzo leapt forward once again. In 1860, not long after Delmonico's had scored the coup of the century by catering a grand ball held for the Prince of Wales at the Academy of Music, he bet once more that the tide of wealth and fashion would surge even further uptown. With war looming on the horizon, he rented the three-story brick mansion of Moses H. Grinnell, a shipping magnate, on Fourteenth Street at Fifth Avenue, overlooking Union Square. After renovations, the new Delmonico's held a grand opening on April 9, 1862.

As usual, Lorenzo invited the press to a preview, a strategy that paid big dividends. There is no more enthusiastic salesman than a well-fed journalist who has had his champagne glass refilled several times, and on this occasion the press was very well fed. The menu, reprinted in full by the *Tribune*, offered a brilliant gustatory procession that began with soup (crème de volaille à la Rachel), ended with desserts (mille-feuilles Pompadour and croquembouche d'oranges), and stopped along the way for Long Island trout, squab, lobster mayonnaise, canvasback duck, and woodcock. The *Times* reporter noted approvingly a pleasing innovation: a separate café with marble-topped tables "in the true Parisian style," and no bar.

Management of the new restaurant was entrusted to the twenty-two-year-old Charles Delmonico, Lorenzo's nephew. Already familiar to New York diners as the manager of the upstairs dining room on Chambers Street, he possessed a rare combination of culinary and business instincts. It was Charles who decided that customers should no longer be presented with a bill. A customer worthy of Delmonico's would request one himself at appropriate intervals. The honor system worked, for a simple reason: anyone who violated it was frozen out. In a style that anticipated the masterly snubs of Henri Soulé of Le Pavillon, Charles would permit the offender to enter the restaurant, place an order, and then languish. No food would arrive. After twisting in the wind for as many agonizing minutes as he could bear, the malefactor would get the point and pay up.

Charles benefited greatly from Lorenzo's inspired hiring of Charles Ranhofer, the chef who would lead Delmonico's from triumph to triumph over the next thirty-five years. He would keep the restaurant's position of preeminence secure, despite a host of competitors catering to the new crowd of affluent New Yorkers.

When the new Delmonico's opened its doors, Ranhofer was working in the kitchens of a rival, the Maison Dorée, one of the more spectacular failures in the city's restaurant history. Little survives of the Maison Dorée but its lofty reputa-

Delmonico's attracted top chefs from France, many of whom went on to elevate culinary standards at other restaurants in the city. This 1902 photograph shows the kitchen of the Fifth Avenue restaurant.

tion. Conceived quite deliberately as a challenge to Delmonico's hegemony, it opened in 1861 to universal acclaim. The lawyer George Templeton Strong, in his diary for July 19, 1861, mentions a dinner "at the Maison Dorée, a new and very nice restaurant established in Penniman's house on Union Square," where he became a devotee. A year later, he humorously noted an evening when the owner, a Mr. Martinez, "discovering that I was the individual who had paid him some thousand dollars for beef-stock during the last two months, became warmly interested in us and insisted on getting up a little artistic recherché dinner for us of his own devising." It was a brilliant success. "Very pretty little dinner it was, and full of elegant but surprising effects," Strong wrote. When the restaurant closed just six years after opening, the collapse seemed ominous to some observers, a judgment on the city's future as a cosmopolitan center. It was not the restaurant that had failed, but New York. "The Maison Dorée enterprise was an attempt to engraft a Parisian institution upon New York," wrote the *Brooklyn Daily Eagle* in a grim postmortem. It then put forward the intriguing theory that Delmonico's, although French in cuisine, had succeeded by developing an American style of service and atmosphere.

The Maison Dorée probably succumbed to the economic turbulence of the 1860s. (Delmonico's, on the alert, bought the contents of its wine cellars.) In any event, Ranhofer was left high and dry, and Delmonico's snapped him up. He came with an impressive résumé. Born in 1836, the product of two generations of chefs, he apprenticed at the age of twelve as a patissier at Fleuret's bakery on the rue de la Madeleine in Paris. After working as head baker at Mercier, on the boulevard du Temple, and at Malpièce, on the rue des Saussaies, behind the Elysée Palace, he took an apparent demotion by entering the service of the Prince d'Hénin, working as a kitchen boy at his château near Nogent-le-Rotrou in northwestern France. The allure of a noble house might explain the move. Or it might have been the promise of rapid advancement, which occurred, quite unexpectedly, when Mollard, the head chef, left in a huff after an argument with the prince over the proper temperature of an ortolan pâté. The kitchen staff, in a hasty caucus, nominated the young Ranhofer as Mollard's replacement. And so it was that the sixteen-year-old took over the top spot. Several years later, looking for broader horizons, he returned to Paris and the kitchens of Benois, a caterer to the rich and famous. His references in good order, Ranhofer then entered the establishment of the Duc de Noailles, a position he parlayed into a job with the Baron Rothschild.

In 1856, Ranhofer set sail for New York, where he cooked for the Russian consul and, not incidentally, adopted the new Russian style of service, in which courses were presented to diners one by one. After stints in Washington and New Orleans, he returned to France, where he orchestrated the grand banquets given by Napoleon III in the Tuileries. Then, in 1861, he went back to New York and the Maison Dorée. Lorenzo Delmonico later recalled his first meeting with the chef as inauspicious. "He was perfect in dress and manner, and his attitude was such as to make me feel that he was doing me a great favor by coming into my employment. He gave me to understand that he would be 'chief' indeed."

The luxurious Maison Dorée set up on Union Square in 1860 as a rival to Delmonico's.

Ranhofer proved invaluable. He knew how to organize large-scale banquets and how to strike the note of luxury, essential ingredients in Delmonico's success. Night after night, year after year, Delmonico's played host to dinners organized by civic clubs, fraternal organizations, and businessmen's associations. When a dignitary, a famous author, a visiting statesman, or a conquering hero visited New York, a banquet at Delmonico's was de rigueur. Over the years, Ranhofer cooked thousands of meals and created hundreds of dishes. More surprisingly, toward the end of his career, he published his recipes in a grand encyclopedia, *The Epicurean*, which offers a comprehensive look at the style of cuisine that he developed at Delmonico's.

Along with the rest of the city's French-style restaurants, Delmonico's followed the dictates of haute cuisine as set forth by Antonin Carême earlier in the century. Chef to Talleyrand, Alexander I of Russia, and other noble employers, Carême codified the dishes, the presentation, and even the pots and pans for French cooking in its most opulent phase. Presentations were ornate, sauces rich, dishes heavy. But Ranhofer kept his eyes and ears open. When new ingredients and new dishes came into view, he responded. Like many a transplanted French chef after him, he absorbed the experimental American ethos. *The Epicurean* abounds in both international dishes and homegrown American classics like jambalaya. Far from being a by-the-numbers classicist, Ranhofer accepted influences from near and far, seized on local ingredients, innovated, and showed

For most of its long life, Delmonico's was the favored restaurant of the city's elite, like the women eating lunch in 1902 at the Delmonico's on Fifth Avenue at Forty-fourth Street.

himself to be a truly great chef. The dishes associated with his name include lobster Newberg and baked Alaska, but Ranhofer's real achievement was to keep Delmonico's on top at a time when New York was becoming a genuine world capital, with restaurants to match.

5

New York Becomes a Restaurant City

When he bet on the rising fortunes of his adopted city, Lorenzo Delmonico was backing a winner. The city's economy, rocked by the Panic of 1837, rebounded and then surged in the 1840s and 1850s, an era of transformative growth and increasing prosperity. Lower Manhattan became a strictly commercial district as the rich and fashionable moved uptown. They built mansions on Bleecker Street and did their shopping on Broadway above City Hall, already a prime tourist attraction renowned for its brilliant shops and mad congestion. For the other half, there was the Bowery, a broad thoroughfare given over to popular theaters, gaudy entertainments, street vendors, and cheap restaurants.

Long before the age of electricity, the New York of nonstop entertainment and endless diversion was taking shape. In other towns, Americans labored and then retired when the sun set. In New York, the hustle and bustle continued after dark and into the wee hours, when die-hard roisterers, after a night at the theater, stopped for a quick oyster dinner before heading back uptown or across the river to Brooklyn on the ferry, just in time to meet the grocery wagons on their way to the Fulton and Washington markets. At dawn, and again in the afternoon, newsboys fanned out from the dozens of newspaper buildings across from City Hall, where a powerful media district had taken shape, a constellation of newspapers and magazines that disseminated images of the nation's most vibrant city to the rest of the world. Modern New York was coming into focus, a city devoted to getting and spending and public display.

The barren restaurant landscape of the 1830s had changed beyond recognition. The problem now was not finding a place to eat, but making a decision. An 1846 guidebook counted no fewer than 123 "eating houses or refectories," oyster saloons not included, but "those places only where breakfast, dinner, and tea can be had at all hours."

In truth, no one really knew how many restaurants there were in the city. "We once undertook to count these establishments in the lower part of the City, but got surfeited on the smell of fried grease before we got half through the first street, and were obliged to go home in a cab," the journalist George G. Foster wrote in a series of humorous sketches for the *Tribune* in 1849. "We believe, however, that there can't be less than a hundred of them within half a mile of the Exchange."

Although French cuisine was gaining a foothold, the dominant cooking style in New York was still English, reflected in the profusion of oyster saloons and chophouses near the theaters, the markets, and the centers of commerce. The venerable Holt's, whose rude service so annoyed Sam Ward, was gone.

In its place appeared a new breed of lunchrooms and eating houses, like Gosling's on Nassau Street, designed to feed large crowds at low prices. The press of hungry humanity required large establishments that could handle anywhere between 1,000 and 3,000 diners during the lunchtime rush, a stampede that became, for foreign visitors, one of New York's required sights. In the larger downtown refectories, the mob swarming up the stairs would collide with an equal number of customers on the way out, creating an ungodly scrum. Inside, lucky diners could grab a seat. The rest ate standing up, gobbling a quick lunch in twenty minutes or less and then sprinting back to work.

"Everything is done differently in New York from anywhere else, but in eating the difference is more striking than in any other branch of human economy," Foster wrote. "A thorough-bred diner down-town will look at a bill of fare, order his dinner, bolt it and himself, and be engaged in putting off a lot of goods upon a greenhorn, while you are getting your napkin fixed over your nankeens (we think the cotton article preferable) and deciding whether you will take oxtail or mock-turtle. A regular down-towner surveys the kitchen with his nose as he comes up-stairs—selects his dish by intuition, and swallows it by steam and the electro-galvanic battery. As to digesting it, that is none of his business."

Any innovation that smoothed the flow was regarded as pure genius. Haley and Sabin's refectory on Nassau Street introduced the self-serve concept by arranging lighter dishes along a large table, allowing customers to pick and choose according to their pocket, their appetite, or their time. "Here one can graduate his feeding precisely to his appetite, and can luxuriate from a penny's worth of bread and butter up to the full capacity of his purse," the *Tribune* reported. "Warm cakes morning, noon and night, good coffee, tea and chocolate, good steaks, etc. pies, cakes, etc. and one may fill with these for a New York shilling."

Hard-pressed restaurant workers toiled for a pittance. In the 1840s, adult waiters earned ten to twelve dollars a month (about $250 to $300 in current dollars), with room and board included. Boys earned seven dollars (or $175 in current dollars). Cooks could earn eight to ten dollars, and dishwashers half that.

The Manhattan business lunch disrupted the domestic circle. No longer was it possible for families to gather at home for a leisurely midday meal. For older New Yorkers, this break in tradition marked the beginning of the modern era. It was yet another reminder that the city was now a money-driven powerhouse where the gentler manners of the Knickerbocker era no longer applied and women could take their meals outside the home. The propulsive energies carry-

In the downtown business district, lunchrooms like the Rotunda at the Astor House, shown in an 1888 engraving, served thousands of diners at lightning speed. The office boy in the foreground is taking a bowl of soup back to a superior at the office.

ing New York into the future conspired against private life, and private dining. "As the fathers, brothers, and sons do not go home to dinner, the mothers, wives, and daughters have no inducements to eat their meals in solitude," *Putnam's* observed in 1853. "So while the male members of the family are eating their little dinners at Delmonico's, Frederick's, or Sweeney's, as the case may be, the female members are solacing themselves with fricandeaus, meringues, and ices at Thompson's, Taylor's, or Weller's; so that it may be said that nearly half the people of New-York dine out every day in the week but Sunday."

Where women fit in remains a puzzling question. To a great extent, public dining was segregated by sex, either explicitly or implicitly. Unescorted women were not admitted to most hotel dining rooms and fine restaurants, and, by preference, they did not venture into masculine haunts like the downtown lunch rooms and oyster saloons. Yet not all doors were closed. Charles Richard Weld, an Englishman, paid a visit to the same Taylor's mentioned by *Putnam's* and, with some surprise, noted the presence of female parties at several tables. For the benefit of his English readers, he added that "this is not at all uncommon in New York." In fact, at the Brevoort House he witnessed the very same phenomenon: a party of women who sat down, ordered, ate ("a little too speedily for English taste"), and departed "without attracting the slightest notice from any one, I believe, but myself." The evidence is scant and contradictory. Did the gender policy depend on the type of restaurant, the management, or the neighborhood? It is difficult to say. The inventory of restaurants was in constant flux, and the welcome an unescorted woman might expect probably varied enormously.

So many new restaurants! George G. Foster, indulging in a favorite newspaper stunt, created a taxonomy of the city's restaurants based on price and clientele. The main categories, proceeding from cheapest to most expensive, were the *Sweeneyorum*, *Browniverous*, and *Delmonican*, references instantly recognizable to every New Yorker. Delmonico's, of course, was the city's most renowned restaurant, but any reader would understand *Browniverous* as an allusion to Clark and Brown's chophouse. Sweeney's needed no introduction, either. Daniel Sweeney's restaurant, founded on Ann Street in the 1830s, and after 1850 located on Chatham Street at Duane, was a byword for plain fare served at rock-bottom prices. The clientele was rough. Sweeney's was a favorite resort of the notorious rabble-rouser Isaiah Rynders, boss of the Sixth Ward, whose constituents included gangs like the Dead Rabbits and Plug Uglies, all of them ready to storm any antislavery gathering at a signal from their warlord. Sweeney's also attracted peaceful working-class New Yorkers looking for humble dishes like meat pies, corned beef, and pork and beans.

At the low end, in Foster's taxonomy, the fare ran to "warm swill" for soup, "perspiring joints" for the main course, and corn bread and molasses for dessert. One step up the ladder were the chophouses, where the waiters were marginally more polite and diners subsisted on the standard shilling plate of "roast beef mixed": a slice of roast beef and gravy with mashed turnips, potatoes, and bread. It was a huge upward leap from the *Browniverous* to the *Delmonican*, a genus with only a handful of representatives.

Journalists, whether foreign or local, tended to write about the extremes. Their pens came to life when describing lavish feasts or culinary crimes. Meanwhile, the average citizen dined on average food. In between the exquisite French fare at Blancard's and the no-frills shilling plate, one finds the sort of meals served at the Atlantic Hotel, an establishment of no great distinction and therefore typical of the period. An 1843 menu suggests an abrupt falloff from the likes of Delmonico's and the Astor House (soon to be joined, in prestige, by the St. Nicholas Hotel). The fish was limited to boiled bass. A core menu of meats, either boiled (turkey, ham, fowl) or roasted (beef, turkey, chicken, duck), was supplemented by a handful of specials (stuffed breast of lamb, veal cutlet, crusted mutton chop, Italian macaroni). A second course of pheasant, quite glamorous to the modern eye, preceded a fairly uninspiring list of desserts on the order of custard or pancakes. Assuming the kitchen was competent, the fare at the Atlantic might have been perfectly satisfying, but nothing about the menu suggests that New York was giving Paris a run for its money.

As Foster and his fellow journalists knew all too well, usually from personal experience, there were cheaper places even than Sweeney's, namely the all-night coffee and cake shops frequented by newsboys, firemen, and clerks. At Buttercake Dick's, the most famous, an order of three biscuits and butter cost three cents, the same as a cup of coffee. A slice of pumpkin pie cost four cents. Richard Marshall, a former newsboy, ran his biscuit parlor in the basement of the Tribune Building on Park Row at Spruce Street, and grew rich on the pennies handed over the counter for his "sinkers"—biscuits with a pat of butter in the center.

New Yorkers short of cash relied heavily on coffee and cake shops like Buttercake Dick's. Among their number was Horatio Alger's Ragged Dick, a junior connoisseur of the restaurants along Nassau and Ann streets in the 1860s. After

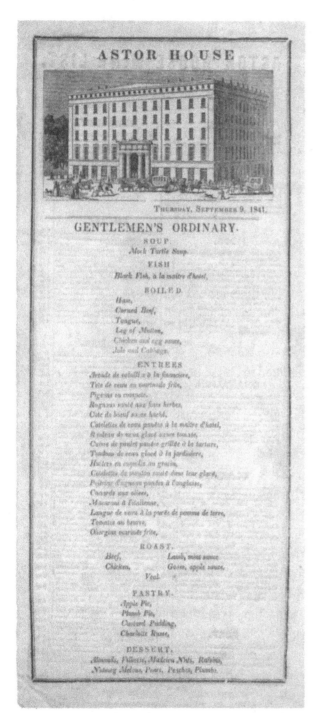

ASTOR HOUSE

THURSDAY, SEPTEMBER 9, 1841.

GENTLEMEN'S ORDINARY.

SOUP.
Mock Turtle Soup.

FISH
Black Fish, à la maitre d'hotel,

BOILED.
Ham,
Corned Beef,
Tongue,
Leg of Mutton,
Chicken and egg sauce,
Jole and Cabbage,

ENTREES
Broade de volaill a à la financiere,
Tête de veau en tortinade frite,
Pigeons en compote,
Ragoux veroll aux fines herbes,
Cote du boeuf sauce haché,
Cutelettes de veau panées à la maitre d'hotel,
Risleau de veau glacé sauce tomate,
Cotes de poulet panées grillée à la tartare,
Tendons de veau glacé à la jardiniere,
Huitres en coquille au gratin,
Cuidelles de mouton sauté dans leur glacé,
Poitrine d'agneau panées à l'anglaise,
Canards aux olives,
Macaroni à l'italienne,
Langue de veau à la purée de pomme de terre,
Tomates au beurre,
Giorgion escalode frite,

ROAST.
Beef,   Lamb, mint sauce
Chicken,   Goose, apple sauce,
          Veal

PASTRY.
Apple Pie,
Plumb Pie,
Custard Pudding,
Charlotte Russe,

DESSERT.
Almonds, Filberts, Madeira Nuts, Raisins,
Nutmeg Melons, Pears, Peaches, Plumbs.

The Astor House, the city's finest hotel for decades after it opened in the 1830s, printed a menu every day. This one dates from 1841.

shining shoes one morning, Dick heads up Ann Street to "a small, cheap restaurant" where he breakfasts on a nickel cup of coffee and a dime plate of beefsteak and bread. On the days when he has only a nickel, he eats a couple of apples, or cakes. When flush, he orders coffee, beefsteak, and, for an extra nickel, two rolls.

In the taverns and restaurants of Ann Street, the city's volunteer firemen gathered for cheap meals and good fellowship, with an ear out for the next fire alarm. Notable among these was Harry Venn's Porterhouse, at 13 Ann Street. Venn, a fireman himself, occasionally took up the pen, and left to posterity the following ode:

I remember, yes, distinctly, as tho' it
    were to-day,
The pleasures of my early youth that all
    have passed away;
Some were sad, and some were joyous,
    yet all of them I prize,
And the dearest of them all to me, is
    sweet, sweet Mutton Pies.

How grateful was the perfume, when
    brown and smoking hot,
And their juicy fragrant flavor can never
    be forgot;
Though the maker of the edible now in
    the cold grave lies,
His memory I reverence when I think of
    Mutton Pies.

Oh, tell me not of dishes made in French and German style,
And tenderloins and venisons that are first laid out to spile,
I pass my hand on all of these—my appetite won't rise
At no such fancy fixin's—I want my Mutton Pies.

Alas! the one-legged baker was long ago played out,
And never more we'll hear again his welcome cheering shout;
And though he oft was libeled, we heeded not their lies,
But went in top and bottom crust for luscious Mutton Pies.

A world away from Ann Street, genteel New Yorkers satisfied more refined cravings at ice cream saloons like Taylor's or Thompson's. The new shopping district along Broadway, anchored by Stewart's department store, had created a new class of diner, the well-to-do women who spent their afternoons shopping or strolling along the boulevard, looking in the store windows and taking in the sights. The midwestern heroine of "Ada Lester's Season in New York," a serial that ran in *Peterson's Magazine* in 1854, sends letters back home describing "the morning routine of calls, shopping, and luncheon out at Thompson's saloon." (If she had taken the trouble to step upstairs, she would have found the studios of a rising photographer named Mathew Brady.)

Shopping as a prelude to dining out was something new, an up-to-date urban custom that Taylor's and Thompson's catered to with great flair. They carried on the spirit of the old

At fancy ice cream saloons like Taylor's and Thompson's, women could gather after a morning's shopping, and young couples could find a quiet niche and a table for two.

pleasure gardens, where New Yorkers lingered fondly over ices, cakes, and lemonades, especially young couples desperate to spend time without adult supervision.

For sheer splendor, both restaurants rivaled Delmonico's. "On the counter of these temples of confectionery," an enraptured visitor wrote, "may always be seen the choicest and earliest fruits of the season, the rarest productions of the hot-house, and the most delicate bouquets that the conservatory can offer; while the Titians and Raffaelles of candy, daily produce some novelty of sweetness, to tempt the youthful lover of bonbons." A visitor from South Carolina found the fruit displays remarkable—somehow, Taylor's managed to get watermelons even before they appeared in Charleston or Augusta, "two of the greatest melon markets in the world." Thompson's boasted the longer pedigree, having sold its ices and confections since the 1820s. In 1852, James Thompson erected his own building at 359 Broadway near Franklin Street and opened his most lavish ice cream saloon yet. Soon after, John Taylor set up shop a few steps away at 365 Broadway, in Taylor's International Hotel, whose chief ornament was a palatial ice cream saloon occupying the ground floor and basement. Initially, Taylor's offered ice cream, pastries, and oysters. Diners might also order a glass of champagne or a sherry cobbler to enliven the afternoon. Quite quickly, the menu expanded to embrace everything from woodcocks on toast to porterhouse steak. As a boy, Henry James was taken to both. He recalled Thompson's as "grave and immemorial," while Taylor's was "upstart but dazzling."

Isabella Bird, an English clergyman's daughter visiting the United States in the 1850s, called Taylor's "the most superb" of the city's restaurants. ("When I come into a fortun' I shall take my meals there reg'lar," Ragged Dick announces to a pair of out-of-towners.) Taylor's was a temple of sweetness and light, all 7,500 square feet of its main floor glistening with black-and-white marble, its mirrored walls decorated in cream and gilt. Sparkling light from three enormous chandeliers played enticingly over ornate sugar sculptures and brightly colored bonbons and candies arranged atop massive marble counters. Couples could slip into enchanting niches between fluted marble columns and nibble their ices at little marble-topped tables, or take their ease in the two mirror-lined conservatories (one featuring orange trees and a cut-glass fountain rising seventeen feet from the floor). An army of sixty waiters stood ready to serve and advise, no small task given a thirty-two-page menu running to five hundred items. The clientele was mostly female, and profoundly grateful. "For a long time, it was almost the only place where ladies could go unattended by gentlemen and satisfy their appetites, rendered sharp by their shopping excursions," the *Times* wrote in 1866, when Taylor's finally closed its doors.

The ice cream saloon was not quite the same as the modern ice cream parlor, its entirely wholesome successor. Either subliminally or explicitly, ice cream parlors spelled sex. In an era when young couples stretched the limits of ingenuity to find unchaperoned escapes, the ice cream parlor beckoned. Its sweets and candies, not to mention champagne, served in pleasant surroundings, were tempting bait for the young women of the day. A swain seeking to make an impression knew exactly how to do it: propose a delightful detour to Taylor's, or, moving down the social scale, to one of the Bowery's cheap imitations, shiny with foil and tinsel.

Taylor's and Thompson's encouraged the sort of visit that the *Times* described as "not strictly correct," which is why Isabella Bird, in praising Taylor's as one of the city's finest restaurants, felt compelled to add *"but not by any means the most respectable."* "Did a young lady wish to enjoy the society of the lover whom 'Papa' had forbidden the house?" the *Times* wrote. "A meeting at Taylor's was arranged, where soft words and loving looks served to atone for parental harshness, and aided the digestion of pickled oysters." A more mercenary type also haunted the ice cream saloons. Taylor's "numerous stalls were not always innocently employed, for they were often occupied by those whose business it was to frequent public places, and who were not over particular as to the company they kept." Court reports of the day indicate that more than a few crimes of passion involved, somewhere along the way, a visit to Taylor's or Thompson's. "'Tis here that the first step is taken which leads to infamy," intoned the narrator of *Hot Corn*, a moralizing novel about the miseries and temptations of the city's most visible street vendors. It warned of ice cream "drugged with passion-exciting vanilla."

Solidly in the Delmonican category was the St. Nicholas Hotel, built in 1853 on the site of the old Niblo's Gardens, on Broadway at Prince Street. Larger by several orders of magnitude than the previous generation of first-class hotels, the St. Nicholas faced Broadway with an imposing marble façade, a portico supported by Corinthian columns, and something new indeed—a bridal chamber, so "scandalously splendid" that young women were said to "shrink aghast at its marvels of white satin and silver brocade."

The dining rooms deserve special attention. They demonstrated, according to *Putnam's* magazine, "to what a condition the fine art of dining well has been carried in this city." After shifting quarters to the St. Nicholas during his New York stay, the British traveler William Ferguson was pleased to report an immediate improvement in his level of comfort, especially the meals: "An idea of the dinner may be gathered from the fact, that we had our choice of two soups, two kinds of fish, ten boiled dishes, nine roast dishes, six relishes, 17 entrees, three cold dishes, five varieties of game, 13 varieties of vegetable, seven kinds of pastry, and seven fruits, with ice cream and coffee." Previously, Ferguson had wandered the town in search of dinner, but no more. "We dined at the St. Nicholas," a diary entry reads. "Every dinner there is a source of fresh wonder and interest."

With time, the hotel's clientele drew sniffy criti-

The dining room at the St. Nicholas Hotel (*left*) showed "to what a condition the fine art of dining well has been carried in this city," *Putnam's* magazine wrote. The evidence is clear in a menu from 1866 (*right*).

cism. After the Civil War, the St. Nicholas began to attract a certain "dashing element" that fastidious New Yorkers found repellent. "One sees among its habitués," wrote one critic, "an immense number of flashily dressed, loud-voiced, self-asserting people." There would be a lot of these in the postwar period, when the city was attracting all the wrong sorts of people, flush with new money and eager to show it off. The St. Nicholas was hardly alone in opening its doors to such newcomers, whose style and tastes would inaugurate a grand, gaudy era in New York dining. But that lay in the future.

For the present, New York's restaurants catered to every taste, at every price. In a fanciful sketch in the *Broadway Journal* in 1845, a "gentleman in search of a dinner" made a comic tour of the city's restaurants, driven from one dining spot to the next by a series of mishaps that whittled away at his bankroll of "a half eagle and two shilling pieces." First stop is Blancard's, where he orders a dozen Shrewsbury oysters to start, with a few squirts of lemon juice, to be followed by a filet de boeuf aux champignons and meringue and coffee for dessert. The sudden appearance of an unwelcome guest cuts the meal short, whereupon the gentleman races to Delmonico's and tries to re-create his interrupted meal.

Delmonico's he regards as an equal of Blancard's, although perhaps not as tony: "Here the dinners were quite as good, the *carte* as extensive, and the prices as low, perhaps lower; but the company was more promiscuous and the finish was not so high. I had always had an objection to the great mirrors in the dining-room, and the monstrous bronze chandeliers, to say nothing of two unceasing harpers who are forever clanging the songs of the last opera, and worse than all, the black pepper in square salt cellars." Reaching into his pocket to pay for an absinthe at the bar, the hapless gentleman realizes that one of the two shillings he gave the cabman was actually his half eagle. Suddenly, dinner at Delmonico's is off. He is now flat broke.

"I began to think of the 'French and English' dining saloons, in Nassau Street, where a plate of any thing may be had for a sixpence," he writes, but lacking sixpence, he realizes even Gosling's is out of the question. He goes instead to De l'Europe, Napoleon Bunel's café on Broad Street, despite the sand-strewn floor and bad landscape murals. With hunger gnawing, the gentleman orders dinner, adding a fricandeau and charlotte russe to the list of dishes he failed to eat at Delmonico's, and then appeals for credit, only to find that the French prefer cash on delivery. Under the withering glare of Madame Bunel, he makes a hasty exit.

Next stop is the Franklin Coffee House (Clark and Brown's), all heavy wood, long marble counters, and sporting prints, a comfortable refuge for the diner short on funds and set on enjoying good English fare. "What a magnificent sight his larder is," the gentleman exclaims. "Turkies, saddles of mutton, salmon, lobsters, sirloins, rounds of beef, roasting-pigs, cauliflowers, and strawberries. These were a few of the objects that caught my eye. Confound your *potages* and fricandeaus. I will have, I said, as I walked into this glorious eating-house, salmon and melted butter, a mug of ale, roast lamb and mint sauce, with potatoes and cauliflowers, then a magnificent slice of roast beef with asparagus, and bread and butter; then a rhubarb tart and Gloster cheese and a dish of strawberries and cream." Fate again intervenes, dinner is denied, and the search continues.

Or might have, had the gentleman in search of a dinner filed the third installment of his odyssey. Disappointed readers could have filled in the blanks. A modest meal on credit might have been found at the Café Tortoni, on Park Place. Run by a M. Bardotte, it offered stewed beef with macaroni or roast leg of mutton, a garden salad, and assorted vegetables for fifty cents. A pint of acceptable Bordeaux was just two shillings extra.

Alternatively, the by now desperate gentleman could have taken a ferry to Brooklyn to eat at Bell's, Montague Hall, or Van Wart's, three restaurants that, although undistinguished—and virtually indistinguishable—give a clear picture of what the average diner looked for in a meal in 1845. Bell's Refreshment Saloon, or J. E. Bell's House of Refreshment, as it sometimes styled itself, offered not only a menu but a credo: "Let New York take care of itself! Why go to New York to dine?"

Brooklynites who agreed paid a shilling at Bell's for roast meats (beef, lamb, veal, or pork) or a shilling and sixpence for roast fowl (chicken, goose, turkey, or duck). Meat soups and assorted pies (chicken, veal, "meat," and clam) cost sixpence, the same price as pork and beans. Although Bell's offered a dozen desserts, eleven were pies or puddings, with the inevitable apple dumpling rounding out the list. The vegetable policy is hard to gauge. Bell's menu lists none, but presumably a plate of beef included potatoes and a green vegetable. At Montague Hall, "extra vegetables" offered as side dishes on a September menu included lettuce, cabbage, peas, parsnips, beets, and turnips.

With no cooking facilities at home, many New Yorkers took all their meals out, including breakfast. In the days before the dietary revolution started by John Harvey Kellogg and Sylvester Graham, the first meal of the day could be a mighty repast, nearly as meat-laden and robust as dinner. Fried tripe, in the 1840s, counted as a breakfast dish. So did stewed kidneys, fried clams, fish balls, and veal cutlets, along with toast, fried eggs, hot muffins, and buckwheat cakes.

The role of the theater in New York's restaurant life cannot be exaggerated. The city's playhouses brought crowds onto the street, an army of hungry diners who needed to be fed early and late. In the early years of the century, restaurants had lived on the lunchtime trade, closing their doors when the business day ended. But theaters changed the equation. Clustered along lower Broadway, and later around Union Square, they brought in their train oyster saloons and chophouses that stayed open into the wee hours.

The most celebrated of these, as we have seen, was Windust's basement restaurant near the Park Theater. Windust, a Staten Island oysterman who once sold his catch at Washington Market, decorated the restaurant with playbills, framed reviews, costumes, and props, including a sword once wielded by David Garrick on the London stage. Over the entrance hung a Latin motto, *Nunquam Non Paratus* ("Never Unprepared"), that mystified many a visitor. Vendors, after studying it for a moment, would ask to see Mr. Nunquam or his partner, Mr. Paratus. Along the stairway leading to the dining room, an unknown artist had painstakingly depicted beefsteaks on two boards, with the legend "If it were done, when 'tis done, t'were well it were done quickly."

Windust's quickly became the Sardi's of its day, a theatrical haunt that attracted actors, stage managers, journalists, and theatergoers eager to get a glimpse of the stars. Regulars included theatrical luminaries like Edmund Kean and Junius Brutus Booth, along with poets and scribes like Fitz-Greene Halleck and Nathaniel Parker Willis. A sporting element added spice to the atmosphere. William T. Porter, editor of *The Spirit of the Times*—a paper that combined the coverage of *Field and Stream*, the *Daily Racing Form*, and the *National Enquirer*—held regular dinners at which guests were required to contribute fish and game "killed by their own hand."

Such men "nightly crowded the tier of stalls that ranged along one side of the room, making them resound with gay and brilliant talk." Windust occasionally received the patronage of the "mad poet" McDonald Clarke, author of "Elixir of Moonshine," who would leave the restaurant late at night and cross the street to City Hall Park, where he saw visions until dawn. Windust's enjoyed a run of thirty years before failing, like so many others, amidst the economic dislocations of the Civil War.

Like pilot fish trailing ships, eating houses clustered near each theater as it opened, absorbing the patronage and something of the atmosphere of the play-houses they served. The word "synergy" did not yet exist, but the phenomenon was evident at the Sir John Falstaff, a chophouse run by W. H. Norton, a member of the company at Wallack's. Located on Fourth Avenue near Tenth Street, it drew patronage not only from Wallack's and other uptown theaters, but from the Academy of Music on Fourteenth Street, which had opened in 1854.

The Falstaff was not alone in battening on Wallack's. The ultimate convenience for the theater's patrons and staff was the Green Room, right across the street from the stage entrance, run by another member of Wallack's company, George F. Browne. Because the atmosphere was English, patrons assumed the owner was as well. Actually, Browne was from New Hampshire. After being raised in the family of Henry Junius Booth (eminent actor and father of John Wilkes Booth), he made a successful career as a traveling actor-manager. In 1861, after joining Wallack's company, he decided to open a chophouse as a sideline.

Covered from floor to ceiling with autographed playbills and theatrical portraits, the Green Room served as an unofficial dining club for Wallack's actors, with a citywide reputation for its Welsh rarebit and pig's feet. It lasted, seemingly, forever. When Wallack's moved uptown to Thirtieth Street in 1882, Browne's had already moved to the neighborhood. Browne's final move brought it next to the Empire Theater and across from the new Metropolitan Opera House at Broadway and Thirty-ninth Street, where it lingered until 1925, a curiosity from another time.

The traditional chophouses like Clark and Brown's soldiered on, immune to changing fashion, decade after decade.

Like the oyster cellar, and like the steakhouse of our own times, the chophouse satisfied an almost primal need. No matter how large and diverse New York became, and despite the prestige of French cuisine, the English-style chophouses never lost favor. In fact, their numbers increased exponentially in the 1850s and 1860s. One of the oldest was Old Tom's, a cramped hotel and dining room on Thames Street that started out catering to dry-goods merchants and clerks, but later served "the princes of finance and potentates of the Stock Exchange." (One measure of its fame was the existence, nearby, of an imitator, easily recognized by the swinging sign outside proclaiming it to be "the original old Tom's.")

The place was born old. Patrons in later years remarked on its filthy sawdust-strewn floors, rarely swept, and the cobwebs hanging from its low ceilings.

William Waldorf Astor, a regular, rhapsodized over the groaning board that greeted diners as they entered, "laden with delicately mottled steaks and chops, shining kidneys, glistening fish" with "a bursting cauliflower or two" to the side. In the tiny bar area, three steps above the floor, the proprietor displayed a collection of curiosities: a pair of wooden-soled Confederate shoes brought back from Charleston, a hornet's nest, a Sioux pipe.

Astor and other notables came to Old Tom's for the Welsh rarebit, the pork and mutton pies, the roast beef, and a strange specialty known as a Welsh slip: Welsh rarebit poured over mince or apple pie. The real signature dish, however, was something called "the combination," a mixed grill consisting of a chop, a kidney, a sausage, and a strip of bacon. Old Tom (in fact, son of the founding Tom) waited on customers himself, and many neophytes, unaware that their server was a very wealthy man, would press a coin into his palm. It was always gratefully accepted.

Most, like Farrish's Chop House on John Street, were run by Englishmen. Colonel James A. Farrish emigrated from Leeds and started a grocery business on lower Third Avenue. When the war came, he enlisted in the Seventy-ninth Regiment, New York Highlanders. He was wounded at the Battle of Bull Run, captured by the Confederates, and, after a prisoner exchange, served as army paymaster in the western theater of operations. His probity was legend. Some $8 million passed through his hands, and when the War Department, on auditing his accounts after the cessation of hostilities, found him short by the sum of $1.44, Farrish promptly mailed the difference in postage stamps.

Returning to New York, Farrish opened a chophouse in the grand style, a veritable palace of meat. Customers, their privacy protected by cedarwood screens extending halfway up the front windows, watched as great joints roasted slowly over an enormous fire and then came to the table "with a delicate brown tint, fresh country butter melting over it, and flanked with mealy baked potatoes and a tankard of golden ale." The favored brands were Alsopp's, Bass, and Guinness, served in foot-high glasses or pewter mugs. The steaks, priced at seventy-five cents, fed two. "Those who don't care for steaks can have chops, those who don't care for chops can have steaks, those who have objections to both must go elsewhere, for there is nothing else," a reporter wrote. They could also have dessert: apple pie, mince pie, or Stilton cheese. Each New Year's Day, Farrish would post a statement of the year's sales of chops and steaks. It was always an impressive number.

Farrish's competed with a host of rivals. John Sutherland, a Scot who once tended bar at Delmonico's on William Street, opened a small eating house on Pine Street before moving, sometime around 1860, to a larger building at 64 Liberty Street, which he eventually bought. He ran Sutherland's along strictly British lines. He was the first in the city to serve genuine Dover sole, British turbot, and Irish oysters. He featured Welsh and Southdown mutton, advertising in the newspapers whenever a fresh shipment arrived. Game pies were also an attraction, as well as Scottish grouse in season. Sutherland even catered to Anglo-Indian tastes with curried lobster, made with a curry powder bought in Edinburgh. The restaurant was famous for its Burns Day haggis and black-and-white puddings.

Not surprisingly, Sutherland's drew a heavily English clientele, as well as city notables like Chester A. Arthur, the always-discriminating Sam Ward, and Charles L. Tiffany, the head of Tiffany's, who dined there daily. Sutherland, a lifelong bachelor and natural-history buff, lived above the restaurant, surrounded by caged birds. Late in the evening, he would unleash a team of fox terriers to roam the dining room. On the walls were charts showing edible and poisonous mushrooms, and he often brought strange fungi to the table for guests to sample. Prize specimens went to the government or to various museums. His eccentricities did not stop there. "Irascible, dogged and prejudiced beyond belief," according to one obituary writer, he maintained, for reasons unknown, a wild hatred of the police. When the Sudanese War broke out in the 1880s, he told a customer, "Mark my words, the New York police are at the bottom of this thing."

Cobweb Hall, on Duane Street, the creation of an eccentric Scot named David Pattullo, earned its name from its bizarre decor. "The absence of all pretension is its charm," one magazine writer wrote, understating the case. Every rafter and nook in the place was hung with thick cobwebs. "Gauzy seas of them have veiled every object—the pyramids of ale-casks, and the demijohns at the bar. From every corner and crevice the eye meets them depending by their silken threads." The fare was plain: steaks broiled over an open fire, then served on slices of homemade bread.

Pattullo had started out as agent for Royal Lochnagar whiskey but decided he could make more money selling his product over the counter. His bar and eating house, absent any frills other than the cobwebs and a sign that read "Don't Touch or Speak to the Dog," drew a large patronage from nearby businesses and from carmen on the trolley lines. They made him a very rich man.

Pattullo died a millionaire in 1868, leaving his cobwebs for future generations to appreciate. His successor, Hugh Ferrigan, lovingly tended this legacy until the fateful day, in 1885, when fire broke out in a whalebone factory upstairs, damaging the restaurant's ceiling and eliminating most of the cobwebs. Ferrigan carefully collected the surviving strands and placed them in a glass display case at the rear of the dining room.

William S. Pontin's chophouse, located in a small two-story frame house with a dormer attic on Benson Street, a minuscule dead-end spur off Leonard Street in present-day Tribeca, greeted diners with hams and sides of bacon hanging in a recess in the front hall. Pontin, an Englishman, started out in the kitchens of the Union Club. In 1853 he bought the Erford Cheese, a chophouse on Reade Street, and four years later moved to Benson Street (in 1881 he moved again, to 46 Franklin Street). His chophouse was a favorite with top politicians, who could handle the high prices and enjoyed the casual atmosphere, the old-fashioned iron pepper boxes, and the oil and vinegar in fat flasks. A painted portrait of the owner hung on the wall, along with assorted landscapes, a portrait of Pontin's pug dog, and a picture of Venus rising from the sea. No menus were provided. Instead, diners simply asked for roast beef, roast mutton, chops, or steaks. Pontin himself attended to the patrons, bringing bottles of sherry or claret to the tables, and alerting newcomers to the fact that his mutton came from "the other side"—England. "The fat was firm and white, the flesh as tender as can be imagined," one diner wrote appreciatively. "With the meat, which was as abundant in quantity as it was excellent in quality, were two superbly roasted potatoes. Bottles of piccalilli, royal sauce, walnuts, etc., circulated from table to table, and for those who admire things that bite the tongue and inflame the palate, these were, no doubt, admirable."

Farther north, things were stirring. Once home to the cream of New York society, the streets along Broadway just north of Houston Street were starting to slip by the 1850s, as wealthy homeowners moved farther uptown, and even Bleecker Street, the Park Avenue of its day, showed signs of age. With alarming rapidity, the once-grand mansions along Bleecker, Bond, and Houston streets became "ill-tenanted," as the *Times* delicately put it.

When the rich decamped, theaters and restaurants helped fill the vacuum. John Florence opened his oyster saloon, and theatrical chophouses like the House of Lords and the Clifton Shades moved in, side by side on Houston Street near Crosby.

The De Soto, on Bleecker Street just east of Broadway, consistently ranked near the top of every list of authentic English chophouses. Its flamboyant owner was William H. Garrard, a "burly, jovial mutton-chop-whiskered Londoner" who, in the mid-1850s, accompanied the renowned soldier of fortune William Walker and his private army on a misbegotten expedition to set up a new government in Nicaragua. When Central American politics turned out to be a little too hot for his taste, he signed on as a steward on the *De Soto*, a steamer that sailed between Havana and New Orleans and quite likely earned most of its income from smuggling. After a collision in the Gulf of Mexico, the good ship *De Soto* went up in flames, whereupon Garrard made his way to New York and opened a chophouse on John Street. In 1861, he moved to Bleecker Street and named his new restaurant in honor of his old ship.

The De Soto may have been the most authentically English chophouse of them all, its considerable reputation built on steak and kidney pudding, Yorkshire pudding, broiled kidneys, and, in the words of one guidebook, "toothsome English dishes almost unknown in this country." The nearby Olympic and Winter Garden theaters ensured a steady supply of actors, but Garrard's colorful past seemed to parade before him nightly. His clientele, the *Times* reported, included "every class above the vulgar." Indeed. The crowd jostling at the bar or crying out for steaks included sea captains, "adventurers," detectives, and army officers who often found themselves seated cheek by jowl with Southern sympathizers. Garrard married an American woman, gathered his riches, and died a very wealthy man in 1873.

New Yorkers who knew the great chophouses of this golden era scoffed at their puny descendants and their even punier chops, "a bone scraped quite white, with a small piece of scalloped paper at one end and a morsel of thin, tasteless meat at the other," as *Appleton's Dictionary of New York and Vicinity* put it in 1880. A real chop, the guidebook reminded younger readers, "is a large cut from the loin, 1¼ inches thick, well-outlined with firm white fat, and having a good-sized tenderloin, as rich and juicy as it is tender." After setting the record straight, *Appleton's* surveyed the current chophouse scene, conceding that a "fair" chop could be found at the Astor House. It gave a respectful nod to the De Soto and heartily endorsed Farrish's, where "a nice chop, baked potato, a bit of watercress, plenty of good bread, and English pickles may be had . . . for 30 to 40 cents and two chops for 50 cents," along with broiled kidneys and porterhouse steaks.

New York held no monopoly on steaks. Brooklyn, its twin city, boasted a dozen good chophouses by the 1870s, some with long pedigrees. A proper Brooklyn chophouse had a tiny bar up front, a few mahogany tables in the dining room, and a good selection of English newspapers and magazines on hand. Lunch or dinner was a steak or chop with a bottle of Bass, followed by a choice Havana cigar. Tom Dent may have been the first to set up a genuine English-style house. A native of Nottingham, he opened Chequers in a mansion on Main Street in 1850. After a devastating fire, it reemerged as the Phenix, which found particular favor among "captains of the Atlantic liners, actors, lovers of horse flesh, and newspaper writers," or, more generally, the *Eagle* wrote, "those of a sporting turn of mind." The place did a roaring business in imported hares, pheasants, and legs of Southdown mutton, not to mention tripe, the Saturday-night special.

First among equals was John C. Force's chophouse on Pierrepont Street, which was as famous for the art on the walls as for the food. Force, a Dorset man, exemplified the chophouse owner as public notable and local Medici. A keen Shakespearean and avid art collector, he accumulated a valuable collection of landscapes and animal paintings over the years. A copy of Turner's *Fighting Téméraire* hung on the wall, along with paintings by Asher Durand and forgotten artists like Thomas Earl (represented by *The Hound's Dream*) and the "fin, fur, and feather" specialist Arthur Fitzwilliam Tait. Force, the *Eagle* noted approvingly, was a devotee of the "healthy games" of racket, quoits, and cricket and "regarded the tricks of the turf, and especially of trotting matches, with undisguised contempt."

In nineteenth-century New York, the only dish that could rival a juicy beefsteak or a dozen plump oysters on the half shell was turtle soup, and its partisans were legion. Below Scudder's Museum at Broadway and Ann Street—the museum later taken over by P. T. Barnum—Sandy Welsh operated the Terrapin Lunch, an oyster saloon and chophouse favored by politicians and renowned for its turtle soup and champagne by the glass. Distinction in this arena was no small thing. Although turtle soup has vanished from the American table, it reigned as one of the premier national delicacies from the colonial period into the early years of the twentieth century, usually accompanied by a glass of its equally forgotten companion, Madeira.

The turtles, native to the Caribbean, could weigh several hundred pounds, although smaller turtles of fifteen to forty pounds were also turned into soup. In the old days, when a giant turtle arrived, coffeehouse owners would advertise the event in the newspapers, alerting the public that soup was on the way. Niblo's Coffee House took a more direct approach, setting the turtle out on the sidewalk—upside down and legs wriggling—to entice passersby.

A recipe offered by Crook and Nash's chophouse in the 1880s suggests the complexities and the appeal of genuine turtle soup. The first step was to behead the turtle and let the blood drain for a couple of hours. Next, the top and bottom shells were separated and the organs removed. These, along with any accompanying fat, were put in a pot and boiled. In a separate pot, the turtle meat, limbs, and pieces of shell were boiled until the meat could be separated from the skin and bones. Once the meat was taken care of, the bones were cooked in the turtle liquid with two knuckles of ham, a knuckle of veal, turnips, carrots, and onions. Cloves, allspice, mace, and bay leaves seasoned the broth. Three hours of slow cooking produced a stock to which cubes of light and dark turtle meat were added, as well as cubes of fat. Before serving, the soup stock was flavored with red pepper, Worcestershire sauce, lemon juice, and a little sherry and brandy, then thickened with a roux of flour and butter that had been used to sauté onions. Significantly, Crook and Nash's suggested an alternative—a mock-turtle soup using calf's head, evidence that the real thing was disappearing fast as the turtle population declined.

Sandy Welsh's chief rival for eminence in turtle soup was Bayard's, located in a cottage on State Street near the Battery. "No one who has eaten Bayard's turtle soup can forget it," wrote a nostalgic New Yorker. "It was thick and slab, and made savory by herbs, lemon juice and forcemeat balls." No one did forget it. Charles H. Haswell, in his *Reminiscences of New York by an Octogenarian*, recalled Bayard's soup with uncanny accuracy more than half a century later. The pathetic turtle soup of the 1890s could not be mentioned in the same breath as Bayard's divine product. "Here turtle soup was dispensed which was worthy of the animal of which it was made," Haswell wrote, "not the *puree* of this time, which is served at some of our leading restaurants and clubs; not a thin *consomme* of that which might be calves' head or veal, but *bona fee* [sic] turtle, with callipash, callipee, and forced-meat balls." It was reasonably priced, too. For two shillings and sixpence (i.e., 31¼ cents), customers could dine on a bowl of soup and a glass of punch.

Bayard, alas, had a weakness. He loved the lottery, whose winning numbers were drawn from a big wheel on the steps of City Hall. His fortune vanished, and he ended up working on the streetcars.

Like the theater business, newspaper and magazine publishing played an important role in the restaurant culture of the city. From the 1830s on, New York spawned so many papers and journals that their employees and writers constituted a sizeable market, concentrated for the most part along Park Row. Moreover, journalists tended to regard oyster stands, saloons, food markets, and cafés as good copy. As the city grew, and restaurants of every description proliferated, journalists turned out colorful slice-of-life stories for local and national consumption. Restaurants and their owners—and sometimes even their waiters—received the kind of coverage accorded to politicians in other cities. As a result, dining out in New York became an object of national fascination. In the late nineteenth century, especially, as journalists gravitated toward Bohemia and the delights of the new theater districts around Madison Square and Times Square, restaurants like Maria del Prato's, Mouquin's, Jack's, Lüchow's, and Rector's achieved mythic status. Even sporting newspapers like the *Spirit of the Times* (founded in 1831) and the *National Police Gazette* (1845) devoted coverage to hotels and saloons, adding to the allure of New York's dining scene.

Along Park Row, virtually every newspaper building had a chophouse or coffee-and-cake saloon in the basement. The *Sun* (1833), the *Herald* (1835), the *Tribune* (1841), and the *Times* (1851) set up headquarters along the street, creating their own small world. It was a time when newspapers needed to be near their sources, and Park Row, facing City Hall and within walking distance of Wall Street, proved to be an ideal location. The foreign-language dailies, like the *New Yorker Staats-Zeitung* (1834), took up the north side of the street above Printing House Square. Below the square, the Tribune Building anchored the north end—most impressively after 1875, when the paper put up a new nine-story building—and the Herald Building the south end, with the *World*, the *Sun*, the *Times*, and lesser fry in between. Clustered in nearby streets were illustrated publications like *Harper's Weekly* (1857), *Putnam's Monthly Magazine* (1853), and *Frank Leslie's Illustrated Newspaper* (1855). Nearby were the printing houses, photographers, printmakers, paper manufacturers, and advertising agencies that lived off the newspapers, and their employees, too, contributed to an army of virtually round-the-clock diners. In 1890, when Joseph Pulitzer put up the new World Building, topped with a gleaming golden dome, at the far-north end of Park Row, the street assumed imposing dimensions.

The food in the neighborhood wasn't much, but the restaurants stayed open late. Journalists took a beef-and-beans lunch at Hitchcock's (formerly Buttercake

Dick's) in the basement of the Tribune Building, or at Dolan's next door. Dennett's lunchroom at the corner of Beekman Street and Crook and Nash's in the Times Building also offered cheap meals.

Hitchcock's and Dolan's, the undisputed kings of the "beef and" restaurants, did an enormous business. These were no-frills operations. A big pot of beans sat on the counter next to a large slab of corned beef and a boiled ham. Behind the counter, a griddle turned out buckwheat cakes and biscuit-and-butter sinkers; a coffee boiler dispensed coffee. The owner carved the meat, and the service, such as it was, fell to Irish waiters from the Bowery, who threw plates on the tables and pulled knives and forks out of their pockets. They also spoke a specialized lingo, a precursor of diner slang, that puzzled new customers and thrilled journalists, who explained, in story after story, that the seemingly indecipherable "Ham an'! Draw one—have it in the dark," was, in fact, a plate of ham and beans with a cup of black coffee.

Hitchcock's, founded by Oliver N. Hitchcock in 1854, served "beef and," "ham and," or "pork and"—a ten-cent plate of corned beef, ham, or pork with beans. Cake and coffee on the side cost another dime. This was poor-man's fare that appealed equally to cash-strapped journalists and to businessmen who could easily afford better. It served the conductors and drivers of the Third and Fourth Avenue horsecars, newsboys, and bootblacks, but it also fed the likes of Mark Twain, Horace Greeley, and Bret Harte.

Dolan's, a hole-in-the-wall on the Row with perhaps ten tables, also kept many a struggling cub reporter alive with "beef and," or "Boston and"—the same dish, but its brown beans were baked with pork and not mashed, unlike the white New York–style beans. Three sinkers with plenty of butter and a cup of coffee cost a nickel. "If one was reckless, pie could be had for five cents," recalled Louis T. Golding, the managing editor of the *Commercial Advertiser*. "For the opulent there was fried ham and eggs in various styles at fifteen and twenty cents. It was even possible to get a mutton chop or portion of steak for a quarter, but of this I cannot speak from personal experience." Patrick Dolan, the proprietor, sliced the corned beef himself. Gaunt and spectral, he looked as if he might not last through the lunchtime service, but appearances were deceiving. He carried on for years, leaving an estate worth nearly $1 million when he died in 1903. Like Hitchcock's, Dolan's found favor with rich and poor alike. The banker Jay Gould patronized it, as did Thomas Edison. Teddy Roosevelt promised his Rough Riders a meal at Dolan's when they returned from Cuba. At an uptown dining room, Dolan's served beef and beans for four hundred, at Park Row prices.

Although rough and ready, the "beef and" restaurants represented a small evolutionary advance on the pie shop, typically a hole-in-the-wall where custard or coconut pies, lined up on tin plates, were handed across a counter at a nickel a slice, along with a cup of coffee stirred with milk from a tin can. The pie shops shared business with itinerant hot dog, waffle, and ice cream vendors, some of them nameless near-celebrities, like the Park Row apple woman "with her dusty doughnuts and mysterious Washington pie," or the German who sold two-for-a-nickel frankfurters from a handcart equipped with a little stove. (As the new century dawned, he could still be seen on Ann Street.)

One summer in the 1890s, a group of "coffee-colored men in white jackets" appeared out of nowhere, selling an exotic dish wrapped in corn husks. An enterprising reporter from the *Tribune*, alerted to the presence of the funny men and their strange wares, made his way to the area and buttonholed a vendor who was yelling, "Tamales, chicken tamales, red hot!" Over one shoulder he carried a copper canister about two feet long and ten inches across, divided into three chambers. A small gasoline lamp in the bottom chamber heated water in the chamber above, which released steam into the top chamber, where the tamales were arranged, ready to be transferred to a small paper box for each customer. The "chicken" was actually veal (a cheaper meat at the time). The vendor was unmistakably Irish. The tamale, however, tasted good. For a brief season, it was the fad food of the New York streets.

6

The Melting Pot

By the 1850s, immigration was changing the face of New York. For the next forty years, successive waves of foreigners would bring strange accents, peculiar habits, and new foods. Poverty and political turmoil impelled Germans, French, and Italians in turn to try their luck in America, along with Hungarians, Syrians, Greeks, and, late in the century, Polish and Russian Jews. Chinese immigrants, lured eastward after the completion of the western railroads, gained a foothold in lower Manhattan during the 1880s and quickly introduced New Yorkers to the pleasures of chop suey. The Irish, a mighty force in sheer numbers, added little to the culinary equation, but they took immediately to the restaurant business, working in menial jobs and then establishing themselves as bartenders, saloon-keepers, and chophouse proprietors. By the end of the century, some of the most renowned restaurants in the city owed their fame to Irish owners who knew how to set a table—and a tone.

Anglo-French hegemony yielded a bit, as New York's culinary map became balkanized in an ongoing series of shifts and displacements that continue to the present day. New York's hallmark as a dining city is not the excellence of its best restaurants. Paris has better French restaurants, Madrid has better Spanish restaurants, and Tokyo has better Japanese restaurants. No city, however, offers as many national cooking styles, at all price ranges, as New York does. This diversity became evident in the mid-nineteenth century, and has only increased with each passing decade.

By 1885, New York's fledgling Chinatown had six restaurants. New Yorkers were quick to find them.

Today, New Yorkers in search of "ethnic" food have in mind a meal that is exotic, informal, and cheap. That is exactly what their nineteenth-century counterparts were looking for, too.

The ethnicities, of course, differed. Curiously, the cuisine least represented in New York today once enjoyed enormous popularity and prestige. Hundreds of thousands of Germans poured into New York in the 1840s and settled, for the most part, east of the Bowery just above the present-day Lower East Side, in a neighborhood soon to be called Kleindeutschland. A smaller number put down roots across the river in Williamsburg. The German population in New York increased from about 24,000 in 1840 to more than 200,000 by 1860, or nearly a quarter of the city's population. Natural increase, and a second wave of German immigration in the 1870s, brought the number to nearly 400,000 by 1880. Between 1855 and 1880, only Vienna and Berlin had larger German-speaking populations than New York did. If Kleindeutschland alone had been relocated to Germany, it would have been the country's fifth-largest city.

The Germans quickly opened beer gardens and restaurants, bringing with them a taste for lager beer that Americans adopted, after initial skepticism. Some thought that lager was not beer at all and could be drunk in unlimited quantities without producing any effect. One New Yorker recalled asking for a lager beer at an old-line tavern and being told, sternly, "We don't serve no Dutch drinks here." But lager beer prevailed, as Germans established breweries up and down the East Coast and all over the Midwest.

The centerpiece of immigrant German life in New York was the Atlantic Garden, an immense hall next to the Bowery Theater, on the Bowery just below Canal Street. There, once upon a time, stood the Bull's Head Tavern, a gathering spot for butchers and cattle drovers, and on this hallowed ground newly arrived Germans created a combination theme park, pleasure garden, variety stage, and saloon in 1858. It was hugely popular, crowded with families eager to hear German music, sing German songs, drink German beer, and eat German food.

The garden was a garden in name only. The main hall was a vast open room overlooked by a balcony, and the greenery, judging by engravings, was limited to a few wisps of foliage. A large barroom up front was supplemented by smaller barrooms inside, and patrons could amuse themselves at shooting galleries, bowling lanes, and billiard tables. During the day, music thundered forth from an enormous orchestrion—a cross between a player piano and a pipe organ. At night, a band played popular tunes and selections from the classical repertoire.

An influx of German immigrants made German food, beer, and music potent factors in the city's cultural life. All three were on offer at the Atlantic Garden on the Bowery.

The native press was perplexed. The Atlantic Garden could accommodate up to three thousand patrons at a time, yet fighting was unheard of. Germans drank, but did not get drunk. Beer seemed to make them happy. The atmosphere was wholesome. The Germans even brought their wives and children, just as they did to restaurants, which they also considered family entertainment. Very strange.

In a process later repeated at ethnic dining spots all over the city, the good word circulated. New Yorkers who spoke not a syllable of German, and who had never tasted a drop of lager beer, found their way to the Atlantic Garden, and thence to the innumerable German beer gardens scattered all over the city, some with no more claim to garden-ness, in the words of one reporter, than "a fir in a tub, and a few sickly vines."

The Atlantic Garden remained a fixture for generations. It gradually lost its German accent, however, as Germans prospered and moved uptown to Yorkville, creating a second Kleindeutschland, or left the city entirely. By the turn of the century, the Atlantic Garden was a large vaudeville theater featuring an all-female orchestra and a young pianist named Jimmy Durante; in 1928 it was razed.

German restaurants offered an alternative to the English chophouse. Most occupied basements, where the rent was cheaper. A few simple tables and chairs, and some white sand sprinkled on the floor, established a clean, spartan tone. The standard charge, along the Bowery, was thirty-five cents for a five-course table d'hôte dinner consisting of soup, fish, an entrée with vegetables, and a roast. Dessert was pudding or pie with coffee. Plates were piled high with food, for the German appetite was large, and even humble restaurants and cafés made a point of emphasizing abundance, particularly in the meat department. A roving correspondent for the *Atlantic Monthly*, touring Little Germany in 1867, stepped into a café and feasted his eyes on a bar laden with joints and hams, cold corned beef, loin of veal, "pyramids of sausages of every known size and shape," and "several cognate articles of manufactured swine-meat." There were pretzels stacked in baskets, glass jars filled with pickled oysters, earthen jars of caviar, onions heaped in a pile, and Limburger and Swiss cheeses. A keg of lager beer rested on a trestle, and a wine list was posted on the wall. In an upstairs snuggery, outfitted with the obligatory busts of Schiller and Shakespeare, a fountain trickled beneath floridly Romantic murals that introduced tropical palms into a landscape of Swiss chalets and soaring mountains.

Late in the evening, the Bowery's theatergoers would crowd into the little German restaurants nearby, well worth a detour for the thrifty diner ready to taste unfamiliar food cooked "in a distinctly national manner," as a *Times* article on cheap restaurants put it. They could expect to encounter "dishes of whose existence they had never before dreamed," with "flavors distasteful to the native palate." A few slices of bread and a pint of wine at fifteen cents helped erase any offensive flavors.

Sausages and "swine-meat" were central to another kind of German establishment: the delicatessen. The first delicatessens filled a niche by offering foods that Germans could not find in American stores, but these specialty shops soon began attracting Americans as well as Germans. The German delicatessen, the *Tribune* wrote in the 1890s, "has made Kalteraufschnitt a part of the Sunday bill of fare in hundreds of American families, and has given people who otherwise would never have known an idea of Gänseleberpasteten and Geräucherteg̈änse-brust, of Salzgurken, Senfgurken and Rotherubensalat." The enthusiasm was genuine, the spelling shaky. The intrepid reporter did fine with kalter Aufschnitt (cold cuts), Gänseleber-Pasteten (goose-liver pies), Salzgurken (pickles), and Senfgurken (mustard pickles) but wobbled as he attempted geräucherte Gänse-brust (smoked goose breast) and rote Rübensalat (beet salad).

By the 1890s, there were six hundred delicatessens in New York, 80 percent of them on the East Side and all but a dozen or so owned by Germans. Many functioned as cookshops. They roasted meats for their customers and kept pâtés, roast pork, and pig's feet on hand for takeout. The list of takeout foods was astounding: game pies cooked to order, baked beans, smoked beef shoulder, smoked jowls, fresh ham, meat jelly, blood pudding, liver pudding. In time, kosher German delicatessens sprang up on the East Side. Customers came in for gansekleines (small pieces of dressed goose wings, feet, or necks), gänse grieben (cracklings), foie gras, or gestetztes essen (barley and dried peas prepared on Friday for consumption on the Sabbath). Salads galore were sold from stone crocks: potato salad, beet salad, cabbage salad, parsnip salad, and herring salad. Here we see the first stirrings of a great New York institution, the Jewish delicatessen, later modified by influences from Eastern Europe and Russia, and the starting point for celebrity restaurants like Lindy's and Reuben's, which retained the delicatessen atmosphere and many of the dishes, too.

As Germans prospered, so, too, did their restaurants, which moved into the first rank. From the 1880s to the First World War, any list of the city's finest restaurants would have had to include the Hofbräu House, Lienau's, Lüchow's, the Pabst, and the New Faust, names whose prestige was intimately linked with the waves of musicians, composers, and singers who brought German music to New York audiences. Lüchow's, down the street from the Academy of Music on

Fourteenth Street, and across from Steinway Hall, served as an unofficial headquarters for German artists on tour. August Lüchow, the owner, secured the exclusive U.S. license to serve Würzburger beer, which flowed like a mighty river for decades in the dark, timbered dining rooms of his vast restaurant.

August Janssen was a medical student at the University of Göttingen who came down with a bad case of wanderlust. At some point in his European travels he learned to cook at the Hotel Meurice in Paris, after which he headed for America at the age of twenty. In New York, he found work as a waiter at Delmonico's and later became a partner at Purssell's, an important catering company. In 1898, he opened the quaintly timbered Hofbräu House near Daly's Theater at Broadway and Thirtieth Street, where he thrived for the next thirty years, serving dishes like imported Lübeck sausage with sauerkraut and mashed potatoes, and veal with Teltower turnips.

Like August Lüchow, Janssen regarded the beer of his homeland as a sacred beverage. Whenever a new cask was tapped, bells chimed: three for pilsner, four for Munich beer. One day, Janssen tried unsuccessfully to get the attention of a waiter. A busboy shouted across the room, "Janssen wants to see you." It sounded insolent, and Janssen bristled. Later, though, he decided the phrase had a certain ring to it. "Janssen wants to see you" became the motto of the Hofbräu House, as famous for New York diners as "Last call for Philip Morris!"

In the reminiscences of cultural critics like James Huneker, the heavily laden tables of Lüchow's and the Hofbräu House loomed large, monuments to a spirited style of dining and to the splendor of German culture. The love affair soured with the First World War, and the arrival of Prohibition killed one of the glories of the German table, its beer. "A genuine atmosphere of Teutonic gemütlichkeit existed in those times that are no more," Huneker wrote regretfully in September 1914, just a month after the war's outbreak. He was a little premature. The great German restaurants regrouped, and Lüchow's carried on into the 1980s, but nothing quite equaled the heady days when German music and German beer ruled supreme.

Instead, all along Eighty-sixth Street, Yorkville's main artery, small German restaurants appeared with fake Bavarian decor and nearly identical menus devoted to the clichés of Austro-German cuisine. Large steins of beer, heaps of smoking bratwurst, and the sounds of "Schnitzelbank" sung at top volume attracted New Yorkers eager for an evening of kitsch at places like Maxl's Bräustüberl, Restaurant Platzl, and Old München. "Brau Haus Boulevard," Rian

German cuisine enjoyed enormous prestige in the years before the First World War, nowhere more so than at August Lüchow's restaurant on Fourteenth Street, where the Würzburger flowed like a mighty river.

New York's Famous Bavarian Restaurant

Rudi & Maxl's — 239 East 86th Street

ABOVE: Bratwurst, beer, and oompah music drew the tourists to Rudi's & Maxl's and others just like it up and down Eighty-sixth Street. LEFT: This menu dates from the 1930s.

James called it in his restaurant guide *Dining in New York*, reserving particular scorn for Maxl's. "There is a stringy three-piece orchestra," he wrote in 1930, "which stops every other moment to drink and sing a toast to each newcomer—an orchestra with a temperamental leader, who assists in grinding out well-known German ditties and resents all verbal college-boy intrusions; and there is 'Happy,' a three-hundred-pound play-boy who, dressed up in knee-pants and Alpine hat reminiscent of a Swiss yodeler, knows all the words of all the songs."

Two world wars would dim the allure of German cuisine permanently. In time, even the parodies along Brau Haus Boulevard disappeared, taking with them the last traces of a once-vibrant gastronomic culture.

The French never emigrated in numbers to match the Germans, Irish, or Italians, yet they exerted an enormous influence on dining for one simple reason: they brought their cuisine with them. Two streams of immigration fed the hunger of New Yorkers with a taste for French food. The first was the purely professional traffic of trained French chefs who, lured by high wages and the prospect of rapid advancement, crossed the ocean to work at Delmonico's and its successors. Some amassed a bankroll and returned to France. Others started their own restaurants or, pleased with their new surroundings, assimilated. The second group of immigrants, driven from France by the upheavals of 1848 and 1870, resembled more closely their Italian and German fellow passengers, who left Europe in search of economic opportunity and political stability.

The French congregated in the blocks south of Washington Square and in present-day SoHo, which had not yet become a commercial loft district. Here they opened restaurants and cafés, many of them clustered along Wooster Street, that offered simple, soul-satisfying food—*cuisine grand-mère*—at rock-bottom prices. Typical was the Grand Vatel, a sleepy little café presided over by a Monsieur Leroy, who shuffled around the premises in his slippers. His wife, a commanding presence, sat at a small table near the door, where, surrounded by caged parrots, she counted the money. When the parrots acted up, she would rap the cages with a stick and shout, *"Tranquille!"*

The ambience was austere. Patrons sat at wooden tables covered in oilcloth, with a pewter cruet in the center. A plain meal of soup with a plate of beef and bread, or mouton à la ravigote, cost ten cents. Braised beef with onions was also a dime, and soupe aux croutons was a nickel. The cheeses were Gruyère, Neufchâtel, and Limbourg. Sliding down the scale, one entered, if one dared, the Taverne Alsacienne on Greene Street, reputedly the haunt of thieves and fences. Sullen-looking men played cards, drank wine or absinthe, and ignored the worn-out billiard table at the end of the room. The brave were rewarded with a four-course meal for thirty-five cents.

French cuisine could not be contained within a single neighborhood. French restaurants large and small, ambitious and modest, popped up all over the city. Fine dining and French food were synonymous, but frugal dining, too, found a home in humble bistros, although no one yet used that word. The most famous of them all was Mouquin's, a port of entry for lovers of French food for generations.

Like Delmonico's, Mouquin's was the creation of a Swiss, Henri Mouquin, who came from the canton of Vaud, where both his father and his grandfather

Mouquin's provided a budget education in the art of French cuisine. The uptown branch, depicted in this postcard, was on Sixth Avenue at Twenty-eighth Street.

had been hotel-keepers. In 1854, the seventeen-year-old Henri made his way to Paris, and thence to Le Havre, where he boarded the first German steamship to cross the Atlantic. The voyage proved tedious, and Henri, to amuse himself one day, knocked off a priest's hat with a potato. The captain had Henri hung from the mainmast in a sling, and in this manner he entered New York Harbor.

Once in New York, Mouquin found work as a waiter at Delmonico's, but he developed itchy feet. He roamed westward as far as St. Louis, earning money along the way by driving a cab or pitching hay. In 1857, he returned to New York and opened a restaurant, a twenty-five-cent table d'hôte at Fulton and Nassau streets and, at about the same time, a wine-importing business that expanded rapidly. For a time, Mouquin was the largest importer in the United States, and his flourishing restaurant business allowed him to move to a larger building on Fulton Street within a few years. The formula was simplicity itself: a modestly priced table d'hôte with a plat du jour (Friday was bouillabaisse day), good wine at affordable prices, and French cheeses. His wife, Marie, turned out the food.

Soon Mouquin's was commanding a healthy share of the downtown business lunch trade and challenging the mighty Astor House. Georges Clemenceau, the future French premier, ate at Mouquin's. So did the big guns of the newspaper world, men like Charles A. Dana of the *Sun* and Horace Greeley of the *Tribune*, who, preoccupied, usually let the waiter order for him. James Gordon Bennett, of the *Herald*, sent his son over every day to fetch a beefsteak for lunch. Lawyers and bankers ate at Mouquin's, but even reporters could afford it.

Julius Chambers, a reporter for the *Tribune*, received his education in dining at Mouquin's. He was not alone. As a low-priced introduction to the French *art de vivre*, the restaurant was, he maintained, "as important as Delmonico's for the average professional man." It served truffles and snails and artichokes and onion soup at a time when most Americans had never heard of such things. "Not one New Yorker out of 10,000 had eaten Pont l'Eveque, Camembert, Gorgonzola or Port de Salut cheeses until he became a frequenter of Mouquin's," Chambers wrote. The service was attentive, a revelation for Americans dining at the sub-Delmonican level. You could send a dish back to the kitchen—imagine!—and waiters actually bothered to ask customers how they might like their meat cooked. When Mouquin's opened an uptown branch on Sixth Avenue at Twenty-eighth Street in 1898, the new location became a Bohemian headquarters overnight. Officially, it was the Café Bordeaux, but no one called it anything other than Mouquin's—or Mook's. There, the good times rolled, and no evening was complete without a rousing chorus of the Marseillaise.

Mouquin himself was a shrewd character who lived well into his nineties. He kept current with developments in French cooking on annual business trips to France, where he signed deals with winemakers, scouted new products to import, and kept his eyes open when he dined. He was an old-fashioned *patron* who loathed unions—as well as the automobile, female suffrage, Prohibition, and taxes—and treated his employees like family. That is, he expected them to regard his word as law, work long hours for little pay, and keep their opinions to themselves. When crossed, he could indulge in flights of profanity that connoisseurs judged *superbe*.

The Mouquin approach to labor relations was vindicated during the Panic of 1873, when the restaurant nearly went under. Mouquin gathered his staff and told them he could not afford wages but would pay out commissions. In other words, waiters would be paid according to how much they sold. Two-thirds of them left, but the ones who stayed—the go-getters—earned a good living, and Mouquin observed an uptick in the bottom line. In fact, the restaurant had never been more profitable. The lesson was not lost on him. "Do you know what is the cure for hard times?" he told an interviewer who visited him on his ninety-fourth birthday. "I will tell you. It is low wages. When wages are high, then people are too proud to work. When wages come down they are glad to work for what they can get. It is so."

French cuisine arrived in New York with its credentials in order. Italian cooking was another matter. Eventually, it would become by a wide margin the city's most popular ethnic cuisine, but in 1880, when only twenty thousand Italians lived in New York, dishes like minestrone soup and spaghetti were exotic. A few hardy restaurateurs catered to the Italian opera singers and musicians performing in New York, and at their tables adventurous New Yorkers learned the mysteries of macaroni, as pasta was called at the time. One of the earliest was the Caffè Moretti, located in a basement on Cedar Street near the financial district. Rumors abounded that the owner, Stefano Moretti, was a member of the Carbonari, forced to flee Rome or face death by torture "in the dungeons of the Inquisition." Italians were automatically described in the press as dark, dirty, and dangerous. Moretti, who jokingly called himself "a spoiled priest"—apparently he had once been a seminarian—revealed himself in an interview with the *Tribune* in 1880 as an opera expert with a subtle sense of humor, yet he could not escape being depicted as "a burly, unshaven, brigandish Italian who is never known to wear a cravat, or for that matter clean linen."

Already a fixture in the 1870s—James Lauren Ford, the longtime literary critic of the *Herald*, claimed in his memoirs that the restaurant dated to the 1850s—Moretti's built its business on the plainest of fare, nothing more than huge bowls of boiled spaghetti in "beef gravy" with grated Parmesan cheese. "Occasional visitors try to eat it with knife and fork, to the immense enjoyment of everyone in the room," a reporter wrote. "Others try fork and spoon; others spoon and a bit of bread, which is the most satisfactory way, as the bread ought to be dipped in the gravy and eaten plentifully, to do the thing in true foreign style." Later, after moving to Fourteenth Street, and later Twenty-first Street, and acquiring patrons like Jenny Lind and Adelina Patti, Moretti would expand his repertoire— "He gave you a real succulent half chicken," the *Sun* recalled when the restaurant finally closed in 1903—but it was the pasta that patrons remembered. Amazingly, as late as 1920 a guidebook to the city could refer to spaghetti as a "serpentine food" that "draws the innocent and unwary into its maze of intricacies."

Another Italian pioneer was Maria del Prato's, which started out in a basement on MacDougal Street and won a devoted following among artists and newspapermen for its cheap table d'hôte and free-for-all atmosphere. A few coins would buy a meal of minestrone, chicken, and zabaglione with Chianti.

The pleasures of the Italian table soon became known to a wider audience, as the city's Italian population reached a quarter of a million in 1900 and half a million in 1910. Italians displaced the French south of Washington Square, and Greenwich Village acquired a host of Italian restaurants just like Moretti's and Maria del Prato's, some of them still in existence.

Immigration did not simply change New York's taste in dining. It set the stage, and the tone, for the grand, ongoing spectacle known as Bohemia. As the city replaced Boston and Philadelphia as the nation's cultural capital, it fostered a new population of artists, illustrators, journalists, novelists, poets, and hangers-on—a roving army perennially strapped for cash but rich in imagination and hungry for romance. A clam pie and a bottle of beer might nourish the body, but it did little to feed the soul. The Bohemian set, with its large contingent of artists who had traveled to Paris or Italy, and writers who had at least read of and dreamed about such places, formed a ready-made clientele for any foreign restaurant with a fifty-cent table d'hôte.

Bohemians were fickle, of course. Attuned to the finer things, they deserted their familiar haunts as soon as a check arrived. William H. Rideing, a writer for *Harper's* and a devotee of restaurants like the Grand Vatel in the 1870s and 1880s, vividly recalled the "opulent intermissions in our poverty" when a windfall descended "like feathers from an angel's wings." The French Quarter was quickly abandoned:

> Nothing was too good or too dear for us; we made merry at Delmonico's or at Sieghortner's, the old mansion of the Astor family in Lafayette Place, which retained the quietude and dignity of a stately private house and provided epicurean food, old Sieghortner himself, blandest of hosts, hovering over us, unctuous, smiling, and rubbing his hands, while the solemn and unhurried waiter set before us the incomparable gumbo, the pompano and English sole, the chicken so white and tender that it seemed like chicken transfigured into a dove from the bosom of the same angel that had let her feathers smooth us.

In legend, if not in fact, Bohemia was born in the late 1850s at Pfaff's basement saloon at Broadway and Bleecker Street. Pfaff's was crudely furnished, with a few tables and chairs, a counter, a clock, a row of shelves, and some barrels. At one end of the basement was a sort of cave with a long table. Here, underneath the sidewalk, caroused the likes of Walt Whitman (who sang the praises of "the vault at Pfaff's"), Clemenceau (again!), Artemus Ward, Thomas Bailey Aldrich, the short-story writer Fitz-James O'Brien, and the scandalous Ada Clare, a beautiful actress whose hothouse poetry and illegitimate child earned her the title "love queen of Bohemia." There was an eclectic food mix at Pfaff's—regulars feasted on Dutch pannekuchen and American steaks—but it was the long evenings devoted to drinking, smoking, and talking at the long table that defined the Pfaff's experience. Here was the Algonquin Roundtable nearly a century before the fact.

The presiding spirit was Henry Clapp, who, during a long stay in Paris, developed an infatuation with the world depicted in Henri Murger's *Scènes de la vie de bohème*. Drink eventually got the better of him, and he spent long periods drying out in an upstate "inebriate asylum" before descending into beggary and, in 1875, a pauper's grave (from which he was rescued by Whitman). In his heyday in the 1850s, however, when he edited the avant-garde *Saturday Press*, Clapp reigned as New York's lord of misrule. His genial enabler was Charles Pfaff, a German from Baden who knew how to run a rathskeller and showed a high degree of tolerance for self-proclaimed geniuses, most of them future footnote material.

Clapp cracked the whip smartly from his position at the head of the table. Newcomers needed to have a tough skin to earn a place, since Clapp made free with his caustic asides. Horace Greeley he summed up as "a self-made man that worships his creator." During the Civil War, Fitz-James O'Brien received a staff appointment that had been intended for Aldrich. After he was killed in action, Clapp, who despised both men, remarked, "Aldrich, I see, has been shot in O'Brien's shoulder."

William Dean Howells, who had written for the *Saturday Press* and was therefore—in principle—sympathetic to the artistic program at Pfaff's, paid a visit one day in 1860. "I felt that as a contributor and at least a brevet Bohemian I ought not to go home without visiting the famous place, and witnessing if I could not share the revels of my comrades," he wrote in *Literary Friends and Acquaintance*. Since he did not drink beer or smoke, Howells no doubt made a feeble impression. "My part in the carousal was limited to a German pancake, which I found they had very good at Pfaff's, and to listening to the whirling words of my commensals," he recalled. "Nothing of their talk remains with me, but the impression remains that it was not so good talk as I had heard in Boston."

At one point a group of latecomers straggled in, causing a great stir among the company in the vault. "I was given to understand they were just recovered from a fearful debauch; their locks were still damp from the wet towels used to restore them, and their eyes were very frenzied," Howells wrote. "I was presented to these types, who neither said nor did anything worthy of their awful appearance, but dropped into seats at the table, and ate of the supper with an appetite that seemed poor. I stayed hoping vainly for worse things till eleven o'clock, and then I rose and took my leave of a literary condition that had distinctly disappointed me."

This priggish picture, painted in the 1890s, did not sit well with the surviving members of the company, especially the poet William Winter, Clapp's subeditor at the *Press*. He objected to the term "debauchery." Nor were the members of the jolly company especially given to drink, he insisted, with the exception of Clapp. "Revelry requires money," he wrote, "and at the time Mr. Howells met those Bohemians—with the 'damp locks' and 'frenzied eyes'—it is probable that the group did not possess enough money among them all to buy a quart bottle of champagne." The cosseted dude from genteel Boston, Winter suggested, had badly misread the milieu.

The Civil War dispersed the happy company, and in 1879 Pfaff moved uptown to Twenty-third Street and respectability. His version of Bohemia vanished, but not without a trace. The legend of Pfaff's proved to be potent. Its spell lingered over subsequent generations of writers and journalists who made their way to New York seeking freedom and intellectual companionship. Like artists who came to the city after the heyday of the Abstract Expressionist free-for-alls at the Cedar Bar, they arrived with a picture of the ideal creative society clearly in mind. Cheap food and drink, preferably exotic, were an important part of it. In this respect, they were more fortunate than the Pfaff's crowd, for in the meantime, the world had come to them. It was no longer necessary to book passage to Europe, because Europe was pouring into New York, bringing its cafés, trattorias, and rathskellers. For the first time, New York was becoming a truly cosmopolitan city, with the world's cuisine at its fingertips. Bohemia was ready for its second, and grandest, act (to be dealt with in due course).

Strangely, it was Howells, by this time a resident New Yorker, who did more than any other American novelist to provide a detailed, accurate picture of the city's Bohemian restaurants. His timeless depiction of Manhattan apartment hunting in *A Hazard of New Fortunes* has been much remarked upon, but his fond descriptions of the city's cheap table d'hôtes deserve equal attention. Their documentary precision is equaled only in the restaurant paintings of William Glackens and John Sloan. It is one of literature's little ironies that the American writer most associated with placid, middle-class life should have revealed himself, in his dining habits, as an unapologetic Bohemian, and a culinary adventurer of the first rank.

7

The Dawn of the Golden Age

The Civil War was not welcomed in New York. It was bad for business. The city had taken the same attitude toward the Revolutionary War, and it would later resist, with the same self-serving instincts, the great crusade known as Prohibition. New York existed to trade, to accumulate wealth, and to live well. It had always been so. In a moralizing republic, New York was an amoral anomaly, and the rest of the country regarded it warily—although disapproval was mingled with desire.

At best, then, New York managed two cheers for the Union cause. It disturbed commerce, and any disturbance in commerce threatened a style of living that New Yorkers were starting to regard as their birthright. By hook or by crook, though—mostly by crook—fortunes continued to be made. Big fortunes. And the postwar economic boom would produce even bigger ones, as New York transformed itself, with dizzying speed, into an international financial capital, a manufacturing powerhouse, an immigrant haven, and a cosmopolitan pleasure center. For diners, it was a dream come true.

Despite the failure of the Maison Dorée, Lorenzo Delmonico was, as always, absolutely correct in laying a heavy bet on the future prospects of New York. His judgment was ratified by a hotel-building boom, and a continuing push uptown, propelled by a massive infusion of new wealth. A river of gold was flowing through the city, lifting spirits and culinary standards to new heights.

The Union Square Delmonico's, with its spacious banquet rooms and ball-rooms, functioned flawlessly as a social gatekeeper. The right people attended its balls. The right sort of social clubs held their banquets there. It was the favored location for the Assembly Balls and Family Circle Dancing Classes, and, beginning in the 1870s, the best families sent their daughters there to be presented to society. Coming-out parties had traditionally been held in private homes, but in 1870 the prominent banker Archibald Gracie King took advantage of Delmonico's beautifully appointed rooms and broke with precedent, presenting his eldest daughter at a dinner-dance attended by eight hundred people. The rest of New York society followed suit.

The restaurant performed a badly needed social service at a time when barbarians were at the gates. The old-money aristocracy kept one eye on the immigrant hordes arriving daily at the docks, the other on the equally appalling nouveaux riches—wave after wave of them—demanding a place at the city's top tables. Civil War contractors were followed by the new industrial elite, who yielded, in their turn, to the mining and cattle barons of the West. "Absolute in their own territories, they longed for fresh worlds to conquer," wrote Mrs. John King Van Rensselaer in *The Social Ladder*, her popular history of New York's social changes. "Newspaper accounts of the affairs of New York Society pictured this organization in colors that thrilled the newly rich of the West." And so they came.

Ward McAllister—a cousin of Sam Ward's, as it happened—attained near-autocratic power by offering to sort the whole mess out. In 1872, after sponsoring a series of cotillions at Delmonico's, he organized the Society of Patriarchs, a sort of social Politburo made up of twenty-five prominent, impeccably bred New Yorkers from the city's oldest families—names like Astor, Livingston, Duer, and Schermerhorn. Several times each year, the Patriarchs gave a subscription ball at Delmonico's, with each Patriarch inviting four women and five men. The blessed few who passed the scrutiny of the Patriarchs gained admission to the Four Hundred, a figure equal to the number of guests who could fit comfortably into Mrs. William Astor's ballroom, where an annual ball was held on the third Monday in January. As McAllister remarked offhandedly in a newspaper interview, "Why, there are only about four hundred people in fashionable New York society. If you go outside that number you strike people who are either not at ease in a ballroom or else make other people not at ease." McAllister did not just pluck this nice, round number from the air, nor did it refer to some vague, semi-mythical upper crust. In 1892, after years of tantalizing the public, he actually drew up a list of the four hundred names and gave it to the newspapers. Here was Delmonico's natural clientele.

From its headquarters on Union Square, Delmonico's ruled supreme and, after the demise of the Maison Dorée, unchallenged. Neither war nor the social dislocations that came with peace could ruffle its serenity. "On entering from 14th Street," wrote Abram C. Dayton, "one cannot fail to be impressed by the absence of bustle and confusion; no boisterous commands are heard, and the waiters glide about as noiselessly as ghosts. An air of luxury surrounds you as the attentive *garçon* stands motionless before you and respectfully awaits your wishes."

Like New York society, however, Delmonico's was far from impenetrable. It took time to gain the status of a regular; but the international fame of the restaurant drew all sorts of diners with money to spend, along with tourists desperate to visit a restaurant that, by now, was one of the prime New York sights. Dayton, so impressed by Delmonico's hushed elegance, surveyed the dining room and spied a "soft-speaking gourmand, who gloats over his *carte*" and "a freshly fledged millionaire, who furtively glances about in dread (lest he should not be seen), as he *points* to the highest-priced item, having no remote idea what it is." Elsewhere, his critical eye picked out "a puffy dowager, perspiring at every pore," two country girls staring pop-eyed and forgetting to eat, and "a party of prinked-up young men, sporting gaudy neckties and flash jewelry."

Upstairs, the restaurant also pursued two-track diplomacy. While the cotillions, balls, and coming-out parties retained their stamp of exclusivity, the restaurant gladly accepted the shiny coin of arrivistes like Leonard Jerome, August Belmont, and William R. Travers, financiers and racetrack rivals. Together, the three staged a competitive series of dinners that set the town abuzz.

At the Jerome dinner ladies unfolded their napkins to find a gold bracelet engraved with the initials J.P., for Jerome Park, the fashionable racetrack Jerome had built in the Bronx in 1866. This lavish gesture was soon eclipsed. In 1873, an importer named Edward Luckmeyer broke the taste barrier with a $10,000 dinner. Seventy-five guests sat at an oval table nearly as large as the dining room. At the center of the table was a thirty-foot lake surrounded by an artificial landscape featuring waterfalls, streams, and grassy hillocks planted with elaborate floral beds. As the guests ate, white swans—on loan from Prospect Park in Brooklyn—paddled across the lake. The Swan Dinner, as it was known, was merely the first in a series of extravagant events that would enrich the city's restaurants and appall the public.

In 1865, Lorenzo Delmonico opened another restaurant at 22 Broad Street and put his cousin, John Longhi, in charge. This brought the number of Delmonico's restaurants to four, each with its own clientele. High society—dragging with it a horde of imitators and gawkers—patronized Fourteenth Street, whose café attracted the upper strata of businessmen. The Chambers Street Delmonico's, managed by the cigar-puffing Siro Delmonico, brother of Lorenzo, served politicians, lawyers, merchants, and judges clustered around City Hall, as well as the gentlemen of the press a short walk away on Newspaper Row. The Citadel, managed by another brother, Constant, catered to bankers, shipping men, and brokers. The new branch at Broad Street, virtually next door to the Stock Exchange, took on a Wall Street flavor. It became "the great resort of the stock and gold brokers—a dashing, free, animated set, who indulge in expensive liquors, and are notorious for drinking early and drinking often." There was a Delmonico's, it seemed, for every ward in the city with the wealth to support one, each with its own special atmosphere.

Lorenzo Delmonico was not the only New Yorker who knew how to read a map or follow the real estate news. A shrewd developer by the name of Amos R. Eno looked into the future and saw opportunity beckoning in far-off Madison Square, where, in 1859, he opened the Fifth Avenue Hotel, overlooking the west side of what was then little more than a lawn with a few footpaths. Madison Square was remote. Not until 1871 did the park undergo the landscaping that transformed it into one of the city's most elegant green spaces. But Eno had picked the right spot. Proof positive was the arrival of the French chocolatier Henry Maillard, who opened an exclusive shop and ladies' restaurant on the hotel's ground floor in the 1870s. Maillard's quickly became a sparkling jewel in Manhattan's crown, its restaurant a favored resort of the well-to-do women who shopped the great department stores of the Ladies Mile, on Sixth Avenue.

Like a giant magnet, the hotel pulled theaters and restaurants northward. The Hoffman House, erected in 1863 at Twenty-fifth and Broadway, attracted the sporting crowd and art lovers eager to view the frankly erotic Bouguereau painting *Nymphs and Satyr* that hung in the hotel's barroom. Sumptuous dishes like mushrooms under crystal, and Baltimore flaked crab with green peppers and cream sauce, were served in a dining room decorated in the style of a Moorish temple.

The Hoffman House, like the rest of the jewel-like hotels around Madison Square, took pride in its superb restaurant, presided over by the Alsatian chef Francis Kinzler. One of the main attractions was Bouguereau's *Nymphs and Satyr*, in the hotel bar.

Chicanery was afoot at the Hoffman House. Its co-owner, James L. Mitchell, discovered that Charles H. Read, his partner, had renewed the lease on the hotel without including Mitchell's name. He promptly filed suit and was awarded $45,000 plus interest by the court. With the money, and supported by backers indignant at his treatment, he took over an apartment hotel on the north side of Madison Square and created the Brunswick in 1872. Twisting the knife, he stole the Hoffman House's Alsatian chef, Francis Kinzler, who set about creating an exclusive, top-quality restaurant to rival Delmonico's. Indeed, more than a few gourmets thought it better. The kitchen employed eleven French chefs. In its "ice cream apartment," a dozen ice cream machines, fed by an automatic ice shaver, generated the raw material for desserts molded into fantastic shapes.

The Brunswick's frescoed public dining room, with green carpeting to match the plants, was one of the most opulent in the city, with only forty-five tables arranged around a dramatic fountain. In the windows, stained-glass medallions depicting eminent artists and poets admitted a flickering, kaleidoscopic light. In summers, diners could take their meals in the Jardin d'Été, an outdoor garden under a canvas awning.

Julius Keller, a Swiss immigrant who would one day own his own restaurants, signed on as a waiter at the Brunswick in its heyday. Keller had already paid his dues, serving at the Paisley House, a raffish hotel in the city's vice district, known as the Tenderloin, and at the thoroughly genteel Gilsey House, yet another of the posh hotels clustered around Madison Square. He was dazzled by the parade of wealthy New Yorkers who drifted into the Brunswick after the French Ball and the Arion Ball at Madison Square Garden, signal events of the winter season. "The easy manner of the men, the charm and grace of the women, the exquisite gowns, the gorgeous jewels, the murmur of polite conversation, the soft music of the waltzes and polkas, the whole atmosphere of culture and polish—it was a panoply of human behavior so different from the crude life I had lived only a short time before that I had to steady myself to keep from being bewildered," he wrote in his memoirs. This was the world of Edith Wharton, an enchanted circle of wealth and privilege that most New Yorkers could only gaze on from afar. The women, especially, made a deep impression on Keller: "The whiteness of their teeth, the sheen of their coiffures, the delicate texture of their skin, their modulated voices—it all made me think how lucky were the men who laughed and chatted and danced with them."

One by one, grand hotels attached themselves to Madison Square, and with each one came an ambitious dining room. The Albemarle, at Twenty-fourth and Broadway, arrived just before the Brunswick, in 1870. It was followed by the Gilsey House, the St. James, the Victoria, and the Bartholdi, named for Frederic-Auguste Bartholdi, the sculptor of the Statue of Liberty, whose giant upraised arm remained on view in Madison Square from 1876 to 1884. A few blocks south, Richard de Logerot, the Marquis de Croisic, created an intimate, top-quality restaurant at the Hotel de Logerot. Dorlon's, with its oyster clock, arrived in 1875.

Delmonico's came hard on their heels. In 1876, Lorenzo Delmonico, reading the tea leaves, closed the Fourteenth Street Delmonico's and moved to 212 Fifth Avenue, at Twenty-sixth Street, across the street from Madison Square. The building, which had previously been used for assembly balls, was home to the Dodsworth Studios, where Teddy Roosevelt had taken dancing lessons as a boy. A renovation relying heavily on mahogany, parquet, silver chandeliers, and ceiling frescoes reestablished the note of elegance, and without missing a beat, the Delmonicos were open for business yet again.

With startling rapidity, an elegant entertainment district was taking shape on Madison Square, a pleasure nexus of hotels, restaurants, and theaters organized around the city's most attractive small park. The beauty of the setting owed everything to an Austrian landscape architect named Ignatz Pilat, who in 1871 transformed Madison Square from a utilitarian green patch to a romantic garden rivaling Europe's best. Pilat, who had studied botany at the University of Vienna and worked at the Imperial Botanical Gardens at the Schönbrunn Palace, earned his spurs assisting Calvert Vaux and Frederick Law Olmsted in the design of Central Park. At Madison Square, Pilat laid out a series of curved walkways that encouraged pedestrians to slow down and meander among exotic trees and carefully tended flower beds.

Meanwhile, the theater district was creeping north from Union Square. High-toned playhouses like Daly's and the Fifth Avenue Theater rubbed shoulders with variety houses like Koster and Bial's. And more entertainment was on the way. After the New York and Harlem Railroad abandoned its depot on the east side of Madison Square, shifting operations to the new Grand Central Terminal in 1871, P. T. Barnum took over the site and created his Monster Classical and Geological Hippodrome. This was the first in a series of spectacular, large-scale entertainment venues that culminated in the renovated Madison Square Garden of McKim, Mead & White in 1890, illuminated at night by ten thousand lightbulbs, and topped by the rotating, unmistakably nude figure of the goddess Diana.

Madison Square sparkled enticingly in the center of 1870s Manhattan. Its restaurants defined high-style dining for a generation of New Yorkers and made them feel, for the first time with real justification, that their brash, bare-knuckled metropolis could compete with Paris or London in the more civilized departments of life. Augustus Sala, a well-known British journalist who had spent time in New York during the war, returned in the 1870s and marveled at the new city that had sprung up in his absence. Madison Square, in particular, with its broad boulevards branching outward, struck him as positively Parisian.

Fashionable women, after shopping along the Ladies Mile on Sixth Avenue, might take a carriage over to Maillard's for lunch, enjoy a walk through the park, meet their husbands at the theater, and enjoy a late dinner afterward. Men thronged the cafés and bars of Delmonico's, the Brunswick, and the Hoffman House, where professional bartenders served up the latest in mixed drinks. Bars were different then. Fresh fruit and crushed ice were displayed on the counter. The drinks were served in fine crystal, with a starched white linen napkin. This was the era when the Manhattan and the martini first appeared, created by bartenders who were expected to have a repertoire of hundreds of cocktails at their fingertips and to invent new ones virtually every day.

"By eight o'clock Broadway below Canal Street is almost deserted, save in the immediate neighborhood of the Post Office," wrote James D. McCabe, Jr., setting the New York scene in 1882.

> Gradually this region becomes silent also, and below Union Square but little of interest is to be seen. The true night-life of Broadway is to be witnessed chiefly between 23rd and 34th streets. From Union Square to 34th Street the great thoroughfare is ablaze with the electric light, which illumines it with the radiance of day. Crowds throng the sidewalks; the lights of the omnibuses and carriages dart to and fro along the roadway like myriads of fire-flies; the great hotels, the theatres and restaurants, send out their blaze of gas-lamps, and are alive with visitors. The crowd is out for pleasure at night, and many and varied are the forms which the pursuit of it takes.

The parade lasted late into the night, with a surge when the theaters disgorged their patrons, who, unlike their modern counterparts, ate after rather than before the play, filling the nearby restaurants and cafés.

It was in Madison Square that Edith Wharton's genteel characters arranged their lunch and dinner appointments, usually at the terribly chic Café Martin. This favored dining spot took over Delmonico's space in 1904, a few years after the older restaurant made its final northward jump, to Forty-fourth Street and Fifth Avenue. In no time it became the last word in fashion. The old Delmonico's café was updated with leather banquettes—the latest thing in Parisian restaurants—and an orchestra was installed in the balcony. A few Art Nouveau design touches—another novelty—put the icing on the cake. William De Leftwich Dodge's murals of dreamy, peachy-complected nudes floating through space titillated but stopped just short of shocking refined tastes. Jean-Baptiste

Martin, the owner, knew how to generate what a later age would refer to as buzz. One of his clever advertising gimmicks was to print hand-colored postcards with amusing cartoons that used the Café Martin as a subject. If diners wrote a note to a friend or relative, the restaurant would provide a stamp and mail the card.

Martin showcased ingredients that other restaurants barely knew. The menu featured Marenne oysters, French sole, pré-salé lamb, and Bigareau cherries, as well as exotic international dishes like pilaf and moussaka. Most modern of all was the seating policy. Ladies, if accompanied by a gentleman, could eat in the café, a daring new experiment. Martin's was it, "the Frenchest French restaurant." Best of all, for New Yorkers beginning to find Delmonico's just a little stuffy, was its "polished suggestion of naughtiness."

Martin came to Madison Square with an excellent reputation. He and his brother, Louis, had already made their mark downtown, where they ran the Hotel Martin on University Place. Their father had operated a successful restaurant in the French spa town

The naughty Café Martin, which opened in the old Delmonico's on Madison Square in 1904, was "the Frenchest French restaurant."

of Aix-les-Bains, and there the Martin brothers learned the trade. Jean-Baptiste's lucky strike came with the opening of the Panama Canal. He built the Grand Hotel in Colón, made a fortune while the going was good, and came to New York in 1883. The Hotel Martin and its restaurant became a favorite with French visitors and stayed that way, even after Martin sold the hotel and it became the Lafayette. It would remain a mainstay of the Bohemian set well into the 1950s.

Some idea of the fizz and pop of Madison Square can be recaptured by tracing the last night in the life of Stanford White, the society architect who created Madison Square Garden and died there on June 25, 1906. Early that evening, White took his son and a friend to the Café Martin, where they dined in the café, facing Broadway. It was a bad choice. White did not realize it, but he had been spotted by Harry Thaw and Evelyn Nesbit, who were eating with friends in the main dining room. Nesbit was the stunning chorus girl who had been White's mistress while still in her teens. She had since moved on and married Thaw, the highly unstable son of a Pittsburgh coal and railroad baron. Jealous and possessive, he despised White, whom he referred to as "the beast." Nesbit slipped a note to Thaw: "The B. was here but has left." Thaw fumed.

After dinner, White dropped off his son and friend at the New Amsterdam Theater on Forty-second Street, where a George M. Cohan farce was playing on the roof garden. Then he headed to Madison Square Garden's roof to see the musical *Mam'zelle Champagne*. There, it so happened, Thaw and Nesbit were also in attendance. It was a typical evening in Madison Square—fine food, pretty girls, laughter, and sparkling wine. As a line of chorus girls danced around a giant champagne bottle, Harry Short sang "I Could Love a Thousand Girls." At 11:00 p.m., Thaw approached White, pulled out a pistol, and shot his rival three times in the head.

It was the most shocking celebrity crime in living memory, and the local press was primed to offer full coverage. New Yorkers feasted on descriptions of the last supper at the Café Martin. Edward Chlemar, Thaw and Nesbit's waiter, discreetly disavowed any knowledge of the passed note. He did recall that Thaw drank three cocktails, seemed "a little nervous," and paid the check with a hundred-dollar bill. The table talk, he testified, was about horses. "A little nervous" seems to have been an understatement. The man who ran the hat-check concession testified that Thaw presented his ticket with a violently trembling hand. "When I handed him the hat, he literally jerked it out of my hand," the man recalled, "and in putting it on he crushed it down over his forehead and his eyes with a crashing sound which indicated that it had been broken by the violence of his treatment."

The Stanford White murder brought together all the elements that defined the neighborhood: wealth, a glossy social tone, the avid pursuit of nighttime pleasures, an intoxicating whiff of scandal. When Americans in the provinces clucked their tongues over New York City (and secretly fantasized about spending a wild week on the town), they had in mind precisely the life they read about in the trial of Harry Thaw. Nowhere else in America could you find anything close to matching it.

In truth, by the turn of the century, eyes were already turning northward from Madison Square. Like Union Square before it, Madison Square had once marked the northern frontier of the entertainment district, but within a generation it had become the southern border, the point below which the lights dimmed after six o'clock. When Delmonico's moved to Fifth Avenue, in 1897, the square began to look a little forlorn, despite the lingering attractions of the Café Martin and Madison Square Garden. The St. James was torn down. The Brunswick closed its doors. A brilliant chapter was inexorably drawing to a close.

Julius Keller, in his memoirs, recounted a colorful incident in the Brunswick's downward slide. One day, a well-dressed man entered the hotel's restaurant and proposed a dinner for fifty, money no object. A sample menu was drawn up, at a cost of ten dollars a head. The mysterious gentleman paid cash in advance. On the appointed evening, however, the restaurant staff was shocked to see a mob of Bowery toughs and their molls descending on the restaurant, led by the formerly well-dressed gentleman, now in garish clothing and swearing like a sailor. It was none other than Billy McGlory, owner of one of the city's most notorious dance saloons, Armory Hall.

Ignoring the stricken faces of the waiters and the spluttering protests of the maître d', McGlory insisted that his party be seated and fed. They were, and his motley crew rioted into the wee hours. The next day, hotel guests began moving out, leaving the Brunswick's reputation in tatters. The entire farce, it later transpired, had been engineered by Edward Stokes, who took over as manager of the Hoffman House in 1880, fresh from a four-year stretch at Sing Sing for murdering the financier Jim Fisk. It was Stokes who bought *Nymphs and Satyr* in 1882, and Stokes who, according to Keller, hired Billy McGlory to bring ruination on the Brunswick as revenge for Mitchell and Kinzler's treachery in setting up a rival business.

The dinner sounds apocryphal, but it really happened. However, there is a less dramatic explanation for the decline of the Brunswick and the rest of the elegant hotels nearby: the contours of Manhattan's real estate map had changed. More fashionable hotels, like the Plaza, opened farther uptown, taking the moneyed guests and diners with them. It is the eternal New York story. Madison Square burned brightly for its appointed hour and then yielded the stage.

Anyone looking for portents might have focused on ominous news from the house of Delmonico. In 1881, the great Lorenzo died. Homage was paid to the man who, more than any other, elevated the culinary standards of the city, not just in his own restaurants but in all the restaurants that followed, which either emulated his example or drew their personnel from his training ground.

"When he first began, forty years ago, to keep an eating house in New York, little was known of artistic cooking; and for a long time thereafter restaurants were few in number and not usually distinguished by the skillful preparation of their food," the *Sun* wrote.

> Different ones, it is true, had different specialties in the way of dishes, but a really elegant and well-proportioned dinner could not be obtained in New York. The fare was hearty rather than delicate, and the service was never graceful, according to our modern notions. Oyster saloons, distinguished by their red balls of light, abounded in the city a quarter of a century ago, but of restaurants where a man could get an elaborate bill of fare and be sure of good articles thoroughly well-prepared, there were only two or three at most. The cookery at nearly all of the restaurants was of a very primitive kind, and a large part of the delicacies obtainable in our markets—the best in the world— were not used at all, either on private or public tables . . . Pies of different kinds seem to have exhausted the ingenuity of the cooks of that period.

How different the present day, in large part the work of Lorenzo the Magnificent.

Three years later, Charles, the face of the Fifth Avenue Delmonico's, died under bizarre circumstances. For several years he had been exhibiting erratic behavior. He plunged into the stock market and lost. His appearance became slovenly and his temper unpredictable. Shortly after New Year's 1884, he simply disappeared. Then bits and pieces of his property began turning up along the railroad tracks in New Jersey. Two boys walking their dogs in the Orange Mountains discovered a frozen body in a ravine, its beard stiffened with ice. Charles Delmonico was dead. Deranged, he had apparently formed a plan to visit George McClellan, the Civil War general, who lived near Montclair. Darkness and freezing temperatures overtook him as he tried to cross the mountain between the train station and McClellan's home. The Delmonico name lived on, as did the restaurants, but an era had ended. Increasingly, the restaurant was becoming a symbol of the past, yielding to younger restaurateurs who would carry the city forward into the twentieth century.

An alert observer might have spotted among the supernumeraries of Madison Square two men who would help turn the neighborhood into yesterday's news: Louis Sherry and Oscar Tschirky. Sherry, a former busboy and waiter at the Brunswick, took close notes on the society that passed in and out of the restaurant. He watched, listened, and bided his time. "I kept my ears open for pointers," he later recalled. "I listened to every discussion of dishes and meals I could get within earshot of, and after I had served people long enough to take the liberty, I asked them about dishes and dinners and got new ideas. Then I would suggest new dishes and combinations to them. Those were the years of my schooling."

In the summer of 1880, Sherry was invited to manage the restaurant and kitchen of the Hotel Elberon, a fashionable resort on the Jersey Shore, where he further cultivated the right sort of clientele. After the Brunswick refused to let him return to the Elberon for a second summer, he opened a catering firm on Sixth Avenue at Thirty-eighth Street, supplying food and decorations for the private parties of the Four Hundred. Gradually, Sherry extended his influence. When J. P. Morgan traveled to the Episcopal General Convention, held every three years, Sherry would precede him, rent a house, and dispatch a team of chefs and waiters to cater to the great financier.

Sherry's breakthrough came when *The Mikado* arrived in New York in 1885 and took the town by storm, just as it had in London. Overnight, all things Japanese were the height of fashion, and Sherry pounced. "One of the secrets I had learned was that nothing goes further with dainty people than dainty decorations," he later said. Called upon to cater an exclusive post-theater party at a private town house, he created *Mikado*-themed cakes, with ices molded in the shape of the principal characters, each one holding a tiny parasol. The oohs and aahs could be heard up and down Fifth Avenue.

Sherry was on his way. In 1889, he turned the old Goelet mansion on Fifth Avenue and Thirty-seventh Street into a luxurious restaurant with a large ballroom. An immediate success, it cemented his position with the smart set. It is here that Dreiser's Sister Carrie gets her first taste of life at the top, Manhattan style. Trapped in a modest flat, she has read newspaper accounts of dinners and balls at Sherry's, which give her "a distinct idea of the gorgeousness and luxury of this wonderful temple of gastronomy." The reality does not disappoint. The muted colors, the soft lighting, the rich fabrics, the gilt and mirrors, the whispered attentions of the waiters—all this works on her with an almost erotic power.

Dreiser himself usually ate at cafeterias and neighborhood German restaurants like the Kloster Glocke in Greenwich Village when he lived in New York.

His tastes were proletarian, and in *Sister Carrie* he drops a few acid observations about Sherry's and the "showy, wasteful and unwholesome gastronomy" of the city's high-class restaurants. The Sherry's menu, translated by Dreiser, reads like a bill of indictment: "An order of soup at fifty cents or a dollar, with a dozen kinds to choose from. Oysters in forty styles and at sixty cents the half-dozen. Entrees, fish, and meats at prices which would house one overnight in a hotel. A dollar fifty and two dollars seemed to be the most common figures upon this most tastefully printed bill-o'fare."

Carrie loves it. She is a sensualist, and every detail in the restaurant is designed to captivate an imagination like hers. "The tables were not so remarkable in themselves, and yet the imprint of 'Sherry' upon the napery, the name of 'Tiffany' upon the silverware, the name of 'Haviland' upon the china, and over all the glow of the small red-shaded candelabra, and the reflected tints of the walls on garments and faces, made them seem remarkable," Dreiser's narrator observes. "Each waiter added an air of exclusiveness and elegance by the manner in which he bowed, scraped, touched and trifled with things. The exclusively personal attention which he devoted to each one, saying 'soup—green turtle, yes—One portion, yes. Oysters—certainly—half-dozen—yes. Asparagus! Olives—yes.'" As Carrie surrenders to her impressions, her dinner partner, studying the menu, wonders idly if there might be something wrong about spending so much money. Carrie draws a different lesson. To be rich, she decides, is "a wonderful thing."

Louis Sherry made it his business to please, and New York was pleased to make him a very rich man. In 1898, hard on the heels of Delmonico's, he commissioned Stanford White to create a new restaurant on Fifth Avenue at Forty-fourth Street, with large ballrooms to draw the patronage of the younger set, who were finding the cotillions at Delmonico's a little old hat. He read their minds and their tastes with uncanny accuracy. For the next twenty years, Sherry's would host many of the dinner parties that gave the era its reputation for careless extravagance.

At the Hoffman House, a young Swiss immigrant named Oscar Tschirky was also scrutinizing the passing parade with a keen eye. Thanks to an introduction from his older brother, an assistant chef at the Brunswick, Tschirky had found work at the Hoffman House on the day he arrived in New York in 1883. Over the next few years, he worked his way up to room-service waiter and then steward on the private yacht of the hotel's owner, Ed Stokes. Within four years he was a waiter in the Hoffman House's private dining rooms.

Like Louis Sherry, Oscar bided his time, learning and observing. One day, as he later told the story, he caught sight of Lillian Russell stepping out of her carriage and entering Delmonico's. He was dazzled. Lillian represented everything that was beautiful and gay about the Gay Nineties, lurking just around the corner. At a Rubenesque two hundred pounds, she was hard to miss, an eye-filling display of womanly curves. The Gibson Girl and the flapper would render this type as obsolete as ostrich feathers, but on the happy day that Tschirky spied his nymph, Lillian Russell was the Marilyn Monroe of the era. Immediately, he headed over to Delmonico's, presented his credentials, and was hired. Starting out in the men's café, he rose through the ranks, reaching the position of waiter in the private rooms, where a team of four waiters and a manager arranged everything from small dinners for six to big banquets attended by as many as a hundred guests. Eventually, Tschirky was put in charge of the private rooms and the catering department, which arranged dinners at the private tables of the city's elite.

In 1893, when the brand-new Waldorf looked like the coming thing, Tschirky approached its manager, George Boldt, and applied for a job. Boldt, formerly the manager of the Bellevue in Philadelphia, looked skeptically at this squat, square-faced little man and asked for references. Tschirky went back to Delmonico's and the Hoffman House and returned with ten pages of signatures that included most of the leading citizens of New York. Boldt bowed to the inevitable. Thus began the forty-year reign of the man known simply as Oscar of the Waldorf, arbiter of fine dining, guardian of the velvet rope, symbol of the high life in New York when the sky was the limit.

Most diners took meals far from Madison Square, in cheap ethnic restaurants or in the cut-price progeny of the old chophouses and refectories. They dined at the fifteen-cent restaurants known as hash houses, or beaneries, which in time begat the dairy lunchroom, the Automat, and the cafeteria. New York has always been a city of culinary extremes. Nowhere else, in the waning years of the nineteenth century, could you dine so well, and pay so much—or so little. It's still true, more than a hundred years later. Julius Keller embraced the extremes. He arrived in Manhattan, as we have seen, in 1880 and, as he put it in his memoirs, "followed the trail of food." After shucking oysters at Fulton Market, he set his sights on opening a hash house. This was an immigrant's dream, ruthlessly practical. Keller had had ample opportunity to observe hash-house economics, since he ate at one almost every day, either the Jim Fisk or the Boss

Tweed on Chatham Street, two establishments whose blustering names belied the humble dishes to be found within. "An order of what they called liver and bacon, but which in reality was cow's liver and salt pork, cost eight cents, with a bowl of coffee and a puffover thrown in free," Keller recalled. "You paid fifteen cents for corned beef and cabbage and twenty-five cents for a turkey dinner. While you ate you felt your pockets frequently to keep them from being picked. In winter you put your overcoat on the back of your chair so that it would not be stolen."

Typically, there were no menus. Instead, placards, each emblazoned with the name of a dish, were hung like banners. "Sometimes these were of a highly ornamental character and were a strong influence on the choice of food," one old-timer recalled. "A patron yearning for pork chops would discern the legend 'liver and bacon' gloriously emblazoned in gold on a Prussian blue background, while 'pork chops' appeared in a displeasing combination of yellow and red. An

As it is today, New York was a city of extremes in 1905. Diners could spend as much as five dollars for a meal at Delmonico's, or a few pennies on the Bowery.

instant revulsion of feeling, based on aesthetic grounds, would seize upon the customer, that only an instantaneous plate of liver and bacon garnished with fried onion, could assuage."

With a foreigner's fascinated ear, Keller tuned into the new language that was developing at the cheap lunchrooms. The "beef and" lingo of places like Hitchcock's assumed more baroque forms at the Jim Fisk and the Boss Tweed. Fish cakes were "fried sleeve buttons." Oatmeal was "a plate of summertime," and pork and beans were "a band of music with the leader." This lunchroom slang was catnip for newspaper reporters, who pounced on each and every colorful expression, no matter how outlandish. It defies belief that anyone working in a busy kitchen called a Napoleon "fallen greatness." "Soaked bums" (pickled beets) seems possible, and so does "stack of browns" (buckwheat pancakes). But the catalogue of lunchroom argot allegedly included "slaughter in the pan" (beefsteak), "Red Mike wit' a bunch of violets" (corned beef and cabbage), "drop one on the brown" (browned hash and poached egg), "eggs in the dark" (eggs fried both sides), "white wings, with the sunny side up" (eggs fried on one side), "two shipwrecked" (two fried eggs, over easy), and "a sheeny funeral with two on horseback" (roast pork and boiled potatoes).

Real kitchen slang is a kind of shorthand. It allows waiters to transmit information to the cook as quickly as possible, although the phrases that catch on do tend to be clever or racy or have a certain ring to them. Punchy expressions like "draw one, three off" (a cup of coffee with three buttercakes) or "two ham on one" (two ham sandwiches served on the same plate) did the job much more efficiently than the conceptually complicated, polysyllabic expressions beloved of journalists. Most diners were probably treated to the mumbled mishmash that the *Sun* satirized in a sketch called "Gastronomic Condensation."

> YOUNG MAN (*in coffee-and-cake saloon*): Wheat cakes, waiter, brown on top, and coffee with not too much milk in it.
> WAITER (*vociferously*): Wete cakes an' coffy, an' have 'em right.

Outside the food markets, along Newspaper Row, and up and down Wall Street, quick-lunch spots vied with street vendors both mobile and stationary. Food carts were usually nothing more than glorified wheelbarrows, and food stands little more than cobbled-together shacks, but on Wall Street, across from Jay Cooke's bank, brokers bought tarts, cakes, sandwiches, and pies from three deluxe stands, neatly roofed and outfitted with cornices. One stand, which sold French candy and tobacco, featured imitation black-walnut paneling.

The appetite for pie was stupendous. An estimated 22 million pies were consumed in New York in 1895. In bygone days, solitary bakers would toil through the night, baking pies for their small shops or wagons. As demand increased— many an office boy and clerk lunched on two slices of pie and a glass of milk— wholesalers entered the picture, turning out everything from the tiny individual pies known as "buttons," which sold for four cents wholesale, to giant holiday pies that sold for forty-five cents.

The largest pie bakery, just north of Canal Street, baked up to twenty thousand pies a day: apple, peach, custard, rhubarb, plum, lemon, and coconut, as well as cranberry and mincemeat pies for the end-of-year holidays. Its owner, William Thompson, was one of the city's great success stories. At sixteen he threw down his hoe on a Long Island potato farm, walked to an East River ferry, and convinced the ticket taker to accept his last penny for the trip across. "I came over to New York, found work with a baker that night, and have been in the business ever since," he told a reporter, adding that he used to deliver a slice of pie to P. T. Barnum every day at noon.

The downtown trade was brisk. At one busy lunchroom, open day and night, patrons ate their way through 300 pies daily, or 1,800 individual slices. Today, the name of Jay Gould, the financier, is synonymous with the worst excesses of the Gilded Age. For pie lovers, though, he was a hero. When he extended his railroads into North Carolina's huckleberry belt, he added a new flavor to the New York pie menu.

On Newspaper Row, Louis Haims sold sandwiches and coffee at two cents through a small window in the World Building. Haims had started out selling his wares from a cart on Frankfort Street, or "pie alley," where strolling vendors sold cakes and pies from baskets. At noon, hungry newsboys would swarm these "walking lunchrooms," grabbing a penny slice of Washington pie (a chocolate cake with custard filling), gingerbread Bolivars, or a slice of salmon between two crackers. Haims saw an opportunity in the lack of beverages and, fitting out a rolling cart with a kerosene stove, sold hot coffee for two cents and lemonade for a penny, along with a menu of sandwiches, pies, and cakes. Samuel Blumfield, a cafeteria operator in the neighborhood, later claimed that it was Haims who sold the first hot dogs in New York from his cart.

True or not, Haims did a land-office business, and when Joseph Pulitzer put up the World Building in 1890, he bid on a window at the east corner. It turned out to be a prime location. During the noon hour, the line for his sandwiches stretched all the way down the block. Eventually, Haims took over the basement saloon behind him, a bare space with sawdust on the floor, where the customers served themselves and stood up to eat at a wooden shelf along the wall. Similar lunchtime nooks infested the neighborhood.

On the fourteenth floor of the World Building, hungry reporters could eat on credit at the paper's cafeteria during the week and pay up on Saturday morning. One of them was Albert Payson Terhune, who toiled as a *World* reporter from 1894 to 1916 (and would later win fame for dog stories like *Lad of Sunnybank*).

Terhune's dining habits reflected the tastes and aspirations of struggling reporters who earned lunchroom salaries but hankered after finer things. Like many New Yorkers with no kitchen facilities, they ate all their meals out. Terhune started the day with a fifteen-cent breakfast at a creamery or at Childs, a chain lunchroom. Lunch and dinner posed a tougher challenge. Barring a sudden windfall, restaurants like the Café Martin lay well out of reach, so the ethnic table d'hôte filled the gap. Terhune was a regular at Maria del Prato's, and, like the rest of his journalistic tribe, grumbled when the place was discovered by the uptown crowd. He took fifty-cent meals at Dusquesne's or the Black Cat in Greenwich Village. Dinner at Purssell's represented a splurge: $1.25, including wine. With that much money in his pocket, he preferred Jack's, near the midtown theater district, where fifty cents bought a one-pound porterhouse steak with French or German potatoes, rolls with butter, and a saucer of piccalilli on the side. The accepted tip was a dime. Terhune spent his money at Mouquin's (downtown and uptown), the Brevoort, and (when lucky) Martin's. More typical was the twenty-cent dinner at Childs: three "hot and viscid" sinkers, a large cup of coffee, and a pint bowl of beef stew. "I dined thus, one year, for two consecutive months," he recalled ruefully.

Clerks and copyists made their way to Dennett's, a cheap lunchroom whose self-serve system anticipated by a few years the more famous help-yourself policy at the Exchange Buffet, which opened in 1885. Patrons at Dennett's assembled a selection of mostly cold dishes and sat down in a chair specially fitted with one wide arm, which functioned as a tray. A hollowed-out depression in the arm served as a coffee-cup holder.

Alfred W. Dennett, the founder, served plain, wholesome food in plain, wholesome surroundings. His lunchrooms marked a decided step up from the beef-and-beans joints like Dolan's and Hitchcock's. The walls, paneled with white glass, were decorated with rural scenes executed in paint and colored glass, and set off by Bible verses such as "Be ye strong, therefore, and let not your hands be weak, for your work shall be rewarded." At the start of each day, the female staff, dressed in black, gathered for a required religious service. Many grew to loathe the blend of piety and low wages.

The Dennett formula worked like a charm, although there were a few kinks to be ironed out. Initially, Dennett relied on the honor system. Diners told the cashier what they had eaten and were charged accordingly. Word of this policy spread quickly up and down Park Row, with predictable results. In no time, the honor system was dropped, and the restaurant started turning a profit when it switched to a system that became standard for most lunchrooms. Diners, on entering, would pick up a ticket printed with prices (5 cents, 10 cents, 25 cents), and a server would punch the appropriate price when handing over the food. On leaving, the diner would present the punched ticket to a cashier and pay. Astoundingly, the Exchange Buffet survived until the early 1960s relying on the honor system (the *E* and *B* of their logo, it was said, stood for "Eat 'em and Beat 'em"). Any losses due to cheating, the chain reckoned, were offset by time saved and more customers served. The honor system really did inspire honor among some patrons, who lied when their luck was down to the cashier but returned later and made good when their pockets were full.

Dennett was the first to discover that some diners, even newspapermen, actually preferred to eat in a clean restaurant. As the nickels flooded in, he expanded, opening branches in Philadelphia, Chicago, and San Francisco. If he had stuck with the restaurant business, he might have retired rich and happy. Unfortunately, he started dabbling in mining ventures, possibly to support his various religious missions, and the mines absorbed money as fast as his restaurants could make it. He also began showing signs of mental instability. In 1894, Dennett bought the Kentucky farm where Abraham Lincoln was born, with an eye toward creating a Lincoln theme park and hotel. The venture unraveled, and Dennett descended into madness. He died, shortly after being released from a mental asylum in Stockton, California, in 1908, but his central insight about the restaurant business lived on. In time, spic-and-span lunchrooms and dairy restaurants crowded out the old pie sellers and cart vendors. William Childs, a former Dennett manager, would later adopt his boss's squeaky-clean philosophy and build a vast dining empire.

For the cheapest food in town, down-and-out New Yorkers headed to the

A. W. Dennett

140 E. 14th STREET,   140 E. 14th STREET,

BILL OF FARE.

Chicken Soup. 15

Coffee, Tea or Chocolate, per cup 5
Butter Cakes, per plate (*If served separately, 10*) 5
Sandwich, Ham or Corned Beef 5
Baked Beans, Boston or New York Style 10
Pork and Baked Beans 10
Corned Beef or Ham with or without Baked Beans 10
Wheat or Buckwheat Cakes, Pure Maple Syrup 10

For our various houses we melt over 50 tons of pure Vermont
Maple Sugar annually.

Corned Beef Hash. *Browned in the Pan* 15
Fried or Broiled Ham 20
Corned Beef Hash with one fried or poached Egg 20
    "   "   "   "   "   two "   "   "   Eggs 25
    Fish Cakes 15
    "   "   with one Fried or Poached Egg, 20
    "   "   "   two   "   "   "   Eggs, 25
    French Fried Potatoes 5

EGGS AND OMELETTES

Boiled Eggs . . . . (2) . . 15   (3) . . . 20
Fried Eggs . . . . (2) . . . 15   (3) . . . 20
Scrambled Eggs . . . . (2) . . 15   (3) . . 20
Poached Eggs, plain . . . . (2) . . 15   (3) . . 20
    "   "   on Toast . . . . (2) . . . 20
Plain Omelette . . . . (3) . . . 25
Ham Omelette 25
Ham and Eggs 25

DESSERT

Pie, per cut, (All Pies in Season) 5
    Crullers 5
        Prunes 5
            Corn Starch 5
                Cup Custard 5
                    Charlotte Russe 5
                        Chocolate Eclair 5
                            Assorted Cakes 5
                                Ice Cream 10

Special Attention is Called to the Quality of Our Pies.

Alfred W. Dennett was the first New York restaurateur to understand that patrons preferred to eat in a clean environment. His restaurants offered simple fare at modest prices.

Lower East Side, the Five Points, or the Bowery for the nickel meal known as a regular: stew, hash, liver, or porridge with bread and a bowl of coffee. Along the Bowery, tramps ate at the Four and Nine, named after its prices, or the Fiver, a nickel restaurant. For those who could not afford a nickel, around the turn of the century Bernarr Macfadden, a physical-culture fanatic, opened restaurants near City Hall and the Bowery where plain vegetarian dishes—a saucer of beans or cabbage—cost a penny. Evidently, it was possible to turn a profit on the pennies, because a rash of imitators appeared within a few years.

With no government food stamps or social programs of any kind, private charities addressed the widespread problem of hunger among the destitute and the working poor. One of the most innovative programs was promoted by Clementine Lamadrid, the wife of a Colombian import-export merchant, who vowed, when she came down with yellow fever in 1893, that if she recovered she would devote her life to good works. In 1895, she created the St. Andrew's One Cent Coffee Society, which placed mobile coffee stands around Manhattan and Brooklyn selling simple meals for a penny.

The idea was not hers. A similar program in London had already inspired a group of charitable women in Brooklyn to open several coffee stands near the fer-

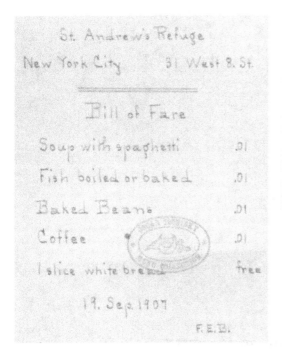

ABOVE: Food stands like the Car Drivers' Coffee-Room on Seventh Avenue and Fiftieth Street, operated by the Woman's Christian Temperance Union, tried to entice workingmen away from the saloon.

LEFT: The down and out could eat their fill for a penny at cafés and coffee stands on the Bowery and the Lower East Side, many of them run by charitable organizations.

ries and the Brooklyn Bridge in December 1886. Over the next three months, they fed 134,000 people. The following winter, three stands were destroyed on election night by overenthusiastic street urchins who used them to make bonfires. Adding insult to injury, the revelers also ate the food supplies within. Nevertheless, the idea of feeding, at nominal cost, "the many discouraged and pitifully poor," and keeping "storm-wrecked souls" from the clutches of the saloon, proved infectious.

In 1893, hoping to offer an alternative to the all-night saloon, the Church Temperance Society, an Episcopalian charity, rolled a lunch wagon into Herald Square. With decorated glass windows and a gaily painted exterior, the Owl looked a little like a circus wagon. Initially, it operated only at night, but hours were extended as the concept took hold. The Herald Square Owl sold 67,600 ten-cent meals in its second year of operation, generating a profit of $1,108, enough to finance a second wagon, the Wayside Inn, which took up the Owl's spot in Herald Square, while the Owl moved to Sixth Avenue, opposite Bryant Park. Eventually, the Society operated eight wagons, strategically located near transportation hubs, so that workers from the cab stands, streetcar stables, or street railways, instead of stepping into the local saloons after their shifts, could enjoy a cheap, alcohol-free meal—"a la cart," as the joke ran.

Under Mrs. Lamadrid's scheme, customers could buy tickets at the One Cent Coffee Society's headquarters at 281 East Broadway and exchange them for plain fare: a half pint of coffee (with milk and sugar) with a slice of bread; beef soup with vegetables and a slice of bread; pork and beans; fish cakes; a sandwich; or, on Fridays, fish chowder. Well-meaning New Yorkers who balked at handing out spare change could buy a pack of a hundred tickets for a dollar and pass them out one at a time to beggars.

The stands themselves were a model of simplicity, nothing more than green-painted pine boxes measuring six feet by twelve feet. From the inside, the manager flipped a counter outward and swung the top section of the front door upward, creating a window through which the food, supplied by a central commissary, was passed. Shoeshine boys and newsboys were the main customers at most stands. At the St. Andrew's stand on the Battery, arriving immigrants stepped up for their first American meal.

The Industrial Christian Alliance, in similar fashion, operated a half dozen People's Restaurants that served meals for five cents. Those with a nickel could simply pay for a meal. The less fortunate could appear at the charity's offices and, if judged deserving, would be issued meal tickets. On the Bowery, the *Christian Herald* operated its own low-price restaurant.

The truly wretched, like Julius Keller, or George Hurstwood in *Sister Carrie*, stood in line at Fleischmann's Vienna Bakery in the dead of night and waited their turn for free bread. This nightly spectacle became one of New York's most haunting images, an emblem of the glittering city's harsh side, and an all-too-vivid reminder of the fate awaiting the weak in capitalism's Darwinian struggle.

Louis Fleischmann, the owner, was no baker. He was an Austrian cavalry officer who twice had his horse shot out from under him at the battle of Sadowa in 1866. Looking for a new career after resigning his commission in 1874, his eyes turned to America, where his brothers had emigrated and made a fortune selling patented compressed yeast. He emigrated, too, and soon hit on the idea of creating a Viennese café for the 1876 Centennial Exposition in Philadelphia.

The Vienna Model Bakery, surrounded by pleasant gardens, scored a direct hit at the fair with its breads, cakes, coffee, and chocolate. The breads and rolls carried off top awards, and when the exposition closed, Fleischmann opened a modified version of the café in Manhattan on Broadway at Tenth Street. It became a favorite afternoon dining spot for visiting German opera stars, and late at night, the aroma of fresh-baked bread attracted hungry New Yorkers down on their luck. At the restaurant one night, Fleischmann began handing out free bread and rolls. The word got around. Each night at 10:00, a line formed, inching forward until 1:00 a.m., when the last bread was handed out. Fleischmann, improving on his original idea, even set up an informal labor exchange to match unemployed men with available jobs.

These private initiatives were highly controversial. The leading thinkers on social policy, as well as many religious groups, denounced the coffee stands and lunch wagons as pernicious: they encouraged the loafers and ne'er-do-wells already in the city, and drew the wrong sort of newcomers from the hinterlands. Cheap lodging houses were criticized for the same reason: they lowered the cost of bare subsistence. The arguments often took on a Dickensian flavor. "We have watched these coffee stands and inquired about them carefully," the *Independent* magazine wrote, "and we are convinced that they are patronized principally by tramps, who thus find an added facility for living without labor, and by newsboys, who thus have more money to gamble by policy-playing"—that is, buying lottery tickets—"and to attend the theater."

Like the soup-kitchen operators and the St. Andrew's Society, Fleischmann was attacked for making no distinction between the deserving and the undeserving poor. Anyone who showed up at the Vienna Bakery was given half a loaf, and if supply exceeded demand, the same man could get in line again and ask for a second half-loaf. Fleischmann was unmoved by criticism. "If a man will stand on a curb for two or three hours in all kinds of weather to get half a loaf of bread or a few rolls, he's hungry," he said. "That's quite enough for me. If I started to find out if each man was worthy, he would probably starve during the investigation."

The merely frugal could eat well in New York, thanks to the cheap ethnic restaurants that became a fixture on city streets. The most dramatic changes in dining came from Italy, as wave upon wave of new immigrants arrived, and a second generation of Italian restaurants inherited the mantle of Moretti's, Riccadonna's, and Morello's near Union Square.

Italy, as we have seen, was a godsend to New York's Bohemians. Exotic cuisine, rock-bottom prices, and the easygoing Italian style suited artists and journalists to a tee. Scarcely a memoir or novel of the period from 1880 to 1910 fails to include a nostalgic scene set in an Italian cellar restaurant in Greenwich Village. The fifty-cent (or even thirty-five-cent) table d'hôte—a stomach-filling multicourse meal with red wine—lived long in the memories of every young man who arrived in New York, pen or brush in hand, and walked the streets in search of a cheap meal and a dash of romance.

The type of crowd could be defined precisely, as James L. Ford did in his 1895 story "Bohemia Invaded." The ideal company at a table d'hôte was as follows: "art, plastic, pictorial and illustrative, 25 percent; letters, poesy, prosody, typewriting and journalism, 25 percent; the stage, lyric, protean and classic, 20 percent; Arctic explorers, tropical travelers and illustrious exiles, 10 percent; ladies, bound by marital or other fragile ties to and usually escorted by atoms of the ingredients already named, 20 percent."

All over the city, ordinary diners followed where the Bohemians led. "Young couples who dwell in furnished rooms and have no cook and servant visit these restaurants constantly," the *Times* wrote in an 1885 article devoted to inexpensive dining. "People who have country cousins 'dine them' there as a 'treat,' and when materfamilias has been given ten minutes' notice by Bridget she often proposes to paterfamilias that the whole brood shall, for a day or two, tone up their stomachs by means of the masterpieces of Signor Bottesini's chef."

The venerable Maria del Prato's on MacDougal Street was the archetypal "red-ink" restaurant, so named for the cheap wine on offer. Sixty cents bought a

Italian immigrants often turned the ground floor of their boarding-houses into inexpensive table d'hôte restaurants, which, like Mori's on Bleecker Street, found favor with the city's Bohemians.

cut-rate feast of soup, spaghetti, and chicken, with zabaglione for dessert. The wines were Chianti, served in straw-covered fiascos, or Lacryma Christi, from the slopes of Mount Vesuvius. A layer of olive oil at the top of the neck kept the wine airtight. Regulars learned to fling it against the wall with a deft snap of the wrist. Guests competed for the honor of mixing the salad, which was then judged for quality by Maria, a benevolent despot who set the dinner hour at 7:00 p.m. and thereafter kept the front door locked against stragglers.

Fame soon attracted a tonier uptown crowd that appalled the original Bohemians. (Some, like Julius Chambers of the *Tribune*, temporarily took their custom to the Pensione di Livorno on Washington Square.) Success drove Maria's uptown to Sixth Avenue and Twelfth Street, where, her patrons warned, she would wither on the vine, cut off from the nourishment of her old neighborhood and deprived of her original fan base. To their amazement and consternation, she prospered as before.

The Italian restaurants of Bohemia numbered in the dozens, and most bore a strong family resemblance. Guffanti's, Roversi's, Mori's, Solari's, Poggi's, Marabeni's—the names roll off the tongue. All of them served virtually identical food. They were located in private houses, with a dining room and small bar on the ground floor and a kitchen in back, where the owner's wife did the cooking. The owner minded the till and sold cigars. In the Village, there would be a back-yard garden with brick walls and potted plants.

It is into such a restaurant, Maroni's, that Basil March, the hero of William Dean Howells's 1890 novel *A Hazard of New Fortunes*, walks one evening with his friend Fulkerson. March, a new arrival from Boston, is an adventurous eater, keen to sample whatever the city has to offer, and in Maroni's, carved out of a private home, he looks forward to an authentic New York experience. He gets it:

There were the corroded brown-stone steps, the mean little front door, and the cramped entry with its narrow stairs by which ladies could go up to a dining-room appointed for them on the second floor; the parlors on the first were set about with tables, where men smoked cigarettes between the courses, and a single waiter ran swiftly to and fro with plates and dishes, and exchanged unintelligible outcries with a cook beyond a slide in the back parlor. He rushed at the newcomers, brushed the soiled tablecloth before them with a towel on his arm, covered its worst stains with a napkin, and brought them, in their order, the vermicelli soup, the fried fish, the cheese-strewn spaghetti, the veal-cutlets, the tepid roast fowl and salad, and the wizened pear and Swiss cheese and coffee, which form the dinner at such places.

One dish is conspicuous by its absence: pizza. It was not until the turn of the century that signs reading PIZZE CAVERE—"hot cakes," in Neapolitan dialect—began appearing in grocery stores and bakeries in Little Italy. Local laborers would drop in for a pie, or a portion thereof, but to the rest of New York the Neapolitan specialty remained a mystery. In 1880, a *Washington Post* writer, reporting on Queen Margherita's visit to Naples, explained that pizza was "a sort of cake beaten flat in a round form, and seasoned with curious condiments." Twenty-five years later, the same paper paid a visit to Spring Street in Little Italy, where Gennaro Lombardi ran a grocery store and made Neapolitan pizzas, which the *Post's* reporter described in loving detail. After spreading a little lard on the dough, the baker sprinkled it with grated cheese, poured tomato sauce on top, and seasoned the pie with oregano. (Already, American adjustments had entered the picture: lard instead of olive oil, grated cheese instead of mozzarella.) Gradually, non-Italian New Yorkers caught on, but it was not until after the Second World War that pizza made the leap from intriguing ethnic specialty to a staple of the New York diet.

The clientele at Maroni's is eclectic: a few journalists and artists, and a sprinkling of regulars, "of all nationalities and religions, apparently," including several "Hebrews" and Cubans. With dinner, Fulkerson orders a small flask of Chianti in a wicker jacket. It reminds March of the containers used to sell cooking oil in country drugstores back in his native Ohio.

Howells, and the dozens of lesser-known writers who fell in love with the city's modest Italian restaurants, described them from the outside, slightly puzzled or amused at Italian ways and Italian cuisine. Maria Sermolino, by contrast, saw things from the inside at her family's restaurant, Gonfarone's, one of the most famous table d'hôte restaurants in the Village.

Gonfarone's building, at Eighth and MacDougal, had been operated as a boardinghouse by Marie Griffou, a Frenchwoman, when the neighborhood was still French. She prospered, bought two buildings on Eleventh Street, and created the Hotel Griffou in the early 1870s, a colorful institution in its own right. Mama Gonfarone, from Turin, took over Griffou's boardinghouse and turned it into a pensione and table d'hôte. Her lucky day came when Anacleto Sermolino turned up. Groaning under the weight of the demijohn of wine he was delivering, he arrived panting and desperate for a drink of water. Mama Gonfarone saw immediately that this was not a man cut out for menial labor. He did have a head for figures, though, and after a brief conversation, she hired him to run the cash register.

Sermolino had more than math ability. He created Gonfarone's famous fifty-cent table d'hôte, lovingly itemized by his daughter. The meal began with antipasto—celery hearts, black olives, salami, sardines, anchovies, sliced tomatoes with basil, imported tuna, pimento—and proceeded to minestrone, spaghetti with meat sauce or tomato sauce, boiled salmon with caper sauce, sweetbreads with a mushroom patty, and broiled spring chicken or roast prime rib. Side dishes were brussels sprouts or spinach, boiled or mashed potatoes, and green salad. For dessert: biscuit tortoni or spumoni, fresh fruit, and assorted cheeses, plus espresso. The price included a pint of California wine. Italian cost a dime extra. On weekends the price rose to sixty cents, but the menu included half a boiled lobster with mayonnaise.

It sounds too good to be true, and perhaps it was. In his 1910 novel *Predestined*, Stephen French Whitman submitted a less than stellar review of the restaurant, thinly disguised as "Benedetto's," where the main character suffers through a meal of "soup redeemed from tastelessness by grated Parmesan, a sliver of fish and four slices of cucumber, spaghetti and a chicken leg, two cubic inches of ice cream, a fragment of Roquefort cheese, and coffee in a small, evidently indestructible cup."

Perhaps it was an off night. Gonfarone's fed legions of hard-up journalists and writers over the years. Originally a tiny place with fifteen tables, sawdust on the floor, and cane-bottomed chairs, it expanded to cafeteria size and on an average weekday served five hundred meals, double that number on weekends. Maria Sermolino, who became a magazine editor after attending the city's public schools, offered a theory to explain the appeal of the place. It offered Americans a "simple, Latin variety of hedonism"—something new in their experience—and Italian hospitality. That combination has spelled success for Italian restaurants all over the world.

As Basil March and his wife settle into their New York life in *A Hazard of New Fortunes*, they evolve into a recognizably modern species, the Manhattan foodie. They begin shopping at an Italian grocery store. They become connoisseurs of the local Italian table d'hôte restaurants. Having mastered Italy, they turn to Spain. Howells does not name any restaurants, but he may have had in mind Pedro's on Centre Street. When not in the mood for Italian or Spanish food, the Marches sit down for a French table d'hôte dinner at fifty cents.

German or Austro-Hungarian food, apparently, is not on the March menu, but if the couple had been so inclined, the budget restaurants of the day included the Café Boulevard, on Second Avenue, and the Café Hungaria, on Union Square, with Fleischmann's Vienna Bakery a somewhat pricier option.

Second Avenue, from Houston Street all the way to Fourteenth Street, presented a German-accented counterpart to Broadway. Curiously, despite the tenements and the red-light houses, it struck more than one observer as the most Parisian of the city's streets, with cafés and theaters lining both sides. It boasted the Café Monopole; Balogh's; the Orpheum Theater (still operating as a theater today); the Café Royale, with tables on the sidewalk; and, most famous of all, the Café Boulevard. The Café Boulevard was the aristocrat of the group. In its previous incarnation, as the Café Manhattan, a modest café with thirty tables, it had put on no airs, but as the greatly expanded Café Boulevard, capable of handling two hundred diners, it catered to the "Vere de Veres of the East Side," as the journalist Benjamin de Casseres put it somewhat snidely, alluding to Tennyson's aristocratic Lady Clara Vere de Vere, "daughter of a hundred earls."

Little Hungary on Houston Street was the neighborhood's big attraction, an atmospheric ethnic restaurant offering slivovitz (Eastern European plum brandy), Gypsy music, a wine cellar, and a menu bearing the motto "You must eat it whether you like it or not." The food at Little Hungary was abundant and filling—beer soup with croutons, goulash, strudel, and a tongue-twisting array of beloved dishes like röte grütze (berry pudding), käse fleckerl (noodles with grated cheese), and Wiener backhändl (breaded fried chicken). The decor was romantic and kitschy, with large paintings of menacing brigands, rural love scenes, and, of course, Lajos Kossuth, Hungary's national hero. "It was the most curious place in New York," de Casseres recalled for the *American Mercury* in "Red-Ink Days," a fond look back at the cheap restaurants he frequented in the 1890s. "Peddlers from the neighborhood would circulate selling shirt studs, ties, socks, and hairpins. In the basement, customers filled their own wine glasses by pushing a button. The wine flowed directly from the cask through a glass tube."

Politically, the neighborhood was a happy hunting ground for Teddy Roosevelt. In 1900, while attending a dinner in his honor given by the Hungarian Republican Club at the Café Boulevard, he promised that if he ever became president he would return to the neighborhood for "a visit of state." And so it came to pass that on Valentine's Day 1905, after being feted at the Waldorf-Astoria the previous night, he descended on Little Hungary for a dinner of chicken paprika, salad with Little Hungary dressing, apple strudel, and Hungarian wines. For readers puzzled by the venue, the *Times* reassuringly noted that Little Hungary was "known to venturesome diners from other parts of the Metropolis as a delightfully Bohemian dining place."

The most venturesome of all found their way to Chinatown, located, as it still is, in the narrow streets between Canal Street and Chatham Square, formerly the notorious Five Points slum. The Chinese presence in New York was limited to a handful of sailors and street peddlers until the 1870s, when the completion of the western railroads led to an eastward migration of laborers. Even with this influx, the city's Chinese population, according to the 1890 census, was scarcely more than two thousand, although that figure seems low. A private survey of local laundries showed that the number was closer to six thousand, and the Chinese themselves put the figure at eight thousand to ten thousand. Most worked in laundries or as candy or cigar peddlers, but some opened restaurants. By 1885, there were six Chinese restaurants in the city, and curious New Yorkers, braving fears of opium dens and white slavery rings, picked up chopsticks for the first time.

In a pattern that continues to this day, the restaurants of Chinatown fed two types of patrons. The Chinese themselves took food seriously. A restaurant meal was an opportunity to feast and splurge. They spared no expense to make a meal a special occasion, and on Sundays the tables in Chinatown would be filled with laundry workers who had saved their pennies for a regal repast. (Hon Heong Lau, at 11 Mott Street, served four thousand diners on a busy Sunday.) A first-class spread, for a table seating up to twelve, cost $50 for forty courses, supplied on two days' notice. Twenty-eight courses cost $40, eighteen courses $25, and eight courses (the cheapest) $8. Americans, by contrast, looked on Chinese cuisine as a steal, since a regular meal cost five cents to twenty-five cents per dish, with each dish serving two or three diners. Black New Yorkers also made the trip to Mott and Pell streets, attracted by low prices and the lack of racial prejudice—to Chinese restaurant owners, white and black Americans seemed equally foreign.

The staple dish was chop suey, a far cry from the vegetarian glop served under that name today. In the nineteenth century, it consisted of chicken livers and gizzards stir-fried over a fire of hay or hickory wood, with mushrooms, bamboo shoots, pig tripe, and bean sprouts. Recipes of the era sometimes mention duck liver, celery, and sliced duck or chicken meat as well. Beyond chop suey, strange marvels awaited. An 1898 guide to Chinatown warned readers to be prepared for shark fins, sturgeon head, eel bladders, and birds' nests. The decor tended to be spartan, with bare wooden tables and chairs, but restaurants like Hong Ping Lo on Mott Street hung lanterns and flower baskets from the ceiling, as well as long scrolls printed in Cantonese, with Chinese maxims: "It is here that heroes met and sages drank; why should we abstain?" or "It is only the superior man who knows what he eats and what he drinks."

The Chinese seduced American taste buds quickly. As early as 1897, a magazine writer could state flatly, "Chinese dinner is the most civilized dinner in the world." Exploratory journalists made a point of dispelling the

What better way to entice the non-Chinese diner than to invoke the city's most famous restaurant?

rumor that rats figured in Chinese cuisine, but one warned that bird's nest soup, "delicious to the Chinese palate, tastes to an American like the steam from a locomotive mixed with the odor of oily-waste smells." Squab with mushrooms, on the other hand, "appeals instantaneously to the American palate"—indeed it "vies with the best dishes of Paris chefs"—and the famous chop suey "is positively addictive." For meat-loving Americans, the Chinese habit of suspending a roast pig from the ceiling and carving off slices as needed only added to the attractions of a strange but beguiling style of cookery that, in response to tourist demand, could sometimes achieve bizarre effects, as with the fad dish called Pineapple Fish: deep-fried cubes of battered pike or shad served with chopped celery, onion, mushrooms, and boiled pineapple. By the turn of the century, Chinese cuisine was firmly entrenched. One restaurateur in Chinatown went so far as to hang out a sign that read "The Chinese Delmonicos." What better way to announce that the Chinese had arrived?

8

The Birth of Times Square

In 1899, a Chicago restaurateur named Charles Rector made a big decision. He would move to New York. His enormous seafood restaurant, Rector's, had earned him a fortune in the city's Loop. Many of his patrons were theater people traveling with road shows from New York, and they convinced him that the big, brash Rector's style would go over big in Manhattan. The timing seemed right, the portents were good, and Rector, a former New York streetcar conductor, knew the city well. Why not roll the dice?

The location Rector had in mind was Long Acre Square, not the obvious choice. Yes, it was situated in the geographical center of Manhattan Island, and it would soon become a teeming crossroads known as Times Square—the name was changed officially after heavy lobbying by *The New York Times*, which relocated there in 1904. But in 1899, Long Acre Square was on the fringes. Located just north of the seedy Tenderloin, an amorphous, wide-open territory west of Fifth Avenue in the Thirties, it had a few hotels, like the St. Cloud (later torn down to make way for the Knickerbocker), and two rooming houses where the grand Hotel Astor would rise in 1904, but its principal function was to serve the horse-and-carriage trade, an important industry at a time when New York's 150,000 horses provided transport and hauled goods.

Up Broadway, at the north end of the square, stood the Brewster carriage factory. At Forty-eighth Street, the Studebaker factory turned out wagons and carriages. William K. Vanderbilt's American Horse Exchange occupied an entire block at Broadway and Fiftieth Street. There were no theaters in the neighborhood, no electric streetlights, and no subway. In December 1895, Oscar Hammerstein, in a daring bid, opened the Olympia, a theater and entertainment complex that, if completed as planned, would have included three theaters, a roof garden, billiard rooms, a bowling alley, a Turkish bath, cafés, and restaurants. Alas, it folded in 1898, just slightly ahead of its time.

The Chicago Rector's, which opened in 1884 at the corner of Clark and Monroe streets, had made a big splash by introducing fresh seafood to midwesterners used to eating oysters from a can. Oysters, clams, and lobsters were shipped express by rail and served in impressive surroundings. Rector's, which could seat three hundred, looked like an oyster cellar for millionaires, and it struck a swaggering, slightly raffish pose that suited brawny Chicago. You had to have money to dine at Rector's, but you did not have to have manners. It put on no airs. At the Columbian Exposition of 1893, Charles Rector won the sole restaurant concession. At his Café Marine, thousands of customers from all over the country got a taste of the Rector style.

Rector settled in at Broadway and Forty-fourth Street, where he hung out his trademark griffin, illuminated at night by green, red, and yellow electric lights. If the bleak surroundings gave him pause, he did not show it. Like the Delmonicos before him, he had looked at the real estate map and saw the city rushing northward to meet him. Good word of mouth from the theatrical community dovetailed neatly with the new generation of theaters that, following the trail blazed by Hammerstein, crept uptown from Madison Square and Union Square.

Rector's took dead aim at the big spenders. In cuisine, it competed with its two main rivals, Delmonico's and Sherry's, which faced each other, like genteel duelists, across Fifth Avenue, two avenues to the east. As for clientele, well, the restaurant suited the neighborhood, which carried a distinct whiff of the Tenderloin, synonymous with vice and police graft for years. Dubbed Satan's Circus by the reformers of the day, the district consisted almost entirely of unsavory saloons, clip joints, gambling houses, and cheap restaurants. Close proximity made Times Square a kind of cousin. Rector's son, George, who trained as a chef in Paris and took over his father's restaurant in its glory days, put it neatly. If Delmonico's and Sherry's catered to the Four Hundred, he wrote, Rector's looked to please both the Four Hundred and O. Henry's Four Million—or those members

RECTOR'S

SPECIALTIES

Onion Soup
Mignon saute, Boivin
Lamb Chops, Draz
Boneless Squab en cocotte

Crab Meat, Mornay
Lobster, Thermidor
Foie-gras, Perigora
Sweetbread, Prince of Wales

Supper

Oysters and Clams

Rockaways 30   Blue Points 25   Lynnhavens 35   Cotuits 30
Little Neck Clams 25   Clams, Estragon 30   Oyster Cocktail 30 in green pepper 35

Broths

Hot or Cold—Beef 30   Chicken 35   Clam 25
Chicken Okra 35   Tomato 30   Celery 30

Imported Fresh Astrachan Caviar 1 75   Hors d'Oeuvres a la Russe 80
Leaves, Rector 60   Tomatoes or Cucumbers, Figaro 75   Canape of Anchovies 60

Shell Fish, etc.

Crab Meat, Mornay or Armenonville 80
Crab Meat, Rector 1 50   Dewey 1 75
Crab Meat, Draz 1 00
Crab, Royale or Schley 80
Stuffed or Deviled Crab 80
Canape, Lorenzo or Martha 80
Fried Oyster Crabs 1 00

Lobster, Remoulade 1 00
Lobster, Newburg or in cream 1 40
Lobster Bonnefoy or Americaine 1 50
Soft Clams, Ancienne 75
Minced Clams on Toast 75
Salmon, Sauce Verte 80
Bismarck Herring 60
Scallops, Tartare 75

Hot

Foie-Gras, Perigord 1 30
Mignon of Beef, Rossini 1 40
Braised Sweetbreads, Financiere 1 50
Breast of Poularde a la King 1 15
Emince of Capon, Creole 1 25
Rail-birds Saute, Hongroise 1 10
Chicken Livers Brochettes, Perigueux,
or Saute with Mushrooms 1 00
Lamb Kidneys, Deviled 70
Sautes, Echalottes 90

Terrapin 2 50
Fresh Mushrooms, Broiled 1 00
Under Glass 1 25
Deviled Veal Kidney 75
Lamb Chops, Signora 1 10
Boneless Squab, Nerac 1 35
Eggs, Tivoli or Opera 60
Chicken Hash, Red Peppers 1 25
Virginia Ham, Cumberland 1 00
Breast of Mallard, Moran 1 90

Cold

Half Partridge 1 25   Quail 1 10
Squab in jelly, Georges Sand 1 25   Royal Squab 1 25   Aspic of foie-gras, Bellevue 1 25
Breast of Chicken, Eventail 1 25   Pickled Lamb Tongues, Potato Salad 80
Beef a la Mode 80   Roast Beef 70   Boned Capon 1 00   Half Chicken 1 15
Pate de Foie gras 1 50   Ham: Jersey 70   Virginia 80   Westphalian 90
Assorted Meat 1 00   Beef Tongue 70   Lamb 70
Egg: A la Russe or Estragon 60

Game

Canvas Back Duck 4 00   Red Head Duck 3 00   Woodcock 2 00
Plover 90   Mallard Duck 2 50   Ruddy Duck 2 00   Teal Duck 1 25   Quail 1 10
Snipe 90   Rail Birds 1 00   Grouse 3 00   Partridge 2 50

Poultry

Broiled Spring Chicken 1 75   Squab Chicken 1 25   Broiled Squab 90   Royal 1 25
Half Turkey 1 75   Half Capon 1 50   Half Duckling 1 25

Salads

Lobster 1 00   Chicken 1 00   Shrimp 90   Crab 1 15   Gauloise 80   Tomato 80   Rector 80
Alligator Pear 75   Lettuce or Romaine 50   Grape Fruit 75   Chicory or Escarole 50

Dessert

Savarin Chantilly 30   Tom Pouce 30   Maraschino Jelly 30
Fruit Salad, Marasquin 60   Assorted Cakes or Eclairs 30

Ices

Vanilla, Chocolate, Strawberry or Peach 30   Mixed 35   Lemon or Orange Water Ice 30
Neapolitan or Biscuit glace 40   Nesselrode or Cafe Parfait 40
Rector's Fancy 50   Jai-alai 50   Souvenir 60   Sherbets 40

Fruits   Cheese
Coffee : French 15   Turkish 20   Special 25

11-26/04   *Dishes not on Bill of Fare will be served on request.*

Rector's, on Broadway at Forty-fourth Street, was the first of the boisterous restaurants known as lobster palaces. Broadway stars, big spenders, and the chorus girls they loved filled Rector's every night and kept the champagne corks popping until dawn.

of it with a fat roll of bills in their back pocket. "It was," he wrote, "the spot where Broadway and Fifth Avenue met."

The diners at Rector's, both men and women, wore a lot more jewelry than their Fifth Avenue counterparts. They were loud, they tipped heavily, and they came for a big show. When the theaters let out, actresses would make their way to Rector's and, timing their entrances to the second, proceed to their tables accompanied by a wave of applause and admiring looks. Chorus girls, usually on the arm of an older male patron, followed in their wake, primed for a lobster dinner with champagne, and, if the evening went according to plan, a diamond bracelet purchased from one of the nearby shops that stayed open until the wee hours for precisely such impulse purchases. The routine inspired a well-known vaudeville joke. "I found a very valuable pearl in an oyster," a man tells a woman. "That's nothing," she answers. "I got a diamond from a lobster over at Rector's last night." One of the hit songs from the 1913 Ziegfeld Follies was "If a Table at Rector's Could Talk," and the implication was clear: at naughty, naughty Rector's, a table would have plenty to talk about. "What a lot of things you'd hear, in your conversation ear," it ran. "You'd know the chumps behind the checks of half the girls in town." The restaurant was, as George Rector put it, "the supreme court of triviality," "the cathedral of froth."

New Yorkers did not quite know what to make of Rector's at first. For one thing, it had a revolving door, a piece of technology so advanced that most of the people who ventured into the restaurant on opening day got no further. They took a spin or two and then went on their way. They soon got the hang of it. And they gave a new name to the kind of restaurant that Rector's pioneered. It was called a lobster palace, and its patrons were known, collectively, as lobster-palace society.

Like moths to the flame, the members of this new society made their way to Times Square in the high-living years after the turn of the century, when the neighborhood sprouted theaters and luxury hotels by the dozen, and transformed itself into a vast entertainment factory. In the 1899–1900 season, Manhattan had twenty-two theaters, only one of them in Long Acre Square. A decade later there were thirty-four theaters in Manhattan. Most were new, and most of them were in Times Square. Tin Pan Alley moved north from Twenty-eighth Street to serve the new theater district. Pretty girls, the stock-in-trade of the musical revues, settled down in rooming houses along the side streets. Journalists, photographers, singers, dancers, actors, and "sports"—the gamblers later accorded mythic status by Damon Runyon—made Times Square and its restaurants their headquarters.

The whirring machinery of Broadway generated bright, alluring images of Manhattan's nightlife. Stock productions sent these images on the road to the farthest reaches of an America that had no radio, film, or television to feed the collective imagination. Even after the advent of film, Broadway still provided color and sound, two dimensions still lacking on the silver screen. Seduced by the Broadway melody, tourists swarmed the area, eager to get a taste of the city's high life as it was lived at places like Rector's or the dozens of other flashy restaurants of lobsterdom.

Even at the time, there was disagreement about who belonged to lobster-palace society. The more jaded journalists dismissed the whole tribe as nothing more than out-of-towners desperate to spend money and whoop it up. Convinced that they were seated amidst real New Yorkers and the cream of the theatrical world, the rubes stared agog at their fellow visitors from Rapid City and Kalamazoo, and endured the close company of big-spending loudmouths like "Mr. Feldman," a composite character created by Julian Street, an urbane Chicago journalist, bon vivant, and shrewd analyst of lobster-palace society.

"The 'Mr. Feldman' kind of man," he wrote, "distributes largesse with a plump and lavish hand. He has cocktails named for him, drinks vintage champagnes, sends for the head waiter, calls him 'Max' or 'Louis,' dresses him down, and gives him a twenty-dollar bill. 'Mr. Feldman' does not pay spot cash in the Lobster Palaces. He merely tips the waiter with a bill and signs his name across the check." The check-signing is key: "It signifies not only that 'Mr. Feldman' runs an account and settles by the month, but that he always has aisle seats, down in front, for the first night of each new 'girl show,' and can pay on credit in the gambling 'clubs.'"

A small industry existed to service the Feldmans and relieve them of their cash, as did legions of chorus girls with expensive tastes. "If a confrere asked a chorus girl where to eat, she would probably say Mink's or Riggs'," Street wrote, "but if a man asked her, she'd say Churchill's, the Marlborough Rathskeller, Burns', Jack's, the Cadillac, Reisenweber's, Pabst's, the Hofbrauhaus, or even the Metropole." Mink's was a small, midpriced cafeteria chain with decidedly nonlobster fare, although "frizzled" beef with cream on toast shaded upward to fancier dishes like Delaware County goose with applesauce and potatoes. Goose notwithstanding, Mink's was the kind of place where the menu warned: "Customers Not Allowed to Help Themselves."

Ironically, all the lobster palaces took pride in their cuisine, even though most of the customers, it seems, were concentrating on everything but their plates. "Nobody of distinction goes to a lobster palace to eat," Street observed. "One goes there in a gaudy mood, or when every other place is filled or closed, or with the kind of man who thinks gaiety means overdressed women, bediamonded men, waiters rushing with champagne as if they had the fire-buckets, and a caterwauling orchestra that repeats the George M. Cohan music every 15 minutes. At midnight the din and the excitement induce a sedate man to ask himself whether he is not in a riot."

James Churchill, a retired police captain who operated one of the biggest, splashiest restaurants in Times Square, tried his best to puncture the myth. The restaurants of the neighborhood, he insisted, were real dining destinations, patronized by ordinary New Yorkers with ordinary motives. "The word Broadway in fiction stands for only one thing—dissipation," he complained. "The phrase 'Broadway life' in fiction

The chic beauty with the knowing eyes epitomizes the sophisticated fun on offer at Churchill's, a vast restaurant on Broadway and Forty-ninth Street. The owner, James Churchill, was a former police captain.

stands for dissipation interpreted by dazzling show girls (they are always 'dazzling'), millionaire youth of bloodless countenance (they are always millionaires and their faces are always pale), lobsters, champagne, cigarettes, taxicabs, shaded electroliers, seductive music, and the other members of the overworked cast of the fiction stock company of Broadway." The truth, he maintained, was quite otherwise. "Broadway restaurants are intended and used as places where persons may get something to eat—also to drink, if they wish," he wrote. "For every broiled lobster, a Broadway restaurant sells six Porterhouse steaks, and for one order of pate de foie gras it will sell 20 orders of poached eggs."

His protests fell on deaf ears. The fantasy of swells and dames strutting on parade, scattering hundred-dollar bills like confetti, had an irresistible appeal—and just enough truth to it to keep the dream alive. George Rector, in his highly colored volume of reminiscences, *The Girl from Rector's* (the title is taken from a play of the period), depicts a rogues' gallery of financiers, theater owners, and gamblers. His patrons included the likes of Berry Wall, known as "king of the dudes," a fop and bon vivant who owned more than five thousand ties and once, according to legend, changed clothes forty times in a single day at Saratoga. The great Ziegfeld would often waltz into Rector's with Anna Held on his arm, beauty incarnate. Diamond Jim Brady, the bejeweled sultan of New York gourmets, often dined with Lillian Russell, the two of them taxing the kitchen's powers to the utmost.

In an age of free spenders, Brady topped the bill, and his exploits with knife and fork made him legendary—a Paul Bunyan of the dinner table. He was a large man, and he ate accordingly, but one grows skeptical at endless accounts of Brady consuming three dozen oysters before tucking into a half dozen canvasback ducks. Was it really true that he offered the doctors at Johns Hopkins $100,000 in gold if they could outfit him with a second stomach? Or that he had diamond bridgework? At Rector's, it was said, a typical Brady meal might begin with a full carafe of orange juice (Brady did not drink), three dozen oysters, a dozen hard-shell crabs, six or seven large lobsters, and, perhaps, a lone steak. Seafood was his love. That and dessert. "When he pointed at a platter of French pastries he didn't mean any special piece of pastry," George Rector recalled. "He meant the platter." A two-pound box of chocolates served as petit-fours. Oscar Tschirky, the maître d' at the Waldorf-Astoria, recalled a much more restrained Brady: a dozen oysters to start, a small filet mignon with a vegetable for the main course, and apple pie or a slice of watermelon for dessert. "If he was a great eater, he must have done his stuffing elsewhere," Tschirky recalled. But the myth was bigger than the man. It symbolized the outsized appetites of a gaudy, grasping, exuberant America, where income went untaxed and a robust mass media panted after images of the rich at play.

Rector's took its food seriously. George, having spent his formative years training in the kitchens of Paris, made a point of keeping up-to-date on culinary trends, and his gourmandizing clients eagerly scanned his menu for the latest thing. He snapped up an Alsatian chef named Emil Hederer to run the kitchen—a little hastily, as it turned out. Hederer came with sterling credentials, having served as a private chef for the Astors, Lorillards, and Belmonts before taking over the kitchen at the Bellevue Hotel in Philadelphia. When the Bellevue's manager, George Boldt, opened the Waldorf Hotel, Hederer came with him. Unfortunately, Hederer did not leave his temperament behind. An autocrat with a short fuse, he wore out his welcome and quickly departed the Waldorf "for a much-needed rest," as Boldt informed the press, adding, sympathetically, "The electric lights with which the kitchen is illuminated have somewhat affected his eyesight." Boldt then created a stir by hiring Xavier Kuesmeier, also of the Bellevue, at the astronomical salary of $10,000, a figure he made sure the press reported. The irascible Hederer, once installed at Rector's, immediately alienated both the staff and the owner. His reign was short-lived, and Charles Perraudin, his saucier, was elevated to the top spot. Perraudin, a native of the Touraine, had served with distinction at Delmonico's, whence the Rectors filched him, and he immediately put a deluxe stamp on the menu.

The food was as rich as the diners. Crabmeat Mornay, straight from France's renowned Café de Paris, was a signature. Crab canapé, Rector style, was another favorite: crabmeat and mushrooms in a thick cream sauce served on toast points spread with anchovy butter and covered with a crisp topping of grated Parmesan cheese and bread crumbs. The disgraced Hederer did leave a small legacy in the form of beef tenderloins, sautéed in butter and smothered in stewed oysters, blanched bone marrow, and Bordelaise sauce. The restaurant scored a coup by obtaining the recipe for sauce Marguery, urged on by Jim Brady, who had sampled filet de sole Marguery at the Café Marguery in Paris and began agitating for the dish to be put on the menu. George was sent to France with strict instructions not to return without the sauce. He triumphed. Diamond Jim took a tentative sip of the sauce and announced, "It's so good I could eat it on a Turkish towel."

Charles Rector turned out to be as sharp as the great Lorenzo Delmonico.

Within a few years, the transplanted Chicagoan could look around and see, where stables once stood, a glittering district of fine hotels like the Knickerbocker, built in 1902, and the Astor, built in 1904, as well as dozens of theaters and a coterie of lobster palaces ready to feed the pleasure-seekers. Oscar Hammerstein, unfazed by the failure of his first theater, rebounded with the Republic (now the New Victory Theater) on Forty-second Street. In short order, he took over a former stable and in 1899 erected the mammoth Victoria next door. Atop both, he created the Paradise Roof Garden.

Less than five years after Rector's hung out its griffin, diners faced a surfeit of choices in Times Square, and not just the high rollers. A favorite with college students was Jack's, a surf-and-turf palace presided over by Jack Dunston, an Irishman from Cork. On the fringes of the Tenderloin, it attracted a high-low crowd of politicians, prizefighters, theater stars, newspaper reporters, and, on fall weekends, swarms of Ivy League students in a rambunctious post-football mood that Jack's indulged. "Jack's tolerated anything short of riot and violence," one regular wrote. "The waiters marveled at nothing."

Jack, born in 1853, had found work as a waterboy at the Fifth Avenue Hotel after emigrating to New York. Like many Irishmen, he moved upward in the business, opening Dunston and Keneally's Manhattan Oyster Bay at Seventy-fourth and Columbus Avenue, on the Upper West Side, where the equally ambitious Tim Healy signed on as a waiter. The oyster restaurant failed, but Dunston found work as headwaiter at Sam Burns's chophouse on Sixth Avenue. Burns was short-tempered, and the relationship was stormy. After a furious row, Dunston quit, swearing that he would come back and buy the place. He did, but it took him twenty-four years to do it, by which time Burns was dead.

In 1891, meanwhile, Jack joined forces with Keneally and Healy to open a restaurant at Sixth Avenue and Forty-third Street, underneath the rattling elevated train. If the location seemed less than ideal at the time, that would change. After 1905, customers could look across Sixth Avenue to the twinkling red and green lights of the Hippodrome, an enormous venue for spectacular entertainments. Over the years, spectators in its 5,300 seats saw circuses, boxing matches, dancing elephants, and, in the Hippodrome's giant water tank, performances by Annette Kellerman, "the million-dollar mermaid." In 1918, Harry Houdini made a ten-thousand-pound elephant disappear onstage.

Officially, the new restaurant was the Manhattan Oyster and Chop House, but no one called it anything other than Jack's, and by that name it passed into legend. The specialties of the house were steaks and chops, steamed clams, broiled lobsters, lobster fat on toast, Welsh rarebit, broiled pig's feet with deviled sauce, and, of course, oysters. Many a late-night rout ended up at Jack's for a wee-hours breakfast of scrambled eggs and Irish bacon. The cooking was impeccable, and the fastidious Jack, a veteran of the oyster trade, had access to the best seafood in town.

The decor was odd. Antlers, animal skins, and stuffed wildlife (including a pug dog that once belonged to Jack) struck an uncompromisingly masculine note, softened a bit by the artwork on the walls. Edward Simmons, a vaguely Impressionist painter known for his murals at the Columbian Exposition in Chicago, and his private work for Rockefellers and Vanderbilts, executed a series of murals illustrating the fairy tales of the Brothers Grimm and Hans Christian Andersen. Two-fisted men, tearing into thick steaks, could look up and enjoy a boldly colored retelling of Little Red Riding Hood.

Jack's never closed. It was the only midtown restaurant with an all-night license, and Dunston, after opening the place, threw away the key. The show began after midnight. "Then the red-hot sports come piling in: rowdy actors, college boys with their tender insides all stirred up by rum, roistering young millionaires throwing dad's hard-earned money to the bow-wows, visiting celebrities, prizefighters, wrestlers, outright bunco steerers, and every variety of sure-thing man and grafter that the city knows," one regular recalled. The famous waiters at Jack's, chosen for size as well as serving ability, dealt firmly with the college boys, most of whom came for the express purpose of trying their luck against the renowned "flying wedge." When matters looked to be getting out of hand, Jack's waiters would wrap cloth napkins around their right hands, close formation, and advance on the troublemakers. Many a Yale or Harvard man, in his autumn years, would fondly recall the night he was thrown out of Jack's and onto the Sixth Avenue streetcar tracks.

Jack himself cut a fine figure. Tall and distinguished-looking, with bushy eyebrows and a large drooping mustache, the Earl of Dunston, as he was jokingly called, "looked far more like an English earl than most English earls even look." Each evening, he changed into formal attire and placed a white carnation in his lapel. Throughout the night, and into the dawn hours, he passed among the tables, radiating charm and good fellowship, "calm amid tumult, and with a keen eye for the cashier's cage." There was a lot of cash to count. Jack annexed the building next door, retaining its azure interior, and created the Blue Room, which opened with great fanfare: it hosted the wedding breakfast of Frank Jay Gould, son of the financier Jay Gould, and Helen Kelly. The Blue Room, a favored haunt of the college rowdies, was soon joined by the White Room, created from a store on the other side of the original Jack's for "the more reserved element." Eventually, a fourth room was added.

When a table at Jack's could not be had, Shanley's beckoned. This was yet another Irish success story. It began in the 1890s, when Thomas J. Shanley, an immigrant from Mohr-Drummond, decided that a career as a lace buyer was not for him. Observing the throngs of shoppers outside the department store where he worked at Sixth Avenue and Twenty-third Street, he decided to open a restaurant. It thrived, and Shanley sent for his six brothers, still in Ireland. Together they set up shop a few blocks uptown, at Broadway and Thirtieth Street, where their restaurant found favor with the actors and patrons of Daly's Theater

Shanley's, in the heart of Times Square, was run by seven Irish brothers who knew how to create a freewheeling, back-slapping atmosphere. It helped that the food was first-rate.

and Weber and Fields Music Hall. As the theater district drifted northward, the Shanleys followed, opening a new branch on Broadway between Forty-second and Forty-third streets. Advertising himself as "the provider of the inner man," Thomas Shanley offered the same sort of slap-on-the-back ambience as Jack's, in an enormous dining room where patrons feasted on chops, lobsters, and broiled kidneys. The third dining room in this vein was Churchill's vast dining hall at Broadway and Forty-ninth Street.

A time-lapse photograph of Times Square between 1900 and 1920 would reveal startling changes. By 1905, with the arrival of the automobile and the subway, the stables and carriage dealers had either disappeared or reinvented themselves as automobile showrooms. Studebaker, with barely a hiccup, bade farewell to the horse and carriage and began selling autos out of its former carriage works on Broadway. Grand hotels like the Knickerbocker and the Astor sprang up, pushing out the cheap rooming houses.

By 1910, the Vanderbilt horse exchange was gone, and even the auto dealers were being pushed northward by new hotels and theaters. "Within six years this section of the city, from 42nd Street northward to about 50th Street, has undergone a transformation almost unparalleled in any other part of the city," the *Times* reported on New Year's Day 1911. Seven theaters now lined Forty-second Street between Broadway and Eighth Avenue, and another dozen could be found in the surrounding blocks. The Astor quickly doubled its size in a 1908 renovation.

In that year came the most attention-grabbing restaurant of all: Murray's Roman Gardens. For all their sumptuousness, the great restaurants of the period inclined toward formulaic interiors, with heavy Victorian furnishings, and tables arranged stiffly in serried ranks. Opulence was suggested by massive wood pillars and coffered ceilings. Murray's, the city's first theme restaurant, shattered the mold. Located on Forty-second Street across from the New Amsterdam Theater, it was designed by Henry Milo Erkins, an architectural decorator, working for the mysterious John Murray, an Irish restaurateur with a crazy dream.

The dream, as realized by Erkins, was straight out of Bulwer Lytton's *Last Days of Pompeii*. Murray's combined, in spectacular fashion, an assortment of ancient styles and subjects. The exterior, modeled on the residence of the Cardinal de Rohan in Paris, greeted visitors with a classical panel, *Horses of the Sun*. Inside, as one architectural writer delicately put it, the eye could feast on "an

When Murray's Roman Gardens opened in Times Square in 1908, New York got its first theme restaurant. The décor mingled Pompeiian, Egyptian, and Japanese elements, with a full-scale Cleopatra barge.

interesting example of the application of Egyptian, Assyrian, Roman, and Pompeiian motifs to modern decoration."

And how. The reception room, in black and gold, led to the Roman gardens themselves, a large atrium whose centerpiece was a thirty-foot terraced fountain, encrusted in glass mosaic tiles and surmounted by a columned temple. Alongside, as though it had just docked, was an enormous Roman barge fit for Cleopatra. Electric stars twinkled in the ceiling, while underneath the tables electric lights radiated a romantic pink glow. Extensive use of mirrors compounded the sense of dislocation—gaping patrons often walked straight into their own reflections.

Erkins beheld his handiwork and pronounced it good. He offered to the New York diner not just a restaurant but the portal to another world. "At his very doors, in the center of the city's theater and hotel section," proclaimed a promotional album published by Erkins's company, "within earshot of the shriek of the noisy iron horse, he can be transported as though on the famous carpet of Mahomet, back to ancient Rome's most ornate homes, of the palaces, villas and pleasure resorts of her wealthiest and most cultured citizens." As an exercise in pure fantasy, Murray's has never been equaled.

Fantasy in decor is easier to realize than fantasy in food. The dining room at Murray's offered a more or less conventional French-influenced menu, but special dishes included deviled dolphin à la Dido (a porcelain dolphin stuffed with flambéed crabmeat, oysters, and lobster), planked lamb à la Ramses II, and a "Cleopatra's needle" salad. The pièce de résistance was an appalling dish dubbed roses à la Potiphar—American Beauty roses stuffed with cheese covered in mayonnaise dressing. The special dinners in the private Dragon Room, with its Oriental theme, beggared the imagination. The centerpiece of the dining room table was a scale model of Peking's imperial gardens, with a miniature railroad that delivered dishes to each place setting. Murray's did more than bring a heightened sense of theater to Times Square; it encouraged mass hallucination.

In the 1890s, New York was on display. Through popular song, vaudeville, the Broadway theater, and newspapers, it exported seductive images of itself to the rest of America. At the same time, New Yorkers preened for one another. The concentration of wealth in the families of the Four Hundred and their parvenu imitators created a new kind of social theater, for which the restaurants of the city provided a convenient stage, with the props already in place. The old Knickerbockers would have turned in their graves at the sight of New York's finest families posing for pictures and not merely permitting but often encouraging the press to chronicle their every movement. The rotogravure sections of the Sunday papers catered to an insatiable appetite for images of the rich at play. Their clothes, their yachts, their polo ponies, and their lavish dinners were all on full view for the millions to gape at, cluck over, and dream about.

The change did not take place overnight. Old-fashioned New York wealth dined behind closed doors. Its celebrations were private. Passersby could walk past the great mansions along Fifth Avenue and stare, but about the lives within they could only fantasize. The Waldorf Hotel changed the rules. The hotel, which opened in 1893 and after 1897 operated jointly with its Siamese twin, the Astoria, was custom-made for a shameless age. Peacock Alley, the corridor running between the Empire Room and the Palm Room, was an early version of the celebrity red carpet, a passageway of amber-colored marble, running three thousand feet along the Thirty-fourth Street side of the hotel, where the wealthy, in full plumage, put themselves on parade. Hordes of curious tourists and ordinary New Yorkers crowded the corridor, peering into the Palm Room from time to time in the hope of spotting a tycoon or social celebrity. Crowd control became a problem. The ingenious Oscar Tschirky hit on the idea of setting up a velvet rope to keep the gawkers at bay. His invention lives on, an unambiguous dividing line separating the ins from the outs. With the ascendancy of the Waldorf, Julian Street wrote, New York "passed the period described by Mrs. Wharton as the Age of Innocence, and began the age of roaring confidence and power."

One evening in particular put its stamp on the Waldorf and crystallized the values of the new era: the Bradley Martin ball. Martin was an impeccably bred lawyer with no desire for public attention. His wife, Cornelia, nourished grand social ambitions, however, and after inheriting a fortune from her merchant father in 1881, she and her husband had the money to translate her dreams into reality. Cash in hand, the Martins began cutting a swath in New York society. They gave lavish dinner parties. With quiet determination, Cornelia worked her way onto the reception committee of Mrs. Astor's Assemblies, a new series of exclusive balls, and mapped out a taxing social schedule designed to put her at the top of the pecking order. In early summer, the Martins made the rounds in Paris and London, where their daughter's marriage to the Earl of Craven gave them instant entrée. In August, during the grouse season, they spent their time at a 65,000-acre estate overlooking Loch Ness.

The Martins might have blended in with their plutocratic peers and slipped unobserved into eternity had Cornelia not decided to give one last ball. It would, she believed, serve as the capstone to her social career and, with a little luck, surpass the renowned Vanderbilt ball of 1883. She settled on a location—the Waldorf—and a date, February 10, 1897. The theme was to be Versailles under Louis XV. The rest is history—a history the Martins would never live down.

Preparations for the event soon took on a life of their own. A breathless press corps reported lavish sums being spent—$250,000 or more (a gross exaggeration). Fabulous jewels were polished for the evening, and guests, in full costume, sat for studio portraits that later ran in magazines like *Harper's Bazaar*.

At a time when crusading journalists like Jacob Riis were plumbing New York's lower depths, and when immigrants toiled endless hours in the city's sweatshops, the Bradley Martin ball struck a nerve. It dramatized, in one let-them-eat-cake moment, the gulf between Ward McAllister's top tier and the heaving masses far below. Rumor spread that anarchists planned to bomb the ball. Theodore Roosevelt, then New York's commissioner of police, positioned a phalanx of his best men to protect the partygoers. Inside, detectives outfitted in period costumes maintained discreet surveillance.

Decorations in the small ballroom, described as "exquisite, unique, and profuse," included a "riot" of roses hurled with abandon at the tapestry draperies and allowed to rest where they fell, creating a deliciously careless effect. Hallways were transformed into woodland bowers, and the grand ballroom, with its fifteen-foot recessed mirrors, was garlanded with mauve orchids. "Sylvan little dells" intended as "flirtation nooks" exhaled the tempting fragrance of clematis (specially imported from the southern states), while a Hungarian band played selections from Wagner and Liszt.

The affair glittered. The seven hundred guests, descending on dealers in antique jewelry, had cleaned out the available supply of period shoe buckles, lorgnettes, snuffboxes, seals, and fobs. Heirloom jewelry came out of private vaults. Cornelia, in Elizabethan costume, wore $50,000 worth of rare stones. As her outfit suggests, the Louis XV theme was interpreted liberally. Guests roamed freely through English, French, and German history from 1500 to 1900 in putting together their costumes. Multiple Marie Antoinettes drifted among Romeos, Juliets, French musketeers, Restoration fops, a lone toreador, a court jester, and—centuries adrift—a Cleopatra.

It was quite a show. "Otho Cushing, a young artist of Boston, was, in fact, thought to have gone rather too far in his impersonation of an Italian falconer of the 15th century," one journalist reported. "His costume consisted of full tights and a short jacket, with a little cap and long locks, while a large stuffed falcon was perched on his left wrist. The costume left little to the imagination as far as the figure was concerned, and, although historically correct in every detail, was so decidedly pronounced that he caused a sensation wherever he moved." Outside the Waldorf, the common folk pressed forward to get a good look as the guests left at dawn and to offer running commentary that occasionally required police intervention.

The Bradley Martin ball quickly became a moral text. From the pulpit, ministers denounced the pomp and pride of the rich. Social reformers proposed alternative uses for the money spent. Newspapers printed thundering editorials. The Martins, stung, fled to Europe and never returned. Years later, Frederick Townsend Martin, Bradley's brother, scratched his head over the affair. "I cannot conceive why this entertainment should have been condemned," he wrote in his memoirs. His bewilderment speaks volumes about McAllister's Four Hundred.

Oblivious, the rich continued to make a spectacle of themselves. In 1903, the Chicago tycoon and horseman C.K.G. Billings took over as head of the New York Equestrian Club. Each incoming president was expected to give a party that outdid his predecessor's, and Billings, the out-of-towner, took the assignment to heart. Initially, a dinner was planned at his new stables in Washington Heights, but Billings, in a ruse, announced a quiet evening at Sherry's instead. Meanwhile, he arranged for several dozen of his most tractable horses to be led over to the restaurant, where, their hooves muffled in cloth, they were transported by elevator to one of the restaurant's private dining rooms.

Billings's guests gathered in a small banquet room, where, a stuffed horse making up the centerpiece, they enjoyed oysters and caviar. Unsuspecting, they were then led to a larger dining room, where the evening's equestrian theme unfolded in full splendor. The room had been transformed into an English country estate, with imitation grass on the floor and burbling brooks flowing through lush meadows. Vine-covered cottages struck a picturesque note.

Waiters, dressed for a fox hunt, invited the guests to hop on their horses, and it was on horseback that the assembled company supped, eating from tray-tables attached to the saddle and sipping, through long straws, champagne from bottles

The infamous dinner on horseback at Sherry's in 1903, where members of the Equestrian Club of New York dined from trays attached to saddles and sipped champagne through long straws. It immediately became a symbol of the excesses of the idle rich.

tucked into saddlebags. A series of variety acts followed, headlined by the English actor-singer Richie Ling and his twelve chorus girls. The horses placidly munched oats.

The dinner on horseback, as photographed by Byron and Associates, has become an emblem of heedless wealth and raw social power in the New York of the early twentieth century. The event did not pass unnoticed. The newspapers had a field day, although one unlucky journalist missed a scoop when his editor simply refused to believe what he was hearing over the telephone. "You're lying to me," he said, and hung up on his enterprising reporter. The scandal sheet *Town Topics* feasted on the Billings dinner for weeks. "Perhaps the only way to surpass Mr. C.K.G. Billings's freak dinner on horseback is to have a dinner on horseflesh, à la Paris during the last siege," it wrote sneeringly. And how on earth, it asked, had Billings failed to serve the only appropriate drink for the occasion—a horse's neck cocktail?

When they were not living it up, the rich went slumming. One of their most piquant pleasures was the beefsteak dinner. A thrilling descent into savagery, the classic beefsteak required guests to sit on the end of a sawed-off barrel and eat sliced beef, pressed between slabs of bread. No knives, forks, or plates were offered, although guests did receive a thick towel to wipe off the meat juices. Usually, an upturned crate served as a table. The origins of the ritual are obscure, but it was well under way by the 1890s, when celebrated "beefsteaks" were given for Robert A. Van Wyck, soon after he was elected mayor, and for assorted Tammany bosses.

Each restaurant specializing in beefsteaks had its own rituals. At Pontin's chophouse on Franklin Street, perhaps the most celebrated of the beefsteak houses, the beef was hung for several weeks, then roasted over hickory coals and served on thick slices of bread, with a mug of ale and a few stalks of celery. Chic restaurants farther uptown, like Reisenweber's on Columbus Circle, began creating "beefsteak garrets," while Healy's (Sixty-sixth Street and Columbus Avenue) opened a beefsteak dungeon. At the Morgue, on West Fifty-eighth Street, the meeting place of the Beefsteak Club, the meat was grilled on sheet-iron stoves, while members sat on soapboxes arranged in a row around three sides of the room. The meat was seasoned with salt, then coated with pepper until the salt was no longer visible. After being broiled over a hickory fire, the steaks were dipped in a pan of melted butter and then cut into slices to be arranged on a slice of bread. As at Pontin's, stalks of celery were passed around, along with tankards of ale. When the beef ran out, lamb chops were circulated.

When Sir Thomas Lipton, the tea magnate, visited the city in 1906, he was ushered into Reisenweber's garret for a genuine New York beefsteak. It had a nautical theme, since Sir Thomas was competing in the America's Cup. Seated on a lager beer cask cut in half, and dining from an empty champagne case, he watched as waiters dressed in sailor suits descended from the ceiling on a rope. A black minstrel sang a comic song, the Irish peer ate his fill, and a good time was had by all. On another occasion, the garret was the scene of a barnyard dinner, with bales of hay on the floor and vegetables hanging from the rafters. Reisenweber's long-suffering waiters, this time dressed in overalls, wigs, and whiskers, served dinner on rusty tin trays. Each guest received a souvenir beef bone on the way out.

The beefsteak eventually became democratized. Saloons got in on the act. Political clubs and social organizations began holding beefsteak fund-raisers, selling tickets that gave each guest the right to eat and drink until he could no longer move. It was emphatically a "he." Joseph Mitchell, anatomizing the beef-steak in *The New Yorker* in 1939, argued that the dinners lost their essential character when they ceased to be all-male celebrations. Women began attending, and that spelled the end of the meat-fest. "They forced the addition of such things as Manhattan cocktails, fruit cups, and fancy salads to the traditional menu of slices of ripened steaks, double lamb chops, kidneys, and beer by the pitcher," Mitchell wrote. "They insisted on dance orchestras instead of brassy German bands. The life of the party at a beefsteak used to be the man who let out the most ecstatic grunts, drank the most beer, ate the most steak, and got the most grease on his ears, but women do not esteem a glutton, and at a contemporary beefsteak it is unusual for a man to do away with more than six pounds of meat and thirty glasses of beer."

As the big spenders swarmed Times Square, Bohemia began moving uptown. Mouquin's, as noted, opened a second restaurant in the Knickerbocker Cottage on Sixth Avenue near Twenty-eighth Street, an old tavern that had once played host to some of the city's strangest meals. In the 1860s, the Cottage was a regular gathering place for large numbers of Freemasons, some of whom branched off to create the Ancient Arabic Order of the Nobles of the Mystic Shrine. They were, in fact, the first Shriners. But they were not the only club to hold court at the Knickerbocker. Captain William Fowler, a builder and Civil War veteran, used the place as headquarters for the Thirteen Club, an organization devoted to a number with special significance for him. Fowler's business had erected thirteen buildings in the city. He had fought in thirteen battles during the war, resigned his commission on August 13, 1863, and on September 13 of the same year bought the Knickerbocker Cottage, where, surely not by coincidence, he became the thirteenth of the original thirteen Shriners. The Thirteen Club, founded in 1880, held banquets on the thirteenth of the month. Its members passed under ladders to take their seats, ignored the overturned salt-cellars on the table, and consumed thirteen courses with thirteen wines. It was an era of funny clubs. The Knickerbocker Cottage also played host to the dinners held by the Five-Pounder Club, so called because members were weighed before the meal and not allowed to leave before they had gained five pounds.

The uptown Mouquin's became the most celebrated Bohemian haunt since Maria del Prato's. It was a particular favorite of the Eight, the circle of American painters that included John Sloan, Robert Henri, Edward Glackens, and George Luks. For artists who had sampled the pleasures of Paris, Mouquin's offered a reminder of the real thing, right in New York. "One might well imagine himself, at certain hours, transported to the Quartier Latin," *Good Housekeeping* wrote in 1909. "There is music, there are Frenchmen, with pointed shoes and luxuriant beards, playing checkers, sipping their Quinquina Raspail or Dubonnet, and listening to French music played by French musicians. When the theater crowd pours in, everyone is gay and sings and rises with uncovered head when the Marseillaise is played."

The Eight also patronized the Café Francis, on Thirty-fifth Street near Wallack's Theater, where Francis Savoureau, a former Mouquin's chef, ran the kitchen, and the owner, a real estate lawyer named James Moore, hung their work on the walls. Glackens returned the favor by putting Moore front and center in one of his most famous paintings, *At Mouquin's*. Moore, a friend to artists and an even greater friend to the attractive women who clustered around them, sits at a table, lifting an aperitif glass. Next to him, with a slightly bored expression on her face, is Jeanne Louise Mouquin, the wife of Henri Jr., and an important figure in the Mouquin kitchen. Glackens's associate Luks also painted Moore at his home base. In the Renoiresque *Café Francis*, a dissipated-looking Moore is depicted taking a feather boa from the shoulders of a blowsy Gibson Girl in a plumed hat.

Farther up the street was Joel's, run by a celebrated eccentric and self-styled philosopher named Joel Rinaldo. Everything about the place was quirky. The wainscoted dining room upstairs, plastered with theater bills, suggested a rustic inn. A wan aesthete, plucking a harp, provided background music. At the downstairs bar, customers imbibed Joel's special Blue Moons, which, one devotee recalled, "would knock you as stiff as Menjou's evening shirts." Although surrounded by political radicals and artistic riffraff, Rinaldo, a Portuguese Jew with an aristocratic manner, sported a gold pince-nez and unfailingly dressed in formal attire, with a fresh flower in his lapel. The city's Bohemians, embracing him as one of their own, deigned to leave their worthless checks in his hands after dining on chili con carne (the house specialty) and corn on the cob. They even regarded his anti-Darwinist treatise, *The Polygeneric Theory of Life*, with utmost seriousness. No one was ever thrown out of Joel's, where the flying wedge was unknown. Instead, Joel, with a look of disappointment on his face, would tap an overly stimulated customer on the shoulder and quietly escort him downstairs. This was considered a great honor.

One New Yorker strolled the boulevards of the town oblivious of Rinaldo's,

Rector's, and Jack's. He was Cortlandt Van Bibber, the fictional creation of Richard Harding Davis, star reporter for the *Evening Sun*. Van Bibber, who featured in a series of popular stories published in the paper, was an American Bertie Wooster, a good-looking, genial chap with a taste for good living and plenty of free time on his hands. His dining habits were a matter of record. He took breakfast every day at Delmonico's, ordering coffee, rolls, and a parsley omelet. In fact, he took all his meals at Delmonico's. In one tale, after losing a big bet at the racetrack, Van Bibber decides to economize. No more Delmonico's. The new policy collapses on the first day. Heading out in the morning in search of budget fare, Van Bibber suddenly realizes he does not know any other restaurant.

In "Van Bibber's Man-Servant," the most famous of Davis's Van Bibber stories, our hero sends Walters, his servant, to Delmonico's with instructions to take a seat and hold the table until Van Bibber and his party of three show up for dinner. Phase one proceeds smoothly. Walters, entrusted with the ordering, decides on littleneck clams with Chablis, followed by pea soup with caviar on toast and oyster crabs with Rhine wine—a Johannesberg Kabinett. To follow: an appetizer of calf's brains and rice opens the second chapter of the dinner, followed by a "roast bird" with cold asparagus and French dressing. Camembert and Turkish coffee finish things off. Suddenly, a messenger arrives with a note, informing Walters that Van Bibber has been called out of town and the dinner party is canceled. Walters, after a violent inner struggle, instructs the waiter to serve the dinner, for one, and eats the meal himself.

The story is instructive. The ornate banquet menus of the period, with their dozens of courses, leave a false impression of how people actually ate. Walters orders the kind of dinner that any New Yorker of means might have eaten, a meal not too different from the one ordered in the 1893 Brander Matthews story "A Thanksgiving Dinner." Again, the restaurant is Delmonico's, specifically the men's café. The narrator and an old friend begin with an order of Blue Points on the half shell, green turtle soup, and filet of sole Mornay. "The sole is flounder, I suppose," the narrator says, "but à la Mornay a man could eat a Hebrew manuscript." Each man orders a canvasback—"real canvasback, not red-head or mallard"—served with samp, or hominy porridge ("of course") and celery mayonnaise. Like Walters, they follow the meal with cheese (cheddar) and coffee.

The canvasback reference is topical. For at least a decade, the consumption of canvasback ducks and diamondback terrapin at fine restaurants had proceeded at a ruinous rate. Merciless hunting in the Chesapeake Bay had brought these two species to the brink of extinction, and many a restaurateur, promising canvasback on the menu, delivered no such thing to the table. George Rector recalled that many kitchens kept a few canvasback heads at the ready to adorn a platter occupied by lesser breeds. When the plate went back to the kitchen, the heads were set aside for the next order. At most banquets, with diamondback terrapin priced at sixty dollars the dozen (they once sold for a dollar apiece), chefs would create a soup using a few diamondbacks mingled with "sliders" from the South or less savory farm-raised terrapin from Maryland.

How expensive was a first-class meal? In 1897, the *Times* conducted an interesting experiment. It decided to see if a party of six could be fed for $20 (about $300 in modern money) at Delmonico's or the Waldorf-Astoria, with a dollar tip included, but not wine. The trick was doable. A Waldorf dinner could start with Blue Point oysters, followed by celery stalks, radishes, and salted almonds—appetizers that seem odd for an expensive restaurant but were a matter of course during the Belle Epoque. Julienne soup and fried whitebait led to main courses of lamb (60 cents per double portion) and quail (75 cents), with potatoes and carrots on the side. A lettuce-and-tomato salad concluded the savory portion of the dinner. Dessert was Nesselrode pudding with assorted fruits, Roquefort cheese, and coffee.

Taller buildings and hot summers led to another dining innovation: the roof garden. Since the early days of the tavern, New Yorkers had flocked to any open space that promised relief from the summer heat. They found it in the pleasure gardens of John Contoit, Joseph Delacroix, and William Niblo, who provided cool green spaces, along with ices, cold drinks, and frivolous entertainment. For theaters, the summer heat posed a seemingly insoluble problem. Before the days of air-conditioning or electric fans, no audience could sit through an indoor performance in July or August, so the theaters simply shut down for the season. This practice continued until the 1880s, when Rudolph Aronson, a conductor and impresario, decided to bring the European-style summer concert garden to New York. Initially, the economics of New York real estate frustrated his plans. There was simply no space in Manhattan to create the kind of garden he envisioned. Then he looked upward. Why not a garden in the sky? In 1882, Aronson unveiled a prototype at his new Casino Theater on Broadway at Thirty-ninth Street. It was nothing much at first, just a few tables and chairs, some potted palms and hanging lanterns, and a small orchestra. Later a stage was added, and on warm nights New Yorkers flocked "to have an ice and see young women in purple tights and the Spanish dances."

The Casino set a trend. Madison Square Garden and Koster and Bial applied more money and imagination to the concept. Madison Square Garden, in particular, caught the public's fancy with its lineup of vaudeville acts.

The New Amsterdam Theater added a roof garden, too. Hotels like the Astor and the Waldorf-Astoria followed suit, as well as restaurants like the Hoffman House. Even Delmonico's and Sherry's got in on the act. Diners could eat their main meal downstairs and go up to the roof for dessert and coffee, surrounded by a post-theater crowd eating a midnight dinner. Of course, even rooftops can get hot in the summer. One trick of the trade was to heat the elevator so that sweltering guests, stepping out onto the roof, felt the blessed relief of cooler air. At the Paradise Roof atop the Republic Theater on Forty-second Street, the ever-inventive Oscar Hammerstein arranged for refrigerated tanks in the basement to pump a constant stream of water over a glass canopy. It seems doubtful that this primitive form of air-conditioning actually lowered the rooftop temperature, but it might have felt that way.

The stagecraft could be ingenious. Hammerstein created a mock country village, with a windmill, a ruined castle, bridges, boats, and stone houses to complement an open-air farm where swains and milkmaids tended live animals. Fitted with colored electric lights, his spinning windmill threw vibrant colors into the night sky, a fantastic touch that inspired other rooftop designers, who quickly realized that it would take more than a few potted shrubs and floral displays to catch the imagination of the public.

The Astor met the challenge head-on. Its 1908 renovation created a series of promenades, fountains, and incandescent archways in a formal garden with grottos and palm trees. Spread out over thousands of square feet, it was magic. As night deepened, its illuminated walkways and gardens took on an air of enchantment. Strolling visitors could amble for hours, taking in a view that encompassed the entire city and beyond—to the dark, looming heights of Weehawken across the Hudson. From the Bella Vista balcony, they could look down on the sparkling lights of Broadway. "The beautiful gowns of the women seem part of the wonderful flowers which abound on all sides, and the three orchestras which are distributed over the surface lend the soothing charm of well selected music to the fairylike scene," *Town and Country* rhapsodized. "It seems impossible that these long lines of pergolas, clustered with growing vines and hanging baskets, these

Hot New York summers forced hotel and theater owners to put entertainment and dining on the roofs. At the Waldorf-Astoria (*top*) and the American Theater (*bottom*), diners could enjoy a light meal, orchestral music, and vaudeville acts.

fountains, lighted as softly and brilliantly as the lamps of the fairies themselves, and placed alluringly in flowering nooks, are a part of a vast hotel in the heart of a vaster city."

The typical rooftop menu was a scaled-down version of the lobster-palace card. On top of the New Amsterdam Theater, where Ziegfeld began staging his Midnight Frolics in 1915, diners fed lightly on oysters, lobster Thermidor or Newburg, broiled lamb kidneys, or sliced cold meats, with ladyfingers or sponge cake and ice cream for dessert—substantial enough fare by present-day standards, but *cuisine minceur* compared with the feasting going on at Jack's or Murray's.

On occasion, though, rooftop dining could be fairly elaborate. One of the principal attractions of the new Astor roof garden was the Belvedere Restaurant. Named for the Belvedere at the Petit Trianon at Versailles, it occupied the rear of the roof under vine-covered trellises that allowed cooling breezes to waft over the tables. A double row of lightbulbs set in green metal leaves swayed "like soft, yet strangely brilliant yellow roses against the mass of emerald." The Belvedere's central feature was a nine-ton block of ice, measuring eighteen feet by six feet, produced by the hotel's gargantuan ice machine. Cold dishes were arranged in a vast buffet: lobster in aspic, paupiettes of bass, Russian borshchok (a vegetable soup), and ices in every color. Hovering over the table was a green-and-white straw fruit basket in the shape of the Astor blimp.

Around 1905, the rooftop gardens seemed to be drawing bigger crowds than ever, and sharp-eyed reporters figured out why: the automobile. Businessmen renting summer cottages by the seashore could now stay in town for a rooftop dinner and drive out later to join the family. The wealthy could drive into the city from their country estates, take in a show and dinner, and make it back to Gatsby-land in time for bed.

As rooftops gained in popularity, shrewd hotel and restaurant managers expanded the entertainment menu. Background music gave way to a full evening of lightweight variety or vaudeville acts. Sleight-of-hand artists shared the stage with comic singers, recitationists, and impersonators. The more ambitious theaters put on leg shows and musical revues on the order of *Mam'zelle Champagne*. At Hammerstein's Paradise Roof, the lineup one evening in 1902 included a cornet quartet, a Russian cat and dog circus, Sparrow the Crazy Juggler, an acrobatic team called the Madcaps, and Patricia, "the electrical billiard ball manipulator." This combination of food and entertainment remained a permanent fixture of the city's nightlife. The jugglers would disappear, replaced by so-phisticated floor shows and torch singers, but the idea that diners needed more than a plate of food to keep them happy spread throughout the restaurant industry and would later find expression in nightclubs like the Stork Club and El Morocco.

Times Square proved a bonanza for the small army of attendants who lived off the cash scattered by free-spending diners, especially at the coat-check and restroom concessions. Busboys dreamed of becoming coat-check attendants, who dreamed of becoming waiters, who dreamed of buying houses and cars with the tips from their best customers. At Rector's, the waiters earned $25 a month in salary but averaged between $600 and $900 a month in tips. Tales abounded of sharp-eared waiters who parlayed stock-market tips into sizeable fortunes. The *Times* reported, in astonishment, that the captain at Sherry's owned an apartment building on West End Avenue assessed at $110,000, and expressed double astonishment that one hat-check girl, after marrying a policeman, presented him with a bankroll of $75,000 after the wedding ceremony.

The saga of Jacob Michaud, the coatroom king, served as an inspiration for all downtrodden restaurant workers. As a hall boy at Delmonico's, he worked hard and saved his tips. When Sherry's moved to Fifth Avenue, he offered to check coats and hats for a one-year rent of $3,000. (A similar proposal to Delmonico's was turned down flat.) The deal turned out to be profitable, and Michaud wangled a ten-year lease with Rector's when it opened, at an annual rent of $6,000. In short order, he signed deals with Murray's, Pabst's, and the Café de l'Opéra, putting him well on his way to becoming a very wealthy man.

Eventually, the public chafed at the outstretched palm of New York's waiters and the outrages of the "hat-check pirates." Some engaged in hand-to-hand combat, refusing to surrender their hats. Others refused to pay the going rate, which seemed to increase monthly. A dime, once considered a respectable tip, became the mark of a piker. One indignant patron at Murray's Roman Gardens ("it's a hanging garden, where they hang you for all you're worth," he fumed) handed a hat-check boy a dollar and asked for change, intending to leave a dime tip. The boy returned two fifty-cent pieces and said, "We don't have no smaller change here than half a dollar."

Unbeknownst to the public, such boys, paid a flat salary of three to four dollars a week, were under strict orders from the boss to coax as many coins as possible from the public. As entrepreneurs bid up the yearly rents for hat-check concessions, they put ever-greater pressure on their underlings to make good. A hat-check boy who did not turn over at least five dollars a day was considered worthless. Tactics became coercive, as guests with modest straw hats were ordered to hand over the headwear and told, "It's the rule of the house." The hat-check workers wore pocketless trousers, so that tips could not be concealed, and a captain was employed to watch their every move, but dull indeed was the hat-check pirate who failed to accumulate a small pile and then strike out on his own.

Tipping, of course, had been a sore point for decades, even when the word did not yet exist, and one spoke of "feeing" the waiter. Old-timers liked to recall the days when service was rendered with a smile, and tips, although graciously received, were not expected. "I can remember when we were mighty glad to get a dime and would dash around very lively for a guest if we knew it was in prospect," a former waiter at the Astor House recalled in 1884. "Now we consider a quarter a fair tip for a lunch or dinner service. If we don't get it, and a guest comes a second time, we get partly even by keeping him waiting for his order as long as we dare, and giving him a poor service generally."

Touchiness about tipping reflected a general unease about the social relationship between server and served. In a democracy, the waiter occupied an anomalous position. He functioned as a manservant, but as an American citizen he enjoyed equal rights with the Vanderbilts and the Astors, and as a New Yorker he felt a deep antagonism toward anyone who walked in the door. Relations could be smoothed over with the right coin, but the mercenary nature of the waiter-diner exchange was fairly naked. The tip system, one critic complained as far back as the 1870s, was "utterly opposed to the spirit of the New World and modern civilization." Yet, as the century wore on, sheepish customers all over New York were reaching into their pockets to reward the waiter, the bartender, and the coat-check boy, not to mention the frantic team of shoe polishers, clothing brushers, and towel jockeys who lurked in the restrooms of the city's finer restaurants and hotels. Soon after the swanky Café de l'Opéra opened in Times Square, the Ziegfeld Follies of 1910 presented "Café de L'Obster," a comic sketch in which two diners are expertly fleeced by a long line of supplicants that begins with the headwaiter and ends with the "cane boy" and the "glove boy." Everyone dreaded the cold stare of a menial offended by an insufficient tip, or—the reproof churlish—a too-small coin returned with a look of withering scorn.

Underlying the arguments for and against tipping, and the itchy palm of the waiter, lay an incontrovertible fact: waiting tables was now a profession. It embraced a significant segment of the laboring classes, and most of them, far from piling up fortunes in real estate or playing the stock market, barely earned enough to keep body and soul together. Most were men. Even at lunchrooms, women waited on tables only during the day, and their role caused no end of consternation among moral guardians. Where underpaid, unsupervised young women attended gentlemen—some of them well-to-do—trouble loomed.

As lunchrooms gained a foothold in the city, the waitress population swelled. The work was hard and the conditions onerous. In 1907, Maud Younger, an enterprising reporter, went undercover and found work at a lunchroom that, although unnamed, was clearly a Dennett's. The salary was $4 for a week of five-hour shifts, $6 for a week of eight-and-a-half-hour shifts—adjusting for inflation, $85 or $140 a week today. Waitresses had to pay their own laundry expenses. Tips were rare. Besides paying to have their uniforms cleaned, the employees were subject to fines imposed by the head waitress, who was herself fined if she failed to meet her quota. "You're fined if you break anything; you're fined if the ice melts on the butter so that water runs on the table; you're fined if the spoon ain't in the sugar bowl," a seasoned waitress explained. "There's mighty few girls that gets full wages here. The firm sometimes makes a dollar a week off a girl." The list did not stop there at this particular restaurant. Waitresses on the morning shift were expected to turn up at 7:30 for prayers in a small upstairs chapel. There were fines for missing prayers, for showing up late, or for not paying attention while the manager read aloud from the prayer book.

A good-looking waitress with an outgoing personality and a good station assignment—up front, where the men sat—could clear up to $2 a day in tips. These were the rare exceptions that gave the rest false hope. Not surprisingly, betting on the horse races was epidemic in the trade.

A Childs lunchroom was the goal. Although the Childs system ran like clockwork, discipline was much less strict, and the wages were better. Waitresses earned $5 for a week of five-hour shifts, $7.70 for eight hours, and $10 for twelve hours. The tone was more professional (no diner slang allowed) and the waitresses thoroughly trained. Consequently, restaurant managers all over town constantly sought the chain's waitresses for their own businesses.

Work at Childs was still work. At about the same time that Maud Younger was toiling at Dennett's, a Childs waitress gave her account of the job to a journalist. Waitresses had to buy three shirtwaists for as much as 99 cents apiece.

Laundry bills ate into their salaries (45 cents for three shirtwaists, 30 cents for three aprons, 24 cents for three sashes). As at Dennett's, the fine system flourished, and head waitresses often used it to settle scores. Breakage was the most common fine. A waitress who lost a check, or whose customer skipped out on the bill, paid for the meal herself. Employees were given fourteen minutes to eat breakfast, and thirty minutes for lunch.

In 1916, the Consumers' League of New York City found that a quarter of the waitresses in the city were under twenty-one and two-thirds were under thirty. Nearly 90 percent earned $9 a week, exclusive of tips, or a dollar less than the minimum needed to subsist and set aside savings. The magazine *Survey*, examining the waitress problem in the same year, found that unremitting toil resulted in "sore feet and a devilish mean disposition." Interviews with 1,107 waitresses revealed that about a third of them worked seven days a week. Nearly 60 percent worked more than 54 hours a week, and 20 percent worked twelve-hour days. Two-thirds were foreign born.

Male waiters had their own problems, even at the fancier restaurants. The top tier of the profession did quite well. But ordinary waiters, even at the big hotel restaurants, toiled long hours for little pay, which could be whittled away by fines for small infractions. As early as 1891, restaurant waiters formed a national union, the Waiters' Alliance, while hotel waiters belonged to the Hotel and Restaurant Employees' Alliance. The fledgling unions tested their muscle with a series of strikes in the early 1890s, but with little success. In April 1893, workers at the tony Holland House walked out just before dinner service, citing a long list of grievances. These included long hours, low wages (83 cents a day), food so bad that most employees took their meals outside the hotel, and a new requirement taking hold at hotels across the city: no facial hair. Newspaper reports took an amused tone. Striking waiters? Imagine!

The strike made good copy. After a ball at Madison Square Garden, hungry patrons poured into Delmonico's, only to find that most of the staff had disappeared. In desperation, some of New York's richest citizens began carving roasts and making their own sandwiches. Charles Delmonico—nephew of the unfortunate Charles found frozen to death in 1884—took the same tough line as other restaurant owners and hotel-keepers. "A walking delegate of the waiters came to me and told me he wanted me to give my men an increase of 17 cents a day," he told a reporter. "I do not propose that outsiders should come in here and dictate to me in my own house, and I told the walking delegate so, and after some time the men went out on strike." Putting his finger on the principal weakness of the waiters' union, Delmonico pointed out that for every man who left, another could be found. "Very many of our waiters came from Alsace and Lorraine, and are pretty good linguists, a necessary qualification in a restaurant like this, which is patronized by people of many nationalities," he said. "There are many other Alsatians in the city who are not waiters, and if the men do not return to work, we shall take others whom we can easily break in."

At the Hotel Logerot, south of Madison Square, the owner, Richard de Logerot, the Marquis de Croisic, took his turn waiting tables, racing back and forth between the kitchen and dining room. Having reached an agreement with his waiters to increase their pay to thirty dollars a month, and putting the mustache issue on hold, he was crestfallen when confronted with a new set of demands. "We want $35 and whiskers, or we go on strike," he was told. At that point, the Marquis threw up his hands. "If I give you $35 now, tomorrow you will make one more demand for $40, and so on until you ask for the hotel itself," he told them. "I do not want to have anything more to do with you."

A month later, the union ordered a strike at nine cafés on the East Side. At issue were wages and hours. The waiters, who earned $5 to $7 a week (or $120 to $170 in today's money), asked for $8 a week and a working day of twelve hours instead of seventeen and a half hours. At some cafés, a compromise was worked out. Others began hiring women, considered more manageable.

The big labor push produced little in the way of results. Waiters at the Waldorf-Astoria still worked fourteen-and-a-half-hour days, seven days a week (7:20 to 10:30 a.m., 11:30 a.m. to 2:30 p.m., 4:45 p.m. to 1:00 a.m.) for $8, a salary that obviously needed substantial tips to equal a living wage. Oscar, who must have forgotten his early days of struggle, presided over a nefarious cost-cutting policy. To staff the banquets in the hotel's private dining rooms, he pulled waiters from their regular stations, where tips were good, and put them to work in rooms where there was no tipping.

Grievances like these led to a series of bitter strikes in 1912 and 1913, as the newly formed International Hotel Workers Union staged a show of strength. All over town, organizers walked into dining rooms just as the lunch or dinner service was about to begin, and blew three blasts on a whistle. As if by magic, waiters, cooks, and busboys vanished. (At the downtown Mouquin's, one organizer hurled a brick through the front window, narrowly missing a diner.) Nearly all the big hotels were hit, and dozens of restaurants as well, as workers left Sherry's,

Shanley's, Churchill's, the Waldorf-Astoria, the Plaza, and the Astor. When more than two hundred waiters unexpectedly walked out of the Knickerbocker on May 27, 1912, dropping their napkins and trays at 7:15 p.m., their confreres across the way at Louis Martin's crowded at the windows to cheer them on. A few days later, they walked out, too.

Violence was in the air. The Plaza Hotel imported black waiters from the South. A crowd of strikers, their ranks swelled by walkouts from Delmonico's and the Savoy Hotel, turned toward the Hotel Netherland, where they tried to enter and drag out nonstriking waiters. A melee ensued, with strikers punching policemen and the police firing back. The waiters' demands were, by modern standards, extremely modest: a salary of $10 for a six-day, sixty-hour week ($7 for busboys), with overtime pay of 50 cents an hour (25 cents for busboys). Many restaurateurs and hotel owners worked out a compromise on wages and hours, but refused to recognize the union. "I'll close my place first," George Rector said. The stalemate persisted.

Storm clouds gathered over Times Square. Labor unrest, looming war in Europe, and the growing agitation of temperance advocates threatened a carefully constructed way of life devoted to pleasure. Oscar Hammerstein's vision of a wide-open entertainment district among the old carriage factories and horse dealers had come to fruition, and much faster than anyone might have supposed. Just as quickly, it would all fall apart. But not just yet.

9
The Party That Never Stopped

From his perch on Broadway and Forty-fourth Street, Charles Rector must have watched with amazed satisfaction as shabby, murky Long Acre Square evolved, virtually overnight, into a great outdoor experiment in modern urban living. Nearly all the revolutionary forces that transformed Victorian America and propelled it into the Jazz Age could be found, on brilliant display, in the new Times Square: outdoor advertising, automobiles, the popular song, the musical, the chorus line, and, as the decade wore on, dancing and smoking.

Physically, the neighborhood was almost unrecognizable. The speed and scale of real estate development was breathtaking, as old buildings fell and new ones rose in their place, most of them temples of amusement in an American society nominally dedicated to hard work, sobriety, and moral probity. Times Square, in nothing flat, had arisen as the anti-America, a raucous, lurid, twenty-four-hour spectacle that mesmerized the rest of the country.

Rector's, the pioneer, had put its stamp on the area, and the little three-story restaurant with the illuminated griffin was bursting at the seams. Charles, never one to think small, decided to raze the place and erect a fourteen-story hotel, designed by the Chicago architect Daniel Burnham. At the new restaurant, on the ground floor, diners who looked up from their plates stared at a $14,000 gilt ceiling.

The hotel would soon prove to be his undoing. Success had already driven a wedge between father and son. George, learning nothing from the behavior of his big-shot customers, had fallen hard for a chorus girl in one of Anna Held's revues and planned to marry her. This is one episode he neglects to mention in his chatty memoirs. Charles Rector strongly disapproved, and a bitter break ensued. George left in 1909 and bought the Café Madrid from James Churchill, who went on to open his namesake restaurant. The venue was not a success. Chastened, George returned to his father's business, but the relationship and the business were on shaky ground.

Rector's had created a monster. Its risqué reputation, broadcast across the land, took dramatic form in 1909 with *The Girl from Rector's*, a frisky farce that proudly advertised itself in the newspapers with a tagline from one of its reviews: "a spicy salad with very little dressing." The restaurant was quickly becoming overexposed, in every sense.

By the time the hotel went up, no middle-class husband heading to New York for a business trip would dare tell his wife that he intended to hang his hat at Rector's. In any case, during the year that it took to build the hotel, lobster palaces like Murray's siphoned off many of its best customers. George M. Cohan, taking pity, decided to make a public show of support. "George, I don't like to see this," he told the younger Rector. "Rector's has always been a great little place, and you're a great little guy, and I always liked you both. I'm going to show you that I'm a great little guy. I'm going to live in your hotel and so are my friends. I'm going to eat in your restaurant again and so are my pals." Cohan already had an apartment in the Hotel Knickerbocker, but he took out a year's lease on a five-room suite at Rector's. It wasn't enough. Within two years of opening, Rector's was in the hands of the receivers, who immediately changed the name of their newly acquired property. Rector's, the name that epitomized Times Square in the lobster-palace era, disappeared in the blink of an eye.

No one really cared. There was too much distraction. John Murray, expansion-minded after opening his Roman Gardens, almost immediately announced plans to transform the Hotel Saranac at Forty-second Street and Seventh Avenue into a restaurant that would seat five thousand diners, making it the largest in the world, and, despite its crazily antique decor, the most modern. New York was about to get its first waiterless dining room. Henry Erkins, the architect, explained to stunned reporters that the main dining room would rely on a device of his own invention, a mechanized table where guests ordered by writing on an "automatic pad" that relayed their commands instantly to the kitchen. A dumbwaiter within the table would carry the food up from the kitchen. The dining room staff would be limited to captains and busboys. Erkins, as it happened, was not alone in pursuing his dream of automation. In 1913, John F. Daschner, founder of the Elite Head Waiters Association of America, patented a similar device: diners checked off their selections on a menu that later reappeared, with the food, as the bill.

The dominant decorative scheme, Erkins announced, would be Assyrian. "There will be so many surprises that New York will be astounded, and many of my most cherished notions will not be divulged, lest imitators steal our thunder," he said. A competitor, hearing of the plans, and the size of the restaurant, predicted failure. "New Yorkers only want to go to places where they can't get a table," he said.

The Café de l'Opéra, one of the great streaking comets in the Broadway night, opened in December 1909. Eight stories tall, it represented an investment of $4 million, much of it devoted to realizing Erkins's Oriental opium dream. Diners entering the black-marble Temple of Music on the

An opium dream of a restaurant, the Assyrian-themed Café de l'Opéra represented an investment of $4 million.

ground floor reached the balconies overhead by ascending a staircase more than twenty feet wide, outfitted from top to bottom with crouching bronze Assyrian lions. The themed rooms included Assyrian palaces and the Japanese Temple of Nikko. (The waiterless system, for whatever reason, never materialized.) Unfortunately, the management insisted on evening dress for all patrons. Broadway rebelled against this stuffy dress code. Also unfortunate was the distance between the kitchen and the tables, so great that the food tended to arrive cold.

Within a year, the Café de l'Opéra was in deep distress. Insanely, Murray and Erkins announced plans for yet another mega-restaurant, along with two new theaters, on the site of the old Brewster carriage factory. This one would be equipped with ten kitchens and seat six thousand diners. Plans called for an ice-skating rink on the roof, topped with a sixty-foot-tall glass dome.

Murray and Erkins quickly went bust. Louis Martin, of the Café Martin, was brought into the Café de l'Opéra to carry out a rescue operation. He renamed the restaurant the Café de Paris, hung his own name outside in flashing letters, and dropped the formal-dress policy, but it was too late for Manhattan's most luxurious restaurant. In 1913, Martin submitted his resignation. Only the flashing sign remained.

Julius Keller, after killing time at several disreputable restaurants in the Tenderloin, finally found his footing. In 1907, in a partnership with the maître d' from the Café Martin, he took over the Café de France on Thirty-eighth Street between Broadway and Sixth Avenue. The spot was cursed. The owner of Morello's, a well-known Italian table d'hôte on Twenty-ninth Street, had sunk $90,000 in the place before giving up. Subsequent owners invested heavily to create a French jewel box called, inevitably, the Café de Paris. It, too, languished. After a week of desultory business, Keller hit on a brilliant idea. Seizing on the big theatrical hit of the moment, Franz Lehár's *Merry Widow*, he renamed the restaurant Maxim's, after the Parisian restaurant featured in the operetta. He outfitted his waiters in a vague approximation of the Louis XIV livery that added such a distinctive note to the Parisian Maxim's and, after adding an orchestra and a few Italian troubadours, threw open the doors for a grand reopening, which was heavily covered by the press. The hash-house days were over. Keller's bitter memories of the Fleischmann's bread line soon dissolved in a pleasant, champagne-scented cloud of gaiety, high living, and ringing cash registers.

Profound cultural change was sweeping over America. Women, increasingly part of the labor force in large cities, were slowly asserting their rights, and the pressures of a

At Bustanoby's, a spinoff of the Café des Beaux Arts, revelers rang in the new century on New Year's Eve in 1899.

At Rector's, a Belle Epoque beauty led the New Year's countdown, circa 1905.

modern economy were breaking down old barriers segregating the sexes. These were formidable. The Victorian code lingered on well after the death of Queen Victoria. With the new century moving briskly along, women still could not go into a bar. They did not dare smoke in public. If they entered a restaurant without a male escort, they were directed to the ladies' café, if one existed, or to a lunchroom specifically designated for women. All this was about to change.

When the Café Martin announced that women would be allowed to eat in the main dining room, it read the future correctly. The old rules were up for revision. Jean-Baptiste Martin struck another blow for freedom when, in December 1907, with New Year's Eve approaching, he announced that women would be allowed to smoke anywhere in his restaurant. This was big news, and the newspapers covered it accordingly. If successful, Martin promised, the New Year's experiment would be extended. "Smoking by ladies is never objectionable," he said. "The smartest women in New York smoke, so why should puritanical proprietors rule against this mode of procedure any more than against the drinking of cocktails or highballs?"

In fact, women had been cheating for quite some time, with the connivance of restaurateurs like Martin, who had already established a women's smoking lounge upstairs, and then spread the word that waiters would look the other way if a woman, seated at her table, should take a puff from her escort's cigarette. The single puff, when hidden by a fan, often lasted for many minutes. Almost immediately, Rector's followed suit for New Year's Eve. Sherry's and Delmonico's held firm, as did most of the hotels. But official policy often bent before necessity. As the *Times* put it, "In every case, it is likely to depend on the sort of woman who wants to smoke." When an ambassador's wife lit up a cigarette at one (unnamed) conservative hotel, no one on the staff dared confront her. As New Year's Eve approached, women all over New York looked forward to smoking in total freedom.

A backlash ensued. After one evening of delicious liberty, the city proposed legislation forbidding women to smoke in public, sending a chill through the restaurant world. At the Café Martin, a notice was posted on the front door advising women that "as a rule," they would not be allowed to smoke in the dining rooms. "If a lady is with her husband and smokes decorously, we do not see her, but I must revoke the official privilege," Martin told reporters. "I believe now that the bulk of the American public is averse to this innovation."

It was a momentary setback. Within a few years, women smoked when and where they liked. "We think our clientele know better than we do what is proper and what is not," said Andre Bustanoby, an owner of the fashionable Café des Beaux Arts, in 1911. "They are adults."

More far-reaching was the introduction of musical and stage acts to the restaurants around Times Square, which had been forced to compete for attention with the roof gardens and flashy revues like the Ziegfeld Follies. Music, of course, had long provided sweet accompaniment to the food at better restau-

CAFÉ DES BEAUX·ARTS

FORBIDDEN FRUIT

LOUIS BUSTANOBY

80 WEST FORTIETH STREET
BRYANT PARK SOUTH

NEW YORK CITY

The four Bustanoby brothers, from the Basque country, catered to "smart Bohemia" at their Café des Beaux Arts across from Bryant Park. Its signature drink was Forbidden Fruit liqueur.

rants and hotels. In fact, music was everywhere, from the lunch hour until well after midnight, and competition for the best orchestras was keen. The programs ran to light classics, operatic melodies, and a few popular tunes. In 1908, it was estimated that New York's hotels and restaurants were spending more than $1 million a year on music. Louis Sherry paid top dollar to import an ensemble formerly led by Johann Strauss. The Waldorf-Astoria employed three orchestras. In an ingenious twist, the management also installed a giant Victrola on the roof garden. As Caruso recordings played, a twenty-five-piece orchestra provided the accompaniment, creating the illusion of a live operatic performance.

In 1911, Jesse Lasky, an up-and-coming vaudeville producer, decided that New York was ready for a European-style music hall with full orchestra, lavish revues, and a sumptuous dinner. Lasky, who would later make a fortune producing Hollywood films, convinced his partner, a seasoned theater producer named Henry B. Harris, that the public would gladly support a theater offering shows to rival the Ziegfeld Follies while enjoying a dinner up to Delmonico's standards, all for $2.50, just fifty cents more than the top price of the Ziegfeld Follies.

The Folies Bergere (from the French Folies-Bergères), advertising itself as "more Parisian than Paris," opened in April 1911 on Forty-sixth Street and introduced New Yorkers to a new word, "cabaret"—so new that advertisements explained how to pronounce it. Opening-night patrons dined to the sounds of a concealed Gypsy orchestra and then, for the next three hours, remained at their tables as two revues and the mildly erotic ballet *Temptations* unfolded before their enchanted eyes. Later in the evening, at a second show, an expanding stage slid out over the orchestra pit, allowing the audience to sit close to the entertainment—cabaret and vaudeville artists who performed until 1:00 a.m. Diamond Jim Brady himself attended, straddling two seats in the front row, and he returned on succeeding nights, his fancy taken by a member of the chorus named Justine Johnstone, a standout on two counts. Only fifteen, she was "already as luscious as Marilyn Monroe," Lasky recalled in his memoirs. Also, "she was never quite in step with the other girls."

Across town, at Lexington Avenue and Fifty-eighth Street, the Terrace Garden, a combination opera house and restaurant with an outdoor garden, went Lasky and Harris one better. It offered a package deal: opera, dinner, and cabaret, plus a free taxi ride home, for two dollars. On opening night, patrons sat down at six-thirty for a dinner of clams, asparagus soup, lobster, sweetbreads, and duck. An hour and a half later, they filed into the adjoining Lexington Opera House to hear

BELVEDERE SUPPER RESTAURANT

Saturday, July 17, 1909

Astrachan Caviar 90
Buffet Russe 50   Grapefruit Cocktail 60
Shinnecock Bays or Little Necks 30   Clam Cocktail 35

Broths
Cold en tasse
Chicken Consommé or Gumbo 30
Bortchok 30

Shellfish
*Lobster, Newburg 1 25;   *Cardinal 1 50
Lobster, cold (½) 65
Lobster or Crab Salad 75   *Crabflakes, Astor 1 50
Crabflakes, Ravigote 60

Hot
Royal Squab étouffé with fresh mushrooms 1 40
*Sweetbreads, Maryland in chafing dish 1 75
Squab Chicken au cresson 1 25   Canapé Lorenzo 60
Canapé Marie Antoinette 60   Club Sandwich 40
Broiled Sardines 50

Cold
Poached Egg, demi-deuil 35
Aspic of Lobster, Bellevue 65
Paupiette of Sole, Epicurienne 50
Filet de Bœuf, Andalousienne 75
Noisette of Veal glacé, Clamart 65
Lamb Chops, Princesse 50   Boned Capon en gelée 60
Veal and Virginia Ham Pie 60
Pâté de Foie gras en terrine 75
Stuffed Tomato, Thermidor 45
Assiette à l'Anglaise 75
Sandwiches: Chicken or Sardine 35   Plain 25

Salads
Russe 75   Kuroki 45   Romaine 30   Lettuce 30
Tomato stuffed with cucumbers 40

Dessert
Plain 25   Mixed 30   Café Parfait 30
Biscuit Tortoni 35   **Biscuit Belvedere 60**   Parfait Tosca 50
Crêpes Suzette 50   Peach, Melba or Princesse 60
Coupe Astor 75   Coupe Hélène 50
Glace Rosadelle 45
Gâteaux Assortis 25

Café
Demi-tasse 15   Turkish 20
Special 25   **Astor 30**
Diable 40

The above Prices are per Person, except dishes preceded by a *

HOTEL ASTOR

The Hotel Astor roof garden covered twenty-eight city lots, with landscaped gardens, winding paths, waterfalls, and music provided by three orchestras. At the Belvedere Restaurant, a cold buffet was served on a nine-ton block of ice.

Carmen. After the opera, they were directed to an outdoor garden, where, as an orchestra played excerpts from *The Spring Maid* and Mendelssohn's "Spring Song," they were entertained by juggling waiters, table dancers, and singers.

The lavish production numbers at the Folies Bergere made it impossible to recoup costs. Within six months, it had been converted into a conventional theater (now the Helen Hayes), but it did stay open just long enough for an eighteen-year-old brunette named Mae West to make her debut in the revue *A la Broadway*. Harris fled to Europe for rest and recuperation, and then made the unfortunate decision to return on the *Titanic*. Lasky had nothing to show for his visionary project beyond the satisfaction of having introduced a number of innovations that lived on into the nightclub era. "Such now-commonplace service items as glass-topped tables with doilies under the plates, silent flag signals on silver ash trays to call waiters without disturbing performer or other diners, and sealed programs for sale were so novel in 1911 as to be conversation pieces," he wrote. Mulling over the failure of the Folies, Lasky singled out the dance floor as the source of his problems. The Folies did not have one. Too forward-looking for its own good, it opened just a little too early to catch Broadway's next wave: ballroom dancing.

Traditionally, dancing for the well-to-do had been restricted to formal parties in which partners arranged themselves in strict formation and performed "set and figure" dances like the quadrille, the cotillion, and the german. As the twentieth century dawned, however, new music and new steps to go with it swept across the variety stage. With a few modifications, the new dances made the transition to Broadway. Blossom Seeley, "the Queen of Syncopation," breezed in from San Francisco in 1911 and sang a ragtime number called "Toddlin' the To-dalo" in *Hen-Pecks* at the Broadway Theater. As part of the act, she jumped on a table and executed a few shaking, shimmying moves familiar to San Francisco audiences but totally new to New York. They stopped the show. Seeley followed up with a dance called the Texas Tommy, lifted from the black vaudeville stage, and before long, American feet were moving wildly to strange melodies and rhythms. Slim-hipped dancing stars from Europe introduced the Apache and the tango. Popularized by the svelte team of Vernon and Irene Castle, dances like the Turkey Trot, the Grizzly Bear, the Bunny Hug, and the Castle Walk sparked a nightlife revolution that transformed dozens of top-flight restaurants.

All over the Great White Way, restaurateurs, bowing to popular demand—and sensing a golden opportunity to build business during the dead daytime hours—hired orchestras and entertainers to promote dancing. Some observers found this amusing. The same diners who once paid to watch dancers perform were now doing all the footwork themselves. Society women clamored for lessons from teachers like Maurice Mouvet, a French import (born and raised in New York) whose "sinuous gyrations" could be studied during private lessons or at small demonstration classes held at Sherry's or the Plaza. As his fame grew, Maurice, as he was universally known, became a cabaret headliner, treating mildly scandalized New Yorkers to the frightening attractions of the Apache dance. "Mischief dances in his blue eyes," Julian Street wrote, "and something more than mischief hangs about the corners of his cruel, complacent, full-lipped mouth." It was said that his first wife had died from Apache-related injuries sustained at his hands.

Tea dances, dinner dances, even breakfast dances could not meet the frenzied demand. Smooth string ensembles and strolling troubadours gave way to full-fledged dance orchestras, hired at enormous expense. The staid Waldorf tried to ban the Turkey Trot but failed to stem the tide. Restaurants hired professional dancers to fill in for men who had not yet learned the new steps. Maxim's hired a former car washer named Rudolf Valentino to guide its female customers around its hastily constructed dance floor.

At the Café de Paris (formerly the Café de l'Opéra), the Castles fell in with the enterprising French headwaiter, Jules Ansaldi, who proposed taking over a basement restaurant next door on Forty-second Street and creating a cabaret, the Sans Souci. The Castles lent their cachet to the new club, and Jules worked his special brand of magic, which Irene Castle had noticed back at the Café de l'Opéra. "He combined all the talents of a social dictator with the acquisitive habits of a business tycoon," she wrote in her memoirs. "He probably made more money at the Café de l'Opéra than we did. If you wanted a table at the café, it was Ensaldi [sic] who first looked you over with his discerning French eye and determined whether you should pass the velvet rope or not. Once you passed the first barrier, it was Jules who ranked you socially and placed you at a table according to your fame or prominence."

The Castles, a refined alternative to the ordinary run of vaudeville entertainers, found themselves in constant demand in the private homes of the wealthy, where they gave demonstrations and lessons. Their presence at the Sans Souci drew a tony crowd, and the dancing habit spread throughout the upper reaches of Manhattan society. The fabulous Maurice, now teamed with his second wife,

Florence Walton, opened Chez Maurice, a dance room and restaurant. Primitive dances and low-rent pleasures were now officially acceptable for the sons and daughters of the Four Hundred.

A new breed of restaurant jumped to the head of the Broadway queue, geared toward dancing and entertainment as much as fine dining. In 1901, the four Bustanoby brothers, from the Basque country of France, had opened the sumptuous Café des Beaux Arts on Fortieth Street, across from Bryant Park. André, who had worked at the Café Martin and Delmonico's, placed a premium on haute cuisine, offered at top prices, but he also understood the more mysterious arts of creating atmosphere and catching the attention of a fickle public. A strange new food, the grapefruit, was beginning to make an appearance in New York produce markets, and the Bustanobys used it as the basis for an exotic liqueur, Forbidden Fruit, an early name for grapefruit. The high-flying atmosphere, epitomized by this exotic after-dinner drink, made the Beaux Arts an overnight sensation among the set they called "smart Bohemia."

The brothers put their distinguished theatrical patrons to work. On Thursday nights they held a Soirée Artistique, at which stars of the musical stage held forth. Guests could thrill to Anna Held singing "I Just Can't Make My Eyes Behave," or Lillian Russell performing "Come Down, My Evening Star." In 1912, Jacques and André closed the Café des Beaux Arts after a falling-out with Louis and opened Bustanoby's, on Thirty-ninth Street near Sixth Avenue. Their pianist, the then-unknown Sigmund Romberg, convinced André that his restaurant should have a dance floor. In typical Bustanoby fashion, the restaurant pulled out all the stops. Among other entertainments, it hosted an Apache night, redecorating the dining room to resemble a louche Parisian nightclub. Guests dressed like Parisian gangsters and watched intently as professional teams demonstrated the thrillingly violent dance.

The frantic activity at Bustanoby's completely overshadowed a pioneering restaurant down the block, just east of Fifth Avenue. In 1913, the furniture designer Gustav Stickley leased a twelve-story building to showcase his designs and convert the public to the ideas of the Arts and Crafts movement. The Craftsman Building, as Stickley called it, included a fascinating experiment called the Craftsman Restaurant. Located on the top floor and decorated in the Stickley style, it offered an inspired alternative to stuffy French dining rooms and Art Nouveau froufrou. Dark, solid wood—the floor was unadorned oak, as were the tables and chairs—and richly colored walls created an uncluttered sense of comfort. Along the Gobelin-blue walls ran a patterned frieze of nasturtium leaves and blossoms in dark green and deep red. Framed sepia photographs of the Craftsman Farms reminded diners that the food on their plates reflected a socio-artistic vision. "We are not starting a restaurant because we feel that we want to go into the restaurant business," Stickley wrote in his magazine, *The Craftsman*, "but because we feel that certain ideals of cooking and furnishings should be expressed in connection with a restaurant."

Like the Craftsman Building itself, the Craftsman Restaurant was intended as a showcase for certain ideas—in this case, ideas about the relationship between food, design, pleasure, and the good life. "We want to see just how comfortable, how simple, how beautiful such rooms can be made," Stickley continued. "We want people to be happy in them, to brighten their ideals of life through contact with them."

Even more revolutionary, at a time when industrialized food production was ascendant, the Craftsman promised to shrink the distance between farm and restaurant. "My theory about a restaurant is that to be the right sort of an eating place it must be closely related to its source of supplies," Stickley wrote, more than half a century before Alice Waters made a religion of the idea at Chez Panisse and inspired a new wave of contemporary farmer-chefs such as Dan Barber at the Stone Barns Center for Food and Agriculture in Westchester, New York.

Stickley looked to his Craftsman Farms in Morris Plains, New Jersey, to put butter, milk, eggs, poultry, fruit, vegetables, and even flowers on his elegantly designed tables, where a fairly orthodox menu was offered. Standard dishes of the day predominated: oysters in all styles, celery and salted almonds sold as side dishes, lobster Newberg, steaks and chops, duck and guinea hen. Instead of rich desserts, the restaurant offered brandied peaches, or figs with cream.

The menu does pose a few tantalizing questions. What went into a Craftsman Salad? Or the Craftsman planked sirloin? Or stewed oysters, Craftsman style? Alas, we do not know. A promotional booklet for the Craftsman Building hinted that the Craftsman menu would include some exotic pleasures as well—"appetizing items from the kitchens of India, China and Japan." The original chef, T. Moto, was Japanese, as were most of the kitchen and dining room staff, but the only Asian note on the menu, besides tea, seems to have been mango chutney. Since Stickley went bankrupt in 1915, the restaurant remained a work in progress, an experiment whose outcome will never be known.

In quirkiness, the only restaurant to compare to the Craftsman was an experimental lunchroom in the city's Department of Health building, where the calorie count and protein content of each dish were printed on the menu. City health officials wanted to demonstrate that the average New Yorker could eat good, nutritious meals on a limited budget.

Elsewhere, dance mania continued to rage. Uptown, on Columbus Circle, it gave a new identity to the fascinating Reisenweber's. The restaurant first appeared in 1855 as a small café called the Halfway House, on what was then Bloomingdale Road (later Broadway), the main route from Greenwich Village to Harlem. The location was ideal: brewery drivers making deliveries to Harlem stopped in the mornings, and stage coaches stopped later in the day. In time, the little café grew to enormous proportions. By the turn of the century, it boasted a dozen dining rooms and a staff of one thousand. The main dining room was an eyeful, with green marble columns, red carpets, bird's-eye maple tables, and an

In 1897, Delmonico's moved for the last time, to Fifth Avenue at Forty-fourth Street, where Prohibition finally killed it in 1923.

outsize Tiffany window in the rear. The men's café, called the Klondike Room, was a masculine set piece in dark mahogany.

Louis Fischer, John Reisenweber's son-in-law, took over the restaurant in 1905 and immediately introduced some new ideas. Fischer, an Austrian immigrant, saw limitless potential in the place. The bicycling craze had brought younger patrons to the restaurant, and he was determined to keep them. Not only did he open the floors to dancing, but he staged complete floor shows with principals, chorus, and sets.

Over time, Fischer reorganized Reisenweber's into a multilevel entertainment center, with different revues and stars on each floor. In the 400 Room, a small restaurant within Reisenweber's that opened in January 1917, he made history by booking the Original Dixieland Jazz Band. This would prove to be a turning point in American popular culture. Almost immediately, record companies were knocking at the door. "Livery Stable Blues" and "Dixie Jass Band One-Step," released in February 1917 by the Victor Talking Machine Company, is now recognized as the first jazz recording, the spark that ignited the Jazz Age. When Sophie Tucker's star began to rise, she was given the 400 Room as her personal showcase for extended engagements. For the hula dancer Doraldina (née Dora Sanders), Fischer created Doraldina's Hawaiian Room. To pay for Ned Wayburn's lavish revues in the Paradise Room, Reisenweber's imposed New York's first cover charge, a whopping twenty-five cents. Customers howled at first. It was unthinkable. But the unthinkable soon became the unavoidable all over town, as restaurants put on stage shows to rival the Ziegfeld Follies.

The Bustanobys, too, planted a foot in Columbus Circle, opening the Domino Room to showcase Emil Coleman's dance orchestra, and an outdoor café, the Café de la Paix. One by one, restaurants up and down Broadway followed suit. Cabaret was king. Murray's installed a revolving dance floor. Thomas Shanley, gritting his teeth, bowed to fashion and slapped on a cover charge. "I don't demand the cabaret but the public does, and so the public has to help pay for it," he groused. "What do you think it costs me? One hundred thousand a year."

The music and the dancing never stopped, or so it seemed. In the afternoon, New Yorkers crowded the dance floor for *thé dansants*. At dinner, they jumped up between courses to swirl across the floor. After dinner, they moved along to yet another restaurant to dance into the morning hours. The new dance regime infuriated the city's professional gourmets. "The old-fashioned dinner with its social and intimate conversation is a thing of the past," one irritated diner complained. Under the new rules, diners slurped down their oysters, then raced to the dance floor for a quick spin before the next course arrived. "In the meantime, all the wicky-wicky boys and girls in grass skirts cavort around the open space you have just abandoned to the tune of countless ukeleles, tom-toms, and clanking castanets. In a few moments the performers disappear, your soup has been served, and there is time for another whirl before the fish comes, and you whirl."

A revolution was under way. The discreet feminine smoke signals from the Café Martin signaled the incineration of the old code and the transformation of the Gibson Girl into the flapper, keen for a little thrill—Broadway's stock-in-trade. Dance broke down all sorts of social barriers, as once-segregated social classes mingled freely in the Broadway melee. Enthralled audiences, after observing the new dances, ached to try them out on the restaurant floor. But with whom? Just about anybody, apparently. "Practically any well-dressed person who is reasonably sober and will purchase champagne and supper for two, may enter," Julian Street wrote. "This creates a social mixture such as was never dreamed of before in this country—a hodge-podge of people in which respectable young married and unmarried women, and even debutantes, dance, not only under the same roof, but in the same room with, women of the town."

And the way they danced! The spirit of the new dances was intimate. The ideal, demonstrated so effectively by teams like the Castles, or the alluringly risqué Maurice and Florence Walton at the Café de Paris and Reisenweber's, was to fuse two partners into one, moving fluidly and sensuously to the music. To the older generation, this was shocking. "The debutante of five years since," Street wrote in 1913, "would have indignantly refused to dance with the young man who held her as he needs must hold her in the dance of to-day."

Newspaper readers first got an inkling that something scandalous was afoot in the theater district when the Eugenia Kelly case made headlines. Kelly, a nineteen-year-old socialite, was arrested at the request of her own mother, who told the police she was fed up with her daughter's wild ways. Since graduating from the Sacred Heart Convent two years earlier, Eugenia had spent nearly every night dancing and living it up in the restaurants and cabarets of Times Square, where she surrounded herself with men whom her mother's lawyer described as "Broadway sports and rounders." Among them was a middle-aged, very married wine agent named Al Davis, chief beneficiary of the young girl's largesse. At the time of her arrest, Miss Kelly, as the newspapers called her, had recently borrowed somewhere between $4,000 and $5,000, and could not account for $4,000 worth of jewels that she once owned.

Eugenia Kelly smoked. She drank absinthe, champagne, and white mint frappes. She danced until dawn at places like the Café des Beaux Arts, the Domino Room, Maxim's, Murray's, and Reisenweber's. "She told me a girl was no good in New York City these days unless she went to at least five cafés every night and it wasn't possible to cover the ground before three or four o'clock in the morning," her distraught mother told the court. Exactly. The sentiment was captured in a snappy poem.

> *If you've never dined and wined*
> *With a show, all combined*
> *You are not*
> *(Pardon me)*
> *Anywhere.*

Initially defiant, Eugenia knuckled under after a team of lawyers and relatives explained the meaning of the word "inheritance." Head bowed, she told the court that mother knew best. She was sorry. She had been blinded by the lights of the Great White Way.

There was a name for men like Al Davis. It was "tango pirate," close cousin to the lounge lizard and the parlor snake. Members of the species had no visible means of support. Unlike the rest of the criminal class, they operated in daylight hours, haunting the fashionable restaurants of the town, where rich women gathered to lunch and to dance, easy prey for a breed of men easily identifiable by their plumage. "During the Fall, Winter and Spring these young fellows invariably wear a silk hat, usually tilted at an angle of 45 degrees," the Manhattan district attorney told reporters. "In the summer they wear, before dark, the most fashionable straws. And cutaway coats. And spats—always spats. I have seen fifty of them, and never one without spats." A smooth talker and dancer, the tango pirate was after money, not sex, unless sex was required to get the money. He wheedled cash and jewelry from gullible young women—or their mothers, whose unwitting husbands made them easy blackmail victims.

The tango pirate appeared in deepest dye one afternoon in 1917, when the naked body of Elsie Lee Hilair, a thirty-five-year-old married woman from

Brooklyn, was found sprawled across a bed in the Hotel Martinique. Her jewels and cash were missing. Hilair, it turned out, liked to attend afternoon tango dances in Times Square. She was also in the habit of wearing a lot of jewelry, whose sparkle caught the eye of a posse of tango pirates lurking at her favorite spots: Rector's, Bustanoby's, and the ballroom at the Biltmore. For days, the "Brooklyn matron" with the double life dominated the front pages and motivated the police to crack down hard on the lobster palaces, rooting out the young men in spats and encouraging them to find jobs. At one point, the police sent a team of female detectives to hit the dance floor, mingle, and learn what they could about the devious ways of this new predatory class. All to no avail. The Hilair murder was never solved. And the dancing went on.

Later, when the First World War and Prohibition had extinguished the bright lights of Broadway's brilliant dining scene, and the postmortems began, the finger of blame often pointed straight to the dance floor as the prime cause of the decline and fall of the city's restaurant culture.

10

The Future Is Now

Henry Erkins's waiterless dining room was not a joke. It was a portent. The wave of modernization that had swept over Times Square was radically changing the technology of dining at lower-priced restaurants. Sherry's and Delmonico's, of course, maintained a stately pace. Haute cuisine prizes slow perfectionism, and change comes slowly. But on the lower culinary slopes, the scientific spirit was transforming artisanal workshops into a streamlined industry dominated by three goals: better, cheaper, faster.

Already, Alfred Dennett had pioneered a new kind of quick lunch in his chain of sanitary restaurants, which offered humble American fare at low cost to legions of office workers (many of them now women). The Dennett model led to the Exchange Buffet (twenty-five New York lunchrooms in 1916), Hartford Lunch (sixteen lunchrooms), Hanover Lunch (thirteen), and, biggest of all, the lunchroom empire founded by the Childs brothers.

Samuel S. and William Childs grew up with their eight brothers on a farm in Basking Ridge, New Jersey. In 1886, they both headed out to the wheat fields of North Dakota to work a land claim. Their farming venture fizzled, but the brothers did not return empty-handed. "On our trip we were much distressed by the poor, badly cooked food that was served to us in the restaurants along the way," William later recalled. "The average was worse than poor, and at times our experiences were well nigh revolting. When we returned to New York the idea occurred to us that clean, good restaurants were a needed thing."

They were right. Other pioneers, like James A. Whitcomb of the Baltimore Dairy Lunch chain, had already sensed a change in customer tastes and responded accordingly. Whitcomb stumbled into the business. In 1887, a dairy in Washington, D.C., began selling buttermilk by the glass at its central depot, simply as a way to get rid of surplus milk. Before long, it was selling whole milk, half-and-half, and buttermilk, along with Maryland biscuits at a penny apiece. As business increased, it added crullers, pie, and coffee to the menu. Since all the food was cooked in advance, it could serve customers quickly.

One of the dairy's customers was Whitcomb, who decided to open a similar business in Baltimore, with improvements. He patented the one-arm chair with coffee-cup holder and, responding to a customer's complaints, offered utensils, cups, and saucers, decorated with a fanciful picture of a farmer milking a cow. The formula caught on, and Whitcomb opened branches in New York and other cities—140 of them by 1916.

At about the same time, the Childs brothers were making headway. Set on learning the restaurant business, Sam entered a management-training program

The Childs lunchroom chain signaled its emphasis on cleanliness and wholesome food with white tile interiors and waitresses whose starched uniforms made them look like nurses.

for the Dennett chain, and persuaded William to join him. The brothers embraced the Dennett corporate culture a little too enthusiastically. Nakedly ambitious, they bombarded Dennett with criticisms and suggestions. They insisted on working overtime, alienating their fellow workers. After six months, William was fired and Sam quit.

In 1889, the Childs brothers took out a two-month lease on the ground floor of the Merchants Hotel on Cortlandt Street, a well-spotted location near the New Jersey ferries. The lease was, in effect, a private bet: if the restaurant was not taking in forty dollars a day within two months, they would quit. After borrowing money to open the restaurant, the brothers were broke, so they built the interior themselves on the family farm. They also installed electric lights, still a novelty. It was only seven years earlier that the Edison Electric Light Company, as a demonstration, had installed electric lights in the chandeliers at Sweet's, a seafood restaurant near Fulton Market, dazzling a large crowd of onlookers when it pulled the switch.

After opening their first lunchroom in 1889, the Childs brothers built a multimillion-dollar empire that survived into the 1960s. Pictured here: the Childs at Union Square

Like Dennett, the brothers put a premium on cleanliness, which they communicated to customers by outfitting waitresses in white aprons and starched white lace caps, making them look a little like nurses. The walls were covered in glazed white tile, the tabletops finished in white porcelain. The hospital aesthetic greatly appealed to the architecture critic Lewis Mumford, who praised Childs for the "hard brilliance" and "antiseptic elegance" of its uncompromisingly modern interiors. The early Childs restaurants, in his opinion, represented the beginning of "a real machine-form." What the Childs brothers made of this is unknown.

The chain became a byword for sanitary dining. ("He's clean, perfectly clean, as clean as a Childs restaurant," a detective tells his partner after frisking a suspect in *House of Glass*, a 1916 Broadway play.) Moreover, service was quick and efficient. To draw the attention of passersby, an employee stationed at a stove in the front window of every Childs restaurant cooked its signature yeast pancakes and buttercakes throughout the day. "Childs' buttercakes, baked in their window on a griddle together with their famous griddlecakes, were sumptuous to my mind and taste," wrote Gertrude A. Parkhurst, a New Yorker born the year the first Childs lunchroom opened. "Actually they were like freshly cooked English muffins . . . and were the same as dough for bread rolls, only cooked on a griddle instead of in an oven." The front-window performance, and the flavor of the cakes, immediately entered New York mythology.

The Childs brothers opened five more lunchrooms in the next five years. By 1928, they operated 112 restaurants in thirty-three American and Canadian cities. Unlike most of their competitors, they nurtured a strong corporate culture. Each restaurant had a bowling team, and the league results were posted in *Childs*, the company magazine. Procedures at the lunchrooms were strictly standardized, and the food consistent from one restaurant to the next. Besides the pancakes (plain or wheat), diners could choose from simple dishes like corned-beef hash, roast-beef hash with mashed potatoes, ham cakes with tomato sauce, corned-beef sandwiches, and eggs served every which way. Clam chowder and fish cakes with tomato sauce were served on Fridays. The menu also included a long list of dairy specialties, like rice and milk or hominy and cream.

The lunchroom competition was stiff. William Childs, after his brother's death in 1925, was looking farther afield for expansion and cast his eyes northward, to Fifth Avenue in the Forties, where retail businesses were invading what once was a great boulevard of private mansions. At the turn of the century, the

Fifth Avenue Association had fought to keep stores like B. Altman's off the street, but it was no use. Fifth Avenue was taking on a commercial character. Shops meant shoppers, and to the Childs brothers, shoppers meant customers. In an impudent move, William Childs took out a lease on the old Russell Sage residence between Forty-eighth and Forty-ninth streets and prepared to replace it with upper Fifth Avenue's first fast-food restaurant. Shrewdly, he hired a first-rate architect to come up with a design appropriate to the street: William Van Alen, who had already designed a Childs farther south on Fifth Avenue and would go on to design the Chrysler Building. Van Alen's sophisticated Fifth Avenue Childs, with its Art Moderne curves, silenced even the most skeptical members of the Fifth Avenue Association. There would be more surprises to come from William Childs, some of them disastrous for the company. But for the moment, his touch was golden.

In December 1902, a strange new restaurant opened on Broadway at Twelfth Street. It was called the Automat. The word was new to New York and so was the concept. Inside, perplexed diners discovered that there were no waiters, only busboys, and no traffic between the kitchen and the dining room, for the simple reason that there was no kitchen on the main floor. Instead, customers confronted a vending machine along one wall, with a card next to it that read: "Insert coin opposite the dish desired. Pull handle below and retain check delivered. When dish ordered appears in adjoining apparatus, insert check. Your order is electronically communicated and at once freshly prepared." This was the hot-food station. At a cold-food station, stocked with salads and desserts, patrons could drop a coin in the slot beside each dish and remove their food immediately. A coin-operated drinks station dispensed beer, wine, coffee, whiskey, and assorted liqueurs. (One newspaper report listed highballs and absinthe frappes as well, which seems highly unlikely.)

Customers at the hot-food station could not see or hear it, but by turning the handle to get their brass check, they initiated a complex operation. A bell sounded one floor below, in the kitchen, where their coin had just dropped into a holder monitored by the staff. After preparing the requested hot dish and placing it into a dumbwaiter, workers sent the food upstairs, at which point the customer's coin dropped from the holder—a signal that the order had been completed. To prevent theft, the dumbwaiter rose to a level just above the retrieval niche. Only when the brass check was inserted into the slot did the dumbwaiter drop into proper position, allowing the food to be removed.

Although the Automat soon became one of the city's most visible symbols, New York was not the first city to get one, nor was it an American invention. Automats were developed in Europe and had quickly become popular in Berlin by the 1890s. London had one, too. The first American Automat opened in Philadelphia just a few months before the Harcombe Restaurant Company introduced its Automat to Manhattan, part of an ambitious rollout of the new technology. Harcombe's German parent company had plans for a dozen more Automats, but tepid public response, after the first flush of curiosity, led the company to abandon its crusade. The Automat, it appeared, was an idea whose time had not yet come. It was at this critical juncture that a Philadelphia company called Horn & Hardart entered the picture.

The meeting of Joe Horn and Frank Hardart strongly suggests the hand of fate. In 1888, Horn was a twenty-seven-year-old with a passion for the restaurant business that drove his mother to despair. She had raised seven children on the income from her late husband's surgical-appliance business, and two sons already ran a restaurant. That was enough. But after endless pestering by Joe, she agreed to put up $1,000 to help him create a quick-service lunchroom in

New York's first Automat opened in 1902 on Broadway near Twelfth Street. It failed, but Horn & Hardart improved the technology and built an empire.

Philadelphia. Frank Hardart, meanwhile, was waiting tables in the same city. Now thirty-eight, he had come up the hard way, the son of German immigrants who started a fruit-and-vegetable business in New Orleans. After working menial restaurant jobs from the time he was thirteen, Hardart moved to Philadelphia, a city he had fallen in love with after visiting the Centennial Exposition. There, fortune frowned. After failing to get a soda fountain off the ground, he wound up toiling in a lunchroom in a bad neighborhood.

One day, Hardart noticed a newspaper advertisement placed by Joe Horn, who was looking for a partner with restaurant experience. Hardart ripped a piece of paper off a sugar bag, wrote, "I'm your man," and mailed it off. By the end of the year, Horn and Hardart had opened a lunchroom, where Hardart insisted on serving coffee the way it was made in New Orleans, using the French drip method. More lunchrooms followed. Then, in 1898 a salesman representing Quisisana, a German manufacturer of Automat equipment, paid a visit and described the wonders of the waiterless restaurant. Hardart, intrigued, took a trip to Germany to look at the machinery for himself. He was sold on the idea, and in 1902, the first Horn & Hardart Automat opened in center-city Philadelphia.

After the last Automat closed in the early 1980s, former patrons grew nostalgic over the meringue pies of yesteryear.

The partners quickly identified weaknesses in the first-generation Automats. The drink dispensers worked fine: a coin, once inserted in a slot, released a premeasured quantity of liquid. But the circuitous hot-food system needed refinement. Horn & Hardart's engineer, John Fritzsche, developed a unit that allowed workers behind the scenes to slide hot dishes into open compartments on a rotating metal drum. When the slots were filled, the drum turned to face the customer, who could simply drop a nickel into a slot and pull out the food. A metal jacket heated by hot water kept food in the drum warm. Similarly, jackets cooled by cold water chilled the cold-food drums.

When Joe Horn and Frank Hardart came to New York in 1912, they were ready. They had experience in the lunchroom trade and their Automat technology was on the cutting edge. Just as important, they understood the aesthetics of the business, and they knew how to advertise. Determined to open with a bang, they decided to put their first restaurant right in the middle of Times Square.

The partners knew that it would take more than a coin-operated lunchroom to make an impression amidst restaurants like Rector's, Murray's, and the Café de l'Opéra. They hired Nicola D'Ascenzo, the glass sculptor responsible for the windows of the Cathedral of St. John the Divine, to create a two-story stained-glass façade in the Arts and Crafts style. The word "Automat," prominently displayed, was framed by brightly colored fruits and flowers. The interior, with its ornate columns, was pure spectacle. All along the walls of the enormous dining room, glassed-in food compartments, as precisely arrayed as letter boxes in a post office, contained the dishes of the day, ready for delivery as soon as customers dropped their nickels in the slot. Display ads in the newspapers made a simple pitch: "Automat Lunch Room Opens To-Day. New Method of Lunching. Try It! You'll Like It!!"

New Yorkers did like it, once they got the hang of it. Initially, befuddled customers kept tapping on the little glass windows separating them from the food. Consequently, busboys spent most of their time running back and forth explaining the system. Once diners mastered the technology, they found that the Automat offered surprisingly good food at a bargain price in attractive surroundings. After taking their food from its little compartment, and dropping a nickel in the slot for a cup of coffee (precisely measured by a pump device, and delivered via a dolphin spout), they took their seats at round tables covered in white milk-glass. At the center of each table, in addition to the standard sugar, salt, and pepper, were celery salt and Worcestershire sauce.

By 1920, Horn & Hardart had opened another fourteen Automats in New York. Two years later, they created their first combination cafeteria and Automat. It was the largest restaurant in the city, capable of feeding ten thousand customers a day. By 1933, there were forty-three Automat cafeterias in New York, supplied by huge commissaries that allowed the company to buy in bulk and produce their signature dishes in mass quantities. From humble beginnings as a traditional lunchroom, Horn & Hardart developed the first truly industrialized restaurant system run on an assembly-line basis.

For millions of New Yorkers, and countless tourists, the Automat was modern living at its best: American food served in a sleekly designed space using the latest technology. Ilf and Petrov, the great Soviet satirists, made a point of eating at one on their tour of America in 1935, and no wonder. The Automat expressed something essential about capitalist America. Here "the process of pushing food into the American stomach" had been carried "to the point of virtuosity." Ilf and Petrov found the sight of individual dishes imprisoned in small glass-fronted cages poignant, and, needless to say, they smelled a capitalist rat lurking behind the whole operation. Surely the bosses had devised a waiterless restaurant in order to put "poor marcelled girls with pink headdresses" on the street and pocket their wages themselves. Besides, all American food was tasteless.

New Yorkers quickly embraced the Automat, a waiterless restaurant where they put coins in a slot to get their food and beverages.

Americans, too, recognized the Automat as emblematically American and modern, one of the milestones marking the country's transition from the nineteenth to the twentieth century. As such, it served as an endless inspiration for cartoons, jokes, and comedy routines. As early as 1914, in the Irving Berlin revue *Watch Your Step*, W. C. Fields experimented with a promising-sounding Automat sketch that, for some reason, never made it past out-of-town tryouts. The picture of innocence, he walked into an Automat,

By 1925, when this photograph was taken, the Horn & Hardart's Automat was a New York institution, feeding busy businessmen, office workers, and actors waiting for that first big break.

dropped a nickel into one of the food slots, and reached for a slice of pie. Instead, a billiard table dropped down in front of him.

For New Yorkers, the Automat attained mythic significance. Horn & Hardart's baked beans and macaroni and cheese were soul food for generations of budget-conscious diners, remembered with affection in their later, more affluent days. As the Automat worked itself into the fabric of the city, it came to represent a particular kind of American experience. It was ostentatiously democratic, for one thing. Lacking the gatekeepers associated with traditional restaurants, it attracted diners from every social level. *The New Yorker* feasted on cartoons depicting Park Avenue matrons or top-hatted blue bloods dropping into the Automat, a social contrast that was inherently funny, but no great exaggeration. A bit of verse in the *Sun*, printed in the Depression year of 1933, caught the spirit precisely:

Said the Technocrat
To the Plutocrat
To the Autocrat
And the Democrat—
Let's all go eat at the Automat!

Down-and-outers sidled in and made free tomato soup by stirring ketchup on the table into a mug of hot water, or made lemonade by squeezing the lemon wedges set out for iced tea. (In the two years after the 1929 Wall Street crash, business at the Automats increased by 50 percent.) Clerks and typists sat at the same table with time-pressed businessmen. Struggling actors eked out their nickels at the Automat as they dreamed of their first big break. Around Times Square, and across from Bryant Park, the Horn & Hardart Automats, free from supervision, developed into prime cruising grounds for gay New Yorkers.

Writers could sit and think for hours over a nickel cup of coffee. "When I first came to New York, before 'Studs Lonigan,' I ate out of those slots," James Farrell recalled. "For breakfast, coffee and muffins for a dime; for lunch, a bowl of pork and beans; for dinner, the same." The Automat was the headquarters of the lonely crowd, the natural setting for the anonymous, the unattached, and the disconsolate, like the pensive woman in Edward Hopper's *Automat* (1927), balancing a coffee cup with one hand, alone with her thoughts.

The nickel coffee stayed a nickel until November 1950, when increased wholesale prices forced Horn & Hardart to double the price, at just about the time that the subway fare went from a nickel to a dime. For many New Yorkers, this double whammy marked the end of the city's heroic era.

Automation would reach a final pitch of absurdity in the hands of Charles Fuller Stoddard, an inventor who struck it rich with his designs for a pneumatic mailing tube and the Ampico player piano. Stoddard, a nervous fussbudget with wire-rimmed spectacles, grew irritated at the inconsistency of fried chicken from one restaurant to the next. That, and wasted human movement, preyed on his mind, so in 1930 he opened Stoddard's Restaurant. Located near Columbia University, it was intended to be the last word in efficiency. To address the fried-chicken problem, Stoddard invented an automatic frying pan that measured the temperature and weight of the chicken being prepared. He also installed automated measuring, mixing, and cooking devices, including an automatic pastry roller that was eventually bought by Stouffer's and Schrafft's. To streamline service, he invented a timing machine that monitored eight tables at once. With it, he determined that a waitress walking two steps at an ordinary gait cost him one-fiftieth of a penny. Less scientifically, if diners lingered too long at their table, he asked them to leave. The experiment came to an end in 1956, when Stoddard suffered a stroke. It had been a surprisingly successful run that nevertheless left Stoddard disgruntled. "There was no precision to it," he complained. "You were at the mercy of the chefs, and chefs make mistakes."

The rush toward more modern ways of eating led to a brief enthusiasm for "capsular restaurants," where the food came in pill form. Truly, the new century promised an age of wonders. Americans had already been softened up by the dietary warning of cranks like the Reverend Sylvester Graham and Dr. John Harvey Kellogg, who waged holy war against steaks, fried foods, and pies. Their efforts brought about a revolution in the American breakfast, formerly heavy on meats, now a gentler beginning to the day that relied on cereal and fruit. Scientists discovered the vitamin and the calorie, mysterious entities that captured the public imagination. At the same time, stomach ulcers and dyspepsia became the signature ailments of the new century.

In 1901, the first "tabloid" restaurant opened in Manhattan, followed almost immediately by one in Brooklyn, on Fulton Street, opposite the entrance to the Brooklyn Bridge. The word, coined by two Americans in the pharmaceutical business as a catchier, more marketable substitute for "tablet," came to be applied to just about anything in compressed form. The tabloid menu, using compressed and ersatz foods developed by Kellogg at his sanitorium in Battle Creek, Michigan, included such delights as compressed "beefsteak," nut roast, protose (a wheat and peanut meat substitute), nut meat, and nuttolene, a sliceable peanut loaf. A reporter for the *Eagle*, ordering the "beef," received a meatlike entrée with brown gravy, sweet potato, and three slices of bread for fifteen cents. "In appearance compressed beef steak looks like Hamburger steak and it is decidedly palatable," he wrote. "It tastes like meat, yet its composition is not so firm." Customers enchanted with the tabloid concept could also order bromose, a caramel-like tablet of nuts, cereals, and fats that could be chewed or dissolved in hot water and drunk like coffee.

The breakfast foods created by Kellogg and his patient C. W. Post became major industries and a permanent part of the American diet. But futuristic foods like nuttose—precursors of Space Food Sticks and Tang—never caught on, perhaps understandably. An unsuspecting character in a period novel, sampling

11 WEST 18TH STREET
NEW YORK CITY
E. W. COATES, Proprietor

DINNER

FOR THE

VEGETARIAN SOCIETY

WEDNESDAY, JAN. 27th, 1904

MENU

NUT CHOWDER

PINEAPPLE NECTAR

NUTTOLENE CUTLETS—
GREEN PEAS

LAUREL FRUIT SALAD
CREAM STICKS

FIG ICE CREAM

"NO FLOCKS THAT RANGE THE VALLEY FREE
TO SLAUGHTER I CONDEMN;
TAUGHT BY THE POWER THAT PITIES ME,
I LEARN TO PITY THEM."
—*Goldsmith.*

At the turn of the century, vegetarian restaurants came on the scene. Some served well-prepared nonmeat dishes. Others offered strange meat substitutes such as nuttose and protose.

nuttose for the first time, describes the taste as a mixture of "whale oil and dead beetles." Vegetarianism, however, did make small inroads. New York's first vegetarian restaurant, rather unimaginatively named Vegetarian Restaurant Number One, opened in 1895 on West Twenty-third Street. The venture was backed by the New York Vegetarian Society, which took the position that no food should be eaten that had been obtained through the destruction of life. This ruled out meat and fish, including scallops and oysters, a shocking thought for a city as oyster-mad as New York. Dairy products, however, were permitted. In addition to dishes like fruit soup, baked cauliflower, and spaghetti with tomato sauce, diners could feast on Bohemian cream with fruit sauce or milky rice pudding with lemon sauce. The Physical Culture Society also operated several vegetarian restaurants. But vegetarians swam upstream in a muscular culinary environment that, as yet, saw no particular reason to forgo fat, cholesterol, and double portions.

11

Decline and Fall

As the clock neared midnight on January 16, 1920, New York, along with the rest of the nation, went dry. At 12:01 a.m., the Volstead Act, outlawing the sale of alcohol, went into effect, ushering in what would prove to be thirteen years of Prohibition.

The momentous occasion passed quietly. Resignation rather than defiance was the mood. Several bars and restaurants staged mock funerals. At the Park Avenue Hotel, where the dining room tables and walls had been draped in black, somberly dressed mourners paid their respects to a coffin filled with booze bottles. Healy's uptown restaurant, at Ninety-fifth and Broadway, handed out miniature caskets to its patrons. Colonel David L. Porter, chief of the internal revenue agents for New York, made it clear that he would not be staging any dramatic raids at the stroke of midnight. Prohibition tiptoed in politely.

Broadway had been sagging for years. The waiters' strikes of 1912 and 1913 were warning shots in a coming labor war that would plague the restaurant business for the next half century. Overambitious and out of control, the great lobster palaces—Rector's, Churchill's, Louis Martin's—began to fold, one by one. With the outbreak of war in 1914, government-imposed rationing and a temporary ban on distilling slimmed down the fabulous menus and cast a pall over the bars. Patriotic Frenchmen like Jules Ansaldi at the Sans Souci headed back to Europe to fight.

The growing prospect of a U.S. entry into the war changed the national mood. The mayor of New York, deciding that it was "unseemly" for Americans to be celebrating late into the night while young men were fighting in Europe, revoked the late-night liquor licenses that had kept Broadway up until dawn. Starting on May 1, 1917, cabarets and restaurants would no longer be allowed to sell liquor after 1:00 a.m. This was a grievous blow. "The lights of Broadway twinkled in the face of dawn this morning as they have twinkled in the past, but the heat was gone out of them," the *Times* reported the day after the new law went into effect. It was obvious, even at the time, that a new, less frivolous era was in the making. Already the newspapers were sounding an elegiac note: "The passing of the 24-hour day on Broadway," one reporter noted, "means the end of the age of splendor and luxury that reached its height the world over in 1914." The fun was over.

As a purely practical matter, wartime meat restrictions and food guidelines imposed new challenges for chefs. *The Caterer*, a restaurant trade magazine, printed creative fish recipes, like shark with salt pork, to help restaurants deal with the meat shortage, but even the most imaginative editor could do nothing about the Eighteenth Amendment. Although no one paid much attention at the time, the Volstead Act hurt restaurants just as badly as it hurt the saloons, not only by robbing them of their principal source of profits, but also by snatching a key ingredient from the hands of the chef. It is possible—just—to enjoy a French dinner without wine, but it is impossible to make one. Sauce Bordelaise without red wine cannot be done. New Yorkers found this out only when it was too late. In a show of mercy, the government allowed the importation of wine with 1 percent salt added, but chefs found it unsatisfactory. Julian Street sampled lobster Newberg made without sherry. It tasted "like superior grade wet newspaper." Everywhere, portions shrank, substitute ingredients were introduced, and standards slid, even at the grand hotels, which prided themselves on their lavish tables. Deprived of the income from wine and liquor sales, they cut back on their kitchens and doubled their room rates overnight. Meanwhile, speakeasies cut into the profits of restaurants.

Service standards declined. Street blamed the abandonment of the French system, in which each waiter had an assistant, or *commis*, to take orders and deliver the food, leaving the waiter to preside over the meal and shape the experience for guests, offering the small attentions that made for a memorable evening. Over time, diners would develop close relationships with their waiters. This was a standard feature of dining life at the best restaurants. Adding insult to injury was the national mania for dieting and calorie-counting, reflected in the pencil-thin flapper ideal. Restaurants were put on notice that the grand cuisine of the old century was increasingly a thing of the past.

Many New York restaurant owners and their patrons regarded the new law as a joke, which could explain the lack of drama when Prohibition first came into effect. Kansans might want a republic of virtue, but not New York. French and Italian restaurateurs, in particular, saw Prohibition as a fit of temporary insanity, an experiment in cultural sadism that no civilized diner could long endure. They intended to carry on pretty much as they had before.

They were in for a rude awakening. Some of the most illustrious names in the restaurant world soon found themselves standing in front of a judge, as federal agents raided, and raided again, in the early, aggressive days of Prohibition. One of the first to go was Julius Keller, when agents raided Maxim's and found that liquor was being served. This was hardly a surprise. Maxim's without cocktails and champagne was inconceivable. Keller, along with two waiters and a bartender, was sentenced to a short jail term. Mysteriously, his memoir makes no mention of this episode.

In an impressive show of zeal, federal agents blanketed Broadway in the early 1920s, swooping down on restaurants and cafés. Inevitably, they found what they were looking for. In one assault, on New Year's Eve 1922, five squads hit restaurants, cafés, and cabarets throughout the theater district, arresting more than 150 people. The following spring, cabarets began closing their doors. Slapped with injunctions, Reisenweber's, Shanley's, Murray's, and a host of lesser fry folded forever. In a desperate move to stay solvent, many introduced cover charges of one to three dollars, but it was too late. Diners rebelled. If the entertainment was no longer free, why not go to the theater instead? Postwar wages were also squeezing profits. The dishwasher who earned $25 a month before the war could now earn $25 a week or more. Hotel dining rooms and restaurants, imposing a "Prohibition tax," hiked prices on everything from rolls and butter to filet of sole.

"The Roman Gardens of Murray's are like a classic cemetery," the *Times* reported. "The revolving floor has long since ceased to pulse and thrill. The mirrored walls reflect only the image of the overalled and jumpered caretaker where once they shimmered with the bright hues of Paquin gowns." The current owner, "sitting like a wraith of other days in the ruins of a coliseum," predicted that it was only a matter of time before all the big cabarets folded, and, along with them, every restaurant of note in the city. Murray's premises were taken over by a flea circus (and eventually by a gay brothel, where the over-the-top Roman decor finally made sense).

In 1923, the mighty Delmonico's served its last meal. In a bow to new customs, it had allowed dancing. It even gave afternoon tea dances on its upper floors. But in the last decade of its long, long life, the old place seemed marooned, the sad relic of a gentler, more refined era. Edmund Wilson made a wistful entry in his journals after seeing the FOR RENT sign outside the old place: "No name, no sign, the last stronghold of the old Fifth Avenue. Alec McKaig told me that his aunt from Pittsburgh always used to insist upon eating there; she seemed to have a blind inherited faith in its reliability: if you ate there, you were always safe." Louis Sherry followed soon after, vacating Fifth Avenue and setting up a smaller, much less ambitious restaurant operation on Park Avenue. Henceforth, Sherry's would be associated not with high society but with candies and ice cream.

The Mouquin family tried every possible ruse to dodge the new law, providing newspapers with colorful copy. Old Mouquin had retired in 1900 to his farm in Virginia, leaving the two restaurants in the hands of his sons, Louis C. and Henry F. Mouquin. Louis, faced with the challenge of Prohibition, took a defiant stance. He and his chauffeur became the first citizens arrested for transporting liquor from a city home to a country residence—105 cases of vermouth were intercepted en route from Brooklyn to Mouquin's summer home in Belle Harbor, Long Island.

After Henry closed the downtown restaurant, Louis continued to sell alcohol uptown, a fact not lost on the authorities. In a raid conducted in 1923, agents discovered a secret passageway leading from Mouquin's cellar into an office building that, ironically enough, once served as Federal Prohibition Headquarters. There they came upon nearly a thousand empty wine and liquor bottles.

The uptown Mouquin's closed in August 1925, but Louis was not done yet. With remarkable speed, he established a highly profitable bootlegging syndicate. His traveling salesmen took orders all over the Midwest and then sent them, with payment, to a post office box in New York. Mouquin then shipped the liquor by express rail. Discretion was not a hallmark of the operation. In 1926, the federal authorities dispatched an agent by train to Omaha to look into the matter. As it happened, one of his fellow passengers was a Mouquin salesman, eager for company. In the course of the trip, the agent placed an order for a case of bonded whiskey and listened attentively as the salesman explained the workings of the Mouquin syndicate, at one point showing a list of customers in Omaha, Minneapolis, St. Louis, and other cities. An arrest warrant for Mouquin was issued shortly thereafter.

Mouquin tried to brazen it out. In a spectacular bit of cheek, he appeared at the Federal Building in lower Manhattan to complain that he was the victim of mistaken identity. Either someone with an, admittedly, similar name was at the bottom of this affair, or an imposter was involved. The warrant named Louis A. Mouquin. The man standing in the courtroom was Louis C. Mouquin—obviously a different person, Mouquin's lawyer maintained. The judge remained unmoved. Aside from the very long odds against there being two Louis Mouquins, another problem presented itself. A revenue agent placing an order with one of Mouquin's salesmen had seen the man address a telegram to 454 Sixth Avenue, the address of the uptown Mouquin's.

In a variety of courtrooms, the real story emerged. Rinaldo Micalizio, Mouquin's former chauffeur, testified before an Omaha judge that his onetime boss had ordered him to open a post office box under the name Mike Rinaldo and receive mail for the Mouquin company there. Micalizio, who denied knowing what the mail contained, filed suit against Mouquin for luring him into an illegal scheme under false pretenses. As the heat increased, Louis fled to Paris. The gay Mouquin era was definitively over, although the Mouquin dynasty survived. Henry's wife, Jeanne, had won acclaim for the desserts she supplied to the Sixth Avenue restaurant, and eventually she set up a pastry shop of her own, Henri's. Located next to the Algonquin Hotel, it was much favored by girls from nearby private schools; under different ownership after 1930, it developed into a chic restaurant.

No one could match the record of James Moore, the owner of the popular Dinty Moore's on West Forty-sixth Street. Raids were almost a weekly ritual for Moore, who became something of a folk hero. When agents raided his restaurant on December 9, 1923, for the second time in two weeks, a crowd gathered outside and jeered the police. Moore affected nonchalance. The previous week, after being acquitted on charges of violating the Volstead Act, he sauntered into police headquarters and asked for his liquor back, saying it was "personal stock" for the Christmas holidays. The charade continued for the next decade. At one point, Moore was hauled in after serving drinks to an undercover agent. The agent in question, an attractive twenty-two-year-old named Marjorie Melius (nom de guerre, Miss Meiss), worked as a typist by day, but at night, for a salary of five dollars, she sipped rye highballs for the government. The double life of Miss Meiss made for a thrilling headline.

And so it went. Formerly law-abiding restaurateurs tried to sneak their way past the new law, but soon gave up the fight. Once they tried operating on the square, the iron laws of economics came into effect. Thirsty customers took their business to speakeasies, some of which invested heavily in expensive furnishings and fine food. Others did not but made hefty profits anyway. Before long, one beleaguered restaurateur after another would hang a sign on the door that read CLOSED FOR EXTENSIVE ALTERATIONS AND REDECORATION. The doors never reopened.

For serious diners, this was New York's zero hour—the moment when a century of culinary progress came to a screeching halt. "Broadway has changed," lamented Jack Dunston, before closing down Jack's in 1925. "All the old-timers are gone, dead or scattered. The town is full of cafeterias. Men don't seem to care much for good food, as they did in the old days." The rich retreated to their private dining rooms, where, if they had shown foresight, they drank French wine from personal cellars. The very rich hired private chefs. But the talent pool had shrunk, as restaurant owners soon found out. Tightened immigration laws introduced in 1920 made it much more difficult for French chefs and kitchen workers to come to America, and their numbers had been decimated by the war. For those who remained, what prestige could there be in practicing their art in a restaurant without wine?

The crisis for bartenders was even more acute. Once, the bars in the great hotels and restaurants were waystations on a cocktail route that stretched from Madison Square to the farthest reaches of the Great White Way. Now it was a trail of tears.

Many bartenders left for Europe. Others found work in speakeasies or private country clubs, but the limitations of Prohibition liquor soon took a toll. Bad gin was the universal ingredient, and to accommodate it, cocktails devolved into flavor-smothering drinks that were tossed down fast. It took no great skill to mix rye and ginger ale, or an Alexander, a liquid dessert compounded of gin, cream, and crème de cacao. The bartending art, and decades of creativity, vanished overnight. Genuine artists slipped into the shadows, like the eerie bartender in Fitzgerald's short story "The Rich Boy," whom the narrator spies chilling non-alcoholic champagne in the Plaza Hotel.

The good life and the good times, it seemed, were gone forever. Only the hotels could offer dining in palatial surroundings. Their overhead could be spread among different departments, and their dining business was propelled by the growth of large corporations with multiple divisions. Banquets fit in perfectly with the up-to-date business thinking that encouraged employees in the same firm to mingle, exchange ideas, and develop esprit de corps. The old banquet business, supported by fraternal lodges and social and political organizations, took a new lease on life, as businesses invested heavily in annual meetings and sales conventions.

Times Square, adept at self-reinvention, underwent yet another of its remarkable quick-change acts, shedding one gaudy skin for another in the 1920s. It lowered its sights and pitched its appeal to a broader audience.

The old lobster palaces gave way to enormous new chop suey restaurants. Chinese entrepreneurs were willing to take on the expensive leases that broke the back of the cabarets. With low food overhead and cheap labor, they undercut the nightclubs, offering music and dancing at minimal cover charges. The pioneer was Lee Fook, who had opened the Far East restaurant at Fiftieth Street and Broadway as early as 1917, which put him in an ideal position to reap the benefits from Prohibition. Unlike the cabarets, the Far East and imitators like Chin Lee and the Jardin Royal did a mammoth lunch trade. With meals priced at 55 to 65 cents, they attracted armies of stenographers and salesgirls. Average New Yorkers could easily afford dinners at 75 cents, or $1.75 with show. Lee Fook's second restaurant, the Far East Tea Garden on Columbus Circle, paved the way for the splashy Yeong's, in Churchill's cavernous restaurant. Yeong's, at street level, broke with the practice of placing Chinese restaurants on the second floor, where the rent was cheaper. In another move to capture the public eye, C. M. Joe took over the old Palais Royal at Broadway and Forty-eighth and, after renaming it the Palais d'Or, began offering jazz and a Ziegfeld-style revue. The age of the westernized, modernized Chinese restaurant was off to a flying start.

The mingling of food and entertainment, born in the lobster-palace era, became a permanent fixture of the city's nightlife. In fact, it was hard to say whether diners paid the cost of a meal so they could dance and enjoy the entertainment, or whether they suffered through the entertainment in order to dine. When nightclubs served food, and restaurants offered nightclub entertainment, who could tell which was which?

A talent booker and press agent named Nils Thor Granlund decided that he could make money offering a meal and a cabaret show for $1.50, with no cover charge, if he could fill a large-enough dining room. Backed by the gangster Owney Madden, he enlisted the former manager of the Knickerbocker Hotel's food department to devise a six-course dinner for fifty cents, and then took out a lease on the second floor of the former Rector's, which could seat eight hundred diners without strain.

Granlund put together a top-flight chorus line, hung photographs of film stars and Hollywood sights on the walls, and declared the Hollywood Restaurant ready for business. Customers, timidly peeking in the door, hesitated at first, but once they found that no cover charge meant no cover charge, the money came rolling in. The main attraction was the floor show, anchored by a chorus line of twenty-four dancers dubbed "the most beautiful girls this side of heaven" by the gossip columnist for the *Daily Mirror*. "Epicures, gourmets, and those who just like good food don't go to the Hollywood for the cuisine," one restaurant guide noted. "Soups have been known to refrigerate to an icy temperature and hot entrees to grow cold and soft bread to stale while feverish eyes remain glued to the undraped ladies on the floor."

With the support of another gangster, the quietly lethal Charlie Sherman, Granlund followed up in 1932 with the Paradise, on the second floor of the Brill Building, directly across from the Hollywood. The Viennese Modernist and Ziegfeld designer Joseph Urban, much in demand for the top-end speakeasies, did the interior. Once again, beautiful girls were the attraction. Granlund flew out to California, and, using Busby Berkeley as his talent scout, began rounding up the best-looking dancers money could buy. Thirty pairs of shapely legs proved to be an irresistible draw, and the Paradise, offering "an endless, stupendous, naked floorshow" with a $1.50 dinner served on tables "the size of a poker chip," raised the bar for erotic entertainment on Broadway another couple of notches. The Granlund formula was replicated at the Palais Royal (on the premises of the former Palais d'Or) and the Casino de Paree.

Old-timers wrung their hands. The old Broadway, glamorous and glittering, had sunk to a new low, its pearl-like string of superb restaurants "now a bleak procession of rapid-fire lunches, chain coffee shops and pastry parlors," the syndicated columnist O. O. McIntyre wrote. The transformation was rapid. As early as 1921, *Collier's* magazine, in an article tellingly titled "Broadway Becomes Main Street," complained, "In a street once famous for 'gilded' restaurants, you find today a swarm of middle-class eating places of moderate tariffs, flanked by dairy restaurants, pastry shops, rotisseries, cafeterias, and 'automats.'"

For epicures, Times Square was dead. They were right to shed tears. But the newer, ruder Times Square had its own appeal. The theaters carried on. Broadway still pulsated with energy and life—a different kind of energy and life, and a new cast of characters, lovingly chronicled by a new breed of newspaper columnist in step with the fast Broadway beat. This was Damon Runyon's Broadway, the Technicolor setting for *Guys & Dolls*. It was the Main Stem chronicled by Walter Winchell and a host of violently competitive Broadway columnists writing in telegraphic, staccato prose. Every paper had one, reporting on the stars, the nightlife, the in-jokes, and the show-business scuttlebutt. The manners and the names and the lingo of Broadway were transmitted, in print and over the radio, to an eager audience of millions. The new movers on Broadway gathered at restaurants to exchange gossip, look for work, talk deals, and while away the time until the *Morning Telegraph* hit the streets. Food, in this hectic milieu, was a secondary consideration.

Restaurants like Lindy's, the archetypal show-business canteen, catered to the entertainment industry, but not in the same way that Rector's had. The food and the atmosphere were casual, and Jewish. The waiters bickered with the customers, who bickered back, pretended to be annoyed, and loved every minute of it. Actors and comedians drifted from table to table, greeting friends and trading wisecracks.

Lindy's (thinly disguised by Runyon as Mindy's) opened in 1921 on the east side of Broadway between Forty-ninth and Fiftieth streets. Leo Lindemann, the founder, was the son of a German peddler who apprenticed to a delicatessen owner in Berlin. Leo came to America in 1913, when he was twenty-five, and bused tables at the Hotel Marie Antoinette. After working as a waiter at Feltman's, the big hot dog emporium on Coney Island, he found work at Gertner's, near the Metropolitan Opera House, and married the owner's sister. In 1921, he opened Lindy's, a glorified delicatessen, with a few dishes (gefilte fish, borscht, pickled herring) contributed by his wife.

The sandwiches made the place. The Lindy's Special led the list, a two-hander packed with turkey breast, smoked tongue, Bermuda onions, Swiss cheese, coleslaw, and Russian dressing. There were a host of others, often in unusual combinations, like sturgeon and smoked salmon; turkey breast, pastrami, and chicken fat; or the Tongue Temptation, a layering of tongue, Swiss cheese, tomatoes, and Indian relish. And then there was the cheesecake. No cheesecake on earth could match the cheesecake at Lindy's, for the simple reason that any other cheesecake, whatever its merits, was by definition not from Lindy's.

When Al Jolson and Eddie Cantor, early customers, began touting the restaurant from the stage, Lindemann's fortune was made. Broadway being what it was, the restaurant, along with show-biz headliners, attracted the patronage of a certain Arnold Rothstein, a high-level gangster who decided to make Lindy's his unofficial headquarters. This was bad. Rothstein, the man who fixed the 1919 World Series and served as the model for Meyer Wolfsheim in *The Great Gatsby*, received his minions at Lindy's, listened to their reports, and sent them on their daily rounds. Mrs. Lindemann, in an effort to give Rothstein the slip, took to closing just after midnight. Rothstein simply turned up earlier. Mrs. Lindemann was at her wit's end when Rothstein exited the scene in spectacular fashion, gunned down at the Park Central Hotel for reasons that have never been satisfactorily explained.

In 1930, Lindemann invested heavily in a second restaurant at the northwest corner of Broadway and Fifty-first Street. Business was slow, but fortune smiled. In September 1931, Eugene O'Neill's *Mourning Becomes Electra* opened at the Guild Theater, just a block away. Because the play was six hours long, audiences were released for a dinner intermission, providing a presold clientele for the new Lindy's. And so the legend lived on.

Essentially, Lindy's was a Jewish delicatessen with glorified sandwiches. So was Reuben's, a small delicatessen that its owner, Arnold Reuben, parlayed into a show-business hangout and tourist attraction through his menu of signature sandwiches, each named after a show-business celebrity. At both restaurants, the atmosphere conformed to the New York delicatessen style that evolved slowly over the decades: pastrami, corned beef, turkey, and tongue piled on rye bread, along with soups, knishes, lox, chopped liver, dill pickles, and assorted side dishes. These were brought to the table by waiters of a type unknown at other restaurants, whose sole function was to "frustrate the hungry, intimidate the cautious, and rule the diets of his daily patrons with an iron hand," wrote Ruth Glazer, a delicatessen owner's daughter, in a taxonomy of old-style Jewish delis that she wrote for *Commentary* in 1946.

Manhattan's growing army of clerks and office workers were not looking for entertainment or style during the lunch hour. They wanted an inexpensive meal in pleasant surroundings. For nearly a century, the brisk lunchtime trade had catered to a male clientele. The grubby pie stalls and the "beef and" lunchrooms gave way to the decidedly more appealing Dennett's and Childs chains, but women looking for a modestly priced, welcoming restaurant, rather than a fast-

Arnold Reuben turned his deli into a celebrity hangout by offering overstuffed sandwiches named after Broadway stars of the day.

Reuben's Famous Sandwiches

Imported Unsalted Malossal Caviar	$2.00	Roast Virginia Ham	$ .40
Club a la Reuben	1.00	Roast Beef	.40
Reuben's Special	.85	Prime Rib of Beef	.65
Reuben's Paradise	.85	Spiced Beef	.35
Ina Claire Special	.85	Liver Wurst	.35
Francine Larrimore Special	.85	Liver Wurst and Bermuda Onions	.50
Gladys Feldman Special	.85	Home Boiled Ham	.35
Tartar Sandwich a la Al Jolson	1.00	Home Boiled Tongue	.40
Peggy Joyce Special	.85	Brisket Corned Beef	.35
Reuben's Steak Sandwich	1.00	Salami	.35
Reuben's Superior	.90	Roast Pork	.40
Reuben's Tongue Delite	.65	Imported Swiss Cheese	.35
Marjorie Rambeau Special	.85	Roquefort Cheese	.50
Marilyn Miller Special	.85	Cream Cheese and Bar le Duc	.50
Lilyan Tashman Special	.75	American Cheese	.35
Fay Marbe Special	.75	Camembert Cheese	.50
Reuben's Turkey Sandwich, Russian Dressing	.60	Lake Sturgeon	.65
Roast Virginia Ham and Imported Swiss Cheese	.65	Nova Scotia Salmon	.50
		Anchovy Paste	.40
Turkey and Virginia Ham	.75	Sardellan Butter	.40
Chicken Salad, Russian Dressing	.50	Sardine	.60
Virginia Ham and Egg Sandwich			.75

food convenience stop, were stuck, especially in midtown. Thousands of hungry workers awaited a solution. It was on the way.

The same social changes that were flooding the lunch market with typists and stenographers were also pushing a new breed of restaurateur to the fore— ambitious women who wanted to start their own businesses and understood female tastes. Overnight, they created a new restaurant category, the tearoom. All the big hotels offered afternoon tea, but small, independent restaurants offering tea and a limited menu of light fare did not exist until pioneers like Mary Elizabeth Evans saw a niche and jumped to fill it.

Evans was a determined woman from Syracuse who found her calling the hard way. Her father died when she was quite young, and her grandfather, a judge, left the family some heavily mortgaged property when he died a few years later. With financial ruin looming, Mary Elizabeth, now a teenager, searched desperately for a source of income. Since she and her sisters loved to make candy with their mother, she began selling one-pound boxes to friends. Later she took over a small counter in a downtown Syracuse office building, arranging her wares on a plate. There was no sales staff. Instead, customers were invited to help themselves and leave payment in a wicker tray, making their own change. "Our family lived out of that wicker tray for a year," Evans later recalled.

As the business grew, so did Evans's ambitions. She tried her luck in New York, selling candy in retail stores from counters draped in white dotted-swiss fabric. Even with dozens of employees, she still hewed to the handcrafted approach that allowed her to sell her candies at a premium. She cracked her nuts by hand, rather than buying them in bulk pre-cracked, for example. Sandwiches and cakes followed, as well as more shops. In 1909, she planted her flag on Fifth Avenue, and, in time, the Mary Elizabeth's tearooms achieved legendary status.

"Who does not know this name, synonymous with daintiness and a spick and span installation?" George S. Chappell wrote in *The Restaurants of New York*, one of the earliest restaurant guidebooks. The delights included finger food like marmalade-and-nut sandwiches, cheese-and-olive spread, scones, salmon salad, and diet-defying desserts: chocolate fudge layer cake, marshmallow layer cake, and pineapple-nut ice cream. Like most tearooms, Mary Elizabeth's avoided elaborate cooked dishes, concentrating instead on salads, sandwiches, and baked goods. A lamb fricassee, cheese omelette, or fried filet of sole was about as adventurous as things got in a Mary Elizabeth's kitchen.

Even more extraordinary was the rise of Alice Foote MacDougall. An unlikely business pioneer, MacDougall grew up in a well-to-do family on Washington Square and at twenty-one married a coffee broker with whom she had three children. At the time, the coffee business was divided between "green" coffee wholesalers, who imported the beans but did not roast them, and roasters who did not import. MacDougall thought this was illogical and encouraged her husband to do both. The suggestion amused him. That was "a woman's idea," he told her.

In 1907, her husband died, leaving her with thirty-eight dollars in cash and a business teetering on the brink. After failing to make ends meet by addressing envelopes, MacDougall decided that coffee would have to be her ticket out of genteel poverty. She rented a small office downtown on Front Street near the East River, and bought five pounds of coffee. After roasting and grinding the coffee, she sold it for $1.40, netting seventy cents. MacDougall, at the age of thirty-six, was now a coffee merchant—the only female coffee merchant in town, and not a very successful one, either. Shortly after the war, with the business limping along, MacDougall leased a booth in Grand Central Terminal and opened the Little Coffee Shop as a showcase for her product. At first she sold only coffee, tea, and cocoa, but as time went on she decided that her niche could be "a place of rest and beauty, a little haven to entice the weary commuter." She hung blue silk curtains in the window and arranged brass articles and blue-and-white china next to the coffee bags on the shelves. A percolator exhaled the delicious aroma of freshly brewed coffee. "The setting and the fragrance together began to turn the trick," MacDougall later recalled. "Gradually people came in to buy their pound—or five, or ten—as they dashed for their trains, commuting for dear life. Sometimes they asked to taste my coffee, and before we knew it we were serving coffee from tiny tables and all unconsciously were laying the foundation of the coffee houses."

MacDougall found her way to a multimillion-dollar empire by comparing her own experiences with those of others and then drawing a few useful conclusions. On Front Street, she noticed, it was hard to find a satisfying lunch. The soda fountains were dirty. The restaurants, with their thick china and coarse cotton tablecloths, and the lunchtime cacophony of shouting waiters and crashing dishes, offended both eye and ear. Her secretary, she noticed, ate a single slice of apple pie for lunch. The office boy seemed to subsist on doughnuts. "Gradually," she wrote, "there grew in my heart a real sympathy for the great hungry public that either had to eat like animals at prices they could afford to pay or impoverish themselves to secure a little of the beauty that we all crave as an accompaniment to our food."

The problem had been festering for decades. As far back as the 1890s, women had been entering the workforce in large numbers as stenographers, typists, clerks, and waitresses, creating a new population of dissatisfied lunch customers concentrated in the businesses south of City Hall. So many women workers crowded into one beef-and-beans restaurant on Park Row that it became known as the Typewriters' Exchange. "The proprietors of the downtown restaurants have come to regard their female patrons as an important element, and special pains are taken in many places to cater to the fair lunchers," the *Times* reported in 1890. "While women are not all light eaters, most of them are partial to dainty tid-bits, pastry, and ice cream. Where a man would order a plate of roast beef or spring lamb with peas, a woman would ask for a patty of some kind or the wing of a fowl."

In most areas of the city, however, women searched in vain for an agreeable place to eat. Surely, MacDougall reasoned, there was money to be made in an aesthetically pleasing midpriced restaurant? Indeed there was. An eager clientele awaited, made up of women like Una Golden, the heroine of Sinclair Lewis's novel *The Job*. Una, forced into secretarial work when her father dies, immediately confronts a dining crisis, shared with her wisecracking officemate, Bessie. "Sometimes she lunched at a newspaper-covered desk, with Bessie and the office-boy, on cold ham and beans and some small, bright-colored cakes which the boy brought in from the bakery," Lewis's narrator writes. "Sometimes she had boiled eggs and cocoa at a Childs restaurant with stenographers who ate baked apples, rich Napoleons, and, always, coffee. Sometimes at a cafeteria, carrying a tray, she helped herself to crackers and milk and sandwiches. Sometimes at the Arden Tea Room, for women only, she encountered charity-workers and virulently curious literary ladies, whom she endured for the marked excellence of the Arden chicken croquettes. Sometimes Bessie tempted her to a Chinese restaurant, where Bessie, who came from the East Side and knew a trick or two, did not order chop-suey, like a tourist, but noodles and egg foo-young."

After just a few months at her dead-end job, Una yearns for a restaurant to match her refined sensibilities, something with an artistic touch, and she finds it one day on Sixth Avenue. It's clean, with lace curtains and, between the curtains, a red geranium in a pot tied with a decorative green ribbon. "She entered the new restaurant briskly, swinging her black bag. The place had Personality—the white enameled tables were set diagonally and clothed with strips of Japanese toweling. Una smiled at a lively photograph of two bunnies in a basket. With a sensation of freedom and novelty she ordered coffee, chicken patty, and cocoanut layer-cake."

MacDougall understood the Una Goldens, slaving away at dreary jobs, desperate for a touch of color and a genteel bite to eat at lunchtime. She experienced another brainstorm on a blustery February day in 1921 when a sleet-laden wind forced passersby into Grand Central. Scanning this picture of human misery, MacDougall suddenly thought of hot waffles. She called up her maid and asked her to mix up a pitcher of waffle batter, grab a waffle iron, and rush to the station. In the meantime, MacDougall made up a small sign that read: "Coffee and Waffles, 30 cents." The waffles were an instant hit. MacDougall soon opened a larger store in Grand Central. A year later, she unveiled the Alice Foote Mac-Dougall Coffee House, in the Bar Building on West Forty-third Street.

On a foundation of coffee and waffles, MacDougall built a restaurant business that made her the Martha Stewart of her day. The Forty-third Street coffee shop alone served eight thousand diners a month. Deeply religious, MacDougall believed it was her mission to create loveliness and perfection wherever she walked. "In all you do, in all you think, be beautiful," she advised, applying this gooey philosophy to the food and interior decoration of all her restaurants. The abundant meals of her childhood inspired her, especially the big breakfasts with fruit, oatmeal, hot bread, sausages, buckwheat cakes, and syrup, accompanied by coffee with sugar and "cream we could cut with

Alice Foote MacDougall, the Martha Stewart of the 1920s, created dim, fancifully decorated restaurants like the Cortile that brought a touch of color and beauty to women in the workforce.

a knife." The cuisine was American: consommé vermicelli, poached eggs on toast, broiled chicken with hearts of lettuce, baked potato, baked squash, waffles, baked pears, vanilla ice cream.

By serving smaller portions, she kept costs down. By decorating with taste, she pleased her customers, especially women like herself. "I always think of myself as an average human being in that my wants, my inclinations, my pleasures, and my pains are pretty much those of the rest of the world," she said. "In running my restaurants, I almost invariably shun things which are unpleasant to me and insist upon giving my customers those things that I, myself, want to have."

After a trip to Italy in 1922, MacDougall absorbed a new artistic vocabulary that found its way into three new midtown restaurants: the Cortile, the Piazzetta, and the Firenze, all decorated to resemble rustic Italian streets. The Cortile even had washing hung from overhead balconies, and the waitresses filled their water pitchers from a fountain in the village square. A Spanish-themed restaurant, the Sevillia, followed. All expressed her faith in "the principle of beauty: beauty of surroundings and beauty of service."

Men hated the MacDougall restaurants. Women loved them. "Saturated with quaintness," *The New Yorker* sneered. They were "the paradise of the uptown bridge club, the prosperous Brooklynite, the suburban shopper, the eager sightseer from the hinterland; ladies substantial and ambitious for the better things, whose digestion is aided by a little culture." Lewis Mumford, the great champion of avant-garde restaurant design, regarded the works of MacDougall with despair. With a grand overdecorated flourish, she had turned back the clock on industrial-age triumphs like the Childs lunchrooms.

MacDougall floated serenely above such criticisms. "The extravagances of cubistic and ultramodern art do not seem to me conducive to peace and good digestion," she wrote. "It may be charity to the Russian refugees to eat in a restaurant where wild splashes of red, yellow, and green dart at you from every corner, but I can't think it very restful." At the MacDougall restaurants, "neutral tints and soft colors" prevailed, and tranquil service was provided by "soft-spoken, slow-moving colored women," who evidently picked up the MacDougall tone very quickly. When a rare male diner placed an order and told his waitress to make it snappy, she replied, "You can't be artistic in a hurry." The formula worked. At its zenith in the mid-1920s, the MacDougall empire employed eight hundred waitresses and reported annual revenues of $3 million.

Farther downtown, Frank G. Shattuck also saw possibilities in a midpriced restaurant that offered pleasant surroundings and high-quality food. Shattuck had started out as a traveling salesman for a Brooklyn confectioner, but his life took a sudden turn when he tasted the chocolates of a competitor, Schrafft's. It was love at first bite. He raced to the company's offices in Boston and offered to sell its candies on commission. Shattuck had more faith in the product than Schrafft's did. He believed that the candy could be sold on its own, in a store bearing the Schrafft's name. When Schrafft's disagreed, he went ahead and

opened a Schrafft's store on his own, across from the New York Herald Building at Thirty-sixth and Broadway. The renegade store incorporated his pet ideas about the importance of counter display, wrapping, and freshness but did not really find its footing until the arrival of his sister Jane, who managed the first store while her brother sold candy on the road. It was Jane who came up with the idea of selling tearoom food as well as candy. Soon customers could have ice cream, cake, and sandwiches at the store's soda fountain. In time, a more substantial menu evolved, which Jane supervised until her retirement in 1933.

Shattuck guessed, correctly, that diners would pay a premium for higher-quality ingredients and agreeable surroundings. At local markets, the company advertised its commitment to quality by having merchants put a RESERVED FOR SCHRAFFT'S sign on their best fruit, vegetables, and meat. From the outset, the company imposed a rigorous system of testing new dishes, essentially letting cooks at the various branches compete with one another.

Over the years, Schrafft's became famous for its cheese bread, grilled sandwiches, and ice cream sundaes. On this 1919 menu, the house style is already evident.

Lunchtime diners crowd a Fifth Avenue Schrafft's in 1954. The chain began as a candy store in 1898 and evolved into a dining empire with a feminine tone.

The best version earned a place on the menu after being tasted by the management, and the winning chef was then sent on tour to the other Schrafft's stores as a temporary instructor. The system worked. Some of the chain's signatures, like its cheese bread, became culinary classics.

To keep the tables turning quickly, Shattuck created a special hostess system. A chief hostess would greet guests and then signal the size of the party to an assistant hostess in the middle of the dining room. The assistant hostess, after signaling back information on table availability, would then escort the party to the proper table and point out their waitress. During peak hours, strangers would be seated together to fill a table. In 1912, Shattuck introduced a form of air-conditioning using multiple fans, an innovation he trumpeted in signs

Schrafft's was beloved by women for its light entrees and rich desserts, like the cakes being frosted at its Rockefeller Center restaurant in 1948.

that read: "The air in our shop and luncheon room is changed every eight minutes; in our kitchen it is changed every four minutes." He hired college students to wait tables at night, believing that they added a wholesome tone and youthful enthusiasm. Most unusually, he insisted on promoting women to management jobs. "I have found them good in executive positions," he said. "They are conscientious and efficient in detail work." At Schrafft's, women led the food, candy, and advertising departments.

By 1913, Schrafft's had opened eight stores in New York. It also operated an unusual in-house restaurant in the Mutual Life Building on Nassau Street, where the company's 550 employees ate their lunch in twenty-minute shifts between noon and 1:00 p.m. By 1923, there were seventeen Schrafft's locations in New York and another five in other cities. By the end of the decade, the company was earning $3.5 million on annual sales of $20 million.

The chain aimed squarely at a female clientele. "The 50 cent and 75 cent luncheons are useless to any male with an appetite," a disgusted (male) restaurant critic wrote in 1934. His opinion mattered not a whit. Over its long life, Schrafft's, like the Automat, became an institution. Dependable and genteel, even though it served cocktails, it was the official dining spot for New York women of a certain class and a godsend for any mother who wanted to take her child to lunch or dinner before a show. Like the Automat, it was regularly featured in *The New Yorker*, where the cartoonist Helen Hokinson depicted the typical Schrafft's customer as a plump uptown matron wearing a tiny outlandish hat—the sort of woman, one journalist wrote, who "would nibble on a lettuce sandwich and then devour a chocolate nut sundae submerged under an atomic cloud of whipped cream." When a man was murdered in a Schrafft's in 1951, the shocking thing was not the crime but the location. "They're so damned respectable," exclaimed one patron. "You can drink four martinis and fall over on your face and still feel respectable."

Tearooms, coffee shops, and waffle shacks spread throughout midtown, as competitors followed the lead of Mary Elizabeth and Alice Foote MacDougall. Most catered to women, from well-to-do shoppers down to harried office workers, and they came in every conceivable variety. The Hawaiian craze of the 1920s, which introduced Americans to the ukulele, the surfboard, and the pineapple, brought forth a tearoom, Ka Lana o Hawaii (Torch of Hawaii). Sanka, to advertise its coffees, opened several shops, and the Fifties were infested with small restaurants like the Cabin, Aunt Polly's, the Golden Rod, Le Hibou, and the Kangaroo, "neat, cleanly little places, with painted furniture, gingham tablecloths, and serving maids in attractive costumes," according to George Chappell. Like the MacDougall coffee shops, they offered a quaint decorating theme along with dishes or needlework for sale. Chappell particularly liked the Double Door Tea Room, just west of Fifth Avenue on Fifty-first Street, with its bamboo hangings and tropical screens. A little farther downtown, near the big department stores, shoppers could break up the day at the Cosy, the Chimney Corner, the Fernery, the Colonia, and At the Sign of the Green Parrot. The old beanery of the last century had given birth to daughters.

The theater critic George Jean Nathan spied another trend unfolding in the 1920s—sandwiches. "As little as a half dozen years ago the sandwich industry occupied a position of relatively small importance in the American economic and social history," Nathan wrote. "Today it has become one of the leading industries of this country, taking precedence over soda-water, candy, chewing gum, and the *Saturday Evening Post*." Almost unnoticed, the simple ham sandwich of yesteryear had spawned offspring without number, some of them passing strange. With great assurance, Nathan insisted that in the 1890s, eight sandwiches accounted for the entire repertoire: Swiss cheese, ham, sardine, liverwurst, egg, corned beef, roast beef, and tongue. Writing in 1926, a year in which New York City boasted no fewer than 5,215 shops specializing in sandwiches, Nathan cited the official-sounding number of 926 as the grand total for modern sandwich varieties and proceeded to name a fair percentage of them. In addition to the now classic tuna fish and chicken salad, the list included sandwiches made with Bermuda onion and parsley, pig's knuckle and horseradish, lamb mousse, and fruit salad and snails. Add Lindy's and Reuben's to the list, and the sandwich universe took on awe-inspiring dimensions. Is it possible that anyone ever ate a watermelon and pimento sandwich? Perhaps.

The tearoom cult was not limited to the ladies who lunch. Astonishingly, it took hold in Greenwich Village, the official headquarters of New York's ever-roving Bohemia. By 1910, the French in the neighborhood had been almost entirely displaced by Italians, whose cheap table d'hôte restaurants, as we have seen, lured hungry journalists and artists almost as soon as they opened their doors. They came to eat, and they stayed, attracted by cheap rents, the laissez-faire atmosphere, and the cozy geography—before Sixth and Seventh avenues were extended southward, Greenwich Village consisted entirely of crooked little streets that made it a world apart. In the years leading up to the First World War, the Village swarmed with painters, sculptors, political radicals, journalists, suffragettes, and independent thinkers who made it the national capital of eccentricity, free love, and revolutionary politics.

Naturally, the Villagers ate at Villagey sorts of places. The Brevoort and the Lafayette (the old Hotel Martin) kept the French flag flying, and inevitably attracted the patronage of artists flush from a recent sale of their work. But most days of the week, the Village dined at little Italian red-ink restaurants like Bertolotti's, Baroni's, or Gonfarone's, or at the slightly more elevated Enrico and Paglieri's on Eleventh Street, a relative newcomer that offered an open-air garden and Italian cuisine a cut above the usual fifty-cent table d'hôte. "What restaurants do you have that to compare is / With the cool garden back of Paglieri's?" wrote John Reed in a bit of doggerel. "I challenge you to tell me where you've et / Viands more rare than at the Lafayette!"

Greenwich Village specialized in eccentric tearooms and goofy restaurants like the Village Barn, where city slickers could get on the floor for a square dance and whoop and holler to their hearts' content.

The quintessential Village restaurants, however, were absurdist tearooms like Polly's, the Purple Pup, the Wigwam, and the Mad Hatter. Polly's ruled the roost. Officially it was the Greenwich Village Inn, but its owner, the anarchist Paula ("Polly") Halladay, infused it with her outsize personality. Halladay plunged into radical politics at the Liberal Club soon after breezing into town from Evanston, Illinois. In 1913, she opened a restaurant underneath its headquarters on MacDougal Street, where her husband, the Czech anarchist Hippolyte Havel, sent out shockingly good food from the kitchen. Polly extended easy credit and scored a resounding success with a loose formula that included dancing, poker games, and late-night arguments. Perhaps finding the Liberal Club too timid for her tastes, she moved to Sheridan Square in 1918 and created the Greenwich Village Inn (where the then-unknown Stuart Davis painted the sign outside). Her partner and manager was Barney Gallant, who made history of sorts when he became the first New Yorker to be arrested for violating the Volstead Act.

Sheridan Square was infested with tearooms, twee restaurants, and "goofy clubs." A Smith College graduate named Mary Alletta Crump—"Crumpy" to her friends—operated the Crumperie on the square in 1916, serving "crumpled" eggs, toasted sponge cake, pea soup, and peanut butter sandwiches. For entertainment, Crumpy would play the ukulele and sing folk songs. Nearby, a former art student named Don Dickerman created the Pirate's Den, where guests knocking at the door would be greeted by a pirate in full regalia, including eye patch and cutlass. A treasure map spread out on a table, a dead man's chest, and an ancient macaw named Robert added to the atmosphere, which the police found less than amusing. After hearing testimony that the Pirate's Den "reeked of riotous revel," a judge approved a dispossess order, forcing Dickerman to move to Christopher Street in 1918. There, his troubles continued. On February 21, 1922, a squad of policemen raided the Pirate's Den and stripped the waiters of two flintlock pistols, one cutlass, and a sword. The meek performance by Dickerman's pirate crew gave the newspapers a field day. In truth, the Pirate's Den was good, clean, sophomoric fun, with jazz bands performing on the "decks" of three pirate ships, and diners ordering from a prosaic menu of steak, chicken, and sandwiches, along with a few novelty drinks—the Black Skull Punch and the Pirate Cocktail.

Foolish fun was the order of the day at the Village Barn. Here, patrons play musical chairs in 1947.

Edith Unger, a wealthy sculptor, ran the Mad Hatter tearoom in a basement on West Fourth Street. Patrons descended through the Rabbit Hole and surrendered to the zany atmosphere, carefully contrived. A sign on the wall read: "I'm Mad, You're Mad, You must be or You wouldn't have come here." Come they did, especially tourists eager for a chance to see the funny Village people they had been reading about. At the Pepper Pot, also on West Fourth Street, Timothy Felter, known as Tiny Tim, strolled from table to table selling his "soul candies," each wrapped in a bit of paper inscribed with one of his poems. Felter, a winsome lad who wore a floppy artist's tie, advertised his product in local magazines with the plaintive question, "Have You a Soul?" Customers were assured that in every piece of candy "there is an inspiration for you." If there is one thing that a certified Village character could not abide, it was another Village charac-

"MAIN DECK"
THE PIRATE'S DEN
8 CHRISTOPHER ST.
GREENWICH VILLAGE ~ NEW YORK CITY

At the Pirate's Den near Sheridan Square in the Village, the waiters had their cutlasses confiscated when the police raided in 1922.

ter. Bobby Edwards, who created "futuristic ukeleles" out of cigar boxes, took dead aim at Tiny Tim in one of his celebrated doggerel verses:

> *Tiny Tim, all dressed in white,*
> *Makes the uptown suckers bite.*
> *Makes nice candy, never stale,*
> *Mixes it in the garbage pail.*

Even crueler, a dogged newspaper reporter tracked Wee Tim to his home and filed a scandalized report. "He dwells not in quarters over the Coal Hole," the reporter wrote, "nor in mysterious lodgings above the saffron-and-blue painted barn doors, nor up rickety staircases where are anarchist printing presses and Russian cigarettes." No, Tiny Tim, it was revealed, lived in the Seventies, where he had a wife, and children who attended a good private school.

The Village put on a spirited show, but the reviews were harsh. No sooner had the artists taken up residence than journalists began pining for the "old" Village and the Bohemia of yesteryear, which, in its time, had inspired the same laments. Bohemia—the "real" thing—is always yesterday, when the real artists lived and loved spontaneously, unlike their phony successors. James L. Ford had made the complaint in a humorous sketch, "Bohemia Invaded," back in 1895, describing the stockbrokers who had ruined the atmosphere at the little old Italian restaurants, laughing too loudly, overtipping, and staring at the Bohemians as if they were animals in the zoo.

It is certainly true that the new Bohemia enjoyed something the old did not—extensive press coverage. Unlike the scribblers and philosophizers at Clapp's, who lived their Bohemian lives unobserved, the artists and radicals of the Village strutted across a brightly illuminated stage. Propagandizers like Anna Alice Chapin, in her 1917 book *Greenwich Village*, carefully explained the curiosities of the neighborhood to a broad audience, emphasizing the harmlessness of the natives and the delicious quaintness of their ways.

In no time, the tour buses began rolling. Another Bohemia ruined.

12

The Restaurant Gets Small

The big restaurant of New York is a thing of the past," George Chappell wrote in *The Restaurants of New York*. "The Sherry's and Delmonico's of an earlier day are gone." Chappell's 1925 guidebook began with a nostalgic chapter lamenting the vanished restaurants of a bygone age—one that had ended just five years earlier. Surveying a landscape swept bare by Prohibition, and shedding a discreet tear over the great names, Chappell then led his readers toward the smaller French restaurants that had taken their place, especially along Park Avenue.

Park Avenue today is synonymous with wealth. But when Sherry's and Delmonico's were in their glory, the street was an eyesore. Trains rolled from Grand Central through an open cut, spewing smoke as they traveled northward through the Forties and all the way uptown. Not until the lines were electrified after the turn of the century did the street shed its grim institutional buildings, depots, and factories. As late as 1914, Shaefer operated a brewery on Park Avenue in the Fifties. But as the smoke cleared, the avenue changed. Before long, Park Avenue was lined with high-priced apartment houses, and tony restaurants began popping up along its side streets. Intimate and expensive, restaurants like the Marguery, Pierre's, and L'Aiglon lured the carriage trade with their French cuisine, elegant interiors, and suave maître d's. All of them followed the lead of two brothers from Vienna, Alfons and Otto Baumgarten, pioneers of a genre known as "the bijou apartment restaurant."

The Baumgartens, long since forgotten, deserve a place in New York's restaurant history if only for their visionary collaboration with the Modernist painter and designer Winold Reiss. At the Crillon, and later at Henry Lustig's Longchamps chain, Reiss created some of the city's most visually daring and forward-looking restaurants, real showcases for the latest in European design.

The partnership was pure happenstance. The Baumgartens grew up in the restaurant trade: their father and his father before him had been restaurateurs. After training at the Ritz in Paris and the Carlton in London, they made their way to New York in 1908, where Otto found work at the Plaza Hotel, first as a busboy in the restaurant, later as secretary to the restaurant manager. He then spent time at the Ritz-Carlton, where an inventive chef named Louis Diat was making a name for himself by giving a French twist to American ingredients. (One of his characteristic inventions was a mélange of turkey and stewed corn that he dubbed turkey hash Washington.) In 1913, Otto Baumgarten struck out on his own and took his brother along.

Otto and Alfons decided that the city needed an antidote to the big, bustling restaurants that dominated fine dining. As luck would have it, Alfons, returning from a trip to Europe, struck up a shipboard acquaintance with Reiss, fresh from his studies at Vienna's Royal Academy of Art and the School of Applied Arts. A wholehearted proponent of Viennese Modernism, the German Blaue Reiter painters, and primitive art, he was on his way to America with a portfolio full of fresh ideas about graphics and interior design.

The German artist and designer Winold Reiss gave the Longchamps chain a go-ahead Modernist look evidenced in their eye-catching menus.

Between 1913 and 1919, the Baumgartens, with a Swiss partner by the name of Max Haering, opened three midtown restaurants that became known as the Inner Three.

Reiss's 1950 design for the Longchamps at the Manhattan House (*top*) and his proposed bar and roof garden for the Longchamps at Madison Avenue and Forty-ninth Street (1941).

The pricey Voisin, which opened in 1913 in a basement on Park Avenue at Fifty-third Street, epitomized French formality and became renowned for its flawless, if stiff, service. The Elysée, just east of Fifth Avenue on Fifty-sixth Street, followed in 1918. In 1919, after selling Voisin and the Elysée to their employees, the Baumgartens unveiled their masterpiece, the Crillon, on Park Avenue near Forty-eighth Street. Together, the Inner Three created a style for upper-class dining perfectly attuned to the modern era.

At the Crillon, Reiss dazzled New York with its first Modernist restaurant interior, dominated by bright, prismatic colors—emerald green, ultramarine, and Chinese red—and a motif of stylized birds and flowers treated almost as graphic elements. Instructed by Otto Baumgarten to create "a restaurant that would have none of the earmarks of the conventional restaurant," Reiss broke with the severe spatial organization that made so many traditional restaurants look like meeting halls or refectories. He placed dining areas on different levels, imparting a sense of drama, and created intimate corners and niches. The landlord took one look and recoiled at what he called its "crazy Greenwich Village décor." The smart set loved it. Lunch at the Crillon was "the deb's delight." Next door was another Baumgarten enterprise, the Viennese Bonbonniere, also designed by Reiss, and when Robert Hirsch, the Elysée's maître d', grew restless, he added his own exclusive, if unofficial, restaurant to the Inner Three. Robert's, as it was called, gained renown for its lush, shoe-swallowing rose carpet, its Art Moderne interior with Peter Arno murals, and dishes like pheasant choucroute and sweetbreads à la Eugénie.

Small, exclusive dining spots were the wave of the future. But in the midst of Prohibition, New York did make room for one grand restaurant. It was the Central Park Casino, a throwback to the old lobster palaces, and in its brief heyday it epitomized everything that was right, and wrong, about New York in the 1920s. A glorious disgrace, it was the shining centerpiece to the administration of New York's most flamboyant and corrupt mayor, Jimmy Walker.

There was a Casino before the Casino. When plans were drafted for Central Park, Calvert Vaux designed a building, in the style of a country house, that was originally intended as little more than an ice cream parlor, a respectable place where unescorted women could stop for a treat. In time, the Ladies' Refreshment Saloon, as it was known, evolved into a full-fledged restaurant serving both men and women. It was intended, in part, to solve the growing problem of litter left behind by basket parties. Despite the name, gambling was never a part of the formula; rather, "casino" was intended to suggest the Italian word for "little house."

The Casino, on Seventy-second Street near the Fifth Avenue entrance to the park, was situated on a knoll just behind the Mall bandstand. It was one of the few restaurants in New York that offered outdoor dining. Older residents recalled it fondly as a summer destination in the days of the hansom cab. From the Wisteria Pergola, at the western end of the Casino site, diners could listen to the Wednesday- and Saturday-afternoon concerts on the Mall below. In the summer, food and drink from the Casino were served on tables set up under the archway leading to the Bethesda Terrace. "It is a quaint place with a Victorian flavor," Chappell wrote, "interesting in contrast to the modernity which almost invariably surrounds us."

The city owned the Casino and leased it for a modest fee. Its fortunes brightened in 1896, when two French brothers, Gustave and Ernest Dorval, took over the lease and turned the Casino into a first-rate French restaurant. Gustave was a known quantity. He had opened the Café Savarin in the Equitable Building, one of the city's best French cafés. Together, he and his brother expanded the Casino, adding a glass-enclosed veranda that could be heated in winter and opened up in summer. They put the emphasis on outdoor dining in an effort to compete with the roof gardens and sidewalk cafés elsewhere in the city. Showing great flair, the Dorvals painted the walls of the main dining room Bohemian red, their tribute to the color used in the new wing of the Metropolitan Museum of Art.

Originally called the Ladies Refreshment Saloon, Calvert Vaux's Casino in Central Park became a fancy French restaurant and, after a makeover by the Viennese designer Joseph Urban in the 1920s, an exclusive retreat for Mayor Jimmy Walker and his cronies.

With the passing of the Dorvals after the First World War, however, the Casino entered a sad period of decline, much like the rest of the park, which Walker pledged to rescue as he made his pitch to the voters during the 1925 mayoral campaign. One terrific improvement, he decided, would be a spiffy new restaurant where he and his cronies—a blend of socialites and Tammany politicians and, not least, Walker's latest paramour, the musical-comedy actress Betty Compton—"could entertain without being molested." Compton, a contemporary would recall, "was reminiscent of a morello cherry, that seasonally late, dark red variety which is ripe, sweet, and luscious." Walker found her so, and to enjoy her company in the right surroundings, he proposed a semiprivate club subsidized by the taxpayer.

The idea did not come out of thin air. By chance, Walker had run into a certain Sidney Solomon at the races at Saratoga in 1925, a man to whom he owed a favor—a big favor, in Walker's mind, because Solomon had introduced the clothes-conscious mayor to his tailor. Walker asked if there was something he could do in return. "I'd like to take over the old Casino in Central Park and make it an outstanding restaurant instead of the shanty it is now," Solomon told him.

Solomon, a former hotelier and dress manufacturer, was in fact the front man for the Dieppe Corporation, a group of twenty-eight socialite investors led by Anthony J. Drexel Biddle, Jr., who, casting his eyes over Central Park one day while dining on the St. Regis Roof, decided that the Casino could use a major face-lift. With the right renovations, he reasoned, it could be developed into a smart club, a gathering place for social leaders and bon vivants like himself. Walker immediately saw the genius of the plan.

At the time, the Casino was run by Carl F. Zittel, better known as the publisher of a Broadway sheet called *Zit's Theatrical Weekly*. He had taken over the restaurant from the Dorvals, but the lease was due to expire in 1928. Zittel was eager to renew, but the deck was stacked against him. The Dieppe Corporation, made up of names like Ziegfeld, Zukor, Vanderbilt, and Hearst, outweighed him in power and influence by several orders of magnitude.

In what turned out to be one of the great deals in restaurant history, Solomon secured the franchise for an annual rent of $8,500. The amount was not, on the face of it, outrageous. The Dorvals and Zittel had paid a similar amount. But when rumors started circulating that Solomon had been offered $12,000 a year just for the coat-check concession, his lease began to look like a steal, which it was. His yearly rent turned out to be equivalent to less than a single summer night's receipts.

The Casino was intended to be "a place for the fashionable and fastidious," Biddle told reporters, an architectural gem where the mayor could entertain, in proper style, visiting heads of state, royalty, statesmen, war heroes, and champion athletes, not to mention people like Biddle and his friends. "We feel that New York needs a dining place around which the cultured life of the city can rotate," he said.

Solomon pulled out all the stops, investing a reported $400,000 in renovations. This lavish budget was put at the disposal of the Viennese genius Joseph Urban, one of Biddle's dining partners on the St. Regis Roof, who was encouraged to do his utmost. Urban was well known for his sets for the Ziegfeld Follies and was much in demand among rich hoodlums to design top-class speakeasies like the Park Avenue Club. The Casino project fired his imagination, especially the challenge of creating a modern restaurant and nightclub in a quasi-rustic setting. Rising to the occasion, Urban ingeniously blended city and forest in his design. Throughout, stylized leaves alluded to the trees and gardens outside while keeping the overall effect thoroughly up-to-date. In the Black and Gold Room, with its enormous dance floor, black glass and gold murals struck a sophisticated note. The terrace room was extended to accommodate a tentlike dining pavilion. A rooftop fountain kept the Casino cool.

Walker spent so much time inspecting his Xanadu that Governor Franklin D. Roosevelt could rarely find the mayor of New York. No wonder. The mayor was a man obsessed. When he decided that the entryway did not give René Black, the maître d' (formerly of Café Martin and Sherry's, and known as the "master of forty sauces"), a clear view of arriving parties, he had it done over at great cost.

Urban, for his part, mesmerized the press with lofty pronouncements about his design. "In the ballroom," he declared, "the line of the mural composition is like the wave of a conductor's baton beginning dance music, while dim reflections in the black glass ballroom ceiling give space and movement to the life of the room." In the Pavilion, he told furiously scribbling reporters, the decor was inspired by "the freshness of spring flowers and joyousness of a wind among young leaves." New Yorkers were not sure what to make of all this, but it seemed pretty clear that the city was getting a swell new place.

Nearly 2,500 people competed for the six hundred seats available on the Casino's opening night in June 1929, putting unbearable pressure on a screening committee charged with whittling down the guest list. "Tears and threats of suicide failed to swerve the committee," the *Herald Tribune* noted, describing the opening-night invitees as "the shock troops of New York society, official, and night life."

It was a gala event, nervously monitored by a team of detectives on the alert for gate-crashers and worried that Zittel might stage a protest. The staff was also told to keep a sharp eye out for a certain Urbain J. Ledoux, aka Mr. Zero, a well-known provocateur who, in an annual ritual, tried to shame the rich by leading a group of impoverished war veterans down Fifth Avenue in the Easter Parade.

Neither Zittel nor Zero disturbed the revels, as the cream of New York society (but not the mayor) dined on caviar des Grands Ducs, frivolités Escoffier, boneless chicken Armenonville, and a truly sinful entrée: scalloped lobster layered with foie gras and enrobed in a truffled Mornay sauce.

Seasoned restaurateurs predicted that the Casino would never recoup its costs. They were wrong. It earned a profit of $300,000 in its first three months of operation, and, when a scandalized city finally looked at the books after the Casino's closing, five years later, it turned out that the place had netted $3 million over its short life. High prices and high demand added up to success. After paying a cover charge of $3 ($5 after 11:00 p.m., and $6 on Saturdays), diners could expect to pay $2 for a bottle of soda water and prices for food that gave the restaurant one of the highest per-check averages in the country, $3.65 at lunch and $5.80 at dinner. The kitchen was run by Frederic Beaumont, formerly of the Plaza, and his brother Gabriel, formerly a chef at the British embassy in Vienna and a private chef to Louis Rothschild. They served dishes like green turtle delicioso, braised beef tongue with "italienne noodles polonaise," and sautéed breast of chicken à la parisienne. To justify the expense, Solomon installed two top-class orchestras. Emil Coleman played in the Black and Gold Room, while in the tented pavilion Leo Reisman held sway, broadcasting a "Casino Hour" over the radio. When Reisman demanded more money, Solomon replaced him with his pianist, Eddie Duchin, who went on to become a New York institution.

Right-thinking New Yorkers recoiled at Walker's vanity project, unimpressed with Biddle's insistence that the Casino was the Dieppe Corporation's gift to the city and in no way a private club. "It's a new seizure by royalty of the city's property," fumed John Hylan, Walker's predecessor as mayor. Zittel, when he first got wind of the renovations, and the prices, spluttered in indignation.

"Take a taxicab and go up and look at it yourself and see what they've done," he told a reporter. "Can you imagine a ballroom of black glass and anybody wanting to get in with his wife for a pint of ice cream? Can you imagine us getting in? Can you?" Newspapers tut-tutted in editorials. The *Times*, in particular, took a dim view of the shenanigans at the Casino. The flaunting of wealth in a sylvan setting that, by law, belonged to the people of New York struck the newspaper as unseemly: "To let Sir Gorgeous Midas and Lady Midas loose there to wreak their mistaken ideas of elegance and notoriety would be like plumping down an overdressed and hideously bejeweled woman alongside a shepherdess." Fiorello La Guardia, breathing fire, denounced it as "a whoopee joint."

The Casino's atmosphere was rich. When Walker appeared, with Betty on his arm, the orchestra would break into "Will You Love Me in December as You Do in May?" a Tin Pan Alley tune for which the mayor had composed the lyrics in earlier days. Although liquor was not on the menu, it was near to hand, in limousines parked outside, ready for mixing with those two-dollar bottles of soda. Walker, whatever his faults, tipped big, to Solomon's dismay. Big tips spoiled the musicians. Once, when Walker had left a hundred-dollar bill with the orchestra, Solomon asked him why. Walker, nonplussed, said, "Because I like to do such things." Besides, that was the Casino style. One party spent a record-setting $2,700 at dinner one night. An insurance executive routinely cashed checks for $10,000 and then tipped the orchestra $1,000 before racking up staggering bills, sometimes spending up to $300 on caviar alone. When the market crashed in 1929, he owed the Casino $7,000, which Solomon never collected: the restaurant's favorite customer committed suicide.

The Casino itself disappeared almost as dramatically as the caviar king. In its heyday, it was a stomping ground for big-time columnists like Walter Winchell, O. O. McIntyre, Louis Sobol (Winchell's replacement at the *Evening Graphic*), Mark Hellinger, and Ed Sullivan. Not until the Stork Club arrived did a restaurant command so much newspaper ink. But when Walker departed the mayor's office in disgrace, the future of his pet project became doubtful. The new men in City Hall included a pugnacious parks commissioner named Robert Moses, who loathed the very ground that Walker trod upon. Turning his smoldering gaze directly on the Casino, Moses filed suit to oust the restaurant and its management. At the same time, in a slap to Walker, he devised a replacement restaurant in the quaint old stone sheepfold across from Sheep Meadow. This, too, involved an eviction. Two hundred Southdown sheep were moved to Prospect

Park, and their shepherd was reassigned to the Central Park Zoo. The sheep-fold, built in 1870, was transformed into Tavern on the Green. And then came the coup de grâce. In May 1936, Moses razed the Casino. In the blink of an eye, Walker's glittering palace was reduced to dust and rubble.

The Casino failed to outlive its era, but other restaurants did. Quietly, in the semilegal shadows, Prohibition was nurturing an alternative world that would eventually give New York some of its most famous restaurants and nightclubs. In the Village, for instance, it was widely known that not everything poured into the teacups was tea, especially at a popular little place called the Red Head.

The Red Head was not much to look at. Sitting in the shadow of the Sixth Avenue El, near Fourth Street, it offered the minimum in creature comforts and interior decoration: a few wooden tables and chairs beneath an embossed tin ceiling. On the wall sconces, the parchment lightshades were decorated with the silhouette of a flapper with red hair, hence the name of this modest tearoom-saloon, which would evolve into one of New York's most celebrated restaurants: the '21' Club.

'21' was the nearly accidental creation of two college kids from the Lower East Side. In 1922, Jack Kriendler was a twenty-four-year-old pharmacology student at Fordham University. His cousin Charlie Berns, a recent graduate of New York University's School of Commerce, had his sights set on law school. Tough, ambitious, and smart, both cousins came from Austrian-Jewish immigrant families that had scratched and scrambled to get a foothold in America. Jack's uncle let the two boys earn a little college money by working at his speakeasy on the Lower East Side. The more they worked, the less appealing college seemed. Prohibition had turned New York into a gold mine. Jack wanted in on the action.

Opportunity knocked when a Wall Street friend of Jack's accepted a run-down coffee shop as payment for a debt. He needed a partner to manage the place. Jack borrowed a thousand dollars from relatives, bought into the new business, and enlisted Charlie as his business brains. Jack had a pretty good idea of what college students wanted, and it turned out that what the college kids liked, plenty of journalists and Bohemians did, too. "It wasn't the usual speak where people silently packed down the hooch," recalled Pete Kriendler, Jack's younger brother. "Jack ran the Red Head like a fraternity room." It was "a jivey, jazzy place, good clean fun—everyone dancing the Charleston, playing practical jokes, and shouting 'Nerts to you.'"

The old Jack's and Shanley's crowd, uprooted from Times Square, drifted downtown. Young women flocked to the Red Head, too. The moment Prohibition came into force, the days of sex-segregated drinking ended, one of many social barriers to fall in the 1920s. Women were out to have a good time, and for once there was little to stop them. The flapper was unleashed, her doings wittily chronicled by writers like Anita Loos and Lois Long, *The New Yorker*'s "Lipstick." The Red Head was just their kind of place. Pete, a smitten teenager at the time, recalled the female clientele as "nice girls from uptown, boarding-school types, who thought it was the cat's meow to paint their faces and take the El or the double-decker Fifth Avenue bus downtown to roam the Village tearooms and speaks, without guys to escort them."

The cover charge was fifty cents, and the alcohol, packaged in small flasks, sold for a dollar an ounce. Patrons drank from teacups, using grape juice or ginger ale as a mixer. The menu consisted of sandwiches in three styles: ham, cheese, or ham and cheese. On weekends, Jack and Charlie's, as everyone called the Red Head, served steak and eggs. The cousins had excellent sources for their liquor and cordial relations with the police. At this point, whatever enthusiasm the police and federal agents once had for enforcing Prohibition had evaporated, so operators like Jack and Charlie could operate undisturbed. All they had to do was count the money.

Within three years, Jack and Charlie moved into a larger place across the street called the Fronton, where they established a more subdued atmosphere, upgraded the kitchen, and began attracting an older, more stylish clientele, the kind of power brokers who would later crowd into '21.' The chief ornament at the Fronton was none other than Jimmy Walker, often accompanied by the immaculately tailored Grover Whalen, the city's official greeter and parade organizer. The new and improved Jack and Charlie's, with its selective admission policy and emphasis on well-prepared food, soon set itself apart from thousands of other speakeasies around the city. In 1926, the city announced plans to raze the Fronton and surrounding buildings to make way for a new subway line, a seeming setback that turned out to be a blessing in disguise. Jack and Charlie were more than ready to make the move to midtown.

The two partners leased a handsome town house with an iron gate at 42 West Forty-ninth Street. They named it the Puncheon Grotto, hired an Alsatian chef named Henri Geib, and, sticking to the same philosophy that had made the Fronton a success, operated the place as a fine restaurant with drinks and a wine list rather than as a booze dispensary. The ham and cheese sandwiches of the

Red Head gave way to saddle of lamb, petite marmite, pressed duck, and bouil-labaisse—at top prices. Like many other speakeasies, the Puncheon served spaghetti, but its version had black truffles in the tomato sauce.

Jack and Charlie's soon became a favorite with Robert Benchley and the Algonquin Roundtable. Yale students adopted it as their weekend oasis. The high-toned, fun-seeking element that once patronized the cabarets, and would soon be known as "café society," discovered Jack and Charlie's and gave it a ringing endorsement. Assorted Vanderbilts and other upper-crusters decided that they liked the cut of Jack's jib. Many of them donated lawn jockeys with their personal racing colors—the same jockeys that stand outside the '21' Club today. As time went on, the ranks of the socially prominent were reinforced by the kind of high-powered businessmen who still prop up the price list at '21.'

The new Rockefeller Center displaced Jack and Charlie yet again, but at the end of 1929 the cousins were able to buy a town house at 21 West Fifty-second Street for $130,000. This was a princely sum in the days after the Wall Street crash, but the two partners now had a firm grip on a certain class of New Yorker. Jack and Charlie's '21,' as the new restaurant was called, was not, strictly speaking, a club, but it operated like one. While Charlie tended to the business side, Jack, an outgoing personality and a sharp dresser, coddled the guests. He extended credit, took mail, ran errands, and performed the hundred and one little services that transform customers into loyal friends. When the gossip columnists and the picture press began to zero in on café society, Jack made it policy that no columnists could enter '21,' with the exception of Mark Hellinger of the *Daily News*, a friend and employee from the old Fronton days, and Heywood Broun, another favorite customer. No photographs could be taken, either—that sort of stuff might be fine for the Stork Club and El Morocco, but at '21,' all conversations were off the record and no one was bothered by the flash of a camera. Customers were encouraged to think of '21' as an extension of their own homes. In the 1930s, C. R. Smith, the president of American Airlines, came into '21' with a model airplane, which he hung over the bar. Other executives followed suit, and before long the barroom ceiling was covered with little gewgaws.

Jack radiated the confidence of a man's man, and he gave '21' the unmistakably masculine tone it retains today. The tough Jewish kid from the Lower East Side developed an infatuation with the Wild West and threw himself whole-heartedly into hunting and fishing. He loved to dress in western gear, put on a ten-gallon hat, and strap on a six-shooter. "Two Trigger Jack," as his friends

The '21' Club, originally a speakeasy in the Village, moved to midtown and became one of the city's pre-eminent power restaurants.

began to call him, arranged fishing trips to Alaska and hunting trips in the Adirondacks wtih favored guests. It was no accident that '21' took particular pride in its game menu.

When Jack and Charlie moved uptown, they were invading territory that had been carefully tested by a small restaurant on Madison Avenue and Sixty-first Street called the Colony. Like Jack and Charlie's, the Colony began inauspiciously and then, for somewhat mysterious reasons, soared to unimagined heights. Architecturally, it was awkward. Patrons ascended a narrow flight of steps to enter a cramped lounge, "so small and cluttered," Margaret Case Harriman wrote in *The New Yorker*, "that hardly any woman, however sabled and sleek with jewels, can enter it in a really arresting manner." The dining room was nondescript: a few potted palms in the corners, some colored-glass designs inserted in the windowpanes. That was it. But in its day, the Colony epitomized chic dining in Manhattan. Like Le Cirque in a later era, and for many of the same reasons, it radiated social power.

Gene Cavallero (standing, front), a co-owner of the Colony, doing in this 1943 photograph what he did best: pampering Manhattan socialites

None of this was evident in December 1920, when the Colony opened its doors. The restaurant was less a vision than a whim. Sylvester Haberman, a lawyer, served as trustee for an estate that owned 667 Madison Avenue, a building whose first floor, Haberman reasoned, might well accommodate a restaurant. He shared his thoughts with Joe Pani, who owned a roadhouse on Pelham Parkway called the Woodmansten and managed the prestigious Knickerbocker Grill. Pani, reputedly the first restaurateur to put broccoli on an American menu, liked the idea. He also had a couple of Italian waiters at the Knickerbocker who, he thought, might fit right in with the new plans. Little did he know how well.

Gene Cavallero and Ernest Cerutti, the waiters, came with lengthy résumés. They had both worked at the London Savoy, where Cerutti, a veteran of prestigious restaurants and hotels like the Palast in Berlin, rose to the position of headwaiter. Cavallero, several years his junior, had served under Escoffier at the Carlton Hotel in London. Both men got the itch to try their luck in the United States. Cerutti was brought over to work at the new Biltmore Hotel, while Cavallero wound up in Boston at the Copley Plaza. The two friends reunited at the Knickerbocker Grill, and there they developed a high regard for the night chef, an overqualified Alsatian named Alfred Hartmann. Formerly the head chef at the Vanderbilt Hotel, Hartmann had lost his position after serving in the French army during the First World War. He languished while Cerutti and Cavallero chafed. The Colony came along at just the right time for all three of them.

The Colony had opened as a bistro, and a bistro of uncertain reputation. It was discreet, and gentlemen of a certain sort prized its very private atmosphere, described tactfully in the *Times* as "somewhat clandestine," which is to say, perfect for dining with a mistress. "It was a place frequented by—how do you say—the demimondaines of New York," Cavallero later put it. A gambling club upstairs provided extra revenue in the late-night hours, as poker players drifted downstairs.

The demimondaines began treating the Colony as a kind of club, encouraged by Cavallero's easy credit policy. But Pani, a bit of a showman, contemplated something more along the lines of a nightclub, with a dance floor and musical entertainment. He liked noise and excitement. His customers did not. Cavallero and Cerutti, in league with Hartmann, began plotting a takeover. They schemed, they scrimped, and they bought. And so it came to pass that in 1922, the same year that the Red Head opened its doors, the new and improved Colony threw itself on the mercy of Manhattan.

Manhattan failed to respond. Older men with much younger women continued to patronize the place, but in very small numbers. The Colony was going broke. And then fate intervened. One night, out of curiosity, Mrs. W. K. Vanderbilt and a lady friend stopped in for dinner, which they enjoyed. The word got out. Overnight, the Colony's future was secure (and W. K. Vanderbilt was awarded a permanent table to the right of the entrance). The Vanderbilts brought in their wake the Wideners, the McCormicks, and, inevitably, Jimmy Walker. Charlie Chaplin and the Prince of Wales gave memorable parties in the upstairs dining room. Cholly Knickerbocker, the columnist who gave café society its name, pronounced his blessing on the restaurant, calling it "frightfully inty"—intimate.

"Nowhere in New York will you find such a coterie of cosmopolites, such a consistently smart and impressive collection of people of 'breeding' as gathers daily for luncheon at the Colony," George Ross wrote in *Tips on Tables*, his 1931 restaurant guide. The Colony offered a feminized counterpart to '21', with women outnumbering men by about six to one at lunchtime. It was genteel. "Whatever you do at the Colony," Ross warned, "don't, for the love of Croesus, call to anyone across the room in your best Childs style."

Within a few short years, the Colony's three partners had cleared a million dollars. Cerutti bought a villa in Sicily. Cavallero bought a huge farm near the Lake of Garda that embraced an entire village. Hartmann, cashing in his chips, sold his share in 1927 and retired to a life of leisure in Alsace. "Two waiters starting in business together can do nothing," Cavallero later said, "but two waiters and a chef can make a fortune."

The appeal of the Colony requires some explanation. As early as 1925, George Chappell noted that the restaurant was "very fashionable, clubby, and on the crest of popular favor." This remained true for decades, well after the café society of the 1930s and '40s had passed the baton to the likes of Jackie Kennedy, Richard Nixon, Truman Capote, and Diana Vreeland. For sheer staying power, few Manhattan restaurants of the twentieth century matched the Colony's record.

But why? The cuisine, French-Continental, received high marks. But the real secret to the Colony was Gene Cavallero and a style of service that Margaret Case Harrison called "passionately alert." Elsie de Wolfe knew that her toast would be made with special gluten bread, while Mrs. Frederick Gould, when on a diet, could be sure that the kitchen would send out porridge without salt. At the same time, the customer was, in a sense, always wrong, because the Colony was always right, which is why it attracted a gilt-edged clientele. Sirio Maccioni, later the owner of Le Cirque, made a serious error in his early days as a waiter at the Colony. He asked a table if everything was "okay." Cavallero exploded. "Of course they are okay," he told Maccioni after pulling him aside. "They should be glad that we let them in the door. At the Colony we never ask. We just assume they are happy." Maccioni survived the dressing-down and became the restaurant's maître d' in 1961.

When Cavallero and Cerutti worked as a team, they could convince the most demanding and self-important diners that their table was special, even when it was the worst one in the room. The act was ingenious. Cerutti would greet a party, showering compliments. In the midst of the fuss, Cavellero would rush up and berate his partner for not showing such valued guests immediately to the table that had been waiting for them. If Cavallero did the greeting, then Cerutti would do the berating. The tag team was broken up when Cerutti died suddenly on a voyage to Italy in 1937, but Cavallero carried on at full throttle and the Colony continued to prosper.

The Colony commanded the fierce loyalty of regulars like Mary Elizabeth Leary, who for twenty-seven years ate lunch there nearly every day—lamb chops, salad, and a grapefruit—and dinner two or three times a week. "The coat room boys are practically my secretaries," she told *The New Yorker* in 1953. "They get me theater tickets, and if I have a little card party here—I love poker and canasta—they'll make sandwiches and bring them around at 11 o'clock." When not at the Colony, Leary could be found at the Automat or Childs.

The Gene Cavalleros reappear throughout the history of the city's top dining spots. New York is a socially restless city, and newcomers never quite know where they stand. From the days of Ward McAllister, it has relied on umpires to impose order on the playing field, and restaurants of the top class have always been crucial in this fascinating game. From time to time, multilingual waiters with the right kind of charm and a discerning eye—people like Oscar Tschirky—have wielded enormous power simply by steering the right people to the right table, and providing, with a few well-chosen words, an enormous lift to unstable egos. These cultural ambassadors must have marveled at the galvanizing effect of a few flattering words, embellished with an accent, and a display of simple good manners. What might have passed without notice at an Italian trattoria or a Parisian café took on extraordinary value in New York. It has made the fortune of many a restaurateur.

13

Red Banquettes and Kisses on the Ceiling

The Depression hit New York hard. With the stock market in shock, the economy paralyzed, and unemployment at frighteningly high levels, fine dining was far down on the list of concerns for the average New Yorker. Even midpriced restaurants struggled when diners watched every penny. *Restaurant*, a trade magazine, reported that 33.2 percent of Manhattan's restaurants went under in 1930. The casualties included some famous names. Alice Foote MacDougall, a victim of overexpansion, saw her gross receipts plummet from nearly $1.4 million in 1929 to $400,000 in 1930. In a frantic reorganization, she tried to rally, addressing a poignant appeal to her customers in which she reminded them of her brave efforts to hitch her wagon to a star. "The poor little star blinked and twinkled and was almost dimmed forever by the dark cloud over it," she wrote, promising to carry on at lower prices. It was not to be. In 1932, she declared bankruptcy, as did Don Dickerman, declaring his sole remaining assets "a few suits of clothes three or four years old." His extensive portfolio of funny clubs and restaurants—the Pirate's Den, the Heigh Ho Club, the Blue Horse, and the County Fair—all closed their doors.

Even the mighty Childs empire was rocked to its foundations. Between 1920 and 1926, Childs had never netted less than $1 million a year. The *Magazine of Wall Street* called it one of the five most depression-proof stocks in the United States, but expansion during the flush times had saddled Childs with expensive leases. By 1929, the chain had nine restaurants on Fifth Avenue, making it the largest commercial presence on a street synonymous with wealth and privilege. High-priced real estate, however, was just one of the company's problems.

For years, William Childs had been fixated on the health properties of food. One reason his pancake recipe relied on yeast rather than baking soda was his firm belief that baking soda killed vitamins. When most Americans were just learning the meaning of the word "calorie," Childs lunchrooms were already displaying calorie totals beside each item on its menu. Childs also sensed, or so he thought, a trend toward lighter eating. He wanted every Childs customer to order a meal of 855 calories "with plenty of vitamins sprinkled on top."

In 1920, he began eliminating meat dishes one by one, substituting imposters like "meatless meatloaf." By 1922, the only meat dish available at the Childs lunchrooms was corned-beef hash, a sentimental favorite. Even so, the company grossed more than $24.5 million from the more than one hundred lunchrooms it operated in the United States and Canada in 1925. With his brother Sam's death that year, however, William became positively obsessive about healthy eating, and his vegetarian experiment drove away customers. For a time, the chain raised prices to redress the balance, but its stock price dropped from a high of 74 cents in 1925 to 37 cents in 1928, and sales dropped by $2.5 million—this in a banner year for the restaurant industry. Even William Childs realized that he had made a mistake.

So did the company's board. An angry group of minority shareholders demanded a change in policy, and Childs, who had already reintroduced roast lamb in his restaurants, caved. The company's stock regained some of its luster, but in December 1928 Childs was forced out as president. He rallied and regained control of the company, only to be thrown out again in 1929 by disgruntled shareholders. The pancake flippers in the front windows went, too.

It was downhill from there. In 1930, as the Depression began to tighten its grip, William Childs tried to stage a comeback, opening a series of theme restaurants. At the Old London, a doorman dressed as a bobby patrolled the sidewalk. The Old Algiers tried to suggest the romance of the Casbah. Lewis Mumford, champion of the chain's early interiors, recoiled. "Little did I anticipate," he wrote, "that I should live to see a Childs done up in fake 15th century English or another with vast puffed rice grains spattered over the walls for 'texture.'"

Without Childs at the tiller, the chain struggled. Its hard-won reputation for cleanliness and efficiency no longer proved sufficient to justify its premium prices. Depression-era diners were looking to save every nickel they didn't have. In December 1931, Bernarr Macfadden opened a penny restaurant on Third Avenue near Thirty-fourth Street. This was the same Macfadden who, at the turn of the century, had operated similar restaurants near City Hall and the Bowery. In the meantime, he had achieved notoriety as publisher of the *Evening Graphic*, a racy tabloid, and *Physical Culture* magazine. The advertised price

was no lie. A single penny could purchase a serving of cracked wheat, Scottish oatmeal, green pea or lima bean soup, soaked prunes, or ersatz coffee made from raisins or cereal. Through a $5 million foundation created with his publishing profits, Macfadden would open five more penny restaurants in New York over the next year. Elsewhere, many restaurants lowered the price of a table d'hôte dinner to a dime. Others, rather than cut prices, offered more food at the old rate.

Fighting back, Childs announced a sixty-cent all-you-can-eat menu in one of its New York restaurants. The idea was born when some of the slower restaurants in the chain began offering an extra coffee or dessert, or an extra helping of the main course, to attract more customers. The all-you-can-eat policy was soon extended to all of the chain's restaurants, with interesting results. The Childs near Herald Square doubled its daytime business and tripled its nighttime business. Most customers, managers reported, experimented with gluttony, ordering second and third helpings, but then fell back into their customary dining habits, ordering a more-or-less normal meal but with extra dessert. There were, however, a few who took naked advantage. "Our champion so far,

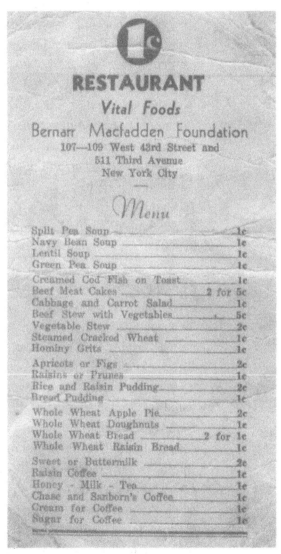

Bernarr Macfadden, fitness evangelist and publisher of the racy *Daily Graphic*, created penny restaurants to feed the poor during the Great Depression.

well I should say he was the man who came in Friday night, a rough-looking customer," one manager told a reporter. "He had a tomato juice cocktail, soup, three orders of liver with onions and potatoes, two salads, four cups of coffee, a pie a la mode, a custard, and some other dessert, a watermelon, I think. For bread, he had crackers, corn muffins, and whole-wheat rolls. I don't think he knew what he was doing when he walked out."

A year later, Childs abandoned the all-you-can-eat plan, which had boosted the bottom line only temporarily. The novelty wore off, and as food prices continued to fall during the Depression, sixty cents looked less and less like a bargain. By the late 1930s, Childs was losing money consistently, although it tottered on, rescued by assorted business interests. In 1950, new owners brought back the pancake flippers, setting up a pancake school in its Forty-second Street restaurant to train a new generation of front-window cooks. There was a new motto for the coffee, too: "The coffee that smiles right back at you." Nothing worked. In 1952, *Fortune* deemed the once-mighty chain, which had flipped 42 million griddlecakes in 1923, "quaint and forlorn." Childs's loss was Horn & Hardart's gain. By the early 1950s, the Automat company was operating the world's largest restaurant chain, its New York outlets alone grossing $42 million in 1951.

One bright spot in an otherwise gloomy picture was the Café Chambord, an exquisite French restaurant created by Roger Chauveron. Chauveron grew up in the trade. His father owned a chain of auberges in the Dordogne, and as a boy he spent his free time in the kitchen, observing, tasting, and, when allowed, helping at the stove. In 1935, after working as a waiter and cook at the Plaza, the Ritz, the Astor, and the Commodore, Chauveron struck out on his own, opening a little restaurant on Third Avenue near Forty-ninth Street. The street, dominated by the elevated train, spelled certain death for a fancy restaurant, or so Chauveron's friends told him. Improbably, it thrived—initially with fairly modest ambitions. Chauveron had in mind an intimate, authentically French bistro. But in 1942, a windfall came his way when a competitor folded and sold its first-rate wine cellar at rock-bottom prices. Chauveron bought the wine and proceeded to upgrade the Chambord, advertised as "the acme in French provincial cuisine." It soon earned a reputation as the most expensive restaurant in the city, with a clientele to match. In its prime, it counted Greta Garbo, Alfred Lunt and Lynn Fontanne, and assorted Rockefellers as devoted customers.

Chauveron's lone star only emphasized the surrounding darkness. The great restaurant names that had glowed so brightly a mere twenty years before were now extinguished. Would New Yorkers ever see their like again?

They would, and sooner than anyone had a right to expect. In 1939, the future lay just around the corner. The Depression was waning and factories were starting to hum again. Technology was making life easier and more enjoyable every day. True, the newspapers brought disturbing news from overseas. In Europe, Nazi Germany had emerged as a psychopathic state bent on terrorizing its neighbors, and democracy was on the defensive. In Asia, the rising power of Japan cast a long shadow over China and the Pacific. But the organizers of the New York World's Fair scanned the horizon and saw only bright promise. Their rosy vision was expressed in the fair's theme, "Building the World of Tomorrow," as well as in the fair's symbolic Trylon and Perisphere, abstract forms suggestive of progress in the sciences and the arts. In the strangest possible way, their vision helped usher in a new golden age for New York diners.

Out in Minnesota, the Reverend J. M. Bartinger had a brilliant idea. He called it the Rail-O-Matic, and he was certain that the New York World's Fair would be missing out on a great opportunity if it failed to jump on this visionary restaurant concept. The Rail-O-Matic was a variation on Bartinger's Automatic Eater, a rolling all-you-can-eat buffet first unveiled at the 1920 Minnesota State Fair. Diners sat down at a long counter, along which eighty-five wooden cars were pulled by a system of cables embedded in a groove. Each car carried a dish listed on the menu. Diners reached out and served themselves as the train passed by. Some cars had an ice-filled drawer that kept cold dishes cold, or a drawer with heated soapstones that kept the hot dishes hot. The Automatic Eater was a hit, although diners at the end of the table sometimes found that there was nothing but boiled cabbage left by the time the train reached their station. For the New York fair, Bartinger proposed an electrified version of his ingenious device.

Like many other fascinating proposals, Bartinger's Rail-O-Matic failed to make the cut. The futuristic spirit behind exhibits like General Motors' "World of Tomorrow" did not extend to plates, forks, and food. The fair's organizers worried more about feeding millions of visitors in the present than experimenting with how they might eat in the radiant future. Purely by accident, however, the fair would shape New York's next generation of restaurants in ways its organizers did not foresee.

The fair stirred things up. Its food concessions and the international restaurants operated by the pavilions of foreign nations injected new energy and a new cosmopolitanism into a listless dining scene. Food and restaurants were suddenly big news again. Tourists from the hinterlands might eat nothing more adventurous than a ham sandwich or a hot dog, but local residents often bought books of tickets and returned to the fair again and again, making the rounds of the foreign pavilions and re-creating the gaudy internationalism that had always been a hallmark of the city's dining culture.

A handful of American restaurateurs set up shop, tried out new ideas, and stayed to try their luck in New York after the fair closed. At the same time, the fair's most celebrated international restaurants—notably those at the Swiss, Belgian, Swedish, and French pavilions—found backers and translated their national cuisines into exciting Manhattan restaurants. One, Le Pavillon, became the most revered, influential New York restaurant since Delmonico's.

All this was distant from the minds of the fair's organizers in 1936, as they began fielding proposals and making plans for cafés, stands, cafeterias, and full-service restaurants aimed at a variety of appetites and pocketbooks. Like quartermasters feeding an army, they spread out maps, drew up charts, generated long lists of figures, and strategically positioned their food stations. The immediate task was to come up with a way to feed hundreds of thousands of visitors every day, most of them interested in a quick, cheap meal, having already invested the princely sum of seventy-five cents (twenty-five cents for children) to get through the turnstiles. At the same time, the organizers understood that food could be an attraction, just like the pavilions showcasing modern marvels like air conditioning, television, and gas heat.

The applications and the ideas came pouring in. In 1936 and 1937, the fair operators entertained hundred of proposals, some of them ridiculous, some intriguing but impractical, others downright tawdry or even shady. The Rail-O-Matic joined a long list of rejects, some of them enormously appealing in retrospect, like the "Babel Tower" proposed by Jacques Gréber, the master architect of the 1937 Paris International Exposition. Gréber envisioned a multistory restaurant tower, rising 150 to 200 feet above the fairgrounds in Flushing Meadows, Queens—tall enough for diners to gaze on the Manhattan skyline in the distance. Each floor would be dedicated to the cuisine of a specific country, making the tower a triumph of internationalism.

It was not to be. Fair operators pointed out that no one would be able to see much of anything from the lower floors, whose restaurants would therefore be the least popular. In addition, every one of the top-caliber chefs required to make the concept work would want to have his own kitchen, an impossibility, and in any case the tower would offer unwelcome competition for the restaurants at the international pavilions. The Babel Tower never left the drawing board.

One of the great near-misses of the fair was a brilliant proposal floated informally by Crosby Gaige, a well-known Broadway producer and gourmet with a radio show and newspaper column devoted to food and drink. Gaige thought that the fair should create an exhibition dedicated to food and wine, with two restaurants attached. The first would be a very small, very expensive restaurant "that would surpass in haute cuisine and service anything existing today," Gaige wrote in a letter to the organizers. Gaige then suggested something radical: a larger, more popular restaurant that would feature the different regional styles of American cooking. On the way out, diners could buy a cookbook that gathered together the dishes served in the restaurant. The proposal, which anticipated by several decades James Beard's missionary work for American food and Time-Life's groundbreaking series of American regional cookbooks, could have been a powerful catalyst for American cuisine at a critical moment, when traditional foodways were under pressure, driven into a corner by industrial food production and the homogenizing forces of modern American life. Alas, like the Babel Tower, Gaige's food pavilion and all-American restaurant ended up in history's dustbin, although Gaige was hired to write an official guidebook, *Food at the Fair*, and went on to publish *New York World's Fair Cookbook: The American Kitchen.*

Many applications came from humble sources. Althea Lepper, of New York, wanted to operate a small restaurant selling nothing but southern corn bread with bacon, ham, and maple syrup on the side. "It would be my idea, too, to have a real southern Mammy as a cook and good Negro serving help," she wrote. Application rejected. A poignant letter, forwarded by Mayor Fiorello La Guardia's office, came from Marie Hanc, wife of the Czech consul, whose country had just fallen to the Nazis. She begged to be allowed to open a small sandwich stand at the fair, since her husband was now unemployed and subject to arrest if he returned to Czechoslovakia. "I am writing this letter without the knowledge of my husband and I ask you to keep it strictly confidential, so that my compatriots here would not suffer more humiliation," she wrote. There is no record of a Czech sandwich concession at the fair.

An initial report by the fair's organizers envisioned several categories of food service. At the cheapest price point, with an average check of twenty-five cents, self-service cafeterias with tables in an outdoor garden court would offer a limited menu of hot dogs, hamburgers, pie, ice cream, and cake. Self-service cafeterias with a full menu and indoor dining would operate at a thirty-five-cent check average. A series of lunch counters and sandwich shops would offer simple meals with an average check price of forty cents. Full-service restaurants, seating three hundred to five hundred diners, would serve meals at an average of $1.20—or $2 with a floor show.

Final plans envisioned 310 eating outlets on the grounds, including mobile stands. The restaurants—one in each of thirty exhibition halls built by the fair, another fifty operated by independent restaurateurs or brewing companies, and dozens more in foreign pavilions, adding up to a total of 43,200 seats—embraced a dazzling array of dining styles for all pocketbooks. "Visitors to the fair will find that the Fair Corporation has anticipated alike the minutest gastronomic demands of the inveterate epicure who dines by the hour and of the quick lunch grabber who gets his lunch as he runs," the official guidebook promised. A 1939 press release was even more breathless. "There will be rendezvous whose internationally known chefs will attract the gourmets," it gushed. "There will be beer gardens, lieder and all. There will be restaurants known for their wine lists and their perfection of serving the ancient beverage. There will be places 'that simply must be seen, m'dear.' It goes without saying that, whatever the type or pretension, all eating places will be festive in spirit and gay with music, and that everyone will have to see the restaurant of Tomorrow."

In the end, the fair corporation approved restaurants operated by owners with a proven track record and good credit. Breweries like Ballantine and Schaefer, which looked at the fair as a golden marketing opportunity, walked through the door with no trouble. The Childs chain won a concession, as did the Borden Company, which operated Borden's Dairy World Restaurant at its exhibit hall. The Brass Rail got the green light to open one of its popular restaurants at the fair, and Jack Amiel, owner of the Turf restaurants (with several locations in Manhattan, Brooklyn, and Flushing), proposed an enormous restaurant to be called the Turf Trylon. In his proposal, Amiel lovingly described the Swiss specialties he intended to serve: geschnetzeltes kalbfleisch (veal sautéed in cream and white wine) and suri leberli (liver sautéed in wine and vinegar). The committee may have been swayed by another part of Amiel's pitch letter, promising that "hors d'oeuvres will be served to all guests at all times by beautiful Swedish girls especially selected for their grace and beauty."

The flamboyant Dario Toffenetti, owner of the popular Triangle restaurants in Chicago and a master of menu mystification, was exactly what the fair needed, organizers decided. He knew how to run a restaurant, and he had the kind of showmanship that would allow him to compete with attractions like Billy Rose's Aquacade. Toffenetti's, with its honey-glazed hams and fulsome menu prose, turned out to be one of the fair's most successful restaurants.

Visitors grumbled about high prices and long lines, but adventurous eaters had a field day. The New York papers sent their women's-page writers to sample the food and report back, giving the fair's restaurants maximum exposure. The curiosities of the national pavilions received special attention, although in most cases the restaurants met American tastes halfway, or better. The Formosan Tea Room at the Japanese pavilion served authentic jasmine and oolong tea, but also such un-Japanese fare as crabmeat egg foo yung and apple pie à la mode. By contrast, the Turkish pavilion offered authentic boreks, kebabs in all styles, and dolmasi, with rose-petal jelly for dessert. The Tel Aviv café, in the Jewish Pavilion, puzzled diners with menu items like jezreel (zucchini with eggs, parsley, and potato), hatzilim (eggplant with sour cream), and dagg makiah, which urban American diners were no doubt relieved to discover was nothing more than pickled herring in cream sauce, a delicatessen standby.

Cuba, Brazil, and Hungary all trotted out their national specialties. Italy uncorked its best regional wines, as a giant bust of Mussolini glowered at visitors. The Soviet Union dished up a healthy serving of proletarian internationalism and workers' rights. The menu, strong on Georgian dishes, included a stern warning to bourgeois American diners: no tipping. Soviet waiters, it explained, were adequately paid for their labor. They needed no charity, unlike their oppressed brethren in the capitalist West.

Stars emerged as the fair went on. The Turf Trylon, home of the fetching Swedish waitresses, did big business. Visitors formed long lines at the Three Crowns, the Swedish pavilion's restaurant, where the smorgasbord was presented on a revolving table that seemed to hypnotize diners and bystanders alike. The maître d' spent most of his time quietly escorting gawkers out the door, while explaining to diners that the concept of the smorgasbord was not to heap one's plate with as much food as it could hold, but rather to select, say, a few raw fish dishes to start, and then return for sausages, meats, and salads, with cheese to end the meal. At fair's end, the restaurant relocated to Manhattan as the Three Crowns.

Toffenetti's proved so popular that in 1941 Dario Toffenetti planted his flag right in the middle of Times Square, creating a thousand-seat restaurant that fed the multitudes, twenty-four hours a day, well into the 1970s. Over the years, the buoyant, endlessly quotable Toffenetti became a darling of the local press, and his menus achieved the status of sacred documents for amateur linguists.

Here was an American success story to warm the heart. Toffenetti was an Italian immigrant who developed an uncontrollable enthusiasm for all-American salesmanship and the latest theories of consumer psychology. As a struggling restaurant owner in 1920, he had hit on the idea of advertising his baked ham by putting a sign on the sidewalk that read: "Hot Roasted, Juicy Sugar-Cured Ham. Finest Oscar Mayer Quality. Very Liberal Sandwich with Sugar Bits, Dill Pickle, Lettuce. Only 15 cents." Then he picked up a knife and stood in the window, carving in full view of passersby. This gimmick sent sales through the roof. By the end of the week he was going through thirty-five hams a day.

At night, Toffenetti attended Northwestern University's School of Commerce, where he studied advertising and psychology. There, as he later put it, he "underwent a thorough mental overhaul." His menu, he decided, suffered from "scatteration." There were too many dishes. He started highlighting a limited set of specialty items, first and foremost his glazed hams. Next came pricing. The ticket to riches, he decided, lay in offering high-quality food at lower prices than could be found in hotel dining rooms.

But how to convince customers that they were getting quality at a bargain price? In his psychology classes, Toffenetti studied the intricacies of stimulus response, and somewhere along the way developed a florid style of English that became the hallmark of his menus. Decades before menu writers adopted selling terms like "line-caught," "day-boat," and "farm-fresh," Toffenetti, after meditating on the essence of his dishes, came up with language that would create a mystique. Chocolate pie, he decided, had three selling points: whipped cream, crust, chocolate. Each could be sold in its own right. The chocolate, for example, was "soft with the fragrance of cocoa, still scented with the tropics." Baked potatoes, one of the restaurant's specialties, and one of the humblest foods imaginable, achieved a crazy poetry in Toffenetti's hands. They were listed on the menu as "Rough Skinned But Tender-Hearted. From the Lava Beds of Idaho. Product of Millions of Years of Evolution." Language like this, Toffenetti believed, was a key ingredient in creating what he called "the psychology of happy eating." Apparently Toffenetti spoke very much as he wrote. When *The New Yorker* paid

Dario Toffenetti, an Italian immigrant, applied psychology and salesmanship to menus like this one from his Times Square restaurant. He was the first to wrap food in seductive language.

him a visit in the 1940s, he was scurrying around his restaurant kitchen, testing, tasting, and exclaiming in Toffenetti-speak. A tomato sauce was pronounced "flavorsome!" Fat baked potatoes were praised as "large and farinaceous!"

A visual counterpart to the menu language was an enormous dining room mural executed by Hugh Troy, a surrealist and practical joker whose instructions for the job were brief and to the point. "I want you to paint the most unusual mural ever painted," Toffenetti told him. Troy, taking the theme of "madness," depicted weirdly metamorphosing forms, with lambs turning into peas, a bass viol into crockery, melons into a talking machine. Troy wanted to paint female bathers on the beach turning into baked potatoes, but Toffenetti balked. Too racy. The women were replaced by musical notes.

The Swiss pavilion operated two restaurants, one expensive, one not, both of them managed by the Swiss-born Max Haering, one of Otto Baumgarten's partners and eventual owner of the Elysée. The garden restaurant, featuring yodelers, two Swiss orchestras, and waitresses in peasant costume, limited its menu to simple Swiss dishes and American food, all intended to be eaten with beer. The Chalet Restaurant, geared to the higher-priced customer, showcased Swiss wines and national dishes, like brochettes Lucernoise (small pieces of chicken liver, bacon, and mushrooms skewered and fried in sweet butter) and délices d'Emmenthal (cheese croquettes filled with a creamy béchamel sauce). After the fair ended, it simply moved to East Fiftieth Street, where it carried on for years as the Swiss Pavilion Restaurant.

Belgium's restaurant, in the country's coolly Modernist pavilion, created a sensation. Outdoor tables overlooked the Lagoon of Nations, where ice-blue fountains splashed and a ring of foreign flags flapped in the breeze. Charlotte Hughes, the *Times*'s food reporter, wrote that dining on the restaurant's terrace was like being on "the deck of a dream liner that never quite docks." The menu made the most of a great cuisine unknown to most Americans, then or now. Diners feasted on waterzooi, carbonnade, slow-roasted chicken with juniper berries, and veal kidneys Liégeoises. The restaurant, in the second year of the fair, was run by André Pagani, an owner of the Carlton Restaurant in Brussels. Sent over by the Belgian government to sort out the restaurant's inefficient management, Pagani stayed on in New York, and, when the fair was over, re-created the restaurant in midtown as the Brussels. Virtually overnight, it jumped to the top tier of the city's dining spots.

The restaurant that overshadowed all others was French. Called, simply, Le Restaurant Français, it opened on May 9, 1939, with a glittering preview dinner attended by the French diplomatic corps and the New York press, which described it in rapturous terms, from the double consommé Viveur to the noisettes of pré-salé lamb Ambassadrice, to the capon in tarragon aspic. France, it was clear, had just given America its greatest gift since the Statue of Liberty. Here, from the nation that invented haute cuisine, was a restaurant truly worthy of flying the tricolor.

This was no accident. It says something about the power of French cuisine that, at a time when leftists and rightists were battling each other in the streets of Paris, the French government, virtually paralyzed in matters of national politics, could move swiftly to put its restaurant front and center at the 1939 fair. The plan was simplicity itself. Government officials called on Jean Drouant, a leading restaurateur, and told him to form a committee capable of giving America a precise replica of a superior-grade Parisian establishment. Drouant was best known as the owner of Drouant, founded by his father in 1880 as a bistro but by the 1920s a luxurious seafood restaurant. Drouant fils, after taking over, expanded. At the time of the 1939 fair, he owned two other celebrated restaurants, the Pavillon Royale and the Bois de Boulogne. His brother-in-law, Louis Barraya, an important figure in his own right, ran the three-star Café de Paris, the Pré Catalan, Fouquet's, and the Pavillon d'Armenonville in the Bois de Boulogne. With backing from the French Line, the two men capitalized the restau-

A menu cover from the Restaurant Français at the World's Fair in 1939. The restaurant would relocate to Manhattan and, as Le Pavillon, become a favorite of the city's elite.

rant at the New York fair, then formed an organizing committee, the Syndicat des Restaurateurs, made up of managers from the Café de Paris, Drouant, Fouquet's, the Meurice, the Pavillon d'Armenonville, the Pavillon Royal, the Pré Catalan, and the French Line. The consortium put together a staff of nearly a hundred kitchen workers, maîtres d'hotel, waiters, and wine stewards from restaurants all over France (and, in the case of the chef de cuisine, beyond). Running the kitchen would be Marius Isnard, the chef de cuisine of the Hôtel de Paris in Monte Carlo. His two sous-chefs came from La Coupole in Paris and Paris Plage in the Normandy resort town of Le Touquet. The dining room would be under the watchful eye of Henri Soulé, the assistant maître d' at the Café de Paris. This turned out to be the most important appointment of all.

Soulé, a short, stout man with a moon face and an impressive double chin, had risen rapidly in his profession. A native of Saubrigues, in the Basque country, he had left home at fourteen to become a busboy at the Continental Hotel in Biarritz and moved on to the dining rooms of the Hôtel Mirabeau and Claridge's in Paris. By the age of twenty-three he was a waiter's captain, the youngest in Paris. By the time he was tapped to run Le Restaurant Français, in part because he spoke English well, Soulé was already gaining a reputation for his imperious manner and exacting style.

Most of the kitchen personnel were young cooks, classically trained, who had caught the eye of their superiors. One such was Pierre Franey, who, like so many of his young peers, signed on for the adventure of New York and wound up with a new life, a new career, and, in his case, lasting fame. Franey, in time-honored fashion, had worked his way through the French apprentice system and in 1939 was firmly ensconced at Drouant, where he had risen to become the second-ranking saucier, near the top of the kitchen's most prestigious department. One day, as he recounted in his memoir, he was summoned to the office of executive chef Jules Petit and informed that he had been named to the team that would be sailing on the *Normandie* to New York. There he would be number two in the kitchen's fish department.

Henri Soulé made Le Pavillon the preeminent French restaurant of the postwar period. He was a benevolent despot to his patrons, and a despot pure and simple to his staff.

Soulé, Isnard, Franey, and their colleagues distinguished themselves in New York. Here was French food and French service unknown since the glory days of the Café Martin, the Brunswick, and Sherry's. Le Restaurant Français was even more uncompromisingly French than those illustrious predecessors, making not a single concession to American taste. Once visitors to the fair entered the French pavilion, they were in France. And when in France, they ate as the French did, on dishes like leg of lamb boulangère, coq au vin, suprême de barbue Mornay, and crêpes suzettes. The wines were stellar: Château Margaux, Clos de Vougeot, and Château Cheval Blanc at fairy-tale prices, three to five dollars a bottle. Every night, just before nine o'clock, the lights were dimmed and diners watched the fireworks display over the Lagoon of Nations. They were the luckiest people in New York. "At its inception, the French restaurant set for itself the lofty aim of presenting French food at its best," an official French pamphlet declared. "It has achieved a rare success." This was no boast. It was the simple truth.

The fair and the French pavilion were thrown into confusion by the outbreak of war. The world of tomorrow had arrived, not as a technological wonderland, but as a descent into barbarism. After Le Restaurant Français closed for the season, its staff returned to France, where many joined the army. Soulé, serving in the First Machine Gun Company of the 168th Infantry Regiment, rose to the rank of sergeant before being informed that the government had decided to reopen Le Restaurant Français for the fair's 1940 season, although with a reduced staff. He and twenty-seven other restaurant workers returned to New York. Two weeks later, the Nazis marched into Paris. The restaurant carried on, braving political disaster back home and ceaseless rain in New York, until the fair closed on October 31. After a brilliant run, Soulé and the rest of his brave company found themselves out of work and without a country.

At this critical juncture, Soulé and Drouant huddled with the ten employees who had decided to risk all and stay in the United States. Here, they decided, was the nucleus of a restaurant. Soulé had $14,000 in hand, most of it borrowed from two silent partners, but his real capital was the goodwill of suppliers and diners. He found suitable premises in a defunct restaurant at 5 East Fifty-fifth Street, took a deep breath, and rolled the dice. On October 15, 1941, he opened the doors to the restaurant he named Le Pavillon, in honor of its origins at the World's Fair. It was a bittersweet moment. "I remember the opening night menu," Soulé later told Joseph Wechsberg, the distinguished epicure who helped immortalize Le Pavillon in the pages of *The New Yorker*. "Caviar, *sole bonne femme*, *poulet braisé* with champagne, cheese, and dessert. Everybody liked it. When it was over, I went up to my office and started to cry, because there was no one to share my success with me."

If Soulé was a gambler, he knew how to hedge his bets. Before opening Le Pavillon, he staged a preview dinner to which he invited precisely the sort of clientele he hoped to feed in the coming years: the socialites and celebrities who would make his restaurant a money spinner and a social power center.

As at the Colony, atmosphere and the personality of the owner counted at least as much as the food. Le Pavillon was Soulé, and Soulé was Le Pavillon. Never for a moment was there any doubt about that. A martinet to his staff, he treated favored guests with carefully calibrated charm, lavishing small attentions that won him slavish devotion. Each day, the kitchen was under instructions to make ten copies of an entrée not on the menu, a *plat bourgeois* showcasing the kind of French cooking dear to Soulé's heart. Looking over the day's reservations, Soulé would choose a lucky customer, approach, and whisper of a very special treat—just one—being held in the kitchen. This little ritual would be repeated nine more times in the course of the evening service.

Soulé could be cool in a crisis, a quality on display in the legendary incident of the roast pheasants. One evening, a party of six had ordered a sumptuous meal in advance. Soulé was hovering over the table when a busboy stumbled into a gueridon and sent several pheasants, fresh from the oven and ready for carving, sliding across the floor. As horrified waiters rushed the birds back into the kitchen, Soulé, with a wave of the hand, said, "Quick, tell the chef to send out the other pheasants." The "other pheasants" were sitting, uncooked, in a refrigerator. Several chefs, in a frenzied repair operation, cleaned off the damaged ones, rearranged the garnish, and sent the refurbished goods out to the dining room again, where they were received rapturously after being carved to perfection by a beaming Soulé. When performing this operation, he was always careful to shoot his cuffs, exposing the cufflinks presented to him by the Duke and Duchess of Windsor.

Soulé's dark side was not pleasant to see. He had a certain angry stare, one Pavillon veteran claimed, "that could curdle a sauce béarnaise." A natural autocrat, he took the view that anyone crossing his threshold entered his personal kingdom. "Le Pavillon, c'est moi," he once declared during a labor dispute that roiled his restaurant, one of many inspired by Soulé's hatred of unions, a by-product of his hatred of interference in any form. Presumptuous diners were included. "No two must be treated alike," he once said of his customers. A real restaurateur, he added, "flatters them, he subtly educates them, and occasionally asserts his authority."

Woe betide the guest who complained of a table assignment or acted up in any way. Soulé was a master of intimidation, of cutting the powerful down to size with surgical precision, like the bumptious diner who loudly requested that Soulé open a credit account for him. Soulé, busy carving a leg of lamb, glanced over at the man and directed him toward a door at the rear of the restaurant. The diner entered what he thought was Le Pavillon's business office. It was the men's room. Again and again, intimidated diners fell into line. The faint aura of menace behind the smile, the iron fist within the velvet glove, had more than a little to do with Soulé's popularity.

The dining room staff found Soulé a merciless taskmaster, always ready to shove a waiter aside unceremoniously and take over if he saw a table requiring his special diplomatic skills. Kitchen workers, fortunately, never saw him. Soulé believed in a strict separation of dining room and kitchen. The chefs and their assistants labored, brilliantly and in complete anonymity, behind doors that their proprietor rarely passed through.

Soulé picked memorable quarrels. He was both stubborn and bursting with amour propre. During the 1960 presidential election, Joseph Kennedy was dining at Le Pavillon with his family when, quite contrary to the restaurant's usual policy, photographers were allowed to take pictures. Kennedy objected. Soulé, sensing a challenge to his authority, intervened. "His son has not even been elected president and already he's acting like a dictator," he said over his shoulder. The Kennedys immediately took their business down the street to La Caravelle, a newcomer in the Pavillon mold.

In 1955, Soulé's new landlords, Columbia Pictures, raised his rent drastically, perhaps, as rumor had it, because the company's president, Harry Cohn, had been denied a prize table at Le Pavillon. Soulé pulled up stakes and moved to the Ritz Towers at Park Avenue and Fifty-seventh Street, where in 1957 he opened a larger version of Le Pavillon. Meanwhile, Columbia Pictures, according to Pierre Franey, relented and offered him his old premises at exactly the price he had indignantly rejected before. In Soulé's mind, he had made his point and inflicted harsh punishment: the landlords could no longer boast of having Le Pavillon. Satisfied, Soulé returned to his old address and created La Côte

Basque. He had been thinking about opening a restaurant devoted to the cuisine of his native region, and now he had the chance. It opened in October 1958 and immediately became a favorite with the tony Upper East Side crowd. It remained so for decades.

Infallible in the dining room, Soulé could blunder badly dealing with employees. His worst mistake came in 1960, when he demanded that Pierre Franey, his chef de cuisine since 1953, reduce the hours of the kitchen staff as a cost-cutting measure. Franey, irate, resigned. Seven other cooks also quit. The split was acrimonious. Several years later, when Franey saw his old mentor on the street, he tried to approach him and say a few words. Soulé, looking straight at the pavement, walked on.

In retrospect, the departure of Franey marked the beginning of Le Pavillon's long twilight. La Côte Basque, which Soulé intended as a lighter, more amusing counterpart to Le Pavillon, siphoned off business from its parent. Spiraling costs and union troubles beset Soulé, who began to flag as he reached his sixties. Both he and his restaurants lost their early vigor. The cuisine suffered and critics took note. In 1962, Soulé sold La Côte Basque to the owners of the Café Chambord—Roger Chauveron had sold his interest years earlier—-then bought it back a few years later, to less than sparkling reviews. In 1966, Soulé dropped dead of a heart attack in the restaurant, reportedly while yelling at a union official over the telephone. Le Pavillon survived him by a half dozen years, but it was never the same. Soulé was right. He was Le Pavillon. Without him, the restaurant was merely a name.

Le Pavillon established the template, and provide the personnel, for nearly every serious French restaurant that followed it for the next twenty years, La Côte Basque being the first but hardly the last of its offshoots. In the late 1960s, Craig Claiborne, *The New York Times*'s restaurant critic, invoked the book of Genesis to indicate its seminal role. "In the beginning Henri Soulé begat Le Pavillon and La Côte Basque," he wrote. "Le Pavillon begat La Caravelle and Le Poulailler. La Caravelle brought forth Le Mistral and the new Le Cygne. Le Pavillon, La Côte Basque, and Le Mistral begat the new Le Madrigal. And Le Pavillon and La Côte Basque and La Poulailler more or less begat the new La Seine." By any measure, this was an impressive roll call, and although some of the restaurants on Claiborne's list were not destined to endure, two of them, La Caravelle and La Grenouille, became New York institutions. In 1960, Roger Fessaguet, a saucier and later sous-chef at Le Pavillon, joined forces with the restaurant's maître d', Fred Decré, to create La Caravelle in the old Robert's space. It survived for more than forty years as one of Manhattan's preeminent French restaurants. Two years later, Charles Masson, another maître d' from Le Pavillon, opened the small but sumptuous La Grenouille, which remains one of the city's most seductive dining spots. Not on Claiborne's list, but worthy of mention, is Le Veau d'Or, a humble but beloved bistro, still in operation. It was created by George Barratin, one of Le Pavillon's waiters.

Two chefs at Le Pavillon never opened their own restaurants but exercised extraordinary influence over American taste buds. Pierre Franey, after leaving Le Pavillon, found work as a consulting chef for the Howard Johnson Company, taking with him a promising young saucier by the name of Jacques Pépin. The matchup sounds improbable, but Howard Johnson, a regular at Le Pavillon, was both discriminating and innovative about the food served at his restaurants. In his memoir *Apprentice*, Pépin describes with great enthusiasm his plunge into commercial American food service, for which he prepared by flipping hamburgers at a Howard Johnson's on Queens Boulevard. Franey eventually entered into an informal partnership with Craig Claiborne at the *Times*, serving as his brain trust, recipe developer, and dining companion. He later wrote the "60-Minute Gourmet" column for the newspaper, as well as several cookbooks. Pépin, after his stint with Howard Johnson's, became a fixture on public television. From a single small restaurant, by a variety of means, Soulé spread the message of haute cuisine throughout the United States.

The influence of Le Pavillon was not all for the good. Sternly traditional, it inscribed, as though in stone, a style of service and an approach to cuisine that lacked the spontaneity of the old Café Martin or Sherry's. This was French cooking and French service by the rule book, immune to change. In time, it would come to seem fussy, antiquated, and, as the forces of globalism revolutionized French cuisine, almost a parody. In France, discontent with the old classical regime led to the innovations (and the excesses) of nouvelle cuisine. These new currents had more influence on American chefs, particularly in California, than on the old-guard French restaurants in New York, which held fast to their ways and to their aging customers. The direct descendants of Le Pavillon limped on well into the last years of the twentieth century, outliving their time and surviving to become museum pieces. It would take a fresh face, the unassuming but exquisite Lutèce, to point the way toward a different kind of French restaurant.

New Yorkers in search of French food did not have to penetrate the forbidding Le Pavillon, though. For years, a string of modest bistros had transformed West Forty-sixth and West Fifty-first streets, where the French liners docked, into French enclaves patronized heavily by French visitors and émigrés. Ambitious cooks and restaurant workers had jumped ship and started their own little dining spots, some of which evolved into dynasties. The Pujol family, for example, operated both Réné Pujol and Pierre au Tunnel.

By far the most stylish venture into moderate-priced French cuisine was Longchamps. The owner, Henry Lustig, started out selling vegetables from a pushcart. From this humble beginning, he created a wholesale fruit-and-vegetable business supplying restaurants, hotels, and passenger ships. He also married the sister of Arnold Rothstein, the flamboyant gambler, who helped Lustig open his first restaurant in 1926. Many more followed. The Longchamps chain made its mark by placing a premium on high-quality, fresh ingredients, especially vegetables, "so recently from mother earth that they are still almost damp from the soil," as the menus boasted.

To put a sophisticated design stamp on his chain, Lustig turned to Winold Reiss, and Reiss did not disappoint. From the gracefully stylized *L* on its tall, narrow menus to its shiny, reflective interiors, Longchamps exuded sleek modernity. The thousand-seat Longchamps in the Empire State Building, with its dramatic descending staircase and multiple dining levels, epitomized Reiss's vision—as did the portraits of American Indians on the wall. Indians were an obsession for Reiss, and Lewis Mumford was quite right to complain that their intrusive presence sometimes made Reiss's interiors look like an adult-education program sponsored by the Museum of Natural History.

At its peak, the Longchamps chain embraced a dozen restaurants, renowned for the quality of their food and for their no-tipping policy—instead, 10 percent was automatically added to the bill. Lustig lived high off the profits. Under the red-and-gold Longchamps colors, he ran top-quality racehorses at the New York tracks. He acquired a Gatsby-like estate in Sands Point, Long Island.

Playing fast and loose, Lustig attracted attention. Early on, Arnold Rothstein forced a showdown when he discovered his brother-in-law fiddling with the company's finances. Sitting in Lindy's one day, he noticed a truck from Lustig's produce business stopping to make a delivery. He asked to see the bill. After doing a little detective work, he found that Longchamps was paying a much higher price for the same fruits and vegetables. Hastily, Lustig raised the money to buy his partner out.

The Internal Revenue Service also began to take an interest in Lustig's books, which turned out to be as skillfully cooked as the signature dishes in his restaurant. In 1947, Lustig was sentenced to four years in prison for evading nearly $3 million in income and wartime excess-profits taxes between 1940 and 1944. The restaurants lingered for decades, coasting on the Longchamps name as the quality of the food declined. In the late 1960s, Longchamps was acquired by a steakhouse owner and folded into the Steak and Brew chain.

If New York worshiped France, it never quite accepted the French notion of the restaurant as a purist exercise in gastronomy. From the outset, the restaurant as a social setting and form of entertainment competed directly with its function as a provider of high-quality food. People-watching, dressing up, and competing for the best table counted as important parts of the dining experience, increasingly so as nightclubs became more influential. Boundaries blurred. Were El Morocco and the Stork Club restaurants with a floor show, or floor shows with drinks and food as necessary accoutrements? Or were the food *and* the entertainment flimsy excuses for their real purpose, to provide a place for socially prominent people to gather and lend their names to the gossip columns? It was hard to tell. In the 1930s and '40s, as the speakeasy gave way to the nightclub, a fevered romanticism took over New York's nightlife, perfectly expressed in restaurants like El Borracho.

El Borracho was the brainchild of a Sicilian immigrant with the unpronounceable name of Niccolo de Quattrociocchi. Nicky Q, as he mercifully allowed friends to call him, was a would-be Valentino who had made a very small splash in Paris and Hollywood before crossing paths with John Perrona, the owner of El Morocco, and the silent film star Monty Banks. Nicky had no money but plenty of charm and a knack for cultivating rich friends, several of whom put their money behind El Borracho. The restaurant was conceived from the outset as a celebrity watering hole with stylish quirks. Nicky installed mynah birds over the bar and devised a menu that included a "Siamese" fish, with a head at each end, priced (jokingly) at $4,127.82. In the Romance Room, the words "I love you" were written in twenty-three languages on the wall. In addition to talking birds, Nicky had a collection of index cards on which assorted girlfriends had planted a lipstick kiss and then signed their names. He put the cards on the walls and encouraged female patrons to add to the collection. By the time *Life* came calling in 1947, the Kiss Room's walls (and ceiling) were covered with 14,283 bright-red lip prints, and El Borracho was crowned by the magazine the most

Romance was in the air—and on the ceiling—at El Borracho, where female patrons were encouraged to leave a lip print for the Kiss Room.

popular restaurant in New York, attracting "a velvety following in theatrical and café society, together with its velveteen hangers on."

El Borracho's two-headed fish faced competition at Nino's Sports Afield Room, a restaurant within a restaurant at Nino's Café on East Fifty-second Street. The draw at the upstairs Nino's was exotic game: sautéed llama steak Rhodesia, or the highly popular New Hampshire black bear steaks with mushrooms. By special order, diners could arrange to have Caribbean barracuda, Mexican armadillo, or beaver (with tail). The prices tended to be steep. Those with a taste for woodchuck had to pay $22 to satisfy it.

Postwar New York was a great time for quirky restaurants, epitomized by the Café Nicholson. The café was the brainchild of a window dresser from St. Louis named Johnny Bulica, who reinvented himself as Johnny Nicholson and, once in New York, began filling the windows at Lord & Taylor with strange junk that he collected along the Bowery and Third Avenue. The company's president promoted Nicholson's castoffs as "the New American Look," an aesthetic that Nicholson transferred to a small antiques shop he opened on Fifty-eighth Street in 1944. The shop became a favorite with the photographers Richard Avedon and Karl Bissinger, who used it as a stage set for their fashion shoots for *Vogue* and *Harper's Bazaar*.

On a whim, Nicholson opened a café in the shop's tiny back garden, intending to sell coffee and a few pastries. His friend Edna Lewis, at that time a seamstress and Communist agitator, convinced him to go all out and create a real restaurant. She did the cooking, he did the visuals. Lolita, a talkative parrot, served as mascot and maître d'hotel. The café, a cheeky retort to all the snooty French restaurants and he-man steakhouses that dominated New York's dining scene, soon attracted a seductive blend of Bohemian New York and high society. It was the haunt of fashionistas, magazine editors, writers, and artists, among them Tennessee Williams, Paul Robeson, Gore Vidal, W. H. Auden, the cartoonist Charles Addams, Brendan Gill of *The New Yorker*, and Alexander Liberman of *Vogue*. It thrived, as so many subterranean places did, on word of mouth. It was the little secret shared by a select in-crowd, and, in the days before instant media exposure of every micro-trend, it managed to stay that way. Lewis, of course, went on to write classic cookbooks devoted to southern food.

Nicholson moved the café to larger quarters on Fifty-seventh Street in the early 1950s (and later to a sculpture studio near the entrance to the Queensboro Bridge). With each relocation, the surroundings seemed to become more idiosyncratic and sumptuous. The decor, a riot of rich fabrics and opulent objets d'art, suggested a nineteenth-century Orientalist fantasy. The food was quite otherwise. There was no printed menu. Diners sat down, and Edna Lewis served them a set meal, with a choice or two for the main course. Simplicity was the ruling aesthetic. A typical dinner might start with a selection of hors d'oeuvres (cold stuffed mussels, a spicy eggplant and tomato mélange, avocado slices with a piquant shrimp mayonnaise), followed by broiled veal kidneys or steak with béarnaise sauce. The entrée par excellence at Café Nicholson was a roasted herbed chicken, "brown as a chestnut fresh from the burr," as Clementine Paddleford, the *Herald Tribune*'s food writer, put it. Dessert was always a chocolate

The Café Nicholson's quirky atmosphere and the cooking of Edna Lewis drew an artistic crowd in the forties and fifties: (left to right) Tanaquil LeClercq, Donald Windham, Buffie Johnson, Tennessee Williams, and Gore Vidal, with Virginia Reed (rear).

soufflé—"light as a dandelion seed in a high wind." Lewis supplied the restraint; Nicholson specialized in excess. At one point, he acquired a Rolls-Royce Silver Cloud and provided chauffeur service to anyone within sixty blocks of the restaurant. Whimsy cut both ways, however. Nicholson would often shut the café for weeks or even months at a time, without explanation. Regulars would simply wait for a reopening and resume their patronage.

The humble hamburger received royal treatment at Hamburg Heaven, a popular spot opened in 1939 by a Connecticut housewife with a history to match Alice Foote MacDougall's. Phyllis Moffett, left stranded by a divorce and desperately in need of an income, came up with the idea of selling hamburgers, since hers had always won raves at backyard cookouts. She came up with a motto—"The Gates of Heaven Never Close"—and put three sample hamburgers with the labels rare, medium, and well-done in the window of her first restaurant, on Madison Avenue just above Sixty-second Street. The menu was limited to hamburgers, pies, tossed salads, and a daily special, but the restaurant developed into a cult, especially after its hamburgers caught the eye of the food writer and bon vivant Lucius Beebe.

"The two-bit hamburgers, served on homemade rolls, are about tops in the field of this particular confection," Beebe wrote, "and are rolled about twice as thick as the average so that it is possible to get the outside nicely browned and the inside white hot without cooking it at all—which is, of course, the way hamburgers should be served." Already, the burgers were attracting an unusual clientele. Beebe spotted two Rolls-Royces whose owners, sitting in the backseats, were chewing furiously at their hamburgers. "For all we know," he wrote, "the chauffeurs and footmen were dining at the Colony, around the corner." A cameo role in *Breakfast at Tiffany's* only boosted the Hamburg Heaven mystique, noted but not always understood by foreign visitors. In 1949, Francis Marshall, an English journalist and Hamburg Heaven patron, tried to explain the pleasures of the classic American dish to readers back home, but words failed. "A hamburger is a kind of soft roll with minced meat (spiced or flavoured) inside," he began cautiously. "New Yorkers are very fussy about hamburgers. I expect this is an acquired taste." The restaurant's kidney-shaped swivel trays and benches did strike him as delightful, however.

Today, American food culture is almost totally dominated by large corporations and national chains, but there really was a time when individual restaurateurs defined the dining experience. Even chains like Horn & Hardart and

Childs, which fed the masses, bore the distinctive stamp of their founders, who presented a certain style as well as a menu. To an extent unimaginable today, entrepreneurial owners like Phyllis Moffett created idiosyncratic restaurants that flourished despite the trend toward homogenization elsewhere in American culture.

One of the most popular restaurants in the city had no name. For convenience it was called Louise's, after the owner and cook, who started out making food for her husband and his friends in a bungalow they rented on Long Beach, Long Island. In the winter of 1933, when the dress company she worked for went under, Louise rented out rooms in her Manhattan house and let guests eat with the family. With an eye to expansion, she rented the bottom floor of a former speakeasy across the street and began cooking for a hundred customers a night, running the kitchen herself to save on expenses. Fashion models began frequenting the little restaurant, and the city's more famous debutantes followed, "It" girls like Brenda Frazier and Barbara Hutton. Before long, Louise's sister opened a similar restaurant, called Louise Jr.

The spirit of the tearoom lived on in dozens of small restaurants devoted to southern cooking, a myth-saturated cuisine that more or less demanded the personal touch provided by a southern owner and a chef from below the Mason-Dixon Line. Hence restaurants like Lottie's Dogwood Room, the Chicken Koop, Helen Lane's in the Village, Tillie's Chicken Grill in Harlem, Mammy's in Rockefeller Center, the Dixie Kitchen, and on and on. Lottie's, the creation of Lottie Pierce, from Talladega, Alabama, epitomized the breed. Fried chicken (served with fried chicken livers) was the main feature, along with Virginia ham, corn bread, hot biscuits, and fruit pies. (In Harlem, chicken with waffles developed into a neighborhood classic that remains hugely popular.) Somewhat more ambitious was the Little Old Mansion Patio. The baked Virginia ham was soaked overnight in milk, basted with cider and spices, and crusted in brown sugar. Desserts were authentic: Mississippi pecan pie, coconut layer cake, and Baltimore amber pie.

The devotion to purely southern cuisine at places like Mammy's did not go much further than fried chicken, although the Chicken Koop offered a New Orleans–style oyster loaf. And many ostensibly southern restaurants encroached on other regions, serving Vermont turkeys and New England clam chowder along with their corn bread. New England, as it happens, was already represented by restaurants like the White Turkey Town Houses, offshoots of the

White Turkey Inn in Danbury, Connecticut. The owner, Harry Davega, had grown restless after retiring from his radio and sporting goods store. A vocational psychologist suggested he keep busy by renovating a hotel or restaurant. Harry and his wife, Dorothy, took over an old colonial inn, put White Holland turkeys from Connecticut on the menu, and soon won a devoted following for their all-American food.

The Town and Country, on Park Avenue, realized Crosby Gaige's dream of a restaurant devoted to American regional cooking. The sumptuous decorating style, all mirrors and chandeliers, suggested French haute cuisine, but the menu spoke pure American, with dishes like New England codfish with creamed egg and Louisiana gumbo.

For decades, food writers had complained that the one cuisine impossible to get in New York was American. "We have always had chop-houses, lunch and tea rooms, American or popular priced restaurants, but I deny that the fudge-shops, beaneries, cafeterias, lunch rooms, or cheap restaurants serve plain American food," argued E. H. Nies, the president of the New York Stewards' and Caterers' Association, back in the 1930s. "That which they serve is not even American food, but faked food camouflaged with cornstarch sauce, burnt flour gravy, nujol mayonnaise, creamed pork shredded to look like chicken, cream of chicken soup which cries out the name of Pillsbury, and marshmallow in place of whipped cream." Progress was slow. Twenty years later, Walter R. Brooks, creator of the Freddy the Pig books and a secret gourmet when he was not busy writing for *The New Yorker*, repeated the charge in his guide to the city. "We have never had a good doughnut in any New York restaurant," he complained. (It's still a problem.) His recommendations included the Consumers Cooperative cafeterias, which served good home cooking and great apple pie.

Charges like these stung because they were true. The Town and Country tried to change the equation with regional dishes like Maryland fried chicken with cream gravy, Bucks County scrapple, pecan buns, and chocolate cream pie. In the Town Room, the menu was southern; in the Country Room, it was New England. In either room, the dishes had the ring of authenticity. By and large, though, New Yorkers hankering after classic American dishes had to head back to their hometowns to find them.

Quirky, personal restaurants added spice to a bland diet. As the 1950s wore on, New York began suffering from gastronomic fatigue. France was no longer a source of innovative cuisine, and proponents of considered, historically minded

American cooking, like James Beard, lacked influence except among a tiny, cultivated minority. Diners in the United States, as Patric Kuh put it wittily in *The Last Days of Haute Cuisine*, faced a stark choice. "In 1950, we didn't have to choose between Northern and Southern Italian, Asian fusion, Cal-Med, Ital-Med, or Franco-Californian," he wrote. "Contemplating a meal at a certain price range, we had one very simple decision to make. Did we want to sit among drapes of red velvet or in a cocoon of red leatherette?" The drapes signaled traditional French. In the red leatherette booths, it was Delmonico steak and baked potato (with creamed spinach on the side). This, in broad terms, was the scene. It was about to change.

14

The Baum Years

Newark Airport is no one's idea of a dining destination. But in 1953, the Port Authority of New York and New Jersey decided that it should be. A Manhattan company called Restaurant Associates was told to make it happen.

This was an odd choice to develop a fine-dining restaurant. Restaurant Associates was known primarily for operating lunch counters, but Jerome Brody, its young president, was intent on expanding into new markets. Eager to win the coffee-shop and snack-bar concessions at the airport's new terminal, he agreed to create a restaurant that would attract higher-end customers—not just the captive audience of airline passengers, but well-to-do local residents who ordinarily spent their food dollars in Manhattan. Brody and his company knew nothing about fine dining, but under pressure they agreed to take on the project. This abrupt left turn would lead, through a chain of unintended consequences, to a complete transformation of the New York restaurant world.

The Newark Airport assignment was truly a mission impossible, but a series of accidents had put Brody in a position to take it on. Restaurant Associates had originated with Philip Wechsler & Son, a coffee company that serviced hotels, restaurants, and steamship lines. In the 1930s, the company acquired one of its clients, the Silver Cafeteria chain, which had overexpanded during the Depression. Then, in the 1940s, it bought out Riker's Restaurant Associates, a chain of thirty-five small coffee shops. At that point, fate intervened. One after the other, three of Wechsler's top executives dropped dead of heart attacks. Abraham Wechsler, who had inherited the business from his father, turned in desperation to Brody, his twenty-five-year-old son-in-law, and more or less ordered him to take over. "It was tough," Brody later said. "I started at the top."

Restaurant Associates (the company dropped the "Riker's" in 1945) made its money selling coffee, doughnuts, pie, and beef stew at its all-night lunch counters and cafeterias in Manhattan and Queens. Volume was high but profits were low. Brody, a graduate of Dartmouth's business school, decided that the company needed to shrink its existing properties, give the remaining restaurants an upgrade (at the company's Corner House lunchrooms, the cooks started adding a splash of burgundy to the beef stew), and expand into new areas: department stores, air force bases, and service plazas along the New York State Thruway between Syracuse and Buffalo. Newark Airport was part of the business plan.

Joe Baum, after leaving Restaurant Associates, created a city's worth of restaurants at the World Trade Center. Here he sits in front of the Big Kitchen, on the concourse, in 1977.

If he was going to create a luxury restaurant, however, Brody needed help. He got it in the person of Joseph H. Baum, a small, tightly wound hotel and restaurant man currently employed as the food and beverage manager of the Schine Hotels in Florida. Baum, as it happened, was in a receptive mood. Florida bored him and he needed a challenge. He said yes.

It was a momentous decision. Together, the two men would turn Restaurant Associates into a fine-dining business, and in a series of innovative, imaginatively designed restaurants, change New York's gastronomic culture forever. As the

Eisenhower era gave way to the Kennedy years, restaurants like the Four Seasons, the Brasserie, La Fonda del Sol, and the Forum of the Twelve Caesars tested new ideas about American and international cuisine, interior design, and the dining experience. Going out to dinner in New York would never be the same.

Baum had grown up in a hotel family. His father ran the Gross and Baum Family Hotel in Saratoga Springs during the summer season. After graduating from Cornell's hotel school, and serving in the navy's supply corps during the war, Baum joined Harris, Kerr, Forster, an accounting and consulting company that worked for hotels and restaurants. There he labored over detailed reports on hotel food and beverage control systems. The drudgery would later pay off.

Eventually, Baum was assigned to manage one of the firm's restaurants, the Monte Carlo in Manhattan, owned by the real estate tycoon William Zeckendorf. It was swanky, with a waterfall and a dance floor, and it did an enormous business. Baum paid close attention to his surroundings, listened to Zeckendorf, and got the hang of running a restaurant. "The Monte Carlo was a very flossy place, and that's where I learned what good but not great meant," Baum later recalled. Zeckendorf, a maniac for detail, thought nothing of calling his young manager at four in the morning to hear about the night's bookings. That obsessiveness stayed with Baum, who went on to apply his lessons at the Schine Hotel chain.

Over time, Baum developed some highly unusual ideas about restaurants and how to make them appealing. His philosophy was a blend of showmanship and mysticism, backed up by intensive research, endless attention to detail, and exhaustive recipe testing. What he needed was a stage. The Newarker, as the new airport restaurant was to be called, offered him his first chance to see if razzle-dazzle, visual flash, and innovative food could put an airport on the dining map.

Baum realized from the outset that he had to give customers a reason to go to Newark. With Albert Stockli, a classically trained Swiss chef with a chameleon-like ability to adapt his cooking, he devised a menu that included exotic curry dishes, flaming entrées, and heaping portions. Diners ordering lobster got a lobster and a half, cleverly listed as a "three-claw lobster." An order of a half dozen oysters came with an extra oyster, served on its own plate. When the restaurant switched to giant Absecon oysters, named after an island off Atlantic City, Baum tore a leaf straight from the Toffenetti playbook, advertising them as "knife and fork oysters" because they were so large you had to use a knife and fork to eat them. Fire was introduced wherever possible, in flaming shish kebabs and in a dessert called the Sparkler, a parfait with its own fireworks display. "The customers like to see things on fire, or accompanied by fiery props, and it doesn't really hurt the food much," Baum explained to a mystified reporter. To promote Thanksgiving dinner, Baum released a live turkey in the terminal. "There was chaos," he recalled, "but everyone got the message there was a restaurant right there in the airport where they could get Thanksgiving dinner." In a masterful bit of understatement, Wechsler told *The New Yorker* in 1964: "Joe had a lot of ideas."

The Newarker lost $25,000 in its first year. "You got snowblindness from the glare of the empty tablecloths," Brody said. But as word spread, it began attracting Newark businessmen and diners from the New Jersey suburbs. By 1955, the restaurant was serving a thousand meals a day, 90 percent of them to nontravelers, and grossing more than $2 million a year. James Beard, who would later become a consultant to Restaurant Associates, dined at the Newarker and liked what he saw. With a sharp eye, he singled out a Zurich specialty that Stockli had sneaked into the menu mix: julienned veal strips sautéed with shallots and served with a white wine and cream sauce. "There was a similar dish made with strips of calf's liver, a tiny bit of vinegar, and cream, which charmed even those who normally shunned liver," he later recalled.

Restaurant Associates now had a quality restaurant division, with Baum its presiding genius. In 1955, the company took over the ailing Hawaiian Room at the Lexington Hotel. Baum went straight to work, flying to Hawaii with Brody and embarking on a nonstop eating and sightseeing tour to soak up atmosphere and poach ideas. On the return trip, Baum and Brody scouted out California tiki restaurants, like Don the Beachcomber and Trader Vic's. They transmitted their findings back to Albert Stockli, who created a series of allegedly Polynesian dishes like baked clams with sesame seeds, and spareribs with pineapple and kumquats. The Hawaiian Room benefited from a publicity windfall when Arthur Godfrey, clutching a ukulele, began broadcasting his television show from the restaurant.

Yes, there was an element of hokum in the concept. There generally was in Baum's productions. But commitment and follow-through lifted the enterprise above the level of kitsch. Baum thought of restaurants as integrated environments, with food, design, and service part of a seamless whole. The look of the place, the language on the menu, the design of the tableware, the waiters' uniforms—all contributed to the overall effect.

"For a guest to be happy, every detail must be carefully considered and thought through," he once said. "This encompasses the temperature of the room, the softness of the lighting, the height of the table, the dressing of the table, the quality and pattern of the china, the fragility of the crystal, the way a fork hefts in your hand, the crispness of the roll, the coldness and sweetness of the butter, the sound of the music, the curve of a rail, the color of the carpet." No one had thought about restaurants this way before, not even John Murray and Henry Milo Erkins in their brief heyday. Gustav Stickley, at the Craftsman Restaurant, applied some brilliant insights about restaurant design, but as he freely admitted, he was not a restaurant man, and his menu never matched the Craftsman's decorative daring.

Baum was just warming up. For years, Restaurant Associates had been angling for a restaurant in Rockefeller Center, and in 1956 an opening developed, on the ground floor of the U.S. Rubber Building on Forty-eighth Street. This was probably the poorest location in the center, but it was a foothold nonetheless, an irresistible opportunity to create a big-idea restaurant. The commerce of Rockefeller Center—a crossroads where the radio and television industries met advertising and publishing—suggested to Baum and his planning team the idea of a forum. By chance, William Pahlmann, one of his interior designers, had just bought a set of large-scale portraits of the twelve Caesars. Thus the Forum of the Twelve Caesars was born, the most flamboyant restaurant New York had seen since Murray's Roman Gardens.

In dead earnest, Baum set about creating an amusement park for the senses. He sent teams of company managers to Rome, Naples, Herculaneum, and Pompeii. He put Albert Stockli to work studying the culinary writings of Apicius, the first-century Roman epicure known for recipes involving nightingale tongues, camel heels, and flamingos. Distinguished classics professors were brought in to lecture new staff members on Roman history and culture. There were field trips to watch *Quo Vadis*, a sword-and-sandals film. Suetonius became required reading for waiters, who, whether they realized it or not, would be working in purple-and-red velveteen jackets, an allusion to the togas worn by Roman rulers.

"He had the knack of putting a lot of talented people together who could collectively come up with ideas and solutions: food people, ad people, artists, graphic designers," said Michael Whiteman, Baum's partner in developing the restaurants at the World Trade Center. "Together they would create a fantasy he had. The point of the research was not to develop a slavish authenticity but to ferret out something obscure, surprising, delightful."

The Forum, Baum liked to tell reporters, was intended to evoke Rome at its height, a time of "lusty splendor." Translated into restaurant terms, that meant wine coolers in the shape of Roman helmets, gladiator wall mosaics, and imperial-sized menus and glassware. Baum, in full obsessional mode, sent the custom-made knives back to Italy again and again to have the head of Bacchus in the handle recrafted. Something about the curl of the lip made the wine god look too triumphant, he decided. A revised version was rejected as "too haughty." In another, the lip had "too much of a semblance to a leer."

Albert Stockli, emerging from his study of Apicius, developed an appropriately excessive menu that incorporated Roman ideas but stopped short of camels' feet. Diners were offered, on menus nearly as large as the tabletop, boneless game hen baked in a clay pot; mussels with roe; gosling on wine-braised sauerkraut; wild boar pâté with a sauce of Damascus plum; truffle-stuffed quail; and a salad dubbed "the noblest Caesar of them all."

The menu language was ripe. Diners were invited to try "the oysters of Hercules, which you with sword will carve"; "Filet Mignon, Caesar Augustus, with a Rising Crown of Pâté and Triumphal Laurel Leaf"; and chicken Varus "in a Shell of Centurian Almonds." Critics, won over despite themselves, wrote respectfully about the food, even as they puzzled over the decor. "It's a shame Rome is under that cloud of 'decline,'" Baum mused to *The New Yorker*. "It's all people think about."

Almost simultaneously with the Forum, Restaurant Associates was planning an entirely different restaurant at the new, uncompromisingly modern Seagram Building, designed by Ludwig Mies van der Rohe and Philip Johnson. Originally, Seagram had planned to use its lobby floor as an exhibition hall, but as soon as the building began to rise over Park Avenue, Brody entered into talks to create a luxury restaurant. Baum envisioned a new kind of restaurant, one that would complement Mies and Johnson's architecture and offer an American answer to deluxe French restaurants such as Le Pavillon, for the simple reason that, as Baum pointed out, "we are not Frenchmen, we are Americans."

The Four Seasons would offer American food, with a Continental accent, in the kind of setting it had never before received. The planning took two and a half years, and in the end Restaurant Associates spent a staggering $4.5 million

The product of two and a half years of planning, costing more than $4.5 million, the Four Seasons was Baum's American alternative to upscale French restaurants like Le Pavillon.

THE FOUR SEASONS

on the Four Seasons and the Brasserie, a late-night bistro on the Fifty-third Street side of the Seagram Building. Johnson, assisted by William Pahlmann, designed the interior. The chairs in the ladies' rooms were by Eero Saarinen. The lobby chairs were by Johnson, Mies, and Charles Eames. The art was by Miró and Picasso. Even the silverware was insistently up-to-date.

Baum was a finicky man, yet his bean-counting mentality coexisted with a visionary streak and a fondness for delphic pronouncements that often left his colleagues scratching their heads. "You have to know the difference between an idea and a BIG IDEA," Baum would tell his assembled brain trust of Restaurant Associates managers. "We must explore all the possibilities, and all the possibilities within the possibilities." Glum silence often followed. "Joe never finished a sentence," said Michael Whiteman. "A sentence would start in Philadelphia, work its way up to the Great Lakes, and dribble out over the Atlantic. Sometimes he did this on purpose. He was always looking for answers he'd never thought of; he always wanted a surprise idea." Baum was fully capable of asking his team to ponder the meaning of a plate, as though it were a Platonic form. "He always reminded me of Merlin," recalled Michael Batterberry, the editor of *Food Arts*. "His eyes would narrow, he'd roll these things around on his tongue, and in a low, mysterious voice he would let loose these fragments that were very haiku-like—sometimes enlightening, sometimes puzzling."

It was a haiku, in fact, that gave Baum the idea for the Four Seasons. As the name implied, the eclectic menu would be seasonal. Ingredients would be uncompromisingly fresh, cooked with herbs from the restaurant's own garden. This in itself was a departure. Reverence for fresh ingredients and seasonality has become axiomatic in American cooking ever since the days of nouvelle cuisine and the pioneering efforts of Alice Waters at Chez Panisse; but in 1959, Baum was offering something revolutionary. He drove home the message in the restaurant's decor, which also changed four times a year, as did the table settings, the floral displays, the glassware, the silverware, and the color of the waiters' uniforms. Four seventeen-foot ficus trees towered over diners when the restaurant opened. Four times a year, new, seasonally appropriate trees would be trucked in and planted.

The menu language was English, not French, and dishes were described tersely: "baby pheasant with golden sauce"; "twin tournedos of beef with woodland mushrooms"; "nasturtium leaves." A few Baumisms, however, did manage to creep in. Baby carrots were sold as "the youngest carrots in butter," and the beefsteak tomato was carved at the table and served with a steak knife.

The Four Seasons was a triumph—the city's "first self-consciously modern restaurant," the architecture critic Paul Goldberger has called it. In one fell swoop, most of the principles that still govern today's restaurants found expression, in a sublime interior. The notion of dining as a theatrical experience; the close attention to design and interior decor as a shaping force in the dining experience; a more relaxed, American style of service; the elevation of American cuisine; women waiters and managers—all these innovations would become a permanent part of the dining landscape.

Like so many of his dishes, Baum was on fire. After the Four Seasons, he decided the time was ripe for New York's first serious Latin American restaurant: La Fonda del Sol, in the Time & Life Building. The usual blitz of airplane trips, on-the-ground research, brainstorming sessions, and group tastings ensued. Committed to authenticity, he imported the staff from Latin America. His flair for showmanship led him to commission the futuristic fashion designer Rudi Gernreich—creator of the topless bathing suit—to come up with the staff uniforms: ponchos, serapes, and high-heeled boots. For the interior, Alexander Girard splashed searing colors on adobe walls. The restaurant included one more Baum innovation that would become a cliché in years to come: the open kitchen.

By the mid-1960s, Baum and Restaurant Associates were operating at full tilt, creating restaurants both grand and plebeian. With the same zeal and eye for detail that yielded the Four Seasons, Baum developed Zum Zum, a popular series of German sausage restaurants. Brody, the company's real estate man, was out of the picture by this time. He made the mistake of divorcing the boss's daughter, a move that cost him his job overnight. The free-spending Baum took over as president, and a company called Waldorf Systems was brought in to provide management expertise. By 1968, Restaurant Associates' 130 restaurants were racking up gross revenues of nearly $100 million, and the company's stock price was soaring.

The combination of class and mass worked like a charm. In 1959, just months before opening the Four Seasons, the company acquired Leone's, an enormous Italian restaurant in the theater district with a fine pedigree. Created in 1906 by Gene Leone and his wife, Luisa, who did the cooking, it had once attracted diners like Enrico Caruso and W. C. Fields. (As a tribute to Mrs. Leone, Restaurant Associates renamed the restaurant Mama Leone's.) The food was undistinguished, but the profit margins were stupendous. Leone's alone contributed $4 million a year to RA's bottom line.

Time magazine, in a 1959 profile of the company, infuriated Baum by referring to him as "bagel-waisted." He fumed over the slight for months. But in every other respect, the future looked bright. Baum was, as always, brimming over with new ideas. Dazzled by his own brilliance, he failed to notice troubling warning signs. RA was spending too much and expanding too quickly.

Soon things began to go terribly wrong. Revenues were rising, but profits were falling. In 1969, the company declared a loss on revenues of $110 million. New ventures outside New York fell flat. The Thruway restaurants turned out to be expensive. Worse, when snow fell between Buffalo and Syracuse, which was

With La Fonda del Sol, which opened in the mid-1960s, Baum created the city's first high-end Latin American restaurant. The interior design by Alexander Girard included (*opposite*) splashy graphics and an open kitchen.

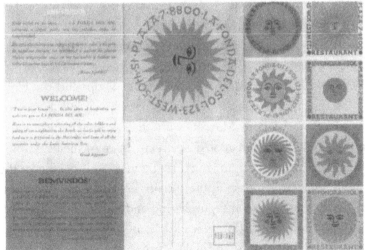

often, they sat empty. Restaurant Associates unloaded them after a year. An experimental European venture—a French resort complex in Divonne-les-Bains to be designed by Raymond Loewy—went nowhere. Ideas for a steakhouse in Paris were dropped. As New York's restaurant economy soured and the city lurched toward insolvency, the company's stock price tumbled. Waldorf Systems seized control of the company and embarked on a cost-cutting campaign. In 1970, Baum was out. Restaurant Associates was, in effect, exiting the luxury restaurant business.

The Baum era was not quite over. Within a few years, he was hired by Hilton Hotels to run Inhilco, its new food-service subsidiary. Almost immediately, the company landed a very big fish: a contract to operate the food stands and restaurants in an enormous new project, the World Trade Center. The trade center, on the drawing board since the early 1960s, was a massive urban renewal project pushed through by the Port Authority of New York and New Jersey. It envisioned seven buildings dominated by two identical towers, 110 stories tall, that would drastically alter the skyline of lower Manhattan. They also presented an interesting logistical problem: how to feed an instant city with a population the size of Albany's.

Baum created a central commissary for food preparation, then opened a series of smallish restaurants at different price levels to feed the swarming thousands who poured through the concourse level of the trade center. Some were commuters riding the PATH trains from New Jersey, others were workers from the surrounding buildings. The concourse resembled a city square enclosed by walls, and Baum treated it that way. With a nod to the Washington Market—displaced after more than a century by the World Trade Center—he created a complex of restaurants called Market Square. It included a formal sit-down restaurant and pub-bar, the Market Bar and Dining Rooms; a self-service fast-food operation called the Big Kitchen; the Corner coffee shop; and the Coffee Exchange, a station specializing in light food and snacks. The Big Kitchen really did evoke the spirit of Washington Market, with stalls selling delicatessen sandwiches, clams and oysters, baked goods, ice cream, or roast meats.

Baum's idea was, as he put it, to "fracture the mass"—break down the food-service operation into twenty or so discrete units, each with its own personality. The central commissary unified the purchasing and much of the food preparation, but out on the concourse, diners could choose from a variety of price options, food styles, and degrees of formality, from eat-on-the-run to the more ambitious Market Bar, which earned stellar reviews for its well-executed steakhouse menu. The market idea was key to the restaurant's image. Suppliers of specific ingredients were indicated on the menu—another practice that restaurateurs would jump on in the 1990s. A "vegetable sommelier" wandered from table to table, whipping up enthusiasm for the fresh produce of the day and offering suggestions on how the kitchen might prepare it.

The crown jewel of the project was Windows on the World, a luxury restaurant on the 107th floor of the north tower. Intended as an aerial counterpart to the Four Seasons, with a similarly Modernist bent, it scored an instant hit, and went far toward reconciling New Yorkers to an architectural landmark they initially loathed. The World Trade Center, and the architect Minoru Yamasaki's towers, seemed at the time a grotesque white elephant, a reckless expenditure of scarce public money. For years, the towers remained half empty, a painful symbol of hubris. "It was unthinkable," Paul Goldberger wrote, "to say a good word about the twin towers in polite company."

Windows on the World, if only for the duration of a meal, let New Yorkers look out on a purified city. Sheer altitude eliminated, as if by magic, the insoluble problems below: crime, white flight, labor strife, drugs, police corruption, and all the rest of the evils that made New York, in the 1970s, cinematic shorthand for social chaos and urban decline.

The restaurant, like the towers, represented an enormous bet on a city the rest of the country had written off. Like the bumblebee, it never should have flown, but it did. From the day it opened, Windows was packed. Yes, you could find better food in the city (although not a more impressive wine list), but food was never entirely the point. The view was the selling point. Diners could look down, not up, at helicopters buzzing over the city. There were days when the restaurant was enrobed in clouds. When it wasn't, diners could see for miles. At Windows, New York was the main course.

The restaurant came with a couple of side dishes. The Hors d'Oeuvrerie was a lounge offering smorgasbord by day and sushi by night. Cellar in the Sky, a small dining room designed to look like a wine cellar, but with dappled light to suggest sunlight filtered through grape leaves, gave New York one of its first wine-pairing menus. Like the Four Seasons, Windows on the World and Cellar in the Sky invested heavily in California wines, a radical departure for the East Coast.

"In a way, it was the symbol of the beginning of the turnaround of New

Windows on the World, 107 stories above Manhattan in the World Trade Center, was Joe Baum's most dramatic restaurant project. Here, diners could see the entire city at their feet. The restaurant and dozens of its employees vanished in moments on September 11, 2001.

York," Michael Whiteman recalled. "We were successful because New York wanted us to be successful. It couldn't stand another heartbreaking failure." The scale of that success was astonishing. "We had projected revenues of twelve million dollars the first year, and the critics all said we'd be lucky to do eight million. "The criticism was so insistent that we came to believe it. We did fourteen million, and it nearly killed us." At its peak, in the late 1980s, Windows was one of the top-grossing restaurants in the United States, taking in more than $24 million a year.

After leaving Inhilco, Baum later undertook a $25 million makeover of Windows on the World with Whiteman after the first trade center bombing, in 1993. At the time, Baum was riding high after a remarkable transformation of the Rainbow Room in Rockefeller Center with the architectural firm Hardy Holzman Pfeiffer. (Ironically, Baum's sole venture into creating his own restaurant, Aurora, was not a success.) He also devised a seductive, intimate restaurant called Wild Blue—an allusion to "wild blue yonder"—in the old Cellar in the Sky space. A cozy cocoon in the sky, as snug as a ship's cabin, it was one of the most charming eating spots in the city, though it never really got the chance to catch on. On September 11, 2001, after two jetliners slammed into the Twin Towers, Windows on the World and Wild Blue came crashing down to earth in a matter of minutes. Seventy-three restaurant workers were dead. An inspiring chapter in New York dining was over, but Baum, who had died in 1998, was not there to see it.

It would be an exaggeration, but not a great one, to say that everything after Joe Baum has been a series of footnotes to his groundbreaking ideas. The concept of the restaurant as a *Gesamtkunstwerk*—a fully integrated artistic concept—still holds sway, as does the model of the restaurant group as an incubator of new ideas and the arbiter of a particular style. The group dynamic can be seen in the restaurants of Drew Nieporent's Myriad Group; of Danny Meyer's Union Square Café, Gramercy Tavern, and related spin-offs; in the joint ventures of Mario Batali and Joseph Bastianich; and in the big, boisterous restaurants of Stephen Hanson's B. R. Guest company. The influential restaurant designs of David Rockwell would be hard to imagine without the example of Restaurant Associates. And the current vogue for carefully researched, scientifically mixed cocktails, although few people realize it, owes everything to Baum. It was at Aurora that Baum instructed his bartender, Dale DeGroff, to study an old book called *The Bon-Vivant's Companion*, the first bartender's manual printed in the United

States. At Aurora and, most influentially, at the Rainbow Room bar, DeGroff reintroduced classic cocktails from the pre-Prohibition era and taught a new generation of bartenders how to mix drinks without shortcuts. The result was a genuine renaissance in cocktail-making and, in many restaurants, fruitful collaborations between bartenders and chefs. Just one more reason to thank Joe Baum.

15

California Comes Calling

When Joe Baum and Restaurant Associates went their separate ways, a brief, effervescent period of creativity ended in New York. Baum made his reputation disrupting the status quo. But in the late 1960s and early 1970s, the status quo was reasserting its rights in New York. Elsewhere, momentous changes were unfolding in the restaurant world. Excitement was in the air. American cuisine stood at the threshold of something new and exciting.

But not in New York. For the first time in a very long while, cultural energy no longer radiated from the nation's largest urban center. It had enjoyed a splendid run. After 1945, the futuristic promise of the 1939 World's Fair looked as though it was being realized in the world's most dynamic, forward-looking city. Abstract Expressionism, live television, bebop, and the Broadway musical put Manhattan in the cultural vanguard. Under Mayor Fiorello La Guardia, a cityscape of smooth highways, public housing, and grand public works unfolded. Like a powerful generator, New York transmitted cultural electricity that lit up the world.

By the 1960s, however, the city of the future was showing its age. New York looked dirtier than ever. The middle class was fleeing to the suburbs. The transport system was decrepit. The highways and the bridges were crumbling. The city synonymous with invention and innovation felt old and tired. In a metropolis where everything once seemed possible, nothing got done. New York, for the first time in its life, had run out of energy and ideas. Chaos and bankruptcy loomed.

The restaurants were certainly not coming up with anything new. Le Pavillon was gone, Henri Soulé dead. One by one, the grand restaurants of the postwar years were losing their clientele to old age and sheer boredom. Gael Greene, *New York* magazine's cheeky restaurant critic, toured the once-great Colony in 1971 and turned in a devastating review. "Today lunch in the Colony dining room is like lunch at Forest Lawn except that here the flowers are mostly plastic," she wrote. "A captain picks his nose. Gene Cavallero Jr. picks his teeth with a matchbook. Young couples arrive bubbling and cheerful . . . and soon grow grim and silent in the vast unoccupied spaces of Marienbad in the off-season." This was an obituary not just for one restaurant but for an entire era and its style of dining.

New York's dining culture presented a pitiful spectacle. French haute cuisine at Le Pavillon's successors continued to perform on autopilot. The lunchroom chains and Automats that had enlivened and improved the life of New Yorkers early in the century were either bankrupt or teetering. Television kept people at home, detaching them from restaurants and de-educating their palates. "The restaurant world was in free fall," the food critic Peter Elliot has written of this period. "Even the restaurants at the lower end of the scale were in full retreat: New York classics like Schrafft's, Horn & Hardart and Chock Full o' Nuts." On every front, it seemed, New York's very identity as a world-class city was threatened.

Deliverance was at hand, though New York diners could not have known it. Momentous cultural and economic forces far away were conspiring to change forever the way chefs thought about food, the way restaurants served it, and the way diners consumed it.

As a general rule, cuisines change very slowly. New World fruits and vegetables irrevocably altered the European diet, but the transformative process took centuries. French haute cuisine, first codified in the era of Louis XV, changed little until the early nineteenth century, when the great Carême gave it a thorough overhaul, and his revisions held until the heyday of Escoffier in the early twentieth century. Overall, the restaurants of New York were remarkable not so much for their innovations as for their high quality and their profession. In no other city were so many national cuisines represented, but in every case, the aim was to present as faithfully as possible a traditional array of national dishes. Innovations tended to come in decor, or modes of service, such as the assembly-line approach of the Automat.

In his autobiography, published in 1982, Craig Claiborne called the New York of his early days as food editor of *The New York Times* in the late fifties "a hick town." Not only that, he insisted, but it had been a hick town for quite some time. "It has long been my contention, and I can prove it by thumbing through vintage dining guides, some of them nearly half a century old, that New York was not, fifty years ago, a great city in which to dine," he wrote. Prohibition and the Depression had dismantled the glorious edifice of dining erected at the turn of the century. The Second World War had completed the process. "That is why, when I came onto the restaurant scene, there were relatively few celebrated (I will not say great) restaurants in New York or in the United States, for that matter," Claiborne wrote. "In New York the list of highly touted restaurants included Le Voisin, the Colony, the Café Chambord, the '21' Club, the Brussels, the Quo Vadis, Maude Chez Elle, and Le Pavillon." Only Quo Vadis and '21' survived.

All this was about to change. In France itself, the inflexibility of haute cuisine was producing restlessness among younger chefs. A new approach to ingredients and their use, cheered on by the powerful Gault-Millau guide, led to the revolutionary style dubbed *nouvelle cuisine*, a self-consciously modern way of cooking that placed a premium on fresh ingredients, reduced cooking times, and lighter dishes presented with loving attention to color and geometry. Heavy cream sauces that disguised natural flavors were banned. Lightness and transparency emerged as paramount values, partly in response to diners worried about their waistlines and their calorie intake. The complexities of haute cuisine were subjected to a rigorous simplification. What Frank Lloyd Wright and Le Corbusier did to Victorian architecture, nouvelle chefs did to French cuisine.

Nouvelle cuisine did not appear out of thin air. It reflected underlying changes in lifestyle—a widespread obsession among the well-to-do with health, diet, and fitness, most notably—and in cultural values. The new focus on fresh ingredients and their pure expression reflected the spirit of the 1960s, with their questioning of tradition, hostility to the calcified forms of the past, and search for authenticity. It also reflected a mounting unease about food quality in an age dominated by industrial producers.

All of these concerns coalesced in the mind of a young woman in California named Alice Waters, who, like many of the Americans of her generation who traveled to France, experienced a revelation when she sat down to eat. The country food she encountered in France, and its expression in the cookbooks of an

American expatriate named Richard Olney, impressed her deeply. This was honest food, which, in its simplicity and genuineness, radiated an almost spiritual aura. A child of the Free Speech Movement at Berkeley, Waters subscribed to the values of the counterculture, both its hedonism and its moralism. With missionary fervor, she set about transplanting the values of homey French cooking to Berkeley, where she founded Chez Panisse, named for a character in Marcel Pagnol's *Fanny* trilogy of films set in Provence. In the process, she helped create California cuisine, unleashing creative forces that reverberate down to the present day.

Feeling their way, Waters and her first great chef, Jeremiah Tower, translated French values into American terms, eventually arriving at a regional style that seduced diners and captivated food writers. Waters described her food as "not esoteric, not too intimidating. Sort of straightforward and, at its best, surprising." Tower, a keen student of old cookbooks, and lavish in his tastes—"I was olive oil, he was more cream and butter," Waters said—loved to stage theme dinners based on his reading. One day, he found himself thumbing through Charles Ranhofer's mammoth *Epicurean*. This was a work seemingly remote from the developing ethos at Chez Panisse, but a certain recipe caught his eye. It was a cream of corn soup that carried the descriptive designation "à la Mendocino." Tower, who had spent many hours talking with James Beard about the possibilities of American regional cooking, stopped and puzzled. "What in the world, I thought, was the chef of New York's most famous restaurant doing thinking about dishes local to small regions of California?" he wrote in his memoir, *California Dish*. A switch flipped. If a Frenchman like Ranhofer could regard California as a region, why couldn't an American chef?

Tower pursued his American dream at a spectacular event at the Four Seasons in New York, where he had been invited to devise a menu for an annual dinner held by a California wine association. He seized on the occasion to advertise the new American style taking shape at Chez Panisse. The menu led with appetizers like snapper tartare and shad quenelles, and proceeded to main courses like stuffed quail with pistachios, veal and morels in cream, and duck livers with apples and Cabernet. All the wines were Californian. Not so coincidentally, this was the year that California stunned the French wine world when its Chardonnays and Cabernets swept the top placings in a blind tasting organized in Paris by Stephen Spurrier, a British wine merchant.

The apostles of California cuisine proved to be expert marketers. In a series of staged demonstrations that mesmerized food writers and critics, they argued their case, as it were, on the plate. Tower followed up his Four Seasons dinner with a California regional menu dinner at Chez Panisse that reads like a manifesto. The dinner started with Tomales Bay oysters in ice, a lead-in to the now-sacrosanct Mendocino cream of corn soup, which Tower tweaked with crayfish butter. Smoked trout from Garrapata Creek in Big Sur was steamed over bay leaves—California bay leaves, of course. Monterey Bay prawns and Sebastopol geese figured in the main dishes, followed by a single cheese—dry Monterey Jack from Sonoma County. "My menu, in English, was a celebration of our new sense of place, of where we lived and ate," Tower later wrote.

Two years later, the traveling show returned to New York, where Alice Waters organized a California feast at Tavern on the Green, giving New Yorkers a sneak preview of coming attractions. With even greater fanfare, Tower (now at the Santa Fe Bar and Grill in Berkeley) would upstage Guy Savoy, a rising French star, at a cooking demonstration in 1983 in Providence, Rhode Island. The event, intended to showcase Savoy's "sauceless cuisine," attracted a legion of food writers. They came to celebrate Savoy but rose to their feet and cheered Tower's bravura performance: a California menu cooked entirely on the grill, including the tropical fruit in the dessert compote.

California cuisine was a trend on the verge of becoming a movement. In Santa Monica, a twenty-four-year-old restaurateur named Michael McCarty opened Michael's, where a procession of highly talented young American chefs helped translate French nouvelle cuisine into a California idiom. A young Austrian, Wolfgang Puck, was picking up the language as well, turning out smoked-salmon and caviar pizzas at Spago and earning the adoration of the Hollywood A-list. By sheer force of personality, amplified by his celebrity fans, he broadcast the California style to the nation at large.

The freewheeling experimentation and local-mindedness of the California food revolution quickly spread eastward. In Louisiana, chefs like Paul Prudhomme rediscovered and reinvented Cajun cuisine. In the South and in New England, young chefs began searching out the best of their local ingredients and rediscovering old dishes. In the spirit of nouvelle invention, they put their stamp on regional classics and elevated popular foods to haute-cuisine status.

Older, classically trained French chefs found the new styles both confusing and confused, but young chefs jumped at the chance to try out new ideas, and adventurous diners followed them. Experiment was in the air. Cheap airplane travel was revolutionizing the experiences of diners and the training of chefs. It brought food products to American kitchens from as far away as Asia within twenty-four hours. A globalized vocabulary known as "fusion" gradually emerged, as younger chefs introduced exotic flavors into hybrid dishes that might incorporate influences from Thailand, Mexico, and North Africa on the same menu. Congress, unwittingly, did its part in the early 1970s, changing a long-standing rule that granted French chefs U.S. work permits as a matter of course. Closing the door on France created an incentive for American culinary schools to expand their programs. A new generation of American chefs trained in America emerged from schools like the Culinary Institute of America and lesser institutions, right down to the community-college level.

The aftershocks from California's culinary earthquake eventually reached New York, where a recovering economy coincided nicely with a momentous demographic trend. The Baby Boom generation was now reaching its peak earning years, with plenty of disposable income to spend on travel and food. Trend-sensitive and self-indulgent, they constituted a dream market for upscale restaurants attuned to the new frequencies in cuisine: New American, Pacific Rim, Nuevo Latino, New Southwestern, anything and everything.

After years in the doldrums, New York rebounded. Its restaurants embarked on a frantic new era of relentless innovation, big money, star chefs, media glamour, and powerful chef-entrepreneur partnerships that would not only redefine dining but reshape the city, imparting their own distinctive flavor to new neighborhoods like Tribeca, the Flatiron District, and the meatpacking district, and transforming old ones like the Lower East Side. The rapidity of change, and the torrents of money flowing through the city, recalled the heady days of Madison Square and Times Square a century earlier.

In New York, the free license granted by nouvelle cuisine gained traction among a cluster of chefs strongly influenced by James Beard and the possibilities of applying French techniques to American ingredients and dishes. The idiom that resulted, New American cuisine, proved to be a liberating and highly influential force. The River Café, which opened on a barge on the Brooklyn waterfront in 1977, emerged as a hothouse for young chefs eager to try out new ideas. Larry Forgione, one of its first success stories, opened An American Place in 1983, serving dishes like planked salmon, pan-seared buffalo steak, apple pandowdy, and banana betty. The River Café would continue to produce superior chefs in the New American vein, notably David Burke at the Park Avenue Café and Charlie Palmer at Aureole in the 1980s, and, in the new millennium, Rick Laakkonen at the brilliant if short-lived Ilo in the Bryant Park Hotel.

Gotham Bar and Grill's Alfred Portale (*right*), one of the brightest lights among the new wave of chefs who transformed the city's restaurants in the early 1980s with a style of cooking known as New American

In Greenwich Village, Alfred Portale, a disciple of Michel Guérard, created another culinary proving ground at the Gotham Bar and Grill. The style—streamlined, simple, inventive—showed how flexible New American cuisine could be. Looking back, Portale calls his early menus, only half jokingly, Continental. And so they were: squab with wild mushrooms; swiss chard and spätzle with mustard butter; goat cheese ravioli with pancetta, onions, and tomatoes in an herbed chicken broth; loup de mer with shiitake, sautéed leeks, and tarragon in a red-wine vinegar sauce. The influences and accents came from all over. The Gotham kitchen turned out future stars whose restaurants would have a major impact on the dining scene in the 1990s and the early years of the new century: Scott Bryan of Veritas, Bill Telepan of Judson Grill and Telepan, Diane Forley (who also put in time at the River Café) of Verbena, David Walzog of Arizona 206 and Tapika, Gary Robins of the Biltmore Room, Kerry Heffernan of One Fifth and Eleven Madison Park. One of Portale's most successful graduates was Tom Valenti, who parlayed his reputation as the chef at Alison on Dominick Street into two enormously popular Upper West Side bistros, one French-American (Ouest), the other Italian (Cesca).

Another pioneer was Barry Wine, a self-taught chef who created, at the Quilted Giraffe, a restaurant with a French-style emphasis on fine dining and refined presentation, but with a decidedly American (and, later, Japanese) slant. Wine's response to lamb baked in hay, a specialty at the three-star Les Prés et les Sources d'Eugénie, was to bake American lamb in corn husks and serve it with California wine.

In 1984, Jonathan Waxman, formerly of Chez Panisse and Michael's, planted the California flag in Manhattan at Jams, on East Seventy-ninth Street, with his partner, Melvyn Master, the director of Jordan Winery. The restaurant was a sensation. Menus were written each day, according to the dictates of the market, and the food reflected the breezy California style, with mesquite-grilled meats, barely cooked vegetables, and colorful showstoppers like grilled scallops over yellow and orange homemade pasta. Waxman's grilled free-range chicken with twice-fried potatoes became one of the decade's iconic dishes. The wine was Californian, and so was the service, a laid-back, casual style natural on the West Coast but new in New York.

The city reshaped itself to accommodate the changing culinary currents. A new generation of restaurateurs, like the artists who colonized SoHo and remade it in their image, sought out marginal neighborhoods where the rents were cheap and, in a quiet way, revolutionized the way New Yorkers lived and the way they thought about their city. In 1979, David and Karen Waltuck, a couple still in their early twenties, opened Chanterelle in a cast-iron storefront on Grand Street, in the lower reaches of SoHo. The cooking, a forward-looking, inventive interpretation of modern French cuisine—seafood sausage in beurre blanc sauce quickly became the restaurant's signature dish—caught the attention of critics, but so did the general tone of the place, a relaxed stylishness that amounted to an indictment of the old-fashioned French service built on intimidation and stifling formality.

Creeping California casualness, and a commitment to global experimentation, propelled the careers of two ambitious neighborhood-shapers whose restaurants would help define New York dining in the 1980s and '90s. Drew Nieporent, a graduate of Cornell University's School of Hotel Management and a veteran of Maxwell's Plum and Tavern on the Green, broke new ground when, in 1985, he created Montrachet, whose kitchen featured a restlessly inventive, highly temperamental chef named David Bouley. The restaurant was in a rough-edged industrial area so nondescript that real estate brokers had to invent a name for it: Tribeca for "*tri*angle *be*low *Ca*nal Street." In his review, Bryan Miller of the *Times* advised diners to call the restaurant for directions if driving. The menu was renegade French: chicken livers with cornmeal madeleines, boneless chicken thighs stuffed with sweetbreads and served in an Italian parsley sauce. Montrachet, with its downtown atmosphere, ambitious kitchen, and eye-popping wine list, was a radically reinterpreted French restaurant, and precisely the sort of high-low cultural experience agreeable to hip diners.

With little more than a nudge, Tribeca took off. The area had been invaded, in fact, some five years earlier by two English brothers, Keith and Brian McNally, when they opened the Odeon. Their restaurant was an unpretentious brasserie with a solid kitchen and a vibe perfectly in tune with the city's downtown night creatures, a species forever captured by Jay McInerney in *Bright Lights, Big City*. The cover of this quintessential early 1980s novel featured the Odeon's façade, bathed in a seductive neon glow. Despite the dependable cooking—for most of the decade the highly regarded Patrick Clark served as executive chef—the Odeon was a style statement first and foremost. It was defined not by its food but by the kind of people who ate there: celebrities like the cast of *Saturday Night Live* intermingled with an assortment of downtown hipsters. With and without Brian—the partnership ended in the mid-eighties—Keith would go on to replicate the Odeon's success with an odds-defying run of hits. The list included Café Luxembourg, on the Upper West Side (until quite recently a neighborhood that was pure poison for any restaurant), a nightclub called Nell's, a "Constructivist" bar called Pravda, and, in 1997, Balthazar, a breakfast, lunch, and dinner brasserie that epitomized Manhattan-style high-energy chic. Like the Odeon, it has greatly exceeded the normal life span allotted to trendy restaurants.

McNally was an oddity. Consulting only his own preferences, he somehow managed to create restaurants that defined the latest word in hipness. Age did

Drew Nieporent's Montrachet, where a young David Bouley ran the kitchen, put Tribeca on the map as a restaurant neighborhood.

not seem to loosen his grip on fashion. In 1999, he invaded the meatpacking district. Located around far west Fourteenth Street, this was another marginal neighborhood—so marginal that its streets reeked of animal blood from nearby packinghouses. In this unlikely spot he opened Pastis, a simulacrum of a 1930s French brasserie, complete with fading ochre paint on the exterior. It looked like a stage set for a Marcel Pagnol film, and the fare was determinedly retro: braised beef with carrots, moule frites, and skate with black butter. On cue, the celebrities and models showed up in force, just as they did when he opened Morandi, an Italian trattoria in the Village, in early 2007.

Montrachet, by contrast, had put the stamp of dead-serious dining on Tribeca. It challenged all comers. When David Bouley left the restaurant in a huff in 1987, he strayed no farther than a few blocks. His restaurant, Bouley, instantly became a rival to Montrachet. Refined and inventive—he was a pioneer of the low-temperature vacuum cooking known as sous-vide—Bouley epitomized the new type of American chef, classically trained but freewheeling and far-ranging when it came to ingredients and techniques. In 1990, Nieporent, in partnership with Robert De Niro, opened Tribeca Grill, an American-style brasserie on Greenwich Street. Six years later, he added to his downtown portfolio with Layla, a bistro with updated Mediterranean and North African dishes like lobster pastilla or lamb-shank tagine with okra and pumpkin couscous. Tribeca was his fiefdom—the critics lay at his feet. And then came Nobu.

Nobu Matsuhisa was a Japanese chef who had picked up some unusual ideas while working in Peru. Different fish, and a different culture, changed him. Deliberately and boldly, he broke through some of Japanese cuisine's rigidly defined categories. After moving to Los Angeles, he opened Matsuhisa, a new-wave fusion restaurant that became a favorite of De Niro's. The actor coaxed the chef to New York and, with Nieporent, created a showcase restaurant for him, Nobu. David Rockwell, a former theatrical set designer who would later go on to create the look for a slew of high-end Manhattan restaurants, devised a wild tropical setting for Matsuhisa's iconoclastic food.

Once again, California showed the way. Sushi, slowly but surely, had worked its way into the city's dining vocabulary in the 1970s, but Matsuhisa made it speak a new language. His sashimi was lightly cooked and often prepared with olive oil or garlic, unheard of for a traditional Japanese chef. Latin ingredients like chilies (instead of wasabi) and cilantro also made an appearance, as well as Peruvian tiraditos and ceviches. His yellowtail with jalapeño was pure California. Matsuhisa's most famous dish was black cod glazed with sweet miso sauce—melting, buttery, and sweet, it became an instant star, one of those dishes that express a cultural moment, or a turn in taste, like Le Cirque's pasta primavera or crème brûlée. Of course, there is no such thing as black cod. The fish is sable. No matter.

The Tribeca pattern—food, fashion, celebrity—was soon replicated a little farther uptown in the area around Union Square and the Flatiron Building. Union Square, bounded on the south by scruffy Fourteenth Street (where the slowly moldering Lüchow's was soon to expire), enjoyed a lowly reputation when, in 1985, a fresh-faced midwesterner named Danny Meyer opened the Union Square Café on Fifteenth Street on the site of a former health-food restaurant called Brownie's. The neighborhood's attractions were visible only to a determined eye, but Meyer had an idea. He had grown up eating fine French food on family trips to Europe, and as a college student had spent a lot of time in Italy, where he loved the homey, welcoming atmosphere of the typical neighborhood trattoria. While French restaurants, no matter how humble, operated according to strict rules, Italian trattorias seemed to enforce only one: enjoy

Danny Meyer, the owner of Union Square Café (*bottom*), put warmth and hospitality on the menu. (*top*) He talks to his chef Floyd Cardoz at Tabla, one of his two restaurants on Madison Square.

yourself. Night after night, Meyer returned to his favorite neighborhood places, and an idea took shape, equal parts midwestern and Italian. Might it not be possible to create a fine-dining restaurant that put customers at ease by relaxing the tight formalities normally associated with stylish restaurants?

Michael Romano, Meyer's chef at Union Square, came up with a breezy New American menu with a strongly Italian accent, and Meyer did the rest, creating an open, friendly atmosphere remarkable in a city fueled by snobbery and exclusion. The restaurant caught on immediately with nearby book publishers, who gave the restaurant intellectual cachet. Its success was ratified by the Zagat Survey, an informal tip sheet created in 1979 by Tim Zagat, a lawyer and dedicated restaurant-goer, together with his wife and fellow lawyer, Nina. A decidedly populist food guide, it assigned numerical scores for food, decor, and service based on comments from ordinary diners and tallied the scores to determine the best, or at least the best-liked, restaurants in the city. Not surprisingly, the immensely appealing Union Square Café quickly shot to the top of the ratings, and has stayed there ever since, refusing to budge from the top three.

Soon after the Union Square Café opened, Bryan Miller, the *Times*'s restaurant critic, declared Union Square and the blocks fanning northward to the Flatiron Building the city's newest dining hot spot. "Since 1984, a dozen restaurants have taken root in the neighborhood, the majority of them in the last 10 to 12 months," he wrote. "And the pace seems to be escalating daily. This area may soon rival nearby Greenwich Village as a center for late-night dining." In fact, it quickly eclipsed Greenwich Village entirely. The area experienced such explosive growth that it had to be subdivided, in the minds of diners, into two distinct dining destinations: Union Square and the Flatiron District.

Most of the restaurants listed by Miller no longer exist. His census reflects the cruel economics of the restaurant business. The Metropolis Café, the Fifth Avenue Grill, Positano, Canastel, Joanna, L'Escale, Café du Parc, the cavernous America on Eighteenth Street—where are they now? Their places were soon taken by restaurants like Gramercy Tavern, Danny Meyer's all-American counterpart to the Union Square Café; Union Pacific, a daring Pacific Rim restaurant with a telegenic young chef named Rocco DiSpirito; and Patria, a high-end Nuevo Latino restaurant created by Douglas Rodriguez, an exciting Miami chef.

Over on Fifth Avenue, a few steps away from Union Square, the owners of Gotham Bar and Grill opened Mesa Grill, a loud, exuberant southwestern restaurant with an equally exuberant chef in the kitchen: Bobby Flay, a cocky

Jonathan Waxman brought the revolutionary California style to New York in the 1980s at Jams, where the accent was on fresh ingredients, grilling, and a casual atmosphere.

New Yorker who discovered southwestern food while working for Jonathan Waxman at Jams. Flay would go on to open Bolo, a Spanish bistro near the Flatiron Building, and bring his bad-boy charm to the fledgling Food Network, becoming one of its biggest draws. DiSpirito would leave Union Pacific to create Rocco's, a nostalgic return to red-sauce Italian-American food, just across the street from Bolo. Its painful birth, and premature death, made for excruciating viewing on the reality television series *The Restaurant*, which helped make Rocco's the most public culinary disaster in the city's history.

The ferment in the Flatiron District was remarkable. In the 1990s, Meyer's partner at Gramercy Tavern, Tom Colicchio, would create his own mini-empire in the area, starting with Craft, a high-end exercise in back-to-basics cooking that spawned the more casual Craftbar and 'wichcraft, a sandwich bar that generated its own spin-offs. Like Bobby Flay, Colicchio found a second career on television, as the somewhat menacing taskmaster of *Top Chef*.

From nothing, something. Union Square and the Flatiron District, blank spots on the map in the early 1980s, emerged as prime dining destinations seemingly overnight, vivid examples of the potential for restaurants to alter the shape of the city. They also reflected a general cultural drift away from the center and toward the periphery. Beginning in the 1980s, previously marginal cuisines began asserting their rights. Younger diners, in particular, were not really interested in eating at the kind of French or Italian restaurant their parents loved. As travelers, they were more likely to seek out exotic destinations, and that taste for adventure carried over to their restaurant choices. Vietnam, Spain, Thailand, Korea, Malaysia, Morocco: these were the new ports of call. A heightened sense of regionalism redefined French, Italian, Chinese, Mexican, and American cuisines. In this atmosphere, local cultures had their say because, as never before, they had an audience. Chinese cuisine, once regarded as a single, undifferentiated entity, subdivided. Hunan restaurants came into vogue, followed by Szechuan. In the 1990s, Shanghai soup dumplings achieved star status. As new Chinatowns developed in Flushing (Queens) and Sunset Park (Brooklyn), the options expanded exponentially. In Flushing alone, two restaurants specialized in the cooking style of Dongbei, a region bordering North Korea.

In similar fashion, diners learned the difference between the cooking of Oaxaca and Veracruz, two of Mexico's most important regional styles. Italy, dearly loved but poorly represented in countless red-sauce restaurants, regained credibility as restaurants defined themselves more narrowly, showcasing the cuisine of Emilia-Romagna, for example, or Venezia-Friuli-Giulia, or Istria. French restaurateurs picked up on the taste for bistros and brasseries. It was a momentous change. Restaurants, diners, and food writers were treating Third World cuisines, regional styles, and even street foods with the respect once reserved for French haute cuisine.

Meanwhile, the ghost of the Colony refused to rest. Café society, deprived of life support, no longer existed. The infrastructure of dance bands, nightclub singers, and fine restaurants that defined high-style nightlife before the Second World War gave way to rock and roll, singles bars, and trendy cafés. The chasm separating these two eras could be measured by the success of Maxwell's Plum, a gaudy hamburger palace with a flamboyant Art Nouveau interior and fevered pickup scene that opened in 1965. Sirio Maccioni, the suave former maître d' of the Colony, assessed Maxwell's Plum with a shrewd eye. It was not to his taste, but he saw exciting possibilities in a restaurant that combined the functions of a social club and a dining room in a theatrical setting. The audience he had in mind was the new generation of Manhattan movers and shakers: the investment bankers, business moguls, fashion czars, and media stars who would ride the big Wall Street wave for most of the 1980s. In 1974, Maccioni opened the doors to

Le Cirque, in the Mayfair Hotel, and for the next twenty-five years served as master of ceremonies for one of the city's most popular shows, a disorganized pageant of wealth, social climbing, and snobbery transmitted to the reading public in the pages of *W* and the newspaper gossip columns. This was the world of Tom Wolfe's *Bonfire of the Vanities*. Le Cirque served as home base for Wall Street's masters of the universe and their social X-ray wives—the frighteningly thin, designer-clad women who ate lunch at Mortimer's and picked at tiny portions at Le Cirque.

Although the menu was wasted on most of the clientele, Le Cirque served as a launching pad for some of the city's finest chefs. Maccioni invested heavily in his kitchen, and he attracted talents like Daniel Boulud, who would later take up residence in the Mayfair Hotel and create an institution to rival Le Cirque: Restaurant Daniel. From the Le Cirque kitchen came Geoffrey Zakarian (later of Patroon, 44 at the Royalton, and Town), Terrence Brennan (Picholine and Artisanal), Michael Lomonaco (Windows on the World), David Bouley, and a wildly creative Provençal pastry chef named Jacques Torres, lured to Le Cirque with the promise of a custom-built pastry kitchen. Torres, sizing up Adam Ti-

Sirio Maccioni, who learned the trade of maître d' at the Colony, made Le Cirque a headquarters for Manhattan's money elite when it opened in the 1970s. Here he sits with Daniel Boulud, his chef, in 1990.

hany's zany three-ring decor, responded with some mildly ridiculous dessert conceits appropriate to the setting, like a chocolate stove whose tiny chocolate pans were filled with dollops of apricot and raspberry compote. With a flourish, waiters would lift the pans and pour the fruit over the stove cake. "I am the clown at Le Cirque," Torres liked to say.

Maccioni read his audience correctly. They resisted the hushed formality of restaurants like the Colony. They liked their restaurants a little louder and a little brighter. They had earned their millions and wanted to put them on display, in a flashy setting. Maccioni obliged, though in many respects Le Cirque remained stubbornly traditional. Maccioni was the star, not his talented chefs. Diners craved the little attentions he doled out and swooned when he approached their tables. Status could be measured precisely in Sirio-time. The more of it you got, the bigger you were. Maccioni was simply an Italian version of Henri Soulé.

Elsewhere, however, profound changes were in the offing. Over at the Lafayette, in the Drake Hotel, a young Alsatian chef named Jean-Georges Vongerichten was making noise with his Asian-influenced reinterpretation of nouvelle cuisine, and his inventive use of vegetable broths rather than traditional sauces. Onion juice flavored his rabbit with fried leeks. For cannelloni stuffed with crabmeat and Swiss chard, he came up with a reduced vegetable bouillon and carrot juice spiced with cardamom.

Vongerichten, still in his twenties, was emblematic of a new generation of chefs. Traditionally, French chefs rose through a strict hierarchy with almost glacial slowness. The most talented could hope, after years of unremitting toil, to run the kitchen at a prestigious hotel restaurant or open their own establishments. There they would remain for the rest of their lives. Even geniuses like Fernand Point and Alain Chapel stayed put, forever associated with a single restaurant.

Airplane travel and nouvelle cuisine broke the old mold. Nouvelle cuisine spawned media stars with bankable names. Hotel chains, especially in Asia, craved the prestige that a top nouvelle chef could bring. Suddenly, younger chefs were traveling the world, exposing their French palates to new ingredients and applying their skilled French hands to new techniques, which they incorporated into their culinary repertoire. The same airplanes that whisked them to foreign cities also delivered—overnight, anywhere in the world—the exotic ingredients they discovered and came to love.

Jean-Georges Vongerichten dazzled diners at the Lafayette in the 1980s with his vegetable sauces and went on to build a dining empire with restaurants such as Vong, JoJo, Spice Market, and Jean Georges.

Like many of his peers, Vongerichten was formed in the classical French manner—an apprenticeship at the three-star Auberge de l'Ill in Illehaeusern followed by stints as a line cook under Louis Outhier at L'Oasis in Mandelieu-la-Napoule and as a saucier for Paul Bocuse before heading off to the three-star Aubergine, in Munich. Outhier, a proponent of nouvelle cuisine, recognized in Vongerichten a precocious talent. Without hesitation, he sent the young chef to run the kitchen at his French restaurant in the Oriental Hotel in Bangkok. This turned out to be a life-changing experience. Shopping the markets, Vongerichten discovered an entirely new palette of ingredients—lemongrass, chilies, lime leaves. After opening restaurants for Outhier in Singapore, Hong Kong, Geneva, Lisbon, and London, he arrived in the United States in the mid-1980s a thoroughly internationalized chef.

The brilliant adventure at Lafayette, which earned the maximum four stars from *The New York Times* and rapturous reviews elsewhere, pushed Vongerichten to the front rank of the city's chefs. And then his career took a peculiarly modern turn. One of his devoted diners was a financier named Phil Suarez, who proposed that Vongerichten leave Lafayette and open his own restaurant. The two formed a partnership, and the result was JoJo, a high-end bistro that opened in 1991 and became an instant success. That should have been that. But Vongerichten and Suarez developed an itch to expand, recognizing that the Vongerichten name could be applied to additional restaurant ventures, in a profusion of cooking styles.

Suarez and Vongerichten opened Vong, a French-Thai fusion restaurant in Philip Johnson's Lipstick Building, in 1994. They followed up with Mercer Kitchen in SoHo, a New American restaurant, which begat the four-star Jean

Georges on Columbus Circle. Shanghai cuisine was featured at 66 in Tribeca, Southeast Asian street food at Spice Market, American steaks at Prime in the Time-Warner Center, and Italian trattoria cuisine at Perry Street in Greenwich Village. Vong spawned more Vongs—four of them around the world—while Vongerichten's other New York restaurants generated spin-offs in Las Vegas, Chicago, Shanghai, London, Paris, and Bora Bora.

The Vongerichten empire demonstrated, in Imax dimensions, just how far a talented chef with the right business partners could travel under the new culinary rules. Like Hollywood stars freed from the old studio system, chefs found themselves in a position to realize riches beyond the dreams of avarice. A well-promoted name could provide the foundation for restaurants, frozen foods, kitchenware, cookbooks, and television shows. Vongerichten, a quiet, almost reclusive man who spoke halting English, did not project well on television, but others did, and the growing reach of the Food Network, a seat-of-the-pants operation started in 1993, allowed New York chefs like Mario Batali and Bobby Flay to turn local popularity into national stardom.

The 1990s and the first decade of the new millennium became the era of the entrepreneurial superchef. No longer anonymous artists toiling in the kitchen, new-model chefs raced around the globe, tending to far-flung business interests. They opened mega-restaurants in Las Vegas, spoke at conferences, appeared on television, signed deals with food corporations. In France, Alain Ducasse created an organization that somehow managed to operate a trio of three-star Michelin restaurants simultaneously, along with an expanding portfolio of restaurants ranging in style from the haute-cuisine opulence of the Plaza Athénée in Paris to the diner-chic of Spoon. Gordon Ramsay, in Britain, went Vongerichten one better. After building an international reputation with his three-star namesake restaurant in Chelsea, and inflating it to film-star proportions with a series of popular television shows, he created Gordon Ramsay Holdings, a company that now operates more than a dozen restaurants in Britain, the United States, France, Japan, and Dubai. Ramsay and Ducasse would eventually plant their imperial flags in New York, beneficiaries of a media-saturated age that accorded chefs the kind of attention normally reserved for film stars.

In the past, cuisine and dining aroused comparatively little attention in countries other than France. Even in a city like New York, the audience for fine dining was relatively small, and the doings of chefs and restaurant owners received scant attention except in trade publications. When prominent restaurateurs like Lorenzo Delmonico or Louis Sherry entertained the notables of their day or staged lavish banquets for foreign dignitaries, the names on the guest list might appear in the newspapers, but restaurant publicity generally stopped there. Raymond Orteig, of the Hotel Lafayette, made front-page news when he put up a $25,000 cash prize for the first aviator to make a solo flight across the Atlantic (and was forgotten the moment Charles Lindbergh touched down in France). But restaurants as restaurants, and the food they served, did not normally merit consideration in the popular press.

This changed after the Second World War, so fundamentally that by the time Alice Waters initiated her modest experiment on Shattuck Avenue in Berkeley, the doings of an obscure restaurant in a second-tier city could resound like a shot heard round the world. Restaurants, chefs, and dining out were now news, in a way they had never been before. The rise of consumer and lifestyle magazines, the softening of hard news at traditional newspapers, and the explosive growth of cable television, which nurtured a new breed of culinary star, put food and restaurants squarely in the center of the national consciousness. If nothing else, knowing where to eat, and what to order once you got there, became a status marker for aspiring young city dwellers.

Remarkably, given the number of restaurants and the importance of dining in New York, there was no restaurant guide to the city before the twentieth century. Tourist guidebooks generally included a page or two on places to eat, most of them in hotels, but none of the daily newspapers employed a restaurant critic. It was not until 1903 that an enterprising publisher commissioned an anonymous hungry reporter on Park Row to dine around town and write up a detailed description of the city's top restaurants in an illustrated stand-alone guide, *Where and How to Dine in New York*, a priceless record of New York's first golden age of dining. Public response must have been muted, since no imitators followed, and for the next twenty years, curious diners were left on their own. In 1925, George S. Chappell, *The New Yorker*'s architecture critic, took a professional detour by writing *The Restaurants of New York*, a necessarily nostalgic document, since most of the city's great restaurants had closed their doors soon after the advent of Prohibition.

Over the next forty years, assorted bon vivants and journalistic hacks would turn their hands to the genre. In 1930, Rian James, the nightlife columnist for the *Brooklyn Eagle*, turned his table-hopping to account in *Dining in New York*, a wise guy's take on the restaurant scene. (After cowriting the screenplay for

42nd Street, he left for Hollywood and never looked back.) At about the same time, *The New Yorker's* gentle Walter R. Brooks wrote extensively on restaurants in *New York: An Intimate Guide*. The obscure George Ross, anticipating a surge of interest in dining with the end of Prohibition, covered an impressive 365 restaurants in *Tips on Tables*, published in 1934.

The World's Fair drew millions of tourists to New York and launched a spate of restaurant guides, but the real turning point for readers interested in food came with the creation of *Gourmet* in 1941 and, a few years later, *Holiday*. Both magazines took food and dining seriously, opening their pages to writers like M.F.K. Fisher and James Beard. It was at *Gourmet* that a young Mississippian named Craig Claiborne, fresh out of Swiss hotel school, found his first job in food journalism.

Claiborne, a former public-relations man with a yen to write about food, walked into *Gourmet's* offices in the early 1950s and talked his way into a job as a receptionist. Soon he was writing feature articles, editing recipes, and turning out the "Along the Boulevards" column, which consisted of capsule reviews of New York restaurants. Then opportunity knocked. Jane Nickerson, the food editor at *The New York Times*, left her job. Claiborne lobbied hard for it, got the nod, and in short order, food journalism in New York changed forever.

Like their counterparts elsewhere in the United States, New York newspapers relegated food news to the women's pages. Restaurants and recipes shared space with tips on household management, child care, and fashion. Restaurants qualified as hard news if there was a fire, a strike, or a real estate transaction. This had not always been the case. For a brief, giddy period around the turn of the century, the *Times* frequently ran large, illustrated features on restaurants, never identifying them by name—that would be free advertising—but zeroing in on such hot social topics as tipping, the snobbery of waiters, and the manners of lobster-palace society. This experiment in New Journalism fizzled out sometime around the beginning of the First World War, after which food and restaurants retreated to the women's pages—edited, always, by a woman, such as the enormously popular Clementine Paddleford at *The New York Herald Tribune*.

Claiborne covered chefs and restaurants the same way his hard-news colleagues covered their beats. In 1963, almost as an afterthought, he also began writing reviews of the restaurants he visited. Quite short at first, they gradually expanded, and in time Claiborne began rating each restaurant, assigning it anywhere from zero to four stars, a system still in place today at the *Times*.

From scratch, Claiborne created serious newspaper food journalism and elevated food to the status of news. This innovation coincided with big changes in consumer journalism. Editors gradually woke up to the fact that readers cared just as much about soft subjects like home design, fashion, and gardening—the whole gamut of lifestyle topics—as they did about international affairs and congressional legislation. Magazines like *New York* made it their mission to provide readers with the latest information about restaurants and dining trends. Gael Greene, installed by Clay Felker as *New York's* restaurant critic, helped turn dining out into a competitive sport. Part of being a New Yorker, in the pages of *New York*, was knowing the latest dining news.

Television was also expanding the audience for serious food. Julia Child's missionary work on public television evolved, over time, into a radical new way to excite ordinary people about cooking and dining out. Cable television and the Food Network turned this cottage industry into a big business. With the right packaging, chefs with local reputations could now become major national stars. In New York, a little-known chef named Mario Batali chugged along happily running a tiny Greenwich Village restaurant called Pó. In 1996, the Food Network hired him to do *Molto Mario*, a cooking show that consisted of little more than Batali standing behind a kitchen counter, with a map of Italy in the background. Like Emeril Lagasse, the New Orleans chef whose ebullient personality made him the Food Network's first breakout star, Batali clicked with viewers. His ponytail and bright-orange clogs became virtual trademarks at a series of restaurants that Batali and his new business partner, Joseph Bastianich, rolled out over the next decade: Babbo, Lupa, Esca, Otto, Del Posto. As it gathered steam, the Food Network developed an amazing power to create food celebrities. Bobby Flay parlayed shows like *Boy Meets Grill*, *Iron Chef America*, and *Throwdown with Bobby Flay* into restaurants in Las Vegas, Atlantic City, and the Bahamas. As the Food Network connected with a growing audience, it whetted the appetites of other cable channels for food programming and set the stage for stars like Anthony Bourdain and Tom Colicchio, and shows like the Travel Channel's *Bizarre Foods*.

By the turn of the new millennium, New York's restaurant world had changed dramatically since the days of Joe Baum. Nearly every vestige of amateurism, and localism, had been squeezed out of the system. The old haute-cuisine model that had ruled for nearly two centuries was dead, displaced by a new internationalism and a globalized food economy. Chefs, once hired drudges, now worked under a media spotlight. Their every dish was held up to scrutiny by newspaper, magazine, and television critics, reinforced by Internet bloggers, who reported to a large, educated, affluent audience keen to try anything new. Success was now defined in national or even global terms. The right combination of personal appeal and cooking skill could translate into international stardom, and a business empire beyond the dreams of Escoffier himself.

16

With Knife and Fork in New York

New York is a present-tense city. It lives in the moment, perhaps because the city's full-blast immediacy engages all the senses simultaneously, squeezing the faculties that allow for reflection on the past and speculation about the future. Like riders on a roller coaster, New Yorkers simply hold on tight.

This manic focus afflicts restaurants—doubly so. Restaurants have a collective history but a poorly developed historical sense, for understandable reasons. For chefs and owners, waiters and waitresses, the world begins anew every day. The horizon extends no farther than the lunchtime rush or the evening dinner service. The long, slow arc of culinary development takes place in a parallel time, perceptible to historians but beyond the ken of the people actually moving the great story forward. It is impossible to be on the stage and in the audience at the same time.

As the restaurant critic for *The New York Times* for nearly five years, from 1999 to 2004, I felt this paradox acutely. By inclination, my mind wandered to the past, but my job thrust me into the swirl of the present. I held, as it were, dual citizenship; I lived in two New Yorks. The past, in my mind, was always present, and visible, too, in venerable restaurants that carried on, some with distinction, some not. The mere sight of restaurants like the Oyster Bar in Grand Central Terminal, or the Veau d'Or, near Bloomingdale's, or the miraculously persistent El Faro, a tiny Spanish restaurant on the fringes of the Village that was already old when the novelist Dawn Powell made it one of her haunts, stirred me in a strange, indefinable way. The surviving Pompeiian columns of Delmonico's near Hanover Square, with the restaurant's name engraved in the lintel, exerted a powerful attraction, like an invitation to enter the Manhattan of Caleb Carr's novel *The Alienist*. Signposts like these pointed to a rich and glorious past unknown to present-day diners, racing toward the next hot spot in the Flatiron District or on the Lower East Side. Did the eager young restaurant-goers at the turn of the last century, going out to eat at Jack's or Murray's Roman Gardens, reflect on the past splendors of Madison Square and the Brunswick as they made the trip uptown? Unlikely.

From time to time I wonder what William Dean Howells, or Cortland Van Bibber, would make of the dining scene in present-day New York. In some ways it might seem familiar—New Yorkers still love to eat out, and their city, replenished decade after decade by new immigrants, generates inexpensive restaurants in profusion to take their place alongside the brawny steakhouses and imposing French gastronomic temples. Howells, in search of his beloved French and Italian table d'hôtes, would find their place taken by Asian storefronts, many of them in Queens and Brooklyn. As for the old oyster cellars, they are long gone, and the comfortable old chophouses have evolved into brutally expensive steakhouses, loud and masculine in a style that evokes the old lobster-palace days of Jack's and Shanley's, but socially closer to the downtown Delmonico's.

Street food would come as a shock. Once past the familiar hot dog and pretzel, the time-traveler would have to readjust to a bewildering international snack menu, especially if he ventured outside Manhattan. The hot corn girls no longer ply the streets. Likewise the shellfish vendors of yesteryear—probably a good thing. It must have taken a brave soul to step up to a rickety wooden cart offering oysters on the half shell in 1900. What was the mortality rate? Still, nostalgia might surge for vendors like the yam seller in *Invisible Man*, with his piping-hot roasted yams from South Carolina, served with a spoonful of melted butter on top. It's hard not to romanticize the Italian fish shacks that once dotted the Bowery, lower Third Avenue, and Eighth Avenue above 125th Street at the turn of the last century, where passersby could buy fried soft-shell crabs, fried oysters, or fried eels.

In their place, however, waves of new immigrants have brought new offerings. Buried deep under the Manhattan Bridge, a tiny stall serves a northern

Chinese specialty, fried sesame-dotted buns stuffed with braised mustard greens or cabbage braised in Chinese red wine. Outside on the street, vendors sell buns stuffed with roast duck. A cart in Washington Square Park sells Sri Lanka–style vegetable dosas. In Jackson Heights, Queens, taco trucks line Roosevelt Avenue, and when the stars align, Maria Piedad Cano, a Colombian better known as the Arepa Lady, makes an appearance—weekends only during warm-weather months. She is legendary for her corn pancakes, filled or topped with farmer's cheese. Out in Flushing, food stalls offer specialties from Taiwan, Szechuan, Zhejiang, Shaanxi, and Tianjin. In deepest Brooklyn, at the Red Hook ball fields, Latin American cooks set up folding tables under a tarpaulin to dispense Salvadoran papusas, Ecuadorean ceviche, Chilean tuna soup, and Mexican huaraches. These are potent antidotes to nostalgia.

In any case, the journalistic imperative, for a critic, is not to dwell on the past but to bring fresh news, to sniff out the latest trend, to identify the up-and-comers. Still, the two sometimes collided in curious ways. This was certainly the case with the first restaurant I reviewed, a revival of the old Coach House restaurant by none other than Larry Forgione, the master of New American cuisine.

The matchup made sense. Some forty years earlier, the Coach House had become one of the city's premier restaurants by offering white-glove American dining in an actual coach house on Waverly Street in Greenwich Village. The owner, a Greek immigrant named Leon Lianides, had made his reputation with the Sea Fare, a restaurant that attracted a devoted following by offering only the freshest fish, cooked Mediterranean style. At the Coach House, Lianides indulged an American fantasy, presenting humble dishes like black bean soup and corn sticks in an elevated setting. New York loved it. Over the years, the restaurant (whose premises are now occupied by Babbo) acquired thick layers of mystique. Its passing played on the city's collective memory with unusual power. It was the culinary equivalent of the old Penn Station.

The owners of the Avalon Hotel looked to Forgione to reheat this soufflé, to make the magic live again at their nondescript property on a shabby block of Thirty-second Street. As a longtime fan of the Coach House and its four-square commitment to American flavors, Forgione was the right man for an impossible job. His menu struck the correct note of respect while moving the food forward in time. But the moment had passed. The Coach House was history, a fond memory. Those old enough to know the restaurant in its prime could not possibly be pleased, no matter how good the corn sticks, which Forgione served up like Manhattan madeleines. Anyone under fifty was unlikely to know or care about a restaurant their parents had loved. Forgione, once a prime mover behind New American cuisine, was confronting the harsh reality of a restaurant culture driven by trends. Fifteen years earlier, he had ridden the crest of a wave. Now restless diners had turned elsewhere. In another bit of historical reenactment, Forgione would open a new version of An American Place at the Benjamin Hotel later that year. It did not last.

The Coach House review was my letter of introduction to the readers of *The New York Times*, and as such, it was carefully chosen. A small bistro would have seemed too inconsequential. A confident opening chord was called for, but not played fortissimo. A whale-size proposition like Daniel Boulud's new restaurant on the old Le Cirque premises, which had its sights set on four stars, would have been premature. It takes time for readers to get used to a new critic, to assess his quirks and predilections, to mark out the boundaries of agreement and disagreement, and to develop confidence in (or contempt for) the judgments being served up every week. The relationship can't be rushed.

Like the Coach House, the critic's franchise at the newspaper had its own history. Since the days of Craig Claiborne, the *Times* has had only a handful of restaurant critics. Each, in his or her way, developed an intense relationship with readers of the paper and helped define the dining culture that the paper covered. An atmosphere of nervous expectation accompanies each passing of the baton, at the paper itself and among readers. I was acutely aware of it. Like a performer onstage, I knew I had a limited period of time to win my audience over and make them forget about my predecessor, Ruth Reichl, who, when she took over as critic, faced the unenviable task of erasing memories of the highly talented Bryan Miller, who succeeded the fierce but much-loved Mimi Sheraton, who, amazingly enough, was only the second critic in the newspaper's history, not counting a quick procession of place-holders after Claiborne left the job. The line of succession at the *Times* is quite short.

Ruth did not make my job any easier. Readers loved her warm, intimate approach, heavily reliant on the first person, with generous sprinklings of overheard conversation from nearby tables. She had great flair and a highly developed sense of personal drama, reflected in one of the first reviews she wrote, a diabolical two-pronged assault on Le Cirque, which she visited both incognito and with her cover blown. Dramatics aside, she rendered a big service in emphasizing, at precisely the right cultural moment, the exotic Asian cuisines that she had been reporting on for years in Los Angeles.

My style was entirely different, much cooler and more analytical. Readers looking for warmth were not going to get it. My historical moment was different, too. New York was in the midst of a frenzied restaurant boom fed by a robust economy, but the trend lines were fracturing. The defining movements of the past twenty years were losing steam and becoming diffuse. Stylistically, the dining scene was a complete free-for-all, as chefs dipped into Pacific Rim and Nuevo Latino with equal enthusiasm, borrowed foam from Ferran Adrià in Spain, rediscovered all-American junk food, and fixated on obscure ingredients like crosnes (the squiggly tubers of a plant in the mint family) and percebes (a Mediterranean barnacle). Familiar cuisines divided and subdivided into their smallest constituent parts. (It was my pleasure to review La Grolla, a neighborhood restaurant devoted to the food of the Val d'Aosta, the ultimate in specialization as far as Italy goes.) Lurking just over the horizon was molecular cuisine and its laboratory experiments with industrial ingredients that allowed chefs to stretch foie gras like taffy or deep-fry mayonnaise.

When a paradigm as powerful as French haute cuisine breaks up, it's like the collapse of the Roman Empire. New tribes charge into the vacuum and the map gets redrawn. As a critic, my historical moment was unsettled, which may explain the nostalgic impulse that brought forth the rejuvenated Coach House. It was hardly surprising that some restaurateurs responded to the confusing present by taking a flying leap backward.

One effort to recapture the past delivered a disaster of epic proportions. Warner LeRoy, eager to reapply the Midas touch that had made Maxwell's Plum and Tavern on the Green so successful, tried to resuscitate the Russian Tea Room. He deserved full credit for nerve. The Tea Room, once an institution,

Warner LeRoy, showman extraordinaire, presided over Maxwell's Plum, a swinging singles restaurant in the 1960s, and turned Tavern on the Green into a money spinner.

had in the end simply grown old, along with its clientele. It had a curious history. At one time, it really was Russian and served tea, back when Manhattan teemed with restaurants like the Russian Bear and the Russian Kretchma, most of them featuring Cossack-costumed waiters and balalaika orchestras. Over time, it became a parody Russian restaurant with an endearingly goofy personality. For the actors, singers, musicians, and entertainment-industry moguls connected with Carnegie Hall and the talent agencies and music publishers in the neighborhood, it served as a sort of company canteen. Its appeal was ineffable.

LeRoy, a born showman—his father produced *The Wizard of Oz*—bought the place in 1996 and spared no expense creating a shiny, bombastic Russian-themed playground. Visitors to the main dining room confronted a revolving acrylic bear that doubled as a fish tank stocked with swimming sturgeon. Restaurateurs are a lot like theater producers. Once they have committed heart and soul to a project, they become blind to its shortcomings. LeRoy was convinced that he was giving New York a splendid gift, a giant Fabergé egg that would

LeRoy pulled out all the stops when he renovated the Russian Tea Room in 1999. The centerpiece of the main dining room was a revolving acrylic bear stocked with live fish.

make diners fall in love with the Russian Tea Room all over again. I well remember riding up in a crowded elevator to the main dining floor shortly after the Tea Room reopened. LeRoy, his sizeable midsection encased in a shimmering, multicolored satin vest, radiated childlike joy at his creation, which satisfied all his aesthetic criteria: it was brightly colored, loud, and visually chaotic. And that bear! Who could fail to love the place?

Well, me. I savaged the Russian Tea Room, not simply for the decor, which was almost awe-inspiringly vulgar—it might have been conceived by one of Moscow's newly minted billionaires—but for the abysmal food, which made the restaurant seem more like the Soviet Tea Room. A brief enthusiasm for the new Tea Room, which really did give diners a lot to look at, turned out to be the last flush of a terminally ill fever patient. Once the curiosity seekers had paid an obligatory visit, no one was left to dine, and the Russian Tea Room quickly closed its doors.

LeRoy's exuberance at the Russian Tea Room dumbfounded diners and critics alike.

It was a bad time for nostalgia but a wonderful time for new chefs. New York's dining scene, at the turn of the millennium, was a rapidly expanding universe. Meteor showers lit up the night sky and strange new planets were constantly being discovered. Rarely have so many been so well fed, or at least diverted. A robust economy and a boom in chic new designer hotels generated an unprecedented number of new restaurant openings, with a much higher than normal survival rate. Opening a first-class restaurant in New York almost made sense. For me, the new economics meant that I had to run faster and faster only to fall farther behind.

Dining trends of every description were fighting to gain a toehold even as sub-styles like Nuevo Latino sputtered, nearly out of gas. Around the time I took over as critic, the experiments of Ferran Adrià at El Bulli in Spain were just beginning to mesmerize New York's chefs. Dishes began arriving in a veil of foam. Adrià took the same technique used to get whipped cream out of a can and applied it to ingredients like foie gras or potatoes. This arresting trick quickly became a gimmick. More meaningful were Adrià's relentless interrogations of traditional culinary concepts, his playful subversions. Technological bravado and conceptual reversals became his hallmark, and young chefs all over the world began making pilgrimages to Spain to keep up with him.

One of his most inventive and talented admirers was Wylie Dufresne, formerly a sous-chef at Jean Georges, who opened a tiny restaurant on the Lower East Side called 71 Clinton Fresh Food. The food was exquisite, although initially much more in the Jean Georges vein, with lots of infused oils and striking color effects. A blimpish squid stuffed with morsels of sweet shrimp and fennel puree, for example, was surrounded by a slick of blood-orange emulsion. The severely abbreviated menu had a standout vegetarian entrée, a cube-shaped "lasagna" made of thinly sliced and stacked root vegetables—potato, rutabaga, parsnip, parsley root, black radish—topped with bitter cresses and bathed in a tingling mushroom-vinegar broth. At most non-Asian restaurants, vegetarian courses often have an apologetic air about them. Dufresne's competed with the best dishes on the menu.

Dufresne took a much more experimental turn at his next restaurant, WD-50. Bored with coddling his customers, he laid down a challenge on every plate, offering dishes like foie gras layered with anchovies and served with citrus chutney, or oysters pureed and flattened into a slick, marble-like sheet, then sprinkled with bits of dried olive and Granny Smith apple. Over time, WD-50, like El Bulli, became a sort of culinary laboratory and test kitchen for molecular cuisine.

Dufresne's restaurants were located off the beaten track, but his success inspired a wave of new restaurants that turned the Lower East Side into a dining destination—strange as it might seem. True, it was dining of a certain sort, exemplified by Suba, a clublike space where the subterranean brick-walled dining room was surrounded by an illuminated moat. Going to a table was like descending into the underworld: to reach the dining room you trod carefully through the murk along an iron catwalk and down stairs made of industrial-style grating. The food matched the decor—it was lurid and determined to produce an effect. Shock therapy seemed to be on the menu a lot at the time. It spoke volumes about New York that just around the corner from Katz's delicatessen you could get venison medallions glazed in bee pollen.

Wylie Dufresne, a downtown avant-gardist, made waves at 71 Clinton Fresh Food on the Lower East Side, and took off in an even more daring direction at WD-50, where he introduced molecular gastronomy to the city.

The Lower East Side was one of several trendy new restaurant districts created ex nihilo. The rising price of real estate was sending restaurateurs into uncharted territory—to NoHo, the meatpacking district, and even Brooklyn, which developed a thriving restaurant culture near Park Slope. Demand lured serious restaurants to the Upper West Side, long a culinary wasteland. A new generation of designer hotels, modeled after successful prototypes like the Morgan and the W Hotel chain, required top-level restaurants to establish an identity. This trend provided me with some of my most pleasurable dining experiences as a critic.

Geoffrey Zakarian, formerly the chef at 44, at the Royalton Hotel—a Brian McNally production that fed Condé Nast editors for years—created a sublime restaurant, Town, at the new Chambers Hotel on Fifty-sixth Street. The surroundings were elegant. David Rockwell, who seemed to do the interiors of half the restaurants I reviewed, transformed what could have been a subterranean pit by lining the room in translucent sheets of blond wood and square panels wrapped in taupe suede. Strands of crystal beads suspended from the ceiling caught the light like giant champagne bubbles frozen in mid-ascent. The visuals nicely complemented Zakarian's refined take on New American cuisine, as urbane as the restaurant's name suggested.

Rick Laakkonen, an adventurous River Café alumnus, shot off fireworks at Ilo in the Bryant Park Hotel, a newcomer ideally placed to soak up the business from New York Fashion Week. The venture was short-lived—in the end, management grew tired of investing in Ilo and replaced it with a Japanese restaurant more likely to draw the fashion-industry crowd—but it was brilliant while it lasted. Laakkonen had a gift for full-flavored, inventive dishes with a certain rustic quality to them, like his oxtail terrine wrapped in ribbons of beef tongue. The "tidal pool," a real show-stopper, floated oysters, sea urchins, wakame seaweed, Asian mushrooms, and percebes in a hot, briny broth that was poured at the table, poaching the ingredients on the spot.

Little hotels also gave New York silly, trendy restaurants, like Thom, in the Thompson Hotel in SoHo, or would-be star vehicles like Olives, at the W Hotel near Union Square, intended to showcase the talents of Boston's prince of overkill, Todd English. Sometimes, you'd get a real oddity like Sciuscia, in the Giraffe Hotel, just up the street from Olives. The name was a Neapolitan dialect word for "shoeshine"—just one of many bizarre features in this cheery but clueless restaurant, where the waiters seemed faintly surprised that the people sitting at the tables actually wanted a meal. "One thing I have to tell you," my waiter warned one night. "The cavatelli with fava beans—well, we don't have fava beans, so they are using asparagus tips." I ordered the lobster ravioli instead. "So you'll have the lobster ravioli with fava beans," the waiter said. It went on like that all night. By the time I paid the check, I felt as if I had been drawn into an Italian Abbott and Costello routine.

The maddest of the hotel ventures was a frantic exercise in retro-diner chic at the Hudson Hotel. The hotel itself, yet another painfully hip production from the hotelier Ian Schrager and the French designer Philippe Starck, drew mobs from the moment it threw open its doors, or rather, put up the velvet ropes and stationed bodyguards to enforce discipline. The restaurant itself was the brainchild of Jeffrey Chodorow, a Philadelphia lawyer turned nightclub impresario and restaurateur. His two big New York successes, China Grill and Asia de Cuba (in another Schrager hotel), had given him an air of invincibility. But on my watch, he uncorked some pretty flat bottles of champagne, including the egregious Tuscan Steak in midtown and the honorable failure of Mix, an interesting but flawed Franco-American diner-brasserie created with Alain Ducasse.

The Hudson Cafeteria was not so much a restaurant as a series of postmodern poses. The deliberately dumb menu, Warholesque in its impassivity, actually included chop suey. The point was not to eat and enjoy it—an impossibility—but to savor the idea of ordering such a thing. It was not an entrée but a text, packed with enough social signifiers to keep a poststructuralist busy for months. For actual diners, it was torture. Cherry Coke Jello, served in a large Coke glass and topped with a cloud of whipped cream, gave a hint of what toxic waste must taste like. Beef stew was served in a giant coffee cup. People often forget that restaurant critics, paid to live the high life, also have to make repeat visits to restaurants like this.

In the post-everything era, decor and irony counted for a lot. Restaurants have always been public spaces in which people gathered to show themselves as well as to eat, but dining as social display has gained ground over the past twenty years. By the time I started reviewing, it was commonplace to note that restaurants had taken over many of the functions that once belonged to the theater. Restaurant interiors were a form of set design. The dishes came in three acts—appetizer, entrée, dessert. The audience was its own show. Diners gazed at one another and found that to be entertainment enough.

The experience could often be highly self-conscious in a postmodern way. Often, as at the Hudson Cafeteria, the food was a set of cultural references that required decoding. Likewise the decor. At Ruby Foo's, in Times Square, David Rockwell created a faux-naïve Chinese chop suey parlor intended to evoke the world of Charlie Chan movies and the big Chinese restaurants of the 1930s, a preconscious age in current cultural terms. At restaurants like Tao, nearly the size of an airplane hangar, it was hard not to feel like an extra in a lost Cecil B. DeMille epic. These were nightclubs minus the orchestra and dancers on the floor. The idea of direct experience or unmediated pleasure grew increasingly remote at more than a few high-end restaurants. All the food came with quote marks. Chefs made coy allusions. They riffed, like Alain Ducasse, who invented dessert "pizzas" and played arcane games with the idea of comfort food at Mix.

Daniel Boulud, in yet another little hotel, showed that the high-low concept envisioned at Mix really could work. At DB Bistro Moderne, near Times Square, he created a bustling, extroverted counterpart to Café Boulud, his Upper East Side bistro. Boulud was riding high. After wobbling a bit at first, Restaurant

Daniel had earned its way to four stars. I had found the food somewhat disappointing at first and gave the restaurant three stars rather than the maximum that Boulud's many fans considered mandatory. I received an outraged letter from Robert Parker, the wine critic, implying that my review was a pathetic attempt to gain attention. Later, reading a book about the restaurant, I discovered that a hidden camera had been trained on my table, so that the kitchen could monitor my every facial expression. By sheer accident, I kept turning away from the camera, which convinced the restaurant's employees that I was onto their scheme. This absurd drama went on night after night, apparently. And I thought I was just eating.

By the time I awarded the fourth star, the enormously popular Boulud was already off to the races with his new bistro, an inspired bit of slumming. DB was the restaurant that launched the war of the deluxe hamburgers, a sublimely silly competition that Boulud unwittingly initiated when he introduced a monumental patty of sirloin stuffed with foie gras, truffles, and braised short ribs. Garnished with tomato confit and tendrils of frisée lettuce, it arrived on a Parmesan bun and sported a price tag of $27. It instantly became the most popular dish on the menu. Restaurateurs took notice. Like Everest, it was there, the world's most expensive hamburger, and others decided they needed to climb it. The Old Homestead steakhouse unveiled a deluxe twenty-ounce hamburger made from Kobe beef and set a new price ceiling: $41. You could have it with cheese, too, at no extra charge. Boulud, fighting back, created a $50 burger. In a preemptive strike, he later added a double-truffle version at $99. That settled the matter, although Salón México, a small fusion restaurant, tried to soak up some of the leftover publicity by creating a $45 burrito stuffed with filet mignon, truffles, and the corn fungus known as huitlacoche.

Daniel Boulud shows off the DB Burger, a jaw-breaking combination of sirloin, braised short ribs, and foie gras at DB Bistro Moderne.

Globalism and the example of Ferran Adrià were pushing many chefs toward an increasingly complex culinary vocabulary. But a countervailing impulse gathered strength at the same time, a chastened, simplified style of cooking that emphasized top-quality ingredients, locally sourced where possible. At Craft, Tom Colicchio showcased cooking fundamentals and the relentless exposure of basic flavors. His chef de cuisine, Marco Canora, moved on to create Hearth, a smaller, Craft-like restaurant downtown with a more pronounced Italian slant but the same culinary values. Both restaurants were outstanding.

Waldy Malouf, formerly the chef at the Rainbow Room, installed a wood-burning oven at Beacon and concentrated on open-flame cooking: roasted oysters, slow-cooked pork shank, charred vegetables. There were even roasted desserts, like his vanilla cake with blueberries, topped with roasted peaches and soaked in pan juices. At Blue Hill, on Washington Square, a previously unknown chef named Dan Barber made a point of using ingredients from his family's farm in Massachusetts as well as from the local greenmarket. His deceptively modest restaurant turned out to be a big idea in the making. Barber emerged as a passionate spokesman for local farmers and local ingredients, and against the onward march of industrialized food. He went on to practice what he preached at the Stone Barns Center for Food and Agriculture, a farm and educational complex in Westchester, where he created a rural version of Blue Hill. This was a social experiment in the great American transcendentalist tradition, a sort of culinary Brook Farm dedicated to the idea that deracinated diners could return to the soil and change the way they think and eat. The results have not yet been tabulated, but similar efforts around the country suggest that Barber has tapped into a powerful undercurrent among diners worried about the quality of their food—and their lives. Daniel Orr, the opening chef at Guastavino's under the Queensboro Bridge, and before that the executive chef at La Grenouille, returned to his home state of Indiana and opened Farm Bloomington, a restaurant heavily invested in its relationships with local growers.

Equally daring, in an entirely different way, was Alain Ducasse's attempted invasion of New York. Over the decades, New York has welcomed many French chefs, but none came with quite the advance press of Ducasse, bearer of multiple Michelin stars and would-be world conqueror. With machine-like regularity, and an ambition bordering on insanity, he had rolled out one Ducasse enterprise after another, all based on the idea that a Ducasse team, thoroughly indoctrinated in the chef's way of thinking and his approach to running a kitchen, could replicate Michelin three-star excellence anywhere and everywhere. Quite consciously, Ducasse was taking his cue from Paul Bocuse and creating a new image for the modern French chef, envisaged not as an artisan but as the chief executive officer of a multinational corporation.

New York, for obvious reasons, was an important strategic objective. And Ducasse, by any measure, is a great chef. But the advance hype surrounding his restaurant, in the Essex House Hotel on Central Park South, soured the happy mood. Something about Ducasse made people want to see him, if not fail, then stumble. He did.

Ducasse arrived expecting a coronation. Instead, he got a hazing. Critics—including me—scoffed at the overproduced dining room and its fussy rituals: the array of recherché mineral waters, the pens in a dozen styles for diners to sign the check with, the multiple choice of weapons with which to attack one's squab. Surgical-looking implements were presented for dealing with asparagus spears. The waiters put on white gloves before taking up scissors to snip at herbs for tisanes. The very lettering on the menu irritated, a monumental ADNY executed as though by a Roman stonemason. The visual taste was suspect, from the weird assemblage of brass instruments and dripped paint adorning the rear wall to the glass sculpture of cavorting fish in front of the open kitchen. The food was very good but not great, at prices that only perfection could justify.

For the first time in a long time, Ducasse heard criticism. To his credit, he listened. By merest chance, several months after giving the restaurant three stars, I ate lunch at the Essex House. Ducasse had introduced a new abbreviated lunch menu, and I was curious. It was sheer bliss on the plate. Encouraged, I began revisiting the restaurant. All the pieces, awkwardly fitted at first, had snapped into place with a satisfying click. The famous team, drilled by their master, and led by their superlative chef de cuisine, Didier Elena, had staged a remarkable four-star comeback, and none too soon. The newspapers were filled with predictions that Ducasse, stung by his rude reception in New York, would decide to pack his bags and leave.

It would be pleasing to report a happy ending to the story. After I stepped down as critic at the beginning of 2004, however, Ducasse brought a new chef into the kitchen, none other than Christian Delouvrier, formerly of Les Célébrités (in the space now occupied by Ducasse in the Essex House) and now left adrift after the St. Regis Hotel pulled the plug on his four-star jewel box, Lespinasse. It was a gamble. On the one hand, Delouvrier, after years of service

at Meurice (where his kitchen staff included a young chef named Thomas Keller),
then at Les Célébrités and Lespinasse, enjoyed enormous respect among the city's
diners and—just as important to Ducasse—
critics. On the other hand, he was an out-
sider, not part of the Ducasse team, as
tightly organized and ideologically united
as a Communist Party cell. The experiment
came to grief when Frank Bruni, my successor, downgraded the restaurant to three
stars, absolutely unacceptable to Ducasse.
In the blink of an eye, Delouvrier was out.
ADNY carried on, its status uncertain. It
existed to be a four-star restaurant. Yet it
limped along with three, like an animal
missing a leg. In the end, Ducasse packed
his bags and moved to the St. Regis Hotel,
where he opened Adour in early 2007. The
verdict? Three stars.

Alain Ducasse, despite three restaurants with three Michelin
stars, found Manhattan a tough nut to crack when he opened
Alain Ducasse at the Essex House in 2000.

The obsession with stars—an obsession
for readers and restaurateurs, but not for
me—created problems all down the line. The star system was originally intended as a kind of shorthand for readers, not as a substitute for the full review.
But it gained a malign influence over time. There really are diners who slavishly
organize their evenings out according to ratings. The thought of being seen in a
less than three-star restaurant is intolerable to them. In a way, this simplifies life.
You run down the list of three-star and four-star restaurants and make reservations accordingly. No serious eater could live this way. It runs counter to the
spirit of discovery and adventure that motivates real gourmets. Besides, man
cannot live on four stars alone. Such restaurants, for reasons of price, time investment, and diet, should be reserved for special occasions. Most of the time,
one star will do.

Ah, that one star. How lonely it seemed when I took over as critic. For whatever reason, Ruth Reichl rarely awarded restaurants a single star, which means
"good." Instead, all sorts of nice little neighborhood places got two, which

seemed to be her equivalent of a gentleman's C. I looked on the one-star rating as an underused asset. It was tailor-made for the sort of satisfying but unspectacular restaurant that supports the grand structure of dining in New York. One star, it seemed to me, was an index of health. Cities with lots of them were in good shape.

Accordingly, I gave one star to a charming little restaurant with a clever menu, La Grolla. The owners howled. All restaurateurs, I soon discovered, believe that they deserve one more star than they really do, but in this case the cries of pain mingled with tears at the injustice of it all. This was the sort of restaurant that Ruth would have given two stars to, and my version of tough love guaranteed their ruin. The truth is, restaurants live or die by word of mouth, just like movies. If people leave the place smiling and tell their friends, things will probably turn out all right. As it happened, La Grolla survived and even expanded.

One little restaurant caught me entirely by surprise. Bouley Bakery was intended to be a sort of placeholder while its owner, David Bouley, plotted his next major move. A chef with Napoleonic ambitions, Bouley was mapping out a campaign that would put him at the center of a culinary empire that, depending on which week you read the papers, would include a flagship restaurant, a cooking school, a catering business, a Japanese restaurant, and, for all anyone knew, a line of fragrances. At one time, he had even colluded with Warner LeRoy to remake the Russian Tea Room, an almost hallucinogenic mismatch that, unfortunately for spectators, fell apart quickly.

Out of curiosity, I dropped in for dinner at Bouley Bakery. The experience was electrifying. I kept coming back, and after four dinners a suspicion hardened into a conviction. If this was not four-star cooking, then the stars had no meaning. Out of the blue, I loaded four stars onto the restaurant. What's the point of being a critic if you do not, once in a while, wave the magic wand?

Bouley missed the Trans-Siberian Express with Warner LeRoy, but he turned up in time for one of the most pleasant (if inexplicable) developments of recent years, the vogue for Austrian food and wine. At Danube, just behind Bouley Bakery, he created a jewel box decorated in fin de siècle Viennese style with a gilt-dotted Klimt reproduction dominating one wall. Mario Lohninger, a young Austrian chef trained at the three-star Tantris in Munich, did justice to a cuisine generally represented by tough wienerschnitzel and tougher strudel. This was Austrian cuisine executed with a light, sensitive hand, but faithful to its roots. At the same time, the restaurant took full advantage of the giant strides made by Austrian winemakers in recent decades. Alexander Adlgasser, the bow-tied sommelier fondly known as Alex the Grape, taught New Yorkers how to say *Spätburgunder* and *Grüner Veltliner*, and to kneel before the dessert wines of Alois Kracher.

It was Austria's moment. Kurt Gutenbrunner, a talented Austrian chef who had never found quite the right setting in New York, hit on the perfect formula at Wallsé, an unpretentious Village bistro where he served kavalierspitz, Austria's classic boiled beef dish, and braised rabbit with spätzle. For desserts, Gutenbrunner reached into the traditional repertoire for Austrian favorites that came as a revelation to most American diners, like feather-light dumplings made from quark, an Austrian farmer cheese, or the jam-filled crepes known as palatschinken.

The desserts turned out to be a warm-up act for yet another Austrian venture, Café Sabarsky. Located in a Fifth Avenue town house below the Neue Gallerie, a new private museum of German and Austrian art, the café was Gutenbrunner's homage to the coffee shops of Vienna. Desserts dominated the menu—great Viennese classics like Sachertorte, Dobos torte, and mohn torte—and a few inventions, like the Klimt torte: thin layers of hazelnut cake alternating with bittersweet chocolate icing. The note of authenticity was reinforced with Meinl's coffee, from Vienna, served *mit schlag*.

The Austrian surge served as a reminder that fads and trends can add energy to the dining scene. Most are ridiculous—dessert in a martini glass comes to mind—but others inject color and life. For years, a lone, dedicated figure toiled at Picholine, Terrance Brennan's three-star restaurant near Lincoln Center. His name was Max McCalman, and he styled himself "maître fromageur." This lofty designation should have invited ridicule, but McCalman's wholehearted devotion to cheese, accorded its own menu, swept diners along with him. Cheeses at his side, he expatiated, rhapsodized, and appealed in frankly emotional terms on behalf of his fragrant friends. He eventually won the larger battle of convincing New York diners that cheese deserved serious consideration in their meal plans.

His vision was realized at Artisanal. Brennan, sensing a groundswell of interest, decided to give McCalman a platform for his missionary work. The entire menu was tilted in a cheese direction, with gougères, the classic French cheese puffs, and a variety of fondues priming diners for the grandiose cheese course that followed the meal. An array of great cheeses from all over the world, after

Max McCalman preached the gospel of artisanal cheeses at Picholine for years. At the cheese-centered Artisanal, he got his showcase, along with a cellar for aging cheeses like the Berkswell he sniffs above.

being aged in a cellar near the back of the dining room, were sold retail from a counter. Cheese consciousness spread all over the city, in restaurants of every description. Some devised intriguing mini-courses of cheese paired with a sweet flavoring, like the chunks of Parmesan served with saba, or grape must, at Otto, or the aged Gouda accompanied by apple-maple strudel at Town. At a trendy Spanish restaurant called Meigas, the chef came up with a wonderful ice cream made from torta del Casar cheese.

Raw fish and home-cured meats also fought for the attention of diners. Sushi was second nature to New Yorkers, but Esca, a Mario Batali and Joe Bastianich production in the theater district, introduced a menu of what could be thought of as Italian sashimi—little slices of raw fish doused in olive oil and subtly tweaked with herbs or spices, like sliced scallops in tangerine oil, or fluke with a few spindly sea beans and sliced radishes. This was something new and exciting. It was also in the air. At the four-star Le Bernardin, Eric Ripert added his own take on crudo to the menu, with little raw shrimps in a mignonette of lime zest, salt, and white pepper, or fluke in a marinade of coconut water, lime juice, red onion, and jalapeño pepper. Meanwhile, over at Otto, Batali made a great display of his home-cured meats, or salumi, with top billing accorded to the smoked and salted pork fat known as lardo, which was draped in paper-thin slices across miniature pizzas. A salumi cult quickly developed.

Perhaps more than any other chef in the city, Batali showed a knack for catching the public's attention. Lardo was just one of his clever grace notes. Smart chefs know how to popularize their obsessions. Others simply obsess, like Paul Liebrandt, the most divisive chef to arrive on the New York scene while I was critic. Liebrandt, a British chef still in his mid-twenties, arrived with solid credentials, having worked with Marco Pierre White and Pierre Gagnaire. He landed his first big American job at Atlas, a peculiar restaurant on Central Park South. Formerly a suite of dentists' offices, it was owned by a real estate family that decided it would be exciting to open a restaurant. They got more than they bargained for.

Mario Batali played to a small but devoted audience at his cult restaurant Pó in Greenwich Village before the fledgling Food Network made him a star. Restaurants such as Babbo (*above*), Esca, Otto, and Del Posto followed.

Liebrandt came with a suitcase full of new ideas. For instance, salsify soup, served in a white china cup covered by a thin slice of roasted quince. Atop the thick soup floated a layer of double-fermented Belgian white beer. It was a carefully orchestrated progression of flavors, from tart-sweet to bittersweet to earthy—quite a voyage.

The dish that came to epitomize the Atlas experience, however, was not on the menu. It was an *amuse-bouche*, a small ball of green-apple-and-wasabi sorbet, sprinkled with a little sea salt, over which a waiter drizzled expensive olive oil, from a delicate cruet. Fiery, tart, and sweet all at once, the notorious green ball made, I thought, a brilliant opening move in the impressively complicated game to follow. I found Liebrandt's cooking innovative and exciting. Others scoffed. *Gourmet*, with Ruth Reichl now in charge, went out of its way to cast a no vote on Atlas and Liebrandt. Jonathan Gold, the magazine's New York critic at the time, dismissed Liebrandt's cooking as "critic's food"—a cynical, naked bid to startle jaded palates. This struck me as completely wrong. Liebrandt was something of a bomb-thrower, but it came naturally. He was by temperament an avant-gardist. Recklessness, not calculation, was his problem.

This quickly became evident at Papillon, a modest saloon with a small restaurant attached that, against all logic, decided to install the incendiary Liebrandt in its kitchen. By this time, Liebrandt had fallen under the spell of a deconstructionist pastry chef named Will Goldfarb, who encouraged him to do a little paradigm-busting. Goldfarb rejected with contempt the notion that food should please. Accordingly, in a dessert called Petit Déjeuner d'Irlande, or Irish breakfast, he slipped a bitter cube of Guinness gelée into an orange-water flan. Later he would unveil some very strange inventions at restaurants like Cru—where, in a dessert intended to recall summers at the shore, he presented diners with a spray container of salt water, a vial of golden liquid, and a vial of sand, all wrapped in a beach towel.

Goldfarb helped Liebrandt orchestrate a series of events at Papillon that flirted with performance art. I turned up for one of these séances but took flight when I found out that the evening would consist of more than twenty dishes. A tougher-minded eyewitness later reported to me that, in the course of the evening, which stretched into the wee hours, diners were at various points blindfolded and fed by hand, surrounded by smoke, or required to eat off the back of a nude woman positioned on all fours. This was miles beyond apple-wasabi sorbet.

At Papillon, I ate what may possibly be the worst dish of my tenure as restaurant critic, three seared scallops draped with a tender slice of squab, then lined up and capped, Stonehenge-style, with a large chip of emulsified cocoa paste. Somehow, sea urchin mousse also found its way into the equation. The combination was unspeakable, inedible, and almost indescribable. In the culinary version of a double take, I ordered the dish twice, unable to believe my taste buds. Sadly, they were correct.

New York encourages excess. Risk is often rewarded. Chefs routinely succeed and fail in spectacular fashion, only to rise again, in an entirely new setting. Liebrandt lived to fight another day. After entering into a partnership with Drew Nieporent, he earned three stars, and sweet vindication, as the chef at Corton, in the old Montrachet space. High-wire acts like his keep the city's dining scene lively.

One of the boldest, brashest projects ever unleashed on the public took shape in my final months as critic. The Time-Warner Center, two forbidding towers rising over Columbus Circle, included in its master plan of retail shops arrayed in a mall-like setting a cluster of fine restaurants pretentiously advertised as "The Restaurant Collection." It was to be, in effect, a new restaurant district created from scratch.

The names were big. Jean-Georges Vongerichten was signed up to create a steakhouse called Prime. Gray Kunz, once at Lespinasse, but without a kitchen for several years, was enticed into developing a brasserie, Café Gray. Masa Takayama pledged to give New York a replica of his rarified, astronomically expensive Los Angeles sushi restaurant. At one point, Charlie Trotter from Chicago was poised to come, a potentially thrilling development. But the developers of the center scored their real coup when they convinced Thomas Keller, the chef and owner of the French Laundry in the Napa Valley, to return to New York and create a second restaurant.

Keller, often acclaimed as the finest chef in America, knew the city well. In the early 1980s, he had cooked at La Réserve and at Rakel, an exciting, forward-looking French restaurant that fell victim to the economic downturn that hit later in the decade. In Yountville, in the Napa Valley, he created the kind of personalized, purist restaurant that recalled such temples of haute cuisine as Fernand Point's Pyramide, or Alain Chapel's namesake restaurant near Lyons. Diners ate for hours, transported by Keller's ethereal, French-inspired California dream. More than a chef, he was a cult. His meals were religious ceremonies. And New York was about to get him back.

The restaurant was called Per Se, and expectations were stratospheric. Keller coolly set up shop and put his kitchen into motion. With no visible sign of strain, Per Se ravished the critics, wowed diners, and earned four stars from Frank Bruni. The typical dinner was a challenge, a four-hour tasting menu that pushed both kitchen and diners to the limit. It presumed, accurately, a certain mind-set peculiar to New York dining, and, more broadly, to cultural life in the city: an informed, passionate interest in the new.

Keller's triumphant homecoming put an exclamation mark at the end of my five years as restaurant critic. But year in, year out, it is not restaurants like Per Se that tell the most about the city's restaurant life. When I try to explain the depth and the richness of dining in New York, I often turn to a much less cele-brated restaurant in the Flatiron Disrict called Fleur de Sel. The chef, Cyril Re-naud, cooked at La Côte Basque for years, secretly planning, like many another, to open his own little restaurant one day. That day came in 2000, on a side street just south of the Flatiron Building. Renaud's father came over from France to help make the furniture. Renaud himself decorated the menus, whose contents were brief. Modesty suffused the entire enterprise, but within its clearly defined limits, Fleur de Sel was perfect, a small, romantic restaurant with an expert, im-passioned chef in charge. In nearly any other American city, a restaurant of this quality would immediately jump to the top-ten list. In any mid-size city, it would be the best in town by a wide margin. In New York, it was simply one of many. And in New York, it found an audience. In 2009, ending a successful run, Re-naud closed the restaurant after opening Bar Breton, devoted to the cuisine of his native region. The result was the same. This is the New York story. It's been told a thousand times over, decade after decade. And it never grows old.

Notes

ONE: The City Without a Restaurant

3   John Battin opened: *New York Evening Post*, May 24, 1813, p. 3.

4   *Blunt's Stranger's Guide*: Edmund M. Blunt, *Blunt's Stranger's Guide to the City of New York* (New York: Edmund M. Blunt, 1817).

4   "I remember entering": Lately Thomas, *Delmonico's: A Century of Splendor* (Boston: Houghton Mifflin, 1967), p. 15.

4   "The little place": Abram C. Dayton, *Last Days of Knickerbocker Life in New York* (New York: Putnam's, 1897), pp. 145–46.

5   "democratic nonchalance": Ward, quoted in Thomas, *Delmonico's*, p. 15.

5   "I reveled in the coffee": Ibid.

5   "foreign element": Dayton, *Last Days*, p. 121.

5   "the *filets, macaroni*": Ibid., p. 146.

5   "more excellent in point of material": Thomas Hamilton, *Men and Manners in America* (Edinburgh: William Blackwood, 1833), vol. 1, pp. 21–22.

7   "a stout, burly, red-faced Englishman": "Downtown Lunchrooms: Peculiarities of the Past and Present," *New York Times*, January 11, 1880, p. 2. Also, Dayton, *Last Days*, p. 124.

8   a British naval officer: Basil Hall, *Travels in North America in the Years 1827 and 1828* (Edinburgh: Robert Cadell, 1830), vol. 1, pp. 31–34.

8   chicken potpie and rice pudding: Charles Gayler, "Half a Century Since," *American Magazine*, November 1892, p. 539.

8   Abram C. Dayton, the merchant's son: Dayton, *Last Days*, pp. 121–22.

9   François Guerin: Ibid., pp. 148–51. Also Charles H. Haswell, *Reminiscences of New York by an Octogenarian* (New York: Harper and Brothers, 1896), p. 53.

10   "a man who walks for a wager": Francis Herbert (pseud. for William Cullen Bryant, R. C. Sands, and G. C. Verplanck), "Reminiscences of New York," in *The Talisman for 1829* (New York: Elam Bliss, 1829), p. 322.

10   John H. Contoit, a Frenchman: Dayton, *Last Days*, pp. 159–62; Haswell, *Reminiscences*, p. 59; Thomas M. Garrett, "A History of Pleasure Gardens in New York City, 1700–1865" (Ph.D. diss., New York University, 1978), vol. 2, pp. 409–19.

11   "not inferior to those of Tortoni in Paris": "Fashionable Resorts," *Ladies' Companion*, July 1834, p. 153. On Palmo, see obituary in *New York Herald*, September 6, 1869, p. 5, and *New*

York Times, September 6, 1869, p. 5. On Café des Milles Colonnes and Café Français, see James Grant Wilson, *The Memorial History of the City of New York, from Its First Settlement to the Year 1892* (New York: New York History Company, 1892–93), vol. 3, p. 360.

11 "It were curious to know": "The Heat and Its Incidents," *New York Times*, June 18, 1852, p. 2.

12 "New York abounds": James Kirke Paulding, *The New Mirror for Travellers and Guide to the Springs* (New York: G. & C. Carvill, 1828), p. 11.

13 The claim was preposterous: On early history of Paris restaurants, see Pierre Andrieu, *Fine Bouche: A History of the Restaurant in France* (London: Cassel, 1956); Giles Macdonough, *A Palate in Revolution: Grimod de La Reynière and the Almanach des Gourmands* (London: Robin Clark, 1987); "History of Paris Restaurants," in *Restaurants of Paris: Everyman Guides* (London: David Campbell, 1994); Rebecca Spang, *The Invention of the Restaurant: Paris and Modern Gastronomic Culture* (Cambridge, Mass.: Harvard University Press, 2000).

14 "frequently dispensed with": John Finch, *Travels in the United States of America and Canada* (London: Longmans, 1833), p. 13.

14 "On the first occasion": Henry Tudor, *Narrative of a Tour in North America* (London: James Duncan, 1834), vol. 1, pp. 37–38.

14 "rolls, toast, and cakes": Hamilton, *Men and Manners in America*, vol. 1, p. 23.

15 "The number of dishes": Ibid., pp. 42–45.

15 The table d'hôte menu: Thomas, *Delmonico's*, p. 34.

16 "It was a table d'hôte": Carl Schurz, *Reminiscences of Carl Schurz* (New York: McClure, 1907–1908), vol. 2, pp. 5–6.

16 John Bernard, an English actor: John Bernard, *Retrospections of America, 1797–1811* (New York: Harper and Brothers, 1887), p. 52.

17 "No fowls, no eggs, no oysters": Asa Greene, *The Perils of Pearl Street* (New York: Betts and Anstice, 1834), pp. 38–40.

18 "Like death, no class is exempt": Thomas Butler Gunn, *The Physiology of New York Boarding-Houses* (New York: Mason Brothers, 1857), p. 12.

19 "we have known the beef of tougher consistency": Ibid., p. 36.

19 "Oysters, here's your brave, good oysters!": For street vendors and their cries, see Meryle R. Evans, "Knickerbocker Hotels and Restaurants, 1800–1850," *New-York Historical Society Quarterly* 36 (October 1952), pp. 377–409; also Alvin F. Harlow, *Old Bowery Days: The Chronicles of a Famous Street* (New York: D. Appleton, 1931), p. 173; J. Frank Kernan, *Reminiscences of the Old Fire Laddies and Volunteer Fire Departments of New York and Brooklyn* (New York: M. Crane, 1885), pp. 56–58; and "The Street Venders [*sic*] of New York," *Scribner's Monthly*, December 1870, pp. 113–29.

19 hot-yam vendor: Ralph Ellison, *Invisible Man* (New York: Modern Library, 1992), pp. 256–60.

TWO: From Field to Market: The New York Feast

21 "O for a mouth to eat": James Kirke Paulding, *The New Mirror for Travellers and Guide to the Springs* (New York: G. & C. Carvill, 1828), p. 12.

22 As the city grew, the supply system: Edward K. Spann, *The New Metropolis: New York City, 1840–1857* (New York: Columbia University Press, 1981), pp. 121–28.

22 "Crabs, lobster, mussels": Jacob Steendam, *Jacob Steendam, Noch Vaster: A Memoir of the First Poet of New Netherland* (The Hague: Brothers Giunta d'Albani, 1861), p. 41.

22 "The elders of the passing generation": James Grant Wilson, *The Memorial History of the City of New York, from Its First Settlement to the Year 1892* (New York: New York History Company, 1892–93), vol. 2, p. 453.

22 This New World bestiary: Peter Neilson, *Recollections of a Six Years' Residence in the United States of America* (Glasgow: David Robertson, 1830), p. 47.

23 New York's bounty: The description of produce, vendors, and the economy of the city markets draws heavily on two books by Thomas De Voe: *The Market Book* (New York: privately printed, 1862) and *The Market Assistant* (New York: Hurd and Houghton, 1866).

24 "are ricketty, rotten": "Our Markets," *New York Times*, June 14, 1858, p. 3.

24 "It is a rare thing": De Voe, *Market Book*, p. 228.

24 "I have frequently observed": Ibid., p. 139.

25 "it could claim the merit": Ibid., p. 241.

26 "an aggravated shanty": "Our Markets."

27 "Choose a Saturday morning": William H. Rideing, "How New York Is Fed," *Scribner's Monthly*, October 1877, p. 730.

27 "is without a doubt the greatest depot": De Voe, *Market Book*, p. 454.

28 The bounty is reflected: The Delmonico's menu, in the collection of the Museum of the City of New York, is reproduced inside the front cover of Lately Thomas, *Delmonico's: A Century of Splendor* (Boston: Houghton Mifflin, 1967).

28 In 1801, Elizabeth Kline: De Voe, *Market Book*, p. 347.

28 a certain Mrs. Jeroleman: Ibid., p. 335.

28 a man with a tin box: Cornelius Mathews, *Big Abel and the Little Manhattan* (New York: Wiley and Putnam, 1845), p. 31.

28 Walt Whitman ventured: "Life in a New York Market," in *Walt Whitman: The Journalism*, edited by Herbert Bergman et al. (New York: P. Lang, 1998), p. 57. The original *Aurora* article appeared on March 16, 1842.

29 "There is no privacy in those humble refectories": "A Landmark Vanishing: The Old Fulton Market," *New York Times*, June 9, 1879, p. 8.

THREE: New York on the Half Shell

33 "Well, why the hell don't you": James Grant Wilson, *Thackeray in the United States: 1852–1853, 1855–1856* (New York: Dodd, Mead, 1904), vol. 1, p. 49.

33 "perfect beasts of oysters": Ibid., vol. 1, p. 82.

34 "There are a few places": Peter Kalm, *The America of 1750: Peter Kalm's Travels in North America* (New York: Wilson-Erickson, 1937), p. 237.

34 "twenty different ways of cooking oysters": Francis J. Grund, *Aristocracy in America* (London: Richard Bentley, 1839), vol. 1, p. 278.

34 "oysters pickled, stewed, baked, roasted": Charles Mackay, *Life and Liberty in America: or, Sketches of a Tour in the United States and Canada, in 1857–8* (London: Smith, Elder, 1859), p. 23.

34 By the middle of the nineteenth century: The statistics that follow, including references to the *New York Herald*, come from Ernest Ingersoll, *The Oyster Industry* (Washington, D.C.: Government Printing Office, 1881). Also "Effect of the Oyster Panic on the Oyster Trade," *Citizen*, November 4, 1854, p. 700; as well as annual reports on the oyster harvest and oyster trade in the *Brooklyn Daily Eagle* and *The New York Times*.

35 Thomas Downing, a free black: The following description of Downing relies on John H. Hewitt, "Mr. Downing and His Oyster House: The Life and Good Works of an African American Entrepreneur," *New York History*, July 1993, pp. 229–52; Mark Kurlansky, *The Big Oyster: History on the Half Shell* (New York: Ballantine Books, 2006), pp. 165–70; and Downing's obituary in the *New York Times*, April 12, 1866, p. 5.

35 "a favorite and very popular resort": Charles H. Haswell, *Reminiscences of New York by an Octogenarian* (New York: Harper and Brothers, 1896), p. 253.

36 "the great man of oysters": Philip Hone, *The Diary of Philip Hone, 1828–1851*, ed. Bayard Tuckerman (New York: Dodd, Mead, 1889), vol. 2, p, 118.

36 "by the best company, the best wine": "Death of 'Johnny Joe,'" *Brooklyn Daily Eagle*, September 2, 1880, p. 3.

37 "All a man wanted": "Bits of Fulton Market History," *New York Tribune*, August 19, 1883, p. 10.

37 The great Alfred P. Dorlon: On the various Dorlons, see "The Great Oysterman: Death of Sydney Dorlon, the Fulton Market Dealer," *New York Times*, July 29, 1873; Alfred Dorlon obituary, *New York Times*, October 27, 1881, p. 8; Philetus Dorlon obituary, *Brooklyn Daily Eagle*, April 24, 1889, p. 6; *New York Times*, April 24, 1889, p. 2; and "The Late Alfred Dorlon," *Harper's Weekly*, November 5, 1881, pp. 749–50.

37 "a tall, compact, well-made man": Matthew Hale Smith, *Sunshine and Shadow in New York* (Hartford: J. B. Burr, 1869), p. 685.

37 "Dorlon's oyster stand is inside of the market": "All About Oysters: Oyster Eating in Fulton Market," *The Weekly Ohio Farmer*, September 21, 1867, p. 304 (reprinted from *New York Evening Gazette*).

40 "somewhere uptown": "Real and Bogus 'Dorlon's,'" *New York Times*, November 8, 1885, p. 9.

40 "Fastidious ladies": Smith, *Sunshine and Shadow in New York*, pp. 684–85.

41 "a heavy mass rolling in the air": "Accident and Loss of Life in Wall-Street," *New York Times*, December 24, 1852, p. 1.

41 "It is like a small cart-wheel": "Glimpses of Gotham," *National Police Gazette*, March 6, 1880, p. 15.

41 five hundred "shilling stews": "Something About Oysters," *Harper's Weekly*, September 16, 1882, p. 582.

41 "the red-white oyster moons": Cornelius Mathews, *Big Abel and the Little Manhattan* (New York: Wiley and Putnam, 1845), p. 32.

42 "Aladdin's cave": George G. Foster, *New York in Slices* (New York: William H. Graham, 1849), p. 94.

42 In 1872, the *Brooklyn Eagle*: "The Oyster Trade," September 26, 1872, p. 2.

42 a veteran oyster dealer: "The City's Oyster Market," *New York Times*, September 10, 1883, p. 2.

42 "oyster-eating community": *The Stranger's Guide Around New York and Its Vicinity* (New York: W. H. Graham, 1853), p. 46

42 "A sort of half-light of criminality": "Changes in New York," *New York Times*, November 22, 1875, p. 8.

42 "worthy of the approving nod": N. P. Willis, "Letter from the Astor to a Gentleman Shepherd in the Country," *Brother Jonathan*, April 29, 1843, p. 498.

42 "the resort of fashionable and fastidious parties": "Changes in New York."

43 "It was here . . . that the celebrated fight": Ibid.

43 "indulged in an interchange of courtesies": Ibid.

43 five-inch smelt: "An Enterprising Oyster," *New York Times*, February 28, 1869, p. 4.

44 "The Rockaways and Blue Points have spawned": "Style in Oysters," *New York Times*, August 31, 1889, p. 4.

45 "Nowadays any big fat oyster": "City's Oyster Market," p. 2.

45 "They belong in fries and broils": "Behind the Oyster Stand," *New York Times*, October 8, 1882, p. 13.

FOUR: A Little Restaurant and How It Grew: The Delmonico's Story

48 "On these occasions": Abram C. Dayton, *Last Days of Knickerbocker Life in New York* (New York: Putnam's, 1897), p. 147.

48 "more of a Yankee": *New York Times*, September 9, 1881, p. 7.

49 "The metropolitan education of an intelligent visitor": Sam Ward, "A History of Delmonico's Restaurant," Samuel Ward papers, 1647–1912, box 5, New York Public Library, Manuscript Collection.

49 "We satisfied our curiosity": Philip Hone, *The Diary of Philip Hone, 1828–1851*, ed. Bayard Tuckerman (New York: Dodd, Mead, 1889), vol. 1, p. 25.

50 "at best a dingy place": Dayton, *Last Days*, p. 149.

50 "money, segars and other articles": "Superior Court: Before Chief Justice Jones," *Atkinson's Saturday Evening Post*, July 27, 1833, p. 2.

54 a dinnertime feast of turtle soup: Sarah Mytton Maury, *An Englishwoman in America* (London: T. Richardson, 1848), p. 197.

54 "crowded to excess": "The Globe Hotel," *Spirit of the Times*, February 2, 1839, p. 1.

54 "Madame Grand-this": Charles Briggs (pseud., Harry Franco), "The Impudence of the French," *Knickerbocker Magazine*, May 1844, pp. 500–501.

55 "potage au lay de mush": Charles Frederick Briggs, *The Adventures of Harry Franco* (New York: F. Saunders, 1839), vol. 2, p. 65.

55 "If a New Yorker who had been absent": "Broadway," *New York Times*, April 21, 1860, p. 2.

58 "at the Maison Dorée, a new and very nice restaurant": George Templeton Strong, *The Diary of George Templeton Strong*, ed. Allan Nevins and Thomas Milton Halsey (New York: Macmillan, 1952), vol. 3, p. 168 (entry for July 9, 1861).

58 "The Maison Dorée enterprise": *Brooklyn Daily Eagle*, March 26, 1867, p. 2.

59 "He was perfect in dress and manner": Lately Thomas, *Delmonico's: A Century of Splendor* (Boston: Houghton Mifflin, 1967), p. 88.

FIVE: New York Becomes a Restaurant City

62 An 1846 guidebook: Edward Ruggles, *A Picture of New York in 1846* (New York: Homans and Ellis, 1846), p. 80.

62 "We once undertook to count": George G. Foster, *New York in Slices* (New York: William H. Graham, 1849), p. 67.

64 "Everything is done differently": Foster, *New York in Slices*, p. 67.

64 "Here one can graduate": *New York Tribune*, September 24, 1846, p. 2.

64 "As the fathers, brothers, and sons": "New York Daguerrotyped," *Putnam's Monthly*, April 1853, pp. 366–67.

64 "this is not at all uncommon in New York": Charles Richard Weld, *A Vacation Tour in the United States and Canada* (London: Longmans, 1855), pp. 377–78.

67 "a small, cheap restaurant": Horatio Alger, Jr., *Ragged Dick: Or, Street Life in New York with the Boot-Blacks* (Boston: Loring, 1867), p. 18.

67 "I remember, yes, distinctly": J. Frank Kernan, *Reminiscences of the Old Fire Laddies and Volunteer Fire Departments of New York and Brooklyn* (New York: M. Crane, 1885), p. 96.

68 "the morning routine of calls, shopping, and luncheon": Carry Stanley, "Ada Lester's Season in New York," *Peterson's Magazine*, March 1854, p. 185.

68 "On the counter of these temples": "New York Daguerrotyped," p. 367.

69 A visitor from South Carolina: William Bobo, *Glimpses of New York City, by a South Carolinian* (Charleston, S.C.: J. J. MacCarter, 1852), p. 158.

69 "grave and immemorial": Henry James, *A Small Boy and Others* (New York: Scribner's, 1913), p. 67.

69 "the most superb": Isabella Bird, *The Englishwoman in America* (London: John Murray, 1856), p. 353.

69 "For a long time, it was almost the only place": "Another 'Institution' Gone," *New York Times*, July 31, 1866, p. 8.

70 "Did a young lady": Ibid.

70 " 'Tis here that the first step is taken": Solon Robinson, *Hot Corn* (New York: DeWitt and Davenport, 1854), p. 221.

70 "scandalously splendid": "New York Daguerrotyped," p. 363.

70 "An idea of the dinner may be gathered": William Ferguson, *America by River and Rail* (London: James Nisbet, 1856), p. 52.

71 "One sees among its habitués": James D. McCabe, *Lights and Shadows of New York Life* (Philadelphia: National Publishing, 1872), p. 306.

71 In a fanciful sketch: "The Adventures of a Gentleman in Search of a Dinner," *Broadway Journal*, June 21, 1845, p. 385, and June 28, 1845, p. 401.

73 A visit to the Café Tortoni: "Where to Get a Good French Family Dinner," *Spirit of the Times*, August 10, 1844, p. 277.

73 to eat at Bell's: Advertisement for Bell's, *Brooklyn Daily Eagle*, October 5, 1847, p. 3; advertisement for Van Wart's, *Brooklyn Daily Eagle*, January 7, 1846, p. 5.

74 "nightly crowded the tier of stalls": Charles Hemstreet, *Literary New York: Its Landmarks and Associations* (New York: G. P. Putnam's, 1903), p. 138.

74 "the princes of finance": Eliza Greatorex, *Old New York: From the Battery to Bloomingdale* (New York: G. P. Putnam's, 1875), vol. 1, p. 37.

75 "laden with delicately mottled steaks": "Old Tom Dead in a House Described by William Waldorf Astor," *New York World*, February 12, 1898, p. 7; and "The Death of Old Tom," *New York Times*, February 12, 1898, p. 12.

75 "with a delicate brown tint": William H. Rideing, "English Haunts in New York," *Appleton's Journal of Literature, Science and Art*, September 13, 1873, p. 332.

75 "Those who don't care for steaks": "Queer Lunch-Houses," *New York Times*, April 28, 1872, p. 11.

76 "Irascible, dogged and prejudiced": "Sutherland's Famous 'Eating House,' Its Patrons and Proprietor," *New York Times Magazine*, October 8, 1905, p. 7.

76 "The absence of all pretension": Rideing, "English Haunts," p. 331.

77 "The fat was firm and white": "Queer Lunch-Houses," p. 11.

78 "burly, jovial, mutton-chop-whiskered Londoner": "Stories of Old New York," *New York Times*, April 28, 1889, p. 20.

78 "toothsome English dishes": *Appleton's Dictionary of New York and Vicinity* (New York: D. Appleton, 1879), p. 57.

78 "a bone scraped quite white": Ibid.

79 "captains of the Atlantic liners": "Tom Dent Dead," *Brooklyn Daily Eagle*, March 30, 1887, p. 6.

79 "regarded the tricks of the turf": "The Late John C. Force," *Brooklyn Daily Eagle*, March 26, 1865, p. 4.

80 A recipe offered by the Nash and Crook chophouse: "Green Turtle Soup," *New York Times*, December 18, 1881, p. 13.

80 "It was thick and slab": Charles Gayler, "Half a Century Since," *American Magazine*, November 1892, p. 533.

80 "Here turtle soup was dispensed": Charles H. Haswell, *Reminiscences of New York by an Octogenarian* (New York: Harper and Brothers, 1896), p. 234.

82 "If one was reckless": Louis T. Golding, *Memories of Old Park Row, 1887–1897* (Brookline, Mass.: privately printed, 1946), p. 4.

83 "with her dusty doughnuts": "Slot Machine Lunch," *Washington Post*, September 18, 1904, p. 8.

83 "Tamales, chicken tamales, red hot!": "Tamales in New York," *New York Tribune*, February 11, 1894, p. 15.

SIX: The Melting Pot

88 "a fir in a tub": Henry Junius Browne, *The Great Metropolis: A Mirror of New York* (Hartford, Conn.: American Publishing, 1869), New York, p. 99.

88 "pyramids of sausages": Charles Dawson Shanly, "Germany in New York," *Atlantic Monthly*, May 1867, p. 555. See also "German Restaurants," *New York Times*, January 19, 1873, p. 5; "Delicatessen Shops," *New York Daily Tribune*, November 25, 1894, p. 15; and "Queer Dishes in Shops," *New York Tribune*, December 12, 1897, supplement, p. 12.

88 "in a distinctly national manner": "Cheap Restaurants: Something About the German, French and Italian Dining-Saloons of New York," *New York Times*, August 6, 1871, p. 5.

89 "has made Kalteraufschritt": "A Delicatessen Pioneer," *New York Tribune*, August 2, 1903, p. 8.

90 "A genuine atmosphere": James Huneker, "Huneker Reminisces About the the Maw of New York," *New York Times Magazine*, September 27, 1914, p. 5.

90 "Brau Haus Boulevard": Rian James, *Dining in New York* (New York: John Day, 1930), p. 243; on Maxl's, pp. 119–21.

93 French cuisine could not be contained: William H. Rideing, "The French Quarter of New York," *Scribner's Monthly*, November 1879, pp. 1–9; also Arthur Bartlett Maurice, *The New York of the Novelists* (New York: Dodd, Mead, 1916), pp. 118, 120–21.

95 "as important as Delmonico's": Julius Chambers, *The Book of New York: Forty Years' Recollections of the American Metropolis* (New York: Books of New York, 1912), pp. 369–70.

95 "Do you know what is the cure": H. I. Brock, "M. Mouquin, of the Vintages, Looks Back," *New York Times Magazine*, January 21, 1932, p. 8.

96 "in the dungeons of the Inquisition": "Queer Lunch-Houses," *New York Times*, April 28, 1872, p. 11.

96 "a burly, unshaven, brigandish Italian: "A Modern Boniface," *New York Tribune*, January 4, 1880, p. 5.

96 Already a fixture in the 1870s: James L. Ford, *Forty-Odd Years in the Literary Shop* (New York: E. P. Dutton, 1921), p. 206.

96 "Occasional visitors try to eat it": "Queer Lunch-Houses," p. 11.

96 "He gave you a real succulent half chicken": "The Retirement of Signor Moretti," *New York Sun*, May 5, 1903; reprinted in *Casual Essays of the Sun* (New York: R. G. Cooke, 1905), p. 71.

96 "serpentine food": Henry Collins Brown, *Valentine's City of New York: A Guidebook* (New York: Valentine's Manual, 1920), p. 77.

97 "opulent intermissions in our poverty": William H. Rideing, "A Corner of Bohemia," *Bookman*, February 1911, p. 629.

98 "a self-made man": William Winter, *Old Friends: Being Literary Recollections of Other Days* (New York: Moffat, Yard, 1914), p. 77.

98 "I felt that as a contributor": William Dean Howells, *Literary Friends and Acquaintance* (New York: Harper and Brothers, 1900), p. 64.

99 "Revelry requires money": Winter, *Old Friends*, p. 93.

SEVEN: The Dawn of the Golden Age

102   "Absolute in their own territories": Mrs. John King Van Rensselaer, *The Social Ladder* (New York: Henry Holt, 1924), p. 210.

103   "On entering from 14th Street": Abram C. Dayton, *Last Days of Knickerbocker Life in New York* (New York: G. P. Putnam's, 1897), p. 140.

104   "the great resort of the stock and gold brokers": "New-York Bars," *Appleton's Journal of Literature, Science, and Art*, April 1, 1871, p. 385.

106   "The easy manner of the men": Julius Keller, *Inns and Outs* (New York: G. P. Putnam's, 1939), p. 35.

107   an elegant entertainment district was taking shape: See Miriam Berman, *Madison Square: The Park and Its Celebrated Landmarks* (Salt Lake City: Gibbs-Smith, 2001).

107   Augustus Sala: George Augustus Sala, *America Revisited* (London: Vizetelly, 1882), p. 53.

108   "By eight o'clock Broadway below Canal Street": James D. McCabe, Jr., *New York by Sunlight and Gaslight* (Philadelphia: Hubbard Bros., 1882), pp. 153–54.

109   "the Frenchest French restaurant": Julian Street, "What's the Matter with Food?" *Saturday Evening Post*, January 31, 1931, pp. 14–15.

109   "polished suggestion of naughtiness": Edwin C. Hill, "Ghosts of a Gayer Broadway," *North American Review*, May 1930, p. 544.

110   "When I handed him the hat": "Waiter Declares Thaw Was 'a Little Nervous,'" *New York Times*, June 27, 1906, p. 3.

111   The dinner sounds apocryphal: For Keller's account, see *Inns and Outs*, pp. 44–48. See also "Billy McGlory's Glorious Time," *Baltimore Sun*, December 30, 1882, p. 4; and "The Famous Banquet at a Swell New York Hotel Given by Billy McGlory," *National Police Gazette*, January 11, 1902, p. 3.

111   "When he first began, forty years ago": "What Lorenzo Delmonico Did," *New York Sun*, September 7, 1881, p. 2.

113   "I kept my ears open for pointers": "Stories of Old New-York," *New York Times*, April 28, 1889, p. 20.

113   "One of the secrets I had learned": "Louis Sherry Dies: Famous Caterer," *New York Times*, June 10, 1926, p. 25.

113   "this wonderful temple of gastronomy": Theodore Dreiser, *Sister Carrie* (New York: Penguin, 1981), pp. 331–33. (Dreiser gets the address wrong. He puts Sherry's at Fifth Avenue and Twenty-eighth Street.)

116   "An order of what they called liver and bacon": Keller, *Inns and Outs*, p. 21.

116   "Sometimes these were of a highly ornamental character": *Valentine's Manual of Old New York* (New York: Valentine, 1925), p. 90.

117   "Gastronomic Condensation": Reprinted in *Life*, March 31, 1887, p. 183.

118   Louis Haims sold sandwiches: Helen B. Ames, "When the Hot Dog Was Only a Pup," *Restaurant Man*, May 1926, p. 15.

119   Terhune's dining habits: Albert Payson Terhune, *To the Best of My Memory* (New York: Harper and Brothers, 1930), pp. 114–16.

124   "We have watched these coffee stands": Charles D. Kellogg, "Blundering Charity," *Independent*, December 11, 1890, p. 2.

125   "If a man will stand on a curb": "Unique Among Charities Is 'The Bread-Line,'" *New York Times Magazine*, October 2, 1904, second section, p. 5.

125   The ideal company at a table d'hôte: James L. Ford, *Bohemia Invaded and Other Stories* (New York: Frederick A. Stokes, 1895), pp. 3–4.

125   "Young couples who dwell in furnished rooms": "The Restaurant System," *New York Times*, May 24, 1885, p. 3.

126 It is into such a restaurant: William Dean Howells, *A Hazard of New Fortunes* (New York: Modern Library, 2002, originally published in 1890), pp. 81–82, 295–96.

127 "a sort of cake": "Queen Margaret in Naples," *Washington Post*, July 25, 1880, p. 2.

127 Neapolitan pizzas: "Ever Eat Pizze Cavuie [*sic*] or Tried Tarallucci?" *Washington Post*, June 18, 1905, p. D2.

128 at her family's restaurant, Gonfarone's: Maria Sermolino, *Papa's Table d'Hôte* (Philadelphia: Lippincott, 1952).

128 "soup redeemed from tastelessness": Stephen French Whitman, *Predestined: A Novel of New York Life* (New York: Scribner's, 1910), p. 241.

129 "Vere de Veres of the East Side": Benjamin de Casseres, "Red Ink Days," *American Mercury*, January 1929, p. 101.

130 "known to venturesome diners": "Hungarian Yells Greet Roosevelt," *New York Times*, February 15, 1905, p. 2.

130 The most venturesome of all found their way to Chinatown: On the rise of Chinatown and the range of restaurants and dishes, see Helen F. Clark, "The Chinese of New York," *Century*, November 1904, pp. 104–13; Louis J. Beck, *New York's Chinatown: An Historical Presentation of Its People and Places* (New York: Bohemia Publishing, 1898); Arthur Bonner, *Alas! What Brought Thee Hither?: The Chinese in New York, 1800–1950* (Madison, N.J.; Fairleigh Dickinson University Press, 1997); "Chinese Restaurants," *New York Tribune*, February 3, 1901, p. B6; Wong Chin Foo, "The Chinese in New York," *Cosmopolitan*, August 1888, pp. 297–311; "Two Chinese Institutions," *Harper's Weekly*, August 25, 1888, p. 635; Julian Jerrold, "A Chinese Dinner in New York," *Illustrated American*, September 4, 1897, pp. 312–13; Allen S. Williams, "Chinese Restaurants in New York," *Leslie's Illustrated Weekly*, January 9, 1896, pp. 26–28; "Epicurus in Chinatown," *New Metropolitan*, July 1903, p. 427; Allan Forman, "Celestial Gotham," *Arena*, April 1893, pp. 620–28; "A Glimpse of New York's Chinatown," in *Seen by the Spectator* (New York: Outlook, 1902), pp. 193–206.

131 shark fins, sturgeon head, eel bladders: Louis J. Beck, *New York's Chinatown*, p. 49.

131 "Chinese dinner is the most civilized": Jerrold, "Chinese Dinner in New York," p. 312.

132 "tastes to an American like the steam from a locomotive": Williams, "Chinese Restaurants in New York," p. 26.

EIGHT: The Birth of Times Square

136 "the spot where Broadway and Fifth Avenue met": George Rector, *The Girl from Rector's* (New York: Doubleday, 1927), p. 60.

136 "the supreme court of triviality": Ibid., p. 4.

137 "The 'Mr. Feldman' kind of man": Julian Street, "Lobster Palace Society," in *Welcome to Our City* (New York: John Lane, 1913), pp. 64–65.

138 "The word Broadway in fiction": Captain James Churchill, "Inside Views of Fiction: The Novels of Broadway Life," *Bookman*, October 1910, p. 127.

139 "When he pointed at a platter of French pastries": Rector, *The Girl from Rector's*, p. 18.

139 "If he was a great eater": Karl Schriftgiesser, *Oscar of the Waldorf* (New York: E. P. Dutton, 1945), pp. 37–38.

140 "for a much-needed rest": "New Chef for the Waldorf," *New York Times*, May 9, 1893, p. 8.

140 "eat it on a Turkish towel": Rector, *The Girl from Rector's*, p. 52.

141 "Jack's tolerated anything short of riot and violence": Will Irwin, *Highlights of Manhattan* (New York: Century, 1927), p. 343. On Jack's, see also "Hic Jacet Jack's, *Saturday Evening Post*, November 17, 1928, p. 34; Benjamin de Casseres, "Jack's," *American Mercury*, November 1932, pp. 348–54; and "'Jack' of 'Jack's' Has Passed," *New York Times*, January 1, 1928, p. 16.

141 "then the red-hot sports": Edwin C. Hill, "Ghosts of a Gayer Broadway," *North American Review*, May 1930, p. 551.

142 "looked far more like an English earl": Ibid.

142 "calm amid tumult": "'Jack' of 'Jack's' Has Passed," p. 16.

146 "At his very doors": *New York Plaisance* (New York: Henry Erkins, 1908), unpaginated.

146 special dishes included deviled dolphin à la Dido: Hugo von Kleist, "Some Dishes 'Out of the Ordinary,'" *Caterer*, November 1908, p. 29.

146 The special dinners in the private Dragon Room: "The Dragon Room at Murray's," *Caterer*, November 1908, p. 31.

147 "passed the period described by Mrs. Wharton": Julian Street, "What's the Matter with Food?" *Saturday Evening Post*, January 31, 1931, p. 14.

149 "Otho Cushing, a young artist of Boston": "Echos of the Big Ball," *New York Times*, February 12, 1897, p. 3.

149 "I cannot conceive": Frederick Townsend Martin, *Things I Remember* (New York: John Lane, 1913), p. 242.

150 "Billings's freak dinner on horseback": *Town Topics*, April 2, 1903, p. 6.

151 When Sir Thomas Lipton: "Sir Thomas a Guest at Beefsteak Dinner," *New York Times*, November 11, 1906, p. 6; and "Gives a Barnyard Dinner," *New York Times*, February 19, 1906, p. 9.

152 "They forced the addition": Joseph Mitchell, "All You Can Hold for Five Bucks," in *Up in the Old Hotel* (New York: Pantheon, 1992), pp. 291–92.

152 The uptown Mouquin's: Benjamin de Casseres, "Mouquin's," *American Mercury*, March 1932, pp. 363–71.

153 "One might well imagine himself": Amy Lyman Phillips, "Famous American Restaurants," *Good Housekeeping*, January 1909, p. 23.

153 Farther up the street was Joel's: Benjamin de Casseres, "Joel's," *American Mercury*, July 1932, pp. 360–68.

153 "as stiff as Menjou's evening shirts": O. O. McIntyre, "New York, Day by Day," *New York American*, February 10, 1932, section two, p. 1.

154 "Van Bibber's Man-Servant": Richard Harding Davis, in *Van Bibber, and Others* (New York: Harper and Brothers, 1892), pp. 37–43.

154 "The sole is flounder, I suppose": Brander Matthews, "A Thanksgiving Dinner," in *Vignettes of Manhattan* (New York: Harper and Brothers, 1894), p. 160.

155 How expensive was a first-class meal?: "Cheap and Dainty Feast," *New York Times*, October 17, 1897, p. 10.

155 another dining innovation: See Vance Thompson, "The Roof-Gardens of New York," *Cosmopolitan*, September 1899, pp. 503–14; W. G. Robinson and F. L. Brace, "New York's Open-Air Restaurants," *Town and Country*, September 1, 1906, pp. 10–13; Stephen Burge Johnson, *The Roof Gardens of Broadway Theaters, 1883–1942* (Ann Arbor: UMI Research Press, 1985). Robert A. M. Stern et al., *New York 1900: Metropolitan Architecture and Urbanism, 1890–1915* (New York: Rizzoli, 1983).

156 "young women in purple tights": L. J. Vance, "Metropolitan Nights in Summer," *Frank Leslie's Popular Monthly*, July 1893, p. 9.

156 "these long lines of pergolas": "The Cold Buffet on the Hotel Astor Roof," *Town and Country*, July 9, 1910, p. 33.

158 "like soft, yet strangely brilliant yellow roses": Ibid.

159 the captain at Sherry's owned an apartment building: "All Things Come Around to Him Who Will But Wait," *New York Times Magazine*, June 30, 1912, p. 10.

159 "it's a hanging garden": "The Plutocrats of Hash," letter to the editor, *New York Times*, February 10, 1910, p. 6.

160 "mighty glad to get a dime": "The Tipping Nuisance," *New York Times*, November 30, 1884, p. 3.

160 "utterly opposed to the spirit of the New World": "The Corrosive Nature of Tips," *New York Times*, January 28, 1877, p. 6.

161 "You're fined if you break anything": Maud Younger, "The Diary of an Amateur Waitress," *McClure's Magazine*, March 1907, pp. 543–52; April 1907, pp. 665–77.

162 a quarter of the waitresses in the city were under twenty-one: Consumers' League of New York City, *Annual Report*, 1916.

162 "sore feet and a devilish mean disposition": "The Hard Lot of the Waitresses," *Survey*, November 18, 1916, p. 174.

162 "A walking delegate of the waiters": "Both Sides Remain Firm: Waiters Losing Tips, Employers Doing As They Can," *New York Times*, April 29, 1893, p. 9.

164 "I'll close my place first": "Strike Call Fails," *New York Times*, June 4, 1912, p. 1.

NINE: The Party That Never Stopped

166 "George, I don't like to see this": George Rector, *The Girl from Rector's* (New York: Doubleday, 1927), p. 178.

166 plans to transform the Hotel Saranac: "Restaurant De Luxe to Seat 5,000 Diners," *New York Times*, August 14, 1908, p. 7.

170 "Smoking by ladies": "Ladies May Smoke," *New York Times*, December 30, 1907, p. 2.

170 "likely to depend on the sort of woman": "Two Restaurants Let Women Smoke," *New York Times*, January 2, 1908, p. 3.

170 "If a lady is with her husband and smokes decorously": "Ban on Women Smokers," *New York Times*, January 12, 1908, p. 1.

172 "already as luscious as Marilyn Monroe": Jesse L. Lasky, *Blow My Own Horn* (London: Victor Gollancz, 1957), p. 85.

175 "Mischief dances in his blue eyes": Julian Street, "Oh, You Babylon!" in *Welcome to Our City* (New York: John Lane, 1913), p. 166.

175 "the talents of a social dictator": Irene Castle, *Castles in the Air* (Garden City, N.Y.: Doubleday, 1958), p. 90.

177 "We are not starting a restaurant": Gustave Stickley, "The Craftsman's Birthday Party," *Craftsman*, May 1913, p. 252.

179 "I don't demand the cabaret": Obituary, Thomas J. Shanley, *New York Tribune*, October 8, 1932.

179 "The old-fashioned dinner": Henry Collins Brown, *New York of To-Day* (New York: Old Colony Press, 1917), p. 201.

180 "Practically any well-dressed person": Street, *Welcome to Our City*, pp. 10–11.

180 "Broadway sports and rounders": For the Kelly case, see "Miss Kelly in Court on Mother's Charge," *New York Times*, May 23, 1915, p. C5; "Hints Eugenia Kelly Is Victim of a Plot," *New York Times*, May 25, 1915, p. 8; "Lure of Broadway Palaces Breaks Hearts of Mothers," *New York Tribune*, May 25, 1915, p. 14; "Eugenia Kelly's Rival Unmasks Broadway Life," *New York Tribune*, May 25, 1915, p. 1; "Miss Kelly, Sorry, Returns to Mother," *New York Times*, May 26, 1915, p. 8.

181 *If you've never dined and wined*: Thomas R. Ybarra, "Cabaretting," *New York Times*, April 10, 1912, p. 12.

181 "these young fellows invariably wear a silk hat": "Tango Pirates Infest Broadway," *New York Times Magazine*, May 30, 1915, p. 16.

TEN: The Future Is Now

183 "On our trip we were much distressed": Walter Tittle, "William Childs, Who Feeds Millions and Philosophizes on Food," *World's Work*, March 1928, p. 530.

186 "hard brilliance": Lewis Mumford, "From a City Notebook," *New Republic*, September 18, 1929, p. 126.

186 "they were like freshly cooked English muffins": Gertrude A. Parkhurst, *Nostalgia* (typescript, New York Public Library, 1932), p. 4.

187 a strange new restaurant: "The Automatic Restaurant," *Scientific American*, July 18, 1903, pp. 49–51; see also "The Automatic Lunch Counter," *Scientific American*, December 5, 1896, p. 408; "Drop a Nickel in the Slot for Beans and Pie," *New York Times Magazine*, September 18, 1904, section two, p. 4; and "Slot Machine Lunch," *Washington Post*, September 18, 1904, p. 3.

189 "I'm your man": Lorraine B. Diehl and Marianne Hardart, *The Automat: The History, Recipes, and Allure of Horn & Hardart's Masterpiece* (New York: Clarkson Potter, 2002), p. 21.

191 "the process of pushing food into the American stomach": Ilya Ilf and Eugene Petrov, *Little Golden America* (New York: Farrar and Rinehart, 1937), p. 28.

191 a promising-sounding Automat sketch: "The Comic Mr. Fields," *New York Times*, September 9, 1923, section seven, p. 2.

193 "When I first came to New York, before 'Studs Lonigan,'": James Farrell, "The Last Automat," *New York*, May 14, 1979, p. 46.

193 Stoddard's Restaurant: Robert Louis Taylor, "Stop-Watch Restaurant," *Saturday Evening Post*, June 10, 1944, pp. 22–23.

194 the first tabloid restaurant: "Tabloid Restaurant Open," *Brooklyn Daily Eagle*, November 17, 1901, p. 40.

196 "whale oil and dead beetles": Mary Findlater and Jane Helen Findlater, *Crossriggs* (London: Smith, Elder, 1908), p. 98.

ELEVEN: Decline and Fall

198 "The lights of Broadway twinkled": "All Broadway Sad As 1 a.m. Lid Goes On," *New York Times*, May 1, 1917, p. 24.

198 "The passing of the 24-hour day on Broadway": Ibid.

198 "superior grade wet newspaper": Julian Street, "What's the Matter With Food?," *Saturday Evening Post*, March 21, 1931, p. 10.

199 "The Roman Gardens of Murray's are like a classic cemetery": John Walker Harrington, "Death Marks the Cabarets," *New York Times*, June 3, 1923, section eight, p. 2.

200 "No name, no sign": Edmund Wilson, *The Twenties* (New York: Farrar, Straus and Giroux, 1975), pp. 148–49.

202 "Broadway has changed": "'Jack' of 'Jack's' Has Passed," *New York Times*, January 1, 1928, section eight, p. 16.

204 "Epicures, gourmets, and those who just like good food": George Ross, *Tips on Tables* (New York: Covici, Friede 1934), p.151. See also Nils Thor Granlund, *Blondes, Brunettes, and Bullets* (New York: David McKay, 1957).

204 "an endless, stupendous, naked floorshow": Ross, *Tips on Tables*, p. 149.

204 "now a bleak procession": O. O. McIntyre, "The New Lobsteria," in *White Light Nights* (New York: Cosmopolitan, 1924), p. 191.

204 "In a street once famous": "Broadway Becomes Main Street," *Collier's*, January 29, 1921, p. 16.

206 "frustrate the hungry": Ruth Glazer, "The Jewish Delicatessen," *Commentary*, March 1946, pp. 58–63.

208 "Our family lived out of that wicker tray": Mary Elizabeth [Evans], "A $300,000 Home-made Candy Business," *The Delineator*, September 1912, p. 145.

208 "Who does not know this name": George S. Chappell, *The Restaurants of New York* (New York: Greenberg, 1925), p. 124.

209 "a place of rest and beauty": Alice Foote MacDougall, *The Autobiography of a Business Woman* (Boston: Little, Brown, 1928), p. 114.

209 "there grew in my heart a real sympathy": Alice Foote MacDougall, "Eating Aesthetically," *Forum*, September 1928, p. 394.

210 "female patrons as an important element": "Phases of City Life," *New York Times*, June 8, 1890, p. 12.

210 women like Una Golden: Sinclair Lewis, *The Job* (New York, Harcourt, Brace, 1917), pp. 160–61.

211 "In all you do, in all you think, be beautiful": Alice Foote MacDougall, *Coffee and Waffles* (Garden City, N.Y.: Doubleday, 1826), p. 29. See also Fred L. Palmer, "Selling Atmosphere As Well As Food," *Restaurant Man*, May 1926, pp. 7–8.

212 "I always think of myself": MacDougall, "Eating Aesthetically," p. 394.

212 "the principle of beauty": Ibid.

212 "Saturated with quaintness": Margaret Leech, "Romance Incorporated," *New Yorker*, February 4, 1928, p. 21.

212 "The extravagances of cubistic and ultramodern art": MacDougall, "Eating Aesthetically," p. 394.

215 "I have found them good in executive positions": "Schrafft's," *Newsweek*, October 24, 1936, p. 31. See also Frank G. Shattuck, "We Found Quality the Shortest Road to Volume," *System*, March 1923, p. 314; "Successful Restaurant Men: Frank Shattuck," *Restaurant Man*, March 1926, pp. 15–23; Joan Kamel Slomanson, *When Everybody Ate at Schrafft's* (Fort Lee, N.J.: Barricade Books, 2006).

216 "The 50 cent and 75 cent luncheons are useless": Ross, *Tips on Tables*, pp. 229–30.

216 "would nibble on a lettuce sandwich": William F. Longgood, "Daintiest Beaneries in Town," *Saturday Evening Post*, December 4, 1954, p. 38.

216 "neat, cleanly little places": Chappell, *Restaurants of New York*, p. 128.

216 "As little as a half dozen years ago": George Jean Nathan, "Clinical Notes," *American Mercury*, June 1926, pp. 237–38.

217 "What restaurants do you have": John Reed, *The Day in Bohemia, or Life Among the Artists* (New York: privately printed, 1913).

TWELVE: The Restaurant Gets Small

223 "The big restaurant of New York": George S. Chappell, *The Restaurants of New York* (New York: Greenburg, 1925), p. 99.

226 "none of the earmarks of the conventional restaurant": Fred Brauen, *Winold Reiss: Color and Design in the New American Art* (photocopied typescript, New York Public Library, 1980).

227 "It is a quaint place with a Victorian flavor": Chappell, *Restaurants of New York*, p. 106.

228 "could entertain without being molested": Robert A. Caro, *The Power Broker* (New York: Alfred A. Knopf, 1974), p. 338.

228 "was reminiscent of a morello cherry": Thoda Cocroft, *Great Names and How They Are Made* (Chicago: Dartnell Press, 1941), p. 84.

228 "I'd like to take over the old Casino": Gene Fowler, *Beau James: The Life and Times of Jimmy Walker* (New York: Viking, 1949), p. 246.

229 "a place for the fashionable and fastidious": "'Red Mike' v. 'Tony's' Casino," *Time*, June 17, 1929, p. 16.

229 "the line of the mural composition": "Opening Rehearsed at the Park Casino," *New York Times*, June 4, 1929, p. 30.

230 "Tears and threats of suicide": "Five First Nights to Cover Debut of Park Casino," *New York Herald Tribune*, June 3, 1929, p. 3.

230 "It's a new seizure by royalty": "Park Casino Plans $25 Cover Charge," *New York Times*, May 15, 1929, p. 27.

231 "To let Sir Gorgeous Midas and Lady Midas": "Luxury Out of Place," *New York Times*, May 16, 1929, p. 28.

231 "Because I like to do such things": Fowler, *Beau James*, p. 250.

232 "It wasn't the usual speak": Marilyn Kantor, *'21': The Life and Times of New York's Favorite Club* (New York: Privately printed, 1975), p. 4.

233 "nice girls from uptown": Ibid., p. 5.

236 "so small and cluttered": Margaret Case Harriman, "Two Waiters and a Chef," *New Yorker*, June 1, 1935, p. 20.

237 "the demimondaines of New York": Craig Claiborne, "Food: Colony Host Marks 40 Years, *New York Times*, December 19, 1959, p. 17.

238 "Whatever you do at the Colony": George Ross, *Tips on Tables* (New York: Covici, Friede, 1934), p. 55.

238 "very fashionable, clubby": Chappell, *Restaurants of New York*, p. 106.

238 "Of course they are okay": Sirio Maccioni, *Sirio: The Story of My Life and Le Cirque* (Hoboken, N.J.: Wiley, 2004), p. 126.

239 "The coat room boys": "Colony Regular," *New Yorker*, March 21, 1953, p. 30.

THIRTEEN: Red Banquettes and Kisses on the Ceiling

241 33.2 percent of Manhattan's restaurants went under in 1930: Cited in E. H. Nies, "In Defense of the Classical Kitchen," *Caterer*, February 1931, p. 13.

241 "The poor little star blinked": E. B. White, "Alice Where Wert Thou," *New Yorker*, July 23, 1932, p. 16.

242 "Little did I anticipate": Lewis Mumford, "From a City Notebook," *New Republic*, September 18, 1929, p. 126.

243 "Our champion so far": "All You Want to Eat for 60 Cents," *Literary Digest*, August 1, 1931, p. 34.

247 "that would surpass in haute cuisine and service anything existing today": Crosby Gaige, New York World's Fair Papers, New York Public Library, box 581, folder 19.

247 "It would be my idea, too, to have a real southern Mammy": New York World's Fair Papers, box 576, folder 11 ("Eating and Drinking Places 1939").

247 "I am writing this letter without the knowledge of my husband": New York World's Fair Papers, box 575, folder 14.

248 "the minutest gastronomic demands of the inveterate epicure": New York World's Fair Papers, box 575, folder 18.

248 "beautiful Swedish girls": New York World's Fair Papers, box 578, folder 3 ("Amiel, Jack").

250 "underwent a thorough mental overhaul": Lawrence W. Rogers, "His Food Lyrics Tickled Their Palate," *Forbes*, September 15, 1929, p. 22. See also "The Food-Appeal Man," *Newsweek*, January 12, 1948, p.58.

251 exclaiming in Toffenetti-speak: "Broadway Frontage," *New Yorker*, April 8, 1944, p. 18.

252 "the deck of a dream liner": Charlotte Hughes, "For Gourmets and Others: Dining Out à la Bruxelloise," *New York Times*, June 11, 1939, p. D9.

255 "At its inception, the French restaurant set for itself the lofty aim": *French Participation in the New York World's Fair: Guide to the French Pavilion and to the French-Overseas Pavilion* (French government, 1939).

255 "I remember the opening night menu": Joseph Wechsberg, *Dining at the Pavillon* (Boston: Little, Brown, 1962), p. 28.

257 "No two must be treated alike": Ibid. p. 41.

258 "In the beginning Henri Soulé begat Le Pavillon": Craig Claiborne, "In the Beginning There Was, in All Its Grandeur, Le Pavillon," *New York Times*, May 1, 1969, p. 55.

263 "a velvety following": "El Borracho," *Life*, February 17, 1947, p. 56. See also Niccolo de Quattrociocchi, *Love and Dishes* (Indianapolis: Bobbs-Merrill, 1950).

264 "brown as a chestnut": Clementine Paddleford, "New Discovery in Restaurants," *New York Herald Tribune*, March 24, 1951, p. 11.

265 "The two-bit hamburgers": Lucius Beebe, "This New York," *Washington Post*, August 13, 1939, p. L1.

265 "A hamburger is a kind of soft roll": Francis Marshall, *An Englishman in New York* (London: G. B. Publications, 1949), p. 24.

267 "We have always had chop-houses": E. H. Nies, "In Defense," pp. 42–43.

267 "We have never had a good doughnut": Walter R. Brooks, *New York: An Intimate Guide* (New York: Alfred A. Knopf, 1931), p. 109.

268 "In 1950, we didn't have to choose": Patrick Kuh, *The Last Days of Haute Cuisine* (New York: Viking, 2001), p. 2.

FOURTEEN: The Baum Years

270 "It was tough": "The Showman of Provender," *Fortune*, March 1958, p. 227.

271 "The Monte Carlo was a very flossy place": Geoffrey T. Hellman, "Directed to the Product," *New Yorker*, October 17, 1964, p. 79.

272 "The customers like to see things on fire": Ibid., p. 81.

272 "There was a similar dish made with strips of calf's liver": James Beard, *The Armchair James Beard*, ed. John Ferrone (New York: Lyons Press, 1999), p. 286.

274 "It's a shame Rome is under that cloud of 'decline'": Hellman, "Directed to the Product," p. 73.

275 "You have to know the difference": Irena Chalmers, "Joe Baum: An Exaltation of Larks," *Gastronomica*, Winter 2003, p. 92.

276 "He always reminded me of Merlin": William Grimes, "Joseph Baum, American Dining's High Stylist, Dies at 78," *New York Times*, October 6, 1998, p. B10.

281 "It was unthinkable . . . to say a good word about the twin towers": Paul Goldberger, "Design Notebook," *New York Times*, August 24, 1977, p. 53.

281 "symbol of the beginning of the turnaround": William Grimes, "Windows That Rose So Close to the Sun," *New York Times*, September 19, 2001, Dining section, p. 1.

FIFTEEN: California Comes Calling

286 "Today lunch in the Colony dining room": Gael Greene, "Colony Waxworks," *Bite* (New York: W. W. Norton, 1971), p. 151.

286 "The restaurant world was in free fall": Sirio Maccioni, *Sirio: The Story of My Life and Le Cirque* (Hoboken, N.J.: Wiley, 2004), p. 149.

287 "It has long been my contention": Craig Claiborne, *A Feast Made for Laughter* (Garden City, N.Y.: Doubleday, 1982), p. 140.

288 "not esoteric, not too intimidating": Marion Burros, "What Alice Taught Them: Disciples of Chez Panisse," *New York Times*, September 26, 1984, section C, p. 1.

288 "What in the world, I thought": Jeremiah Tower, *California Dish* (New York: Free Press, 2003), p. 107.

289 "My menu, in English": Ibid., p. 111.

SIXTEEN: With Knife and Fork in New York

311 the first restaurant I reviewed: William Grimes, "Coach House: Attempting a Sequel," *New York Times*, May 19, 1999, p. F1.

315 I savaged the Russian Tea Room: William Grimes, "First the New Russia, Now the New Tea Room," *New York Times*, December 15, 1999, p. F1.

316 a much more experimental turn at his next restaurant: William Grimes, "A Neighborhood Place Without Boundaries," *New York Times*, April 5, 2000, p. F15.

317 exemplified by Suba: William Grimes, "Spanish Notes from Underground," *New York Times*, May 1, 2002, p. F10.

317 a sublime restaurant, Town: William Grimes, "Midtown Elegance, One Floor Down," *New York Times*, May 2, 2001, p. F10.

318 Rick Laakkonen, an adventurous River Café alumnus: William Grimes, "At a Hip New Hotel, Food to Write Home About," *New York Times*, August 15, 2001, p. F1.

318 a real oddity like Sciuscia: William Grimes, "Mediterranean Interlude, Without the Views," *New York Times*, August 1, 2003, p. F8.

318 retro-diner chic at the Hudson Hotel: William Grimes, "The Way We Ate, Somewhat Souped Up," *New York Times*, December 27, 2000, p. F11.

319 Café Boulud, his Upper East Side Bistro: William Grimes, "At the New Daniel, Ambition Meets Restraint," *New York Times*, June 2, 1999, p. F1; "In New York, Promised Fulfilled," *New York Times*, March 14, 2001, p. F1.

320 off to the races with his new bistro: William Grimes, "Midtown Playground for an Uptown Chef," *New York Times*, August 22, 2001, p. F8.

321 At Craft, Tom Colicchio showcased: William Grimes, "With Such Scallops, Who Needs Free Will?" *New York Times*, June 27, 2001, p. F7.

321 His deceptively modest restaurant: William Grimes, "The Food Speaks for Itself, and Says It All," *New York Times*, June 7, 2000, p. F11.

321 Alain Ducasse's attempted invasion: William Grimes, "The Perfect Tempest: A Sneak Preview of Ducasse," *New York Times*, July 12, 2000, p. F1; "At Ducasse, Lots of Luxury (But Just 1 Pen)," *New York Times*, November 1, 2000, p. F1; "At Ducasse, a Ticket to the Stratosphere," *New York Times*, December 19, 2001, p. F1.

324 Out of curiosity, I dropped in for dinner: William Grimes, "Bouley Returns, Deft and Daring," *New York Times*, September 15, 1999, p. F1.

324 At Danube, just behind Bouley Bakery: William Grimes, "Bouley, in His Klimt Period," *New York Times*, February 9, 2000, p. F10.

325 the perfect formula at Wallsé: William Grimes, "A Chef Delivers His Own Private Austria," *New York Times*, September 6, 2000, p. F12; "Where the End of the Meal Is the Beginning," *New York Times*, April 10, 2002, p. F10.

325 His vision was realized at Artisanal: William Grimes, "Say 'Cheese' and Try Not to Smile," *New York Times*, May 30, 2001, p. F10.

327 Paul Liebrandt, the most divisive chef: William Grimes, "A Cheeky Ambassador of the British Scene," *New York Times*, November 29, 2000, p. F1; "Waiter, There's Beer in My Consommé," *New York Times*, February 27, 2002, p. F10.

Selected Bibliography

Ashley, Diana. *Where to Dine in Thirty-nine.* New York: Crown, 1939.

Batterberry, Michael, and Ariane Batterberry. *On the Town in New York.* New York: Routledge, 1999.

Beard, Rick, and Leslie Cohen Berlowitz, eds. *Greenwich Village: Culture and Counterculture.* New Brunswick, N.J.: Rutgers University Press, 1993.

Berman, Miriam. *Madison Square: The Park and Its Celebrated Landmarks.* Salt Lake City: Gibbs-Smith, 2001.

Bonner, Arthur. *Alas! What Brought Thee Hither?: The Chinese in New York, 1800–1950.* Madison, N.J.: Fairleigh Dickinson University Press, 1997.

Botsford, Harry. *New York's 100 Best Restaurants.* Portland, Maine: Bond Wheelright, 1955.

Brody, Iles. *The Colony: Portrait of a Restaurant—and Its Famous Recipes.* New York: Greenberg, 1945.

Brooks, Walter R. *New York: An Intimate Guide.* New York: Alfred A. Knopf, 1931.

Castle, Irene. *Castles in the Air.* Garden City, N.Y.: Doubleday, 1958.

Chambers, Julius. *The Book of New York: Forty Years' Recollections of the American Metropolis.* New York: Books of New York, 1912.

Chapin, Anna Alice. *Greenwich Village.* New York: Dodd, Mead, 1920.

Chappell, George S. *The Restaurants of New York.* New York: Greenberg, 1925.

Churchill, Allen. *Park Row.* New York: Rinehart, 1958.

———. *The Great White Way.* New York: E. P. Dutton, 1962.

Claiborne, Craig. *A Feast Made for Laughter.* Garden City, N.Y.: Doubleday, 1982.

———. *The New York Times Guide to Dining Out in New York.* New York: Atheneum, 1964.

Dana, Robert W. *Where to Eat in New York.* New York: Current Books, 1948.

Dayton, Abram C. *Last Days of Knickerbocker Life in New York.* New York: Putnam's, 1897.

DeVoe, F. *The Market Assistant.* New York: Hurd and Houghton, 1867.

———. *The Market Book.* New York: Burt Franklin, 1970. (Facsimile of the 1862 edition.)

Diehl, Lorraine B., and Marianne Hardart. *The Automat: The History, Recipes, and Allure of Horn & Hardart's Masterpiece.* New York: Clarkson Potter, 2002.

Erenberg, Lewis A. *Steppin' Out: New York Nightlife and the Transformation of American Culture, 1870–1930.* Chicago: University of Chicago Press, 1981.

Foster, George G. *New York by Gaslight*. New York: M. J. Ivers, 1850.

———. *New York in Slices*. New York: William H. Graham, 1849.

Fowler, Gene. *Beau James: The Life and Times of Jimmy Walker*. New York: Viking, 1949.

Franey, Pierre, with Richard Flaste and Bryan Miller. *A Chef's Tale: A Memoir of Food, France, and America*. New York: Alfred A. Knopf, 1994.

Gaige, Crosby. *Food at the Fair: A Gastronomic Tour of the World, New York World's Fair, 1939*. New York: Exposition Publications, 1939.

Garrett, Thomas M. "A History of Pleasure Gardens in New York City, 1700–1865." Ph.D. diss., New York University, 1978.

Golding, Louis T. *Memories of Old Park Row, 1887–1897*. Brookline, Mass.: privately printed, 1946.

Graham, Stephen. *New York Nights*. London: Ernest Benn, 1928.

Granlund, Nils Thor, with Sid Feder and Ralph Hancock. *Blondes, Brunettes and Bullets*. New York: David McKay, 1957.

Green, Gael. *Bite*. New York: W. W. Norton, 1971.

Gunn, Thomas Butler. *The Physiology of New York Boarding-Houses*. New York: Mason Brothers, 1857.

Haswell, Charles H. *Reminiscences of New York by an Octogenarian*. New York: Harper and Brothers, 1896.

Hughes, Rupert. *The Real New York*. New York: Smart Set, 1904.

The Iron Gate of Jack and Charlie's '21'. New York: Jack Kriendler Memorial Foundation, 1950.

James, Rian. *Dining in New York*. New York: John Day, 1931.

Johnson, Stephen Burge. *The Roof Gardens of Broadway Theaters, 1883–1942*. Ann Arbor: UMI Research Press, 1985.

Kantor, Marilyn. *'21': The Life and Times of New York's Favorite Club*. New York: privately printed, 1975.

Keller, Julius. *Inns and Outs*. New York: Putnam's, 1939.

Kernan, J. Frank. *Reminiscences of the Old Fire Laddies and Volunteer Departments of New York and Brooklyn*. New York: M. Crane, 1885.

Kuh, Patric. *The Last Days of Haute Cuisine: America's Culinary Revolution*. New York: Viking, 2001.

Kurlansky, Mark. *The Big Oyster: History on the Half Shell*. New York: Ballantine Books, 2006.

Lasky, Jesse L. *Blow My Own Horn*. London: Victor Gollancz, 1957.

Maccioni, Sirio. *Sirio: The Story of My Life and Le Cirque*. Hoboken, N.J.: Wiley, 2004.

MacDougall, Alice Foote. *The Autobiography of a Businesswoman*. Boston: Little, Brown, 1928.

———. *Coffee and Waffles*. Garden City, N.Y.: Doubleday, Page, 1926.

Mackall, Lawton. *Knife and Fork in New York*. Garden City, N.Y.: Doubleday, 1949.

McCabe, James D., Jr. *Lights and Shadows of New York Life, or, the Sights and Sensations of the Great City*. Farrar, Straus and Giroux, 1970. (Facsimile of the 1872 edition.)

———. *New York by Gaslight*. New York: Greenwich House, 1984. (Fascimile of the 1882 edition.)

McIntyre, O. O. *White Light Nights*. New York: Cosmopolitan, 1924.

McNamee, Thomas. *Alice Waters and Chez Panisse*. New York: Penguin, 2007.

Mariani, John. *America Eats Out*. New York: William Morrow, 1991.

———, with Alex von Bidder. *The Four Seasons: A History of America's Premier Restaurant*. New York: Smithmark, 1999.

Maurice, Arthur Bartlett. *The New York of the Novelists*. New York: Dodd, Mead, 1916.

Moss, Frank. *The American Metropolis*. New York: Collier, 1897.

New York Plaisance. New York: Henry Erkins, 1908. (A portfolio of photographs of Murray's Roman Gardens.)

Pépin, Jacques. *The Apprentice: My Life in the Kitchen*. Boston: Houghton Mifflin, 2003.

Rector, George. *The Girl from Rector's*. Garden City, N.Y.: Doubleday, Page, 1927.

Ross, George. *Tips on Tables*. New York: Covici, Friede, 1934.

Schriftgiesser, Karl. *Oscar of the Waldorf*. New York: E. P. Dutton, 1943.

Schwartz, Arthur. *Arthur Schwartz's New York City Food*. New York: Stewart, Tabori and Chang, 2004.

Sermolino, Maria. *Papa's Table d'Hôte*. Philadelphia: Lippincott, 1952.

Slomanson, Joan Kanel. *When Everybody Ate at Schrafft's*. Fort Lee, N.J.: Barricade Books, 2006.

Spann, Edward K. *The New Metropolis: New York City, 1840–1857*. New York: Columbia University Press, 1981.

Stern, Robert A. M., Gregory Gilmartin, and John Montague Massengale. *New York 1900: Metropolitan Architecture and Urbanism, 1890–1915*. New York: Rizzoli, 1983.

Stern, Robert A. M., Gregory Gilmartin, and Thomas Mellins. *New York 1930: Architecture and Urbanism Between the World Wars*. New York: Rizzoli, 1987.

Stern, Robert A. M., Thomas Mellins, and David Fishman. *New York 1880: Architecture and Urbanism in the Gilded Age*. New York: Monacelli Press, 1999.

Street, Julian. *Welcome to Our City*. New York: John Lane, 1913.

Terhune, Albert Payson. *To the Best of My Memory*. New York: Harper and Brothers, 1930.

Thomas, Lately. *Delmonico's: A Century of Splendor*. Boston: Houghton Mifflin, 1967.

Tower, Jeremiah. *California Dish*. New York: Free Press, 2003.

Taylor, William R., ed. *Inventing Times Square: Commerce and Culture at the Crossroads of the World, 1880–1939*. New York: Russell Sage Foundation, 1991.

Walker, Stanley. *The Night Club Era*. New York: Blue Ribbon Books, 1933.

Wechsberg, Joseph. *Dining at the Pavillon*. Boston: Little, Brown, 1962.

Where and How to Dine in New York. New York: Lewis, Scribner, 1903.

Whitaker, Jan. *Tea at the Blue Lantern Inn: A Social History of the Tea Room Craze in America*. New York: St. Martin's, 2002.

Acknowledgments

Special thanks are due to Paul LeClerc, the president of the New York Public Library, who got the ball rolling when he invited me to organize an exhibition of the vintage menus in the library's collection. I would also like to thank Henry Voigt for his generosity in making his menu collection available and for his enthusiastic help all along the way.

INDEX

Page numbers in *italics* refer to illustrations.

Brody, Jerome, 269–72
Brooklyn, 33, 36, 37, 39, 42, 48, 73, 86, 194, 290, 310, 311, 317; chophouses, 79
Brooklyn Eagle, 36, 37, 42, 58, 79, 194, 304
Brooks, Walter R., 267, 305
Broun, Heywood, 234
Brown, George W., 5
Browne, George F., 74–75
Browne's, 74
Bruni, Frank, 323, 330
Brunswick, 105–106, 108, 111, 113, 114, 255
Bryan, Scott, 292
Bull's Head Tavern, 87
Bunel, Napoleon, 71
Burke, David, 290
Burns, Sam, 141
busboys, 159, 190
business lunch, 64
Bustanoby brothers, 170, 171, 176, 179
Bustanoby's, *168*, 176
butter, 17, 67
Buttercake Dick's, 66–67, 81–82

cabaret, 172–74, 175, 179, 180, 198, 199, 204
Caesar salad, 274
Café Boulevard, 129, 130
Café Boulud, 319–20
Café Chambord, 244, 258, 287
Café de France, 168
Café de l'Opéra, 159, 167, *167*, 168, 175
Café de Paris, 168, 175, 179, 180
Café des Beaux Arts, 168, 170, *171*, 176, 181
Café Français, 11
Cafe Francis, 153
Café Luxembourg, 293
Café Martin, 108–109, *109*, 110, 111, 119, 168, 170, 180, 229, 255, 310
Café Nicholson, 263–64, *264*, 265
cafés, 3, 4, 9, 99, 163; Delmonico's, 4–6, 9, 47–49, 108; early, 4–6, 9–12, 47; turn-of-the-century, 108–10, 122
Café Sabarsky, 325
cafeterias, 15, 248; Automat, 190–91
Café Tortoni, 72
Cajun cuisine, 289
California cuisine, 259, 287–307
calories, 194; counting, 199, 210, 242
Canal Street, 41, 108, 130
candy, 213, 214, 215
Canora, Marco, 321
Cantor, Eddie, 206
capitalism, 191
Capote, Truman, 238

capsular restaurants, 194
Cardoz, Floyd, *296*
Carême, Antonin, 59, 286
Casino, 226–27, *227*, 228–32
Casino Theater, 155–56
Castle, Vernon and Irene, 174, 175, 180
Catherine Market, 28, 34
Cato's Tavern, 35
cattle barons, 102
cauliflower, 28
Cavallero, Gene, 236, *236*, 237–39, 286
Cedar Bar, 99
celebrity, 12, 110, 289; of 1980s, 299–300; nouvelle chefs, 290, 295, 301, 303, 306–307; Reuben's, *207*; turn-of-the-century, 147–51
Central Park, 107; Casino, 226–27, *227*, 228–32
cereal, breakfast, 194
Cerutti, Ernest, 236–39
Chambers Street, 11, 56, 57, 68, 104
champagne, 79, 136, 199
Chanterelle, 292
Chapin, Anna Alice, *Greenwich Village*, 221
Chaplin, Charlie, 237
Chappell, George S., *The Restaurants of New York*, 208, 216, 223, 227, 228, 304
charities, 122, *122*, 123–25
Charley Abel's, 11
Chauveron, Roger, 244, 258
cheese: artisanal, 325–26, *326*; French, 93, 95, 325
cheesecake, Lindy's, 205
chefs, 59, 64, 105, 140; Casino, 230; celebrity, 290, 295, 301, 303, 306–307; Delmonico's, 56–60; farmer-, 177; Hoffman House, 105; Le Cirque, 300, *300*; Le Pavillon, 255–59; nouvelle, 287–307, 316–29; Rector's, 140; television, 259, 298, 303, 304, 306; *see also specific chefs and restaurants*
Chequers, 79
Chesapeake Bay, 45, 155
Chez Maurice, 176
Chez Panisse, 276, 288, 292, 304
Chicago, 120, 133, 134, 249
chicken, 66; fried, 193, 266, 267
Chicken Koop, 266
Child, Julia, 306
Childs, Samuel S., 183, 184–87
Childs, William, 120, 183, 184–87, 242
Childs lunchrooms, 120, 161, 183, 184, *184*, 185, *185*, 186–87, 206, 248, 266; all-you-can-eat policy, 243–44; Depression-era, 242–44
China Grill, 318

Grand Street Market, 28
Grand Vatel, 93, 97
Granlund, Nils Thor, 203–204
Great Keno Raid (1871), 43
Gréber, Jacques, 246
Greeks, 85
Greeley, Horace, 12, 29, 40, 42, 82, 95, 98;
   The Perils of Pearl Street, 17
Greene, Gael, 286, 306
Greene Street, 93
Green Room, 74
Greenwich Street, 11, 16
Greenwich Village, 97, 113, 119, 125–28,
   217–21, 233, 291, 297; "goofy clubs," 218,
   218, 219, *219*, *220*, 221; 1910s–1920s
   restaurants, 217–18, *218*, 219, *219*, *220*,
   221, 232–35; tearooms, 218, 219
Greenwich Village Inn, 218
grilled cuisine, 289
Gruyère, 93
Guerin, Edward, 51
Guerin, François, 9, 50–51
Guerin's, 9, 50–51
guidebooks, restaurant, 208, 297, 304–305
Gunn, Thomas Butler, 18–19; *Physiology of
   New York Boarding-Houses*, 18
Gutenbrunner, Kurt, 325

Haering, Max, 252
Haggerty, James, 43
haggis, 76
Haims, Louis, 118–19
Haley and Sabin's refectory, 64
Halfway House, 178
Hall, Basil, 8
Halladay, Paula ("Polly"), 218
Halleck, Fitz-Greene, 11, 73
ham, 66, 82, 266
hamburgers, 265; deluxe, 320, *320*
Hamburg Heaven, 265
Hamilton, Thomas, 14–15
Hammerstein, Oscar, 134, 141, 156, 164
Hanover Lunch, 183
Hanson, Stephen, 283
Hardart, Frank, 188–90
Harlem, 178, 266
Harper's Bazaar, 148, 263
Harper's Weekly, 81, 97
Harris, Henry B., 172, 174
Harte, Bret, 82
Hartford Lunch, 183
Hartmann, Alfred, 237, 238
hash houses, 115–17
hat-check attendants, 159–60

Hawaiian craze, of 1920s, 216
Hawaiian Room, 272
healthy food, 194–96, 242, 287; nouvelle
   cuisine, 287–307
Healy, Tim, 141, 197
Hearst, William Randolph, 228
Hearth, 321
Hederer, Emil, 140
Heffernan, Kerry, 292
Held, Anna, 166, 176
Hellinger, Mark, 231, 234
Henri, Robert, 152
Henri's, 201
Herald Building, 81
Herald Square, 123
herbs, fresh, 276
Hilair, Elsie Lee, 181–82
Hill, Harry, 42
Hippodrome, 141
Hitchcock's, 81, 82, 117, 119
Hofbräu House, 89, 90, 137
Hoffman, Charles Fenno, 11
Hoffman House, 104–105, *105*, 108, 111,
   114, 115
Holland House, 162
Hollywood Restaurant, 204
Holt's Ordinary, 5, 8, 62
Hone, Philip, 36, 49
honor system, 57, 120
Hopper, Edward, *Automat*, 193
Horn, Joe, 188–90
Horn & Hardart Automats, 188–92, *192*, 193,
   244, 265, 286
horseback dinner (1903), 149–50, *150*
hot-corn girls, 19, 310
Hotel Astor, 133, 141, 144, 156, 164; roof
   garden and menu, 158, *173*
Hotel Lafayette, 109, 217, 304
Hotel Logerot, 106, 163
Hotel Martin, 109, 217
hotels, 4, 5, 14–16, 48, 104–107; American
   plan, 14–15; banquets, 203; Delmonico's,
   49, 50, 54, 106–107; designer, 317–20;
   European plan, 54; luxury, 15, 102–107;
   Madison Square, 104–115; midtown, 111,
   133, 144, 147–49, 156, 165–67; post–Civil
   War, 71, *71*, 104–107; pre–Civil War, 14–16,
   23, 51–55, 65, 66, 70–71; Prohibition and,
   199, 203, 204; rooftop gardens, 156, *157*,
   158, *173*; see also specific hotels
Hotel Saranac, 166–67
House of Lords, 77
Houston Street, 42–43, 77, 78, 129
Howard Johnson's, 259
Howard Street, 35

Howells, William Dean, 98–100, 310; *A Hazard of New Fortunes*, 99, 126–27, 129
hucksters, 24
Hudson Cafeteria, 318–19
Hughes, Charlotte, 252
Huneker, James, 90
Hungarian cuisine, 85, 129–30

ice cream, 10–11, 19, 200; early parlors and saloons, 10–11, *11*, 67–69, *67*; Schrafft's, 213
Ilf and Petrov, 191
Ilo, 290, 318
immigration, 85–100, 102, 310–11; Bohemia and, 97–100; Chinese, 85, *86*; first meal, 123; French, 93–96; Germans, 86–92; Italian, 96–97, 125; laws, 202
Independent, 124
Industrial Christian Alliance, 123–24
industrial elite, 102
Inhilco, 280, 283
Inner Three, 224–26
Irish, 85, 93, 143
Irving, Washington, *History of New York*, 9
Italian cuisine, 10–11, 85, 93, 96–97, 125–26, *126*, 127–29, 199, 217, 250, 277, 295, 297, 299; Gonfarone's, 128–29, 217; Maria del Prato's, 81, 96–97, 125–26; Maroni's, 126–27; Moretti's, 96–97; nouvelle, 299, 303, 306, 313, 326–27; *see also specific restaurants*
Italy, 96, 97, 144, 273, 274

Jack's, 81, 119, 137, 141–43, 144, 202, 310
Jackson, Thomas M., 35
jambalaya, 59
James, Henry, 68
James, Rian, *Dining in New York*, 90–92, 304–305
Jams, 292, 298, *298*
Janssen, August, 90
Japan, 113, 245; cuisine, 85, 177, 249, 295, 318
jazz, 165, 179
Jean Georges, 302–303, 316
Jerome, Leonard, 103
Jews, 85, 205, 249; delicatessens, 89, 206
Jim Fisk, 115, 117
Joel's, 153
Johnson, Philip, 274, 275, 302
Jo Jo, 302
Jolson, Al, 206
Josephs, John, 36–37

journalism, food, 66, 81–82, 119–20, 137, 148, 150, 205, 267, 286, 304–306, 309–30; *see also* newspapers and magazines; *specific journalists and publications*

Kalm, Peter, 34
Kean, Edmund, 74
Keller, Julius, 106, 115–17, 124, 168, 199
Keller, Thomas, 323, 329–30
Kellogg, Dr. John Harvey, 72, 194
Kelly, Eugenia, 180–81
Kennedy, Jackie, 238
Kennedy family, 238, 257, 271
kidneys, 78
King, Archibald Gracie, 102
Kinzler, Francis, 105
Kleindeutschland, 86, 88
Knickerbocker, Cholly, 237
Knickerbocker Cottage, 152
Knickerbocker Grill, 236, 237
Knickerbocker Hotel, 133, 144, 164, 166, 204
Knickerbocker Magazine, 111
Knickerbocker society, 3–4, 9, 64, 146
Korean cuisine, 299
kosher food, 89
Kriendler, Jack, 232–36
Kuesmeier, Xavier, 140
Kuh, Patric, *The Last Days of Haute Cuisine*, 268
Kunz, Gray, 329

Laakkonen, Rick, 290, 318
La Caravelle, 258, 259
La Côte Basque, 257–58, 330
Ladies Mile, 104, 107
Ladies' Refreshment Saloon, 226, *227*
Lafayette, 301, 302, *302*
La Fonda del Sol, 271, 277, *278*, *279*
Lagasse, Emeril, 306
La Grenouille, 258, 259
La Grolla, 313, 324
La Guardia, Fiorello, 231, 247, 285
Lamadrid, Clementine, 122–23
lamb, 24, 66, 73, 155, 292
language, food, 250–51, 273, 274, 276
lardo, 327
Lasky, Jesse, 172, 174
Latin American cuisine, 277–79, 297, 311, 313, 316
Layla, 295
Le Bernardin, 327
Le Cirque, 236, 238, 299–300, *300*, 301, 302

146–52, 175–76; of 1820s–1830s, 3–19, 47–55; of 1840s–1860s, 61–78, 85–88; of 1870s–1890s, 89–100, 101–32, 133–36; food markets, 21–31, 62, 280–81; high society, 102–107; immigrants, 85–100; Knickerbocker society, 3–4, 9, 64, 146; midtown growth, 134; mid-twentieth-century society and wealth, 236–39; 9/11 attacks, 283; nineteenth-century growth of, 12, 13–14, 50–55, 61–62, 101–102; of 1900s–1920s, 133–64, 165–82, 183–96, 197–221, 223–38; of 1930s–1940s, 238–39, 241–68; of 1950s–1970s, 263–68, 269–84, 285–90; of 1980s–1990s, 290–307, 313–16; population, 14, 50, 86; post–Civil War, 101–102; post–World War II, 254–58; Prohibition, 101, 197–221, 226, 233; of 2000s, 316–30; World War I, 197–98; *see also specific streets, neighborhoods, and restaurants*

New York *Aurora*, 28
New York Courier and Enquirer, 51
New York Equestrian Club, 149–50, *150*
New Yorker, The, 152, 192, 212, 216, 233, 236, 239, 250, 256, 267, 272, 274, 304, 305
New York Evening Gazette, 37
New York Garden, 10, *11*
New York Gazette, 24
New York Herald, 29, 34, 81, 95, 96
New York Herald Tribune, 230, 264, 305
New York magazine, 286, 306
New York Sun, 81, 95, 112, 117, 192
New York Times, 24, 29, 42, 55, 56, 69, 70, 81, 125, 130, 133, 155, 170, 198, 199, 231, 252, 258, 287, 293, 297, 302, 305, 309; Claiborne reviews, 305–306; food critics, 305–306, 312–30; star system, 305, 323–24; *See also specific food critics and journalists*
New York Tribune, 12, 18, 29, 37, 42, 56, 62, 64, 81, 83, 89, 95, 126
New York World, 81
New York World's Fair (1939), 245–55, 285, 305; restaurants and stands, 246–55
Niblo, William, 5, 155
Niblo's Coffee House, 80
Niblo's Gardens, 69
nickel meal, 122, 123
Nieporent, Drew, 283, 293, 294, 295, 329
nightclubs, 159, 174, 203, 261–63
9/11 terrorist attack, 283
Nino's Café, 263
Nixon, Richard, 238
Nobu, 295
NoHo, 317

nouvelle cuisine, 259, 276, 287–307; celebrity chefs, 290, 295, 301, 303, 306–307; *see also specific restaurants and chefs*
nuttose, 194–96

O'Brien, Fitz-James, 98
Odeon, 293
Old Homestead, 320
Old Tom's, 7, 62–63, 74–75
Olives, 318
Olmsted, Frederick Law, 107
open kitchen, 277, *279*
opera, 172, 174
ordinaries, 5, 8, 48
Orr, Daniel, 321
Orteig, Raymond, 304
Oswego Market, 28
Otto, 306, 327
Outhier, Louis, 302
Owl, 123
Oyster Bar, Grand Central Terminal, 45–46, 309
oysters, 19, 21, 22, 33–46, 55, 72, 114, 134, 142, 155, 158, 271–72, 310; barges with storefronts, *44*; cooking methods, 34, 35–36, 45; dealers and saloons, *30*, *32*, 35–37, *38*, 39–46, 62, 73, 77, 79; Fulton Market, *30*, *32*, 33, 37, *38*, 39, 40, 41, 46; pickled, 34; pie, 41; stew, 37, 41, 45, 46; street peddlers, 19, 34, 35, *35*, 310; trade, 34–35, *44*, 45; varieties and size, 43–45

Pabst's, 89, 137, 159
Paddleford, Clementine, 264, 305
Pagani, André, 252
Palais d'Or, 203, *204*
Palais Royal, 203, *204*
Palmer, Charlie, 290
Palmo, Ferdinand, 10–11
Palmo's Garden, 10–11
Palmo's New York Opera House, 11, *12*
Pani, Joe, 236, 237
Papillon, 328–29
Paradise, *204*
Paradise Roof Garden, 141, 158
Paris, 4, 5, 13, 48–49, 55, 58, 59, 85, 94, 97, 98, 107, 108, 140, 152, 168, 172, 224, 253, 255, 303
Park Avenue, 223–26, 274; "bijou apartment restaurants," 223–26
Park Avenue Hotel, 197
Parker, Robert, 320

immigrants and, 85–100; as integrated artistic concept, 283–84; of 1900s–1920s, 133–64, 165–82, 183–96, 197–221, 223–38; of 1930s–1940s, 238–39, 241–68; 1939 World's Fair, 245–55, 285, 305; of 1950s–1970s, 263–68, 269–84, 285–90; of 1980s–1990s, 290–307, 313–16; nouvelle cuisine, 287–307, 316–29; oyster, 35–46; post–World War II, 254–68; Prohibition, 101, 197–221, 226, 233; terminology, 12; theater and, 12, 41, 73–75, 77, 78, 89, 104, 108, 136–41, 156–58; Times Square, 133–64, 165–82, 183, 203–206; of 2000s, 316–30; *see also* chefs; design, restaurant; menus; service, restaurant; *specific chefs, cuisines, locations, owners, periods, and restaurants*
Reuben, Arnold, 206, *207*
Reuben's, 89, 206, *207*, 217
Reynière, Grimod de la, 13
rice pudding, 8, 17
Rideing, William H., 97
Rinaldo, Joel, 153
Ripert, Eric, 327
Ritz-Carlton, 224
River Café, 290
roast beef, 65
Robert's, 226
Robins, Gary, 292
Rocco's, 298
Rockaways, 44
Rockefeller Center, 234, 273, 283
Rockefeller family, 244
Rockwell, David, 283, 317–18, *319*
Rodriguez, Douglas, 297
Romano, Michael, 297
Romberg, Sigmund, 176
Rome, 144, 146, 273, 274
rooftop gardens, 141, 155–56, *157*, 158, *173*, *225*
Roosevelt, Franklin D., 229
Roosevelt, Theodore, 82, 106, 130, 148
Ross, George, *Tips on Tables*, 238, 305
Rothstein, Arnold, 206, 260
Ruby Foo's, 319
Russell, Lillian, 115, 139, 176
Russians, 59, 85, 89, 249; style of service, 59
Russian Tea Room, 313–14; 1990s renovation of, 313–14, *314*, 315, *315*, 324
Rynders, Isaiah, 65

Saddle Rock oysters, 43, 44, 45
St. Andrew's One Cent Coffee Society, 122, *122*, 123, 124

St. James Hotel, 106, 111
St. Nicholas Hotel, 66, 69–71, *70*; menu, 70, *70*
salmon, 28
Salón México, 320
sandwiches, 216–17; Automat, *190*; Lindy's, 205–206, 217; of 1920s, 205–207, 216–17; Reuben's, 206, *207*, 217
sanitary dining, 120, 186
Sanka, 216
Sans Souci, 175, 197
Sardi's, 74
Saturday Press, 98, 99
Savoy, Guy, 289
Schermerhorn family, 102
schools, cooking, 290
Schrafft's, 193, 213, *213*, 214, *214*, 215, *215*, 216, 286
Schrager, Ian, 318
Schurz, Carl, 15–16
Sciuscia, 318
Scribner's Monthly, 26
Seagram Building, 274, 275
Second Avenue, 129
Seeley, Blossom, 174
self-serve system, 64, 119, 187, 248
Sermolino, Anacleto, 128
service, food, 59, 108, 113, 159–64, 247, 309; automated, 166–67, 187–93; Baum-era, 272, 276; clientele flattered by, 238–39; Colony, *236*, 238–39; Delmonico's, 57, 59, 103, 115, 162–63; early twentieth century, 159–64, 187; of 1840s, 64; French system, 198, 223, 255; "goofy club," 219, *220*; Jack's, 142; labor unrest, 162–64; La Pavillon, 256, 257, 259; Mouquin's, 95–96; nouvelle, 292, 301; Prohibition and, 198, 199, 202; Russian style, 59; Schrafft's, 215; self-, 64, 119, 187, 248; tipping, 159–61, 163, 249; wages and hours, 159–64; Waldorf-Astoria, 163–64; women, 161–62, 210; World's Fair, 247–48; *see also specific restaurants*
Shaffer, George H., 39
Shanley, Thomas J., 143–44, 179
Shanley's, 143, *143*, 144, 164, 179, 199, 310
Shattuck, Frank G., 212–15
Sheehan, Andy, 43
shellfish, 19, 22, 33, 40; oysters, 33–46; Rector's, 133–41
Sheraton, Mimi, 312
Sheridan Square, 218
Sherry, Louis, 113–14, 172, 200, 304
Sherry's, 113–14, 134, 149–51, 156, 159, 163, 170, 172, 175, 183, 200, 223, 229, 255; horseback dinner, 149–50, *150*

9 780374 532499